Second Edition

Reservations and Ticketing with SABRE®

Dennis L. Foster

Chairman, Mundus Colleges

GLENCOE

McGraw-Hill

New York, New York   Columbus, Ohio   Mission Hills, California   Peoria, Illinois

The Travel Professional Series

First Class: An Introduction to Travel and Tourism
Destinations: North American and International Geography
Reservations and Ticketing with SABRE
Reservations and Ticketing with Apollo
Sales and Marketing for the Travel Professional
The Business of Travel: Agency Operations and Administration

Foster, Dennis L.
    Reservations and ticketing with SABRE / Dennis L. Foster.—2nd ed.
        p. cm.— (Travel professional series)
    Includes index.
    ISBN 0-02-801391-3
        1. SABRE (Computer system)   2. Airlines—United States—
    Reservation systems—Data processing.   I. Title.   II. Series.
    HE9787.5.U5F67   1994
    387.7'42—dc20

                                                    93-41610
                                                        CIP

Imprint 1996

Send all inquiries to:

Glencoe/McGraw-Hill
936 Eastwind Drive
Westerville, OH 43081

ISBN 0-02-801391-3 (Text)
ISBN 0-02-801392-1 (Text w/disks)

Printed in the United States of America.

4 5 6 7 8 9 10 11 12   POH   03 02 01 00 99 98 97 96

Contents

About the Author

Dennis L. Foster is the chairman of the board of directors of Mundus Colleges and the executive director of the World Tourism Institute. He is the author of 35 published books on travel, hospitality, computer science, and business management. He was designated by the Department of Commerce as the U.S. representative for tourism education and technology transfer to the International Trade and Development Conference.

As a consultant to airlines, computer reservation systems, travel agency chains, educational institutions, and foreign governments, Mr. Foster developed a number of travel-related curricula for postsecondary and postgraduate education, industrial training, and agent certification. The Mundus curricula, from which the Glencoe Travel Professional Series originated, have been adopted by private and public postsecondary schools, universities, and graduate schools in 21 countries, helping many schools achieve placement rates in excess of 90 percent.

Preface

Perhaps no other industry has been affected as profoundly by the advent and rapid growth of computer technology as the travel and tourism industry. Until the 1950s, virtually all airline reservations were made by telephone or at airports and airline offices. Automated reservation systems—or, as they are known in the industry, "res" systems—first began to be installed in travel agencies in the mid-1960s. However, these early systems were mostly experimental and contained flight information for only one airline. In 1976, American Airlines, TWA, and United Airlines developed the first true computer reservation systems, containing flight information and fares for multiple carriers. From 1981 to 1992, the percentage of U.S. travel agencies using computer reservation systems grew from 61 percent to 96 percent.

Retail travel agencies are not the only industry segment that has benefited from automation. Today's computer reservation systems represent not only airlines, but lodging establishments, cruise lines, car rental chains, tour wholesalers, travel insurance, and rail and coach lines as well.

Despite the vast importance of this increasingly sophisticated technology, relatively few educational materials have as their primary objective the creation of travel professionals with industry-specific knowledge, problem-solving ability, and technological skill. *Reservations and Ticketing with SABRE* is the most comprehensive, detailed, and practical guide to the SABRE computer reservations system ever developed for educational institutions.

About This Series

The first editions of the textbooks and course materials that comprise the Travel Professional Series evolved from a curriculum developed by a consortium of tourism educators, corporate trainers, industry consultants, and travel agency managers. Through various stages, the development has involved more than 200 educators, corporate trainers, travel agency owners, airline representatives, chain executives, government employees, industry associations, and consultants. Since 1977, over 64,000 travel professionals have graduated from universities, community colleges, vocational schools, travel academies, corporate training programs, high schools, and regional training centers where various components of the curriculum have been used.

Since the first editions of this series were published, numerous developments, including changes in passenger carriers, airline routes, fares, and conventions have affected the travel and transportation industries. The revised editions have been expanded as well as updated, with a strong emphasis on creative thinking, problem solving, and interpersonal skills.

Comprising six textbooks and software simulating the major computer reservation systems, this Series provides:

- Thorough, current knowledge of the principles, practices, and economic, social, cultural, and environmental impact of the industry.

- An understanding of the opportunities, responsibilities, concerns, and ethics of a career in travel, transportation, or tourism.
- Effective reasoning, communication, decision-making, and interpersonal skills.
- Development of individual responsibility, self-esteem, sociability, self-management, and personal integrity.

The Travel Professional Series includes the *SABRE* text and the following titles with accompanying instructor's manuals and computer software.

First Class: An Introduction to Travel and Tourism

This text provides an overview of the history, scope, and functions of the travel and tourism industry and career opportunities within that industry. Procedures for handling lodging; land, rail, air, and cruise accommodations; car rentals; and other major on-the-job responsibilities for the travel agent are discussed. Ticketing procedures and a guide to the OAG with accompanying exercises are also provided.

Destinations: North American and International Geography

This travel geography textbook explores all the major regions of the world in the context of the travel counselor's job responsibilities. The text is designed according to popular traveler itineraries. Accompanying the requisite physical maps for each region, the book provides students with such additional references as transportation maps, maps showing gateway cities, entry and exit requirements, tourist attractions, and cultural profiles. This textbook affords travel students the sound geography background required for their future role as travel counselors.

Sales and Marketing for the Travel Professional

This text explores marketing and selling strategies required for success in the travel industry. Discussions include how to target markets, prepare a marketing plan, position travel products, select appropriate advertising and promotion media, and prepare advertising and promotion pieces. The student will also study personal and telephone selling techniques, practice the skills necessary to overcome obstacles to the sale, and review tips for coping with personal stress and client crises.

The Business of Travel: Agency Operations and Administration

The day-to-day operations of a travel agency are examined in the text. Students will discuss job descriptions of personnel, financial planning and accounting, preparation of sales and ARC reports, client billing, and commissions tracking.

The accompanying software provides numerous fill-in screens with corresponding on-screen client situations. These activities require students to enter data, book ARC and non-ARC segments, and prepare client billing statements.

Reservations and Ticketing with Apollo®

This worktext introduces students to computer reservation systems and is accompanied by software (IBM PC or compatible) that provides users with a simulated Apollo environment. The software was developed in cooperation with the training departments of major U.S. airlines. The software also contains simulations of customer requests to test student skills. A thorough appendix provides advanced Apollo functions.

About This Book

This revised and updated edition of *Reservations and Ticketing with SABRE®* is an in-depth, skills-based learning tool, as well as a valuable professional reference. Filled with case studies, examples, and illustrations, this textbook combines student reading material with hands-on exercises, role play, and practical applications, helping students to develop reasoning and decision-making skills while they learn specific job-related tasks.

Organization

The following aids to learning and to teaching are included in this book:

Outline—Each chapter opens with a topic outline followed by a carefully planned list of learning objectives.

Objectives—This list of objectives enumerates, for the student and instructor alike, the expected knowledge and skills outcomes. The objectives also allow the user to prepare for the review tasks and applications assigned at the end of the chapter.

Student Review—This segment appears at the end of each chapter and includes:

Key Concepts—The student is asked to identify key terms and phrases discussed in the chapter. Answers are given at the end of this section for immediate feedback.

Review Questions—The student responds in written or discussion format. For reinforcement, these questions support the objectives presented at the beginning of the chapter.

Applications—A travel scenario is presented. The student is given an opportunity to develop reasoning and decision-making skills while drawing from the chapter's theory.

Study Guide—This guide contains questions for each chapter and is found at the end of the text. It may be used by the student for additional study material or by the instructor for additional testing material.

Glossary—This alphabetical list of terms and concepts introduced throughout the text appears at the end of the book for reference.

Motivation

The practical experience with SABRE functions at the microcomputer is the chief motivational feature of these materials. Without **hands-on experience**, students do not have clearly defined marketable skills. In addition to students' interest in actually practicing job tasks, they find a microcomputer to be a patient and nonjudgmental tutor, creating a vital learning experience. The accompanying software transforms the microcomputer into a SABRE workstation and provides the "look and feel" of a "live" system.

Instructor Support

An Instructor's Manual and Key accompanies each textbook in The Travel Professional Series. The Manual contains plans and teaching suggestions, references, and materials needed to teach each chapter, transparency masters, testing materials, and keys to all testing materials.

Summary

The travel and tourism field is fast-paced and rapidly growing. Each year, it becomes increasingly more difficult for employers to undertake the training of new entrants to the field. The parallel growth in the use of sophisticated technologies has complicated this situation. At the same time, travelers throughout the world have become more sophisticated, more knowledgeable, and more demanding.

However, as educators we have a higher obligation than just training people to perform specific jobs. We must also help students understand social, organizational, and technological systems; allocate resources; make effective decisions; apply technology to specific tasks; and work, communicate, and interact with people from culturally diverse backgrounds.

Teachers, students, and employers must work together to achieve a commitment to lifelong learning and the dedication to the highest standards of quality, productivity, and professionalism.

Dennis L. Foster

Acknowledgements

The author and editorial team wish to gratefully acknowledge the contributions of the following reviewers, whose considerable efforts, suggestions, ideas, and insights helped to make this text a more valuable and viable learning instrument.

Clifford S. Bernstein
Training and Development
Berkeley Colleges
College for Technology
The Betty Owen Schools, Inc.
New York, New York

Jane Edwards
Business & Travel Teacher
J.P. Taravella High School
Carl Springs, Florida

Edmund Gray
Travel Consultant
Schenectady, New York

Kathryn Hoch
Instructor
School of Food, Hotel, & Travel Management
Rochester Institute of Technology
Rochester, New York

Gayle Olson-Suit
Travel Instructor & Coordinator
Business and Industry Services
Moore-Norman AVTS
Norman, Oklahoma

Barbara Scanio
Travel Consultant
Hyatt Travel
Buffalo, New York

Nina Shattuck
Travel Instructor
Ridley Lowell Business and Technical Institute
Binghamton, New York

Carol Silvis
Chairperson/Instructor
New Kensington Commercial School
New Kensington, Pennsylvania

Marilyn Ward
Travel Consultant
Leisure Travel
Clermont, Florida

Chapter 1

Introduction
to SABRE

Chapter Objectives

After you complete this chapter, you should be able to:

1. Identify the main components of a computer reservation system.

2. Discuss the basic SABRE functions.

3. Sign in and sign out.

4. Encode or decode airlines, cities, airports, equipment, hotel chains, and car companies.

The Impact of Technology

Almost every human endeavor has benefited in one way or another from the invention of the computer. Yet it was not long ago that computers were rare and their role in the affairs of humanity was minor. Only 50 years ago there were very few computers anywhere in the world. In 1950 there were about 250 computers in the United States, and today millions of computers are in use across the globe.

It is, therefore, not surprising that over the last two decades the computer has become an essential tool of the travel professional. More than 90 percent of all airline reservations are made by computer. Travel agents, airline reservation agents, airport ticket agents, tour operators, and others use computer reservation systems—or, as they are commonly called in the industry, "res" systems—to quote fares, determine flight availability, and book reservations.

Until the 1950s, flight reservations were made either by telephone or at an airport. Fares were obtained from printed tariffs, and manual calculating machines were used to calculate ticket prices. In the 1960s the flight schedules and fares of most major carriers were stored on microfilm.

SABRE was developed in 1976 by AMR, the parent company of American Airlines. The name *SABRE* is an acronym for **Semi-Automated Business Research Environment.** By 1992 SABRE had been installed at 14,000 retail travel agencies and branch offices, covering 32.5 percent of all U.S. agencies.

To use the SABRE system, a retail travel agency must subscribe, by signing a contract and paying an ongoing subscription fee. Relations between computer reservation system (CRS) vendors and subscribers are regulated by the **U.S. Department of Transportation** (DOT).

Basic CRS Concepts

To understand how a CRS functions requires familiarity with basic data processing concepts. The following section may be regarded as either a review or an introduction, depending on the previous experience of the student.

Information that can be processed by a computer is referred to as **data.** Flight numbers, passenger names, telephone numbers, and fares are examples of data that can be processed by a CRS. Information that consists only of numbers is referred to as **numerical data.** Information that consists only of letters of the alphabet is referred to as **alpha data.** Information that may consist of numbers, letters, and punctuation is called **alphanumeric data.** Thus a fare, such as 305.72, constitutes numerical data, and a city code, such as LAX, constitutes alpha data. An address containing numbers, letters, and punctuation marks constitutes alphanumeric data.

A data processing system such as a CRS consists of the following basic components (see Figure 1-1):

1. central processor
2. terminal
3. storage

The **central processor** performs arithmetic and logic operations and coordinates the communication, storage, and retrieval of information. The processor performs an arithmetic operation whenever it adds, subtracts, multiplies, or divides numerical data.

A terminal is used to send and receive data. A **video display terminal (VDT)** consists of a keyboard, used to enter data, and a video screen, used to display data entered by the keyboard or received from the central processor. A VDT is sometimes called a CRT, short for *cathode-ray tube,* because of the television tube that makes the display. A ticket printer, which receives data transmitted by the central processor, is another type of terminal. Entering data for transmission to the central processor is an **input operation.** Receiving data transmitted by the central processor is an **output operation.**

The part of a data processing system that keeps data for future retrieval is referred to as **storage.** After data has been processed, it can be transmitted to a terminal or placed in storage. Data in storage can be retrieved by the central processor and then displayed by a terminal.

To illustrate, assume a travel agent desires to use a CRS to display fares. The fare information is kept in the storage area. To obtain a fare display the agent uses a terminal to input the origin and destination. This information is transmitted to the central processor, which retrieves the desired fares from storage. The processor then transmits the fares to the terminal, which displays the data on the video screen.

A CRS has two types of storage: permanent and temporary. **Permanent storage** is used by the central processor to maintain such data as reservations, fares, flight

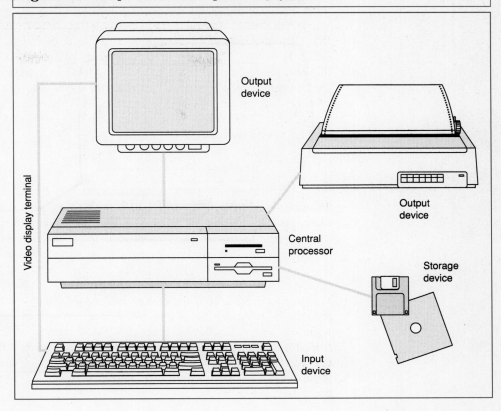

Figure 1-1 Components of a data processing system.

schedules, and hotel lists. A collection of related data kept in permanent storage is called a **record.** A passenger reservation is an example of a record.

Temporary storage is used to assemble information to be transmitted to the central processor. For example, when booking a reservation, a travel agent inputs information about the passenger and the itinerary. This information is stored in the temporary storage area until the agent signals for the data to be transmitted to the central processor.

Together, the central processor and permanent storage area constitute a **mainframe.** All the agent sets in travel agencies, in airports, and at other sites constitute the SABRE network.

In the SABRE system, the following devices are used for input, output, processing, and storage:

1. the agent set
2. the terminal interchange
3. the C system
4. the central processor

Figure 1-2 illustrates how these devices are linked. The agent set used to input and display data may be either a VDT or a desktop computer, commonly called a *personal computer* or *PC*. A PC has its own central processor and storage, in addition to the keyboard and the video screen. It can be used for other purposes besides communicating with SABRE—for example, financial management, record keeping, and word processing. A ticket printer may also be connected to the SABRE system, to enable the travel agency to produce tickets, itineraries, boarding passes, and other documents. A terminal interchange, located at each site where agent sets are

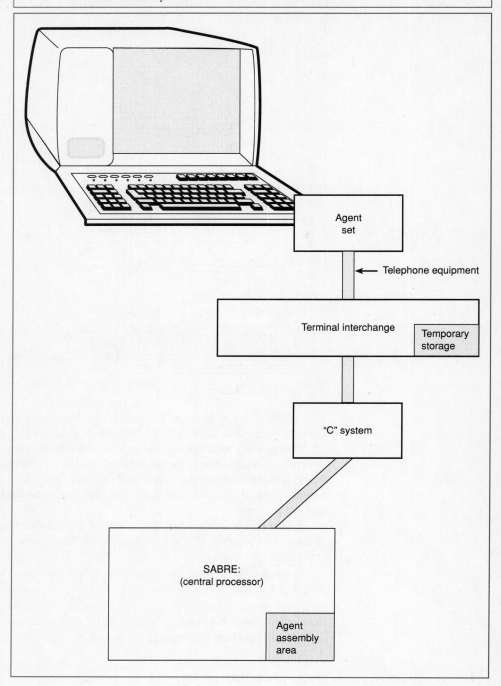

Figure 1-2 The communication chain, a simplified picture of the components of the SABRE system.

present, links the agent set to the central processor. The temporary storage area is located in the terminal interchange.

The C system is an electronic switchboard that coordinates data transmitted by agent sets and relays the information to the central processor. The central processor processes and stores all reservation records transmitted by agent sets throughout the SABRE network. The SABRE mainframe and the C system are located in Tulsa, Oklahoma.

The process of transmitting and receiving data is referred to as **data communication.** Agent sets are linked to the C system by means of telephone lines. Each agent set is connected to a **modem,** which converts computer data into signals that can be transmitted over a telephone line. The term *modem* is short for *modulator-demodulator.* The modem codes, or modulates, information to be transmitted, and it decodes, or demodulates, information received.

ARINC

When an airline reservation is received by the SABRE processor, the record is placed in permanent storage so that it can be retrieved later. However, reservation data must also be communicated to each airline in the itinerary. An independent firm, Aeronautical Radio, Inc. **(ARINC),** maintains a data communication network linking SABRE with the airlines and other travel-related vendors. When SABRE receives a flight booking, the data is transmitted to the airline via the ARINC network.

Basic SABRE Functions

Through SABRE, subscribers have access to the following basic functions:

1. city pair availability
2. flight bookings
3. passenger name records
4. fare quotes
5. preassigned seats
6. special travelers account records
7. queues
8. ticket and document issuance
9. auxiliary services
10. reference information

Understanding how the SABRE system is used requires familiarity with each function.

City Pair Availability

City pair availability is a display of regularly scheduled flights between a specified origin and a specified destination. On each flight, the display shows the number of seats that can be sold in each class of service. The city pair availability function enables an agent to efficiently research, recommend, and book flight segments according to a client's preferences and needs.

Flight Bookings

Booking airline reservations is called **selling space,** or **selling seats.** If the selected class of service is sold out on the desired flight, a reservation can often be waitlisted—that is, put on a waiting list. A waitlisted reservation may later be confirmed if passengers with confirmed reservations cancel their reservations. When seats are sold or waitlisted, the data is transmitted to the airline via the ARINC network. Confirmations are sent back over the network by each airline in the itinerary.

Passenger Name Records

Every reservation booked on the SABRE system is stored in a **passenger name record (PNR).** Each PNR contains the itinerary, passenger names, telephone numbers, ticketing arrangements, and other data. The PNR is transmitted to the mainframe for permanent storage. The PNR remains in storage until the itinerary has been completed or until the passenger cancels the reservation. While the PNR is in storage, the travel agency or the airline can retrieve and display it and make changes in the itinerary or the passenger data fields.

Fare Quotes

A **fare quote** is a display of fares between a specified origin and a specified destination. Fares can be displayed for the current date or for a specified departure date. The agent can view competitive fares for all carriers or only the fares offered by a specified carrier.

SABRE can autoprice most air itineraries; that is, it can automatically calculate the total base fare, tax, and total fare. On request, SABRE can autoprice an entire itinerary, selected segments, or selected passengers.

Prereserved Seats

SABRE can also be used to prereserve seats on flights operated by participating carriers. On many flights SABRE can reserve a seat automatically, considering the client's preference for a window or aisle location. If the flight has a smoking section, a client can also request a seat in either the smoking section or the no-smoking section. (Smoking is not permitted at all by some carriers, nor is it permitted on any domestic flight of five hours or less.)

On many flights a seat map can be displayed so that the agent can assign a specific seat. A seat map shows the location and booking status of each seat on a specified flight.

Special Travelers Account Records

Many SABRE subscribers use *Special Travelers Account Records (STARs)* to store passenger data for their agencies' regular clients. Each line of a STAR contains a particular item of passenger data, such as the name, home telephone number, and form of payment. The data can be transferred to a PNR as needed. STARs provide an efficient means of creating PNRs for frequent travelers, eliminating the need to type out the same data repeatedly for such clients.

Queues

Queue is a French word meaning "a waiting line." In the SABRE system, a **queue** is an electronic holding area where records or messages are stored temporarily for a specific purpose. For example, PNRs that are affected by airline schedule changes are stored in one queue, and PNRs that have been confirmed from a waitlist are stored in another queue. Two types of queues are used: message queues and record queues. Only messages can be stored in a message queue, whereas only PNRs can be placed in a record queue. Queues provide travel agencies with a valuable tool for handling daily workloads. For example, every business day, all PNRs scheduled for ticketing on that date appear automatically in a ticketing queue, and all PNRs with waitlist confirmations appear in the waitlist queue.

Ticket and Document Issuance

SABRE can be used to print tickets and other documents, such as boarding passes, invoices, and itineraries. An **itinerary/invoice** is a document that provides detailed flight information for each segment and a summary of all the charges. Special features enable the travel agent to print messages, called *itinerary remarks* or *invoice remarks,* on the itinerary/invoice. For example, an itinerary remark might be used to print directions to a hotel, or a telephone number to summon a courtesy car.

Auxiliary Segments

Besides airline space, SABRE can also be used to display and book hotels, rental cars, cruises, tours, and other travel products. Such bookings are referred to as **auxiliary segments.**

Reference Information

SABRE can display a wide range of reference information, such as weather forecasts, in-flight services, foreign exchange rates, sports events, and city descriptions. The system even offers daily updates on television serials (soap operas).

The Agent Set

According to statistics compiled by AMR, 72 percent of all SABRE terminals are PCs; the rest are VDTs. The most common type of PC used with SABRE is the IBM PS/2. A PC connected to the SABRE system is referred to as a *workstation.* Several types of VDTs are used with SABRE, including various terminals manufactured by Raytheon, Icot, and IBM.

Video display terminals have been used since the 1970s. Personal computers had not been developed then. Since 1983 the use of PCs in travel agencies has become widespread. Eventually all SABRE subscribers will be using PCs.

A Raytheon or Icot terminal can display a maximum of 30 lines, with 64 characters per line. The display area can be split to display data simultaneously in two windows, called *view ports.* A maximum of 15 lines can be displayed in each view port.

Only uppercase characters can be typed on a Raytheon or Icot terminal. The numerical keys, which consist of the numerals Ø through 9, are in a single row above the alpha keys, as on a standard typewriter or a PC.

On the PC keyboard, a separate numerical keypad is also found to the right of the alpha keys, arranged like a ten-key adding machine. The Num Lock key is used to activate those number keys.

Table 1-1 Special-Purpose Keys for Raytheon or Icot Terminal.

Symbol	Label	Key Name	Purpose
–	NAME	Name	Enter passenger name(s)
*	DSPL	Display	Display PNR data
¤	CHNG	Change	Modify PNR data
Σ	END-ITEM	End-item	Separate multiple entries
‡	CROSS	Cross	Various uses
,	NEW #	New number	Reduce the number of passengers in a party
.	CSS	CSS	Change segment status
/	IAS	IAS	Insert data after a segment

Table 1-2 Special-Purpose Keys on PC Keyboard.

PC Key Label	Symbol	VDT Key Label
-	-	NAME
*	*	DSPL
[	¤	CHNG
\	Σ	END-ITEM
'	‡	CROSS
'	'	NEW #
.	.	CSS
/	/	IAS

The Enter key is used to transmit data to the central processor. Information is displayed on the screen as it is typed, but the characters are not transmitted to the central processor until the Enter key is pressed.

The keyboard of a Raytheon or Icot VDT has several special-purpose keys that are not found on a PC keyboard or a typewriter. Those keys are listed in Table 1-1. On a PC keyboard the keys shown in Table 1-2 are used to perform the functions of the special-purpose keys on a Raytheon or Icot terminal. When the PC communicates with SABRE, the special-purpose keys cause different symbols to be displayed from those displayed when the PC is used for other purposes. For example, when the backslash (\) is typed, the end-item symbol (Σ) is displayed. When the left bracket ([) is typed, a solid box is displayed. When the apostrophe (') is typed, the cross (‡) is displayed.

Figure 1-3 shows the keyboard layout of a PC used as a SABRE workstation.

Basic Operation of the Agent Set

Inputting Entries

An entry instructs SABRE to perform a particular task, such as displaying fares or booking a flight reservation. Each entry must be input in a specified *format;* that is, specified information must be typed in a specified order. Each entry format begins with a code, called a *field identifier* or *entry code.* To input an entry, type the required information and then press the Enter key. A marker called a *cursor* indicates the point where the next character will be typed. The cursor usually appears as a flashing line or solid box.

The Agent Work Area

An agent enters passenger data into the **agent work area,** an electronic holding area assigned to each terminal. In the work area, the agent assembles information such as the traveler's name, contact telephone number, and desired ticketing data. The information may be entered in any order. When all the elements of a PNR have been assembled, the agent enters a command to end the transaction. The record is then transmitted from the agent work area to the central processor, and the work area is erased so that another PNR can be assembled. Six work areas are available for use by travel agents. Each work area is identified by a letter from A to F.

Figure 1–3 The SABRE keyboard.

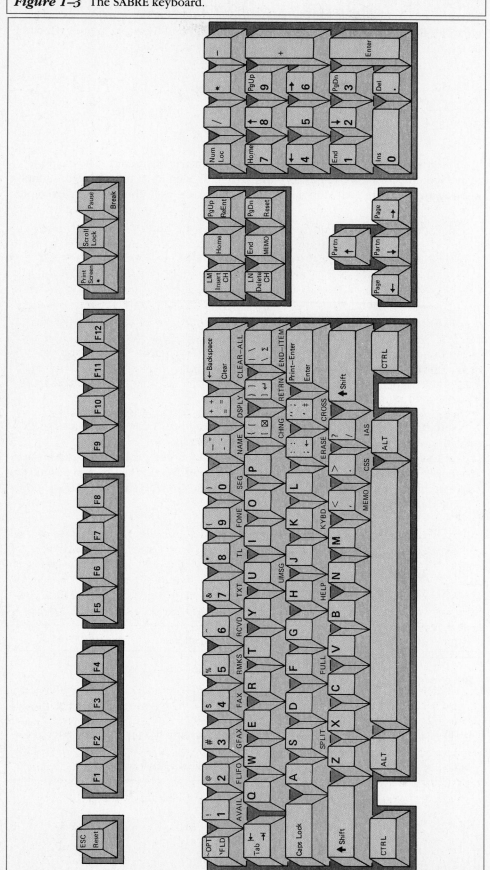

Sign-in

To communicate with SABRE, the agent first must sign in. The sign-in procedure identifies the agent who will be using the computer and the work area in which he or she will be working. The basic **sign-in entry** is as follows:

FORMAT   SI<Work Area><Agent ID Code>

EXAMPLE   SIA53421

The agent ID may consist of up to six alphanumeric characters. The example above would be used to sign in on work area A. To sign in on all work areas simultaneously, type an asterisk (*) in place of the work area, as in the following example:

SI*53421

When the sign-in entry is made, SABRE responds as follows:

```
AGENT SINE-IN
  CURRENT PASSCODE        ID/053421    CTY/Q9X0
DUTY CODE/*/    AREA/A/    NEW PASSCODE
```

Note that SABRE uses the spelling *sine-in* for *sign-in*. Table 1-3 provides an explanation of the information shown in the sign-in response.

Each site where SABRE is used is identified by a four-digit code, called a **pseudo city code.** If a subscriber has multiple sites, each branch office has its own pseudo city code. In the example, the fictitious pseudo city code *Q9X0* is shown for illustration.

The duty code may be one of the following:

*	Full access to reservations functions
/	SABRE-assisted instruction
6	Training mode
9	Management functions

Table 1-3 Information shown in SABRE Sign-in Response.

Response	Information
ID	The agent ID code used to sign in
CTY	The agency pseudo city code
DUTY CODE	The type of work for which the agent has signed in (An asterisk designates reservations duty.)
AREA	The work area (An asterisk indicates all six work areas.)

Note that, in the sign-in response, nothing is displayed after the words *current passcode* or *new passcode*. The cursor appears to the right of the words *current passcode,* prompting the agent to enter the passcode. For security, each agent has a unique passcode consisting of six to eight alphanumeric characters. The passcode may be assigned by the agent, but may not contain two or more characters that match characters in the agent name or ID code. Days of the month and offensive words are also prohibited. Except for these rules, any combination of six, seven, or eight numbers and letters can be used in the passcode.

When the passcode is typed, the characters are not displayed. Thus the passcode is kept secret in case someone else is watching.

To change the duty code, work area, or passcode, position the cursor next to the appropriate word, type in the new information, and then press Enter.

Sign out

Before leaving the agent's set for an extended period, or at the end of the work day, the agent must sign out, as follows:

FORMAT   SO<Work Area>

EXAMPLE   SOA

If the option * was used to sign in to all work areas, the following entry may be used to sign out of all work areas:

SO*

If any unfinished work remains on the screen, SABRE will not allow the agent to sign out.

A terminal that has been left on and not used for a set period of time is automatically signed out. The period can be adjusted, but in most cases it is four hours.

Scrolling the Display

Often the amount of data to be displayed exceeds the size of the screen. A fare quote, for example, may span several screens. A ‡ symbol at the bottom of the screen indicates that additional data exists. The display must be scrolled forward to obtain the additional data. When the display has been scrolled forward, it can be scrolled backward to redisplay the previous data. The first character of the first line of data is referred to as the top of the display, and the last character of the last line is referred to as the bottom.

The following commands are used to scroll a SABRE information display:

MD   Move down (scrolls forward)
MU   Move up (scrolls backward)
MT   Move to top
MB   Move to bottom

The display can be scrolled a specified number of lines, as follows:

MD25

This example will scroll the display forward 25 lines.

The commands for scrolling the display will be illustrated again in later chapters.

In city pair availability displays, fare quotes, and other types of information displays, codes are used to indicate airlines, cities, airports, aircraft equipment, hotel chains, and car rental companies. An agent can encode or decode this type of information. The **encode** function is used to determine the code for a specified name, and the **decode** function is used to determine the name represented by a specified code.

The entry code *W/* is used to encode and decode. Secondary codes are used to specify the type of information sought, as illustrated in Table 1-4.

Carrier Codes

Air passenger carriers are referred to by two-letter carrier codes. For example, the carrier code for United Airlines is UA, and the carrier code for Delta is DL. The carrier codes are assigned by The *International Air Transport Association (IATA),* which represents more than 200 of the world's principal airlines, assigns carrier codes. IATA has also assigned a three-digit airline code to each carrier. For example, the airline code for American Airlines is 001, and the airline code for United Airlines is 016.

Table 1-4 Secondary Codes for Encoding and Decoding.

Code	Function
W/-ALUNITED	Encode carrier
W/*NW	Decode carrier
W/-CCBIRMINGHAM	Encode city or airport
W/*MCO	Decode city or airport
W/EQ*M80	Decode equipment
W/-HLHILTON	Encode hotel
W/HL*SI	Decode hotel
W/-CRAVIS	Encode car rental chain
W/CR*ZD	Decode car rental chain

Airlines Reporting Corporation (ARC) assigns carrier and airline codes to domestic carriers. Its codes, however, are exactly the same as the IATA codes. The main function of ARC is to collect money for ticket sales from travel agencies and distribute it to the airlines.

Examples of carrier and airline codes for major U.S. airlines can be found in Table 1-5.

The following format is used to encode an air passenger carrier:

FORMAT   W/-AL<Carrier name>

EXAMPLE   W/-ALDELTA

Table 1-5 Examples of Carrier and Airline Codes for Major U.S. Airlines.

Carrier Code	Airline Name	Airline Code
AA	American Airlines	001
AS	Alaska Airlines	027
CO	Continental Airlines	005
DL	Delta Airlines	006
HP	America West Airlines	401
NW	Northwest Airlines	012
TW	Trans World Airlines	015
UA	United Airlines	016
US	USAir	037

This example will display the carrier code for Delta Airlines. SABRE will respond as follows:

```
DELTA AIRLINES/DELTA AIR LINES, INC.
DL-OO6-AA  TO TKT OR ACCPT TKT
```

The response includes the airline, the full corporate name, the carrier code, and the IATA airline code. In this example, guidelines for ticketing and ticket acceptance are also displayed.

The following format is used to decode a carrier code:

FORMAT   W/*<Carrier code>

EXAMPLE   W/*AS

This example will display the name of the airline that has the carrier code AS. The response is the same as when a carrier is encoded.

Cities and Airports

In SABRE displays, cities and airports are indicated by three-letter codes. For example, SFO is the city code for San Francisco, and ORD is the airport code for O'Hare Airport in Chicago. For a city served by multiple airports, each airport has its own code. For example, three major airports serve New York City. The city code *NYC* refers to the New York City area, but not to a specific airport. The code for LaGuardia Airport is LGA, the code for Kennedy International Airport is JFK, and the code for the airport in nearby Newark, New Jersey, is EWR.

The **International Standards Organization (ISO),** based in Geneva, Switzerland, assigns city and airport codes. The ISO codes have been adopted by IATA and ARC. All computer reservation systems and airlines use the same codes.

The following format is used to encode a city or an airport:

FORMAT   W/-CC<City or airport>

EXAMPLE   W/-CCALBUQUERQUE

In response, SABRE displays the city code, the city name, and the state, as follows:

```
ABQ    ALBUQUERQUE NM
```

If multiple cities exist with the same name, SABRE displays the code for each. For example, when Burlington is encoded, SABRE responds as follows:

```
BRL    BURLINGTON    IA
BTV    BURLINGTON    VT
```

In this case, two cities named Burlington exist; one in Iowa, the other in Vermont. The following format is used to decode a city or airport code:

FORMAT   W/*<City or airport code>

EXAMPLE   W/*MSY

SABRE responds as follows:

```
MSY    NEW ORLEANS    LA
```

Aircraft Equipment

Each type of aircraft is identified by an equipment code. For example, the equipment code for the Boeing 747 aircraft is 747, and the code for the McDonnell Douglas DC-10 is D10. In flight availability displays, equipment codes indicate the type of aircraft used on each flight. (See Table 1-6 for more examples.)

Some passenger aircraft have more than one model. For example, three basic models of the 727 are used for passenger transportation: the 727, the 727-100, and the 727-200. The equipment codes *72S* and *73S* represent special configurations of the 727 and 737 aircraft. The *S* indicates that the airplanes have been configured for additional passenger seating. These specially configured aircraft are commonly referred to as "stretch jets." Similarly, the code *72M* or 73M indicates a "multiple" configuration, designed to transport both passengers and cargo.

Table 1-6 Examples of Equipment Codes for Common Passenger Aircraft.

Code	Aircraft
A3B	Airbus Industrie A-300B
DC9	McDonnell-Douglas DC-9
D10	McDonnell-Douglas DC-10
D9S	McDonnell-Douglas DC-9 Super Jet
L10	Lockheed 1011 Tristar
727	Boeing 727
72M	Boeing 727-100
72S	Boeing 727-200
733	Boeing 737-300
737	Boeing 737
73M	Boeing 737-200C
73S	Boeing 737-200
747	Boeing 747
757	Boeing 757
767	Boeing 767

The secondary code *EQ** is input to decode an equipment code, as follows:

FORMAT   W/EQ*<Equipment code>

EXAMPLE   W/EQ*M80

The example above will display the aircraft equipment for the code M80. SABRE will respond as follows:

```
M80    MCDONNELL  DOUGLAS  DC9  SUPER  80 JET
       132-172  STD  SEATS
```

Note that the response includes the standard seat capacity. In this example the standard capacity is 132 to 172 passengers.

Hotel Chains and Car Companies

Hotel and car rental chains are also indicated by codes. For example, the code for Holiday Inn is HI, and the code for Budget Rent A Car is ZD.

The following format is used to encode a hotel chain or property:

FORMAT   W/-HL<Hotel chain>

EXAMPLE   W/-HLRADISSON

This example will display the code for the Radisson chain.
The following format is used to decode a hotel chain code:

FORMAT   W/HL*<Hotel code>

EXAMPLE   W/HL*UI

SABRE refers to car rental firms as car companies.
The following format is used to encode a car company:

FORMAT   W/–CR<Car rental chain>

EXAMPLE   W/–CRNATIONAL

This example will display the carrier code for National.
The following format is used to decode a car company code:

FORMAT   W/CR*<Car company code>

EXAMPLE   W/CR*ZE

This example will display the car company for the code ZE.
Note that the following primary and secondary codes are used to encode terms:

W/-AL	Airline
W/-CC	City code
W/-HL	Hotel
W/-CR	Car rental

The following primary and secondary codes are used to decode:

W/EQ*	Equipment
W/HL*	Hotel
W/CR*	Car rental

To decode an airline, a city, or an airport, the secondary code is simply an asterisk (*).

Summary

The SABRE airline reservation system was developed in 1976. If offers flight information, fares, and reservations for different carriers.

The SABRE system consists of a mainframe capable of serving many different sites. Each agent set is connected via modem to the C system, which relays data to the central processor. A travel agency pays a subscription fee for access to the SABRE system.

SABRE can be used for such functions as displaying fares and flight availability, booking reservations, and storing passenger records. When a reservation is booked, passenger data is stored temporarily in an electronic work area. When the record is complete, it is transmitted to the central processor for permanent storage. Six work areas are available for use by travel agents.

New commands included in this chapter:

SIA54321	Signs in on work area A
SI*54321	Signs in on all work areas
SO*	Signs out of all work areas
SO	Signs out of current work area
MU	Moves up
MU25	Moves up 25 lines
MD	Moves down
MD25	Moves down 25 lines
MT	Moves to top
MB	Moves to bottom
W/–ALDELTA	Encodes an airline
W/*DL	Decodes a carrier code
W/–CCBIRMINGHAM	Encodes a city or airport
W/*MSY	Decodes a city or airport code
W/EQ*D9S	Decodes an equipment code
W/–HLWESTIN	Encodes a hotel chain
W/HL*UI	Decodes a hotel chain code
W/–CRTROPICAL	Encodes a car company
W/CR*ZL	Decodes a car company code

STUDENT REVIEW

KEY CONCEPTS AND TERMS

Identify the word or phrase for each of the following concepts:

1. The full name for which SABRE is an acronym.

2. The government branch that regulates relations between CRS vendors and subscribers.

3. Information that can be processed by a computer.

4. Information, such as a fare, consisting only of numbers.

5. Information, such as a city code, consisting only of letters of the alphabet.

6. Information, such as an address, consisting of a combination of numbers, letters, and punctuation.

7. In a data processing system, the component that performs arithmetic and logic operations, and coordinates the communication, storage, and retrieval of information.

8. A data processing component consisting of a keyboard to enter data and a video screen to display data.

9. Inputting data to a computer for processing.

10. Receiving data from a computer for display, printout, or storage.

11. The type of storage that is used to maintain reservations, fares, and flight schedules.

12. A collection of related data, such as a passenger reservation.

13. The type of storage that is used to assemble information to be transmitted to the computer.

14. Hardware consisting of a powerful central processor and a large storage area.

15. The process of transmitting and receiving data.

16. A device that converts computer data into signals that can be transmitted over a telephone line.

17. An independent data communication network that links SABRE with airlines and other travel-related vendors.

18. A display of regularly scheduled flights between a specified origin and a specified destination.

19. The act of booking an airline reservation.

20. A computer record containing the itinerary, passenger names, contact telephone numbers, ticketing arrangements, and other data relating to a reservation.

21. An electronic holding area in which passenger data items are entered by the agent.

22. A display of fares between a specified origin and a specified destination.

23. An electronic holding area where records or messages are stored temporarily for a specific purpose.

24. A document that provides detailed flight information for each segment and a summary of all the charges.

25. Bookings other than flight reservations, such as hotel, rental car, cruise, and tour bookings.

26. The type of entry that identifies the agent and gains access to the computer.

27. A code that identifies each site where SABRE terminals are installed.

28. The function that is used to determine the code for a specified name.

29. The function that is used to determine the name represented by a specified code.

30. The organization that designates official city and airport codes.

Answers:

1. Semi-Automated Business Research Environment; 2. the U.S. Department of Transportation (DOT); 3. data; 4. numerical data; 5. alpha data; 6. alphanumeric data; 7. central processor; 8. video display terminal (VDT); 9. input operation; 10. output operation; 11. permanent storage; 12. record; 13. temporary storage; 14. mainframe; 15. data communication; 16. modem; 17. ARINC; 18. city pair availability; 19. selling space *or* selling seats; 20. passenger name record (PNR); 21. agent work area; 22. fare quote; 23. queue; 24. itinerary/invoice; 25. auxiliary segments; 26. sign-in entry; 27. pseudo city code; 28. decode; 29. encode; 30. International Standards Organization (ISO).

REVIEW QUESTIONS

1. What entry code is used to sign in to SABRE?

2. What entry code is used to sign out?

3. If the information in a display is longer than the screen, what entry would be used to scroll the display forward?

4. What entry would be used to scroll forward 12 lines?

5. What entry would be used to scroll the display up?

6. Write the entry to scroll back to the top of the display.

7. Write the entry to scroll forward to the bottom of the display.

8. What entry code is used to determine the carrier code for an airline?

9. What entry code is used to determine the airline name from a carrier code?

10. Write the entry to determine the carrier code for Continental.

11. Write the entry to display the airline name for the carrier code CP.

12. What entry code is used to determine the code for a city or airport?

13. What entry code is used to determine the name from a city or airport code?

14. Write the entry to display the city for the code BTV.

15. Write the entry to display the city code for Colorado Springs.

16. What entry code is used to determine the aircraft name from an equipment code?

17. Write the entry to decode the equipment code B11.

18. Write the entry to display the hotel chain code for Holiday Inn.

19. Write the entry to determine the hotel chain from the code IC.

20. Write the entry to display the car company for the code ZD.

APPLICATIONS

Read the following scenario, and decide what should be done to satisfy the client's preferences and needs. Briefly describe how you would handle the situation, and then write the required entries.

You have just arrived at the office, and you need to use the agent set to make an airline reservation. A client requests information about flights from Des Moines to Denpasar, Bali. You are not certain of the city codes. When you obtain the flight information, you notice the carrier code GA in the display. You are not familiar with the airline. One of the flights requires a change of planes in NRT, and you are not sure what city has this code. The client asks what type of aircraft is used on a segment from Des Moines to Los Angeles. According to the display, the equipment code is M80, but you are unsure of the type of aircraft.

Chapter 2

Flight Availability

Outline:

The Itinerary	Return Availability
City Pairs	Follow-up Availability Entries
City Pair Availability	Alternative Availability Entries
Specifying a Departure Date	Last-Seat Availability
Specifying a Departure Time	Specific Flight Availability
The Availability Display	

Chapter Objectives

After you complete this chapter, you should be able to:

1. Display city pair availability.

2. Interpret the information in a city pair availability display.

3. Display return flight availability.

4. Use follow-up entries to modify an availability display.

5. Customize an availability display to match a client's preferences and needs.

PROBLEM

A client wants to travel from Los Angeles to the Miami area. He has not decided whether to fly into Miami or Ft. Lauderdale. He would like to arrive around 6 P.M. on 17 August. He wants to return to Los Angeles three days later.

SABRE SOLUTION

Display city pair availability on 17 August from Los Angeles to Miami, specifying a 6 P.M. arrival. If a suitable flight and class are not available, change the destination point to Ft. Lauderdale. When the client has selected a flight, display return flight availability for 20 August.

In this chapter, you will learn various methods of checking flight availability, modifying an existing availability display, and customizing an availability display.

The term **itinerary** refers to the origin, the destination, and all the intermediate points in a trip. Each portion of the itinerary is referred to as a **segment.** The first city or airport in a flight segment is the **departure** or **origin point,** and the second city or airport is the **arrival** or **destination point.**

As an example, consider the following trip:

1. ORD–SFO
2. SFO–ORD

This example includes two flight segments. The first segment in the itinerary is called the originating or outbound segment. The first point of the first segment is called the **originating point.** In this example, Chicago-O'Hare (ORD) is the originating point, and San Francisco (SFO) is the turn-around point or destination. The flight that returns from the destination to the originating point is called the return flight. The passenger will travel from Chicago-O'Hare to San Francisco on the outbound segment, and from San Francisco back to Chicago-O'Hare on the return segment.

In the case of a multi-airport city, the selection of an airport may depend on passenger preference. If the passenger requests a particular airport, the appropriate airport code should be used. Otherwise, the city code can be used to display availability for all airports in the vicinity. For example, the city code CHI would refer to all airports in the Chicago area, including Midway (MDW) and O'Hare.

If a trip involves a connection, a separate segment is included in the itinerary for each connecting flight. A point where a passenger transfers from one flight to another is called a **connecting point.** Any point that is not a connecting point is called a *stopover point.* For example, assume a passenger will travel from Phoenix to Boston, connecting in St. Louis. After attending a meeting in Boston, he will return on a nonstop flight to Phoenix. This passenger's itinerary will consist of the following air segments:

1. PHX–STL
2. STL–BOS
3. BOS–PHX

The passenger will depart from Phoenix (PHX) and disembark in St. Louis (STL) to board another flight to Boston (BOS). The St. Louis-Boston portion of the trip is a separate segment. In this example, St. Louis is a connecting point, and Boston is a stopover point.

City Pairs

Together, the departure point and arrival point make up a **city pair**. The following are examples of city pairs:

BOSPHL	Boston–Philadelphia
SFOMIA	San Francisco–Miami
LAXHNL	Los Angeles–Honolulu

The city pair availability function used to display flight availability between two specified points is called *city pair availability.*

City Pair Availability

The entry code **1** is used to display city pair availability. The following format is used to display availability on the current date:

FORMAT   1<City pair>

EXAMPLE   1INDDFW

This example requests flights departing today from Indianapolis and arriving at Dallas-Ft. Worth.

Specifying a Departure Date

Unless a departure date is specified, SABRE will display only flights scheduled for the current date. However, most flight reservations are for future dates. Since flight schedules and seat availability frequently change, it is important to specify the exact departure date.

When a date is input, the day of the month is typed first, as one or two digits. The month is abbreviated to the first three letters. For example, 10 March is entered as 10MAR, and 23 July is entered as 23JUL. If the day of the month consists of one digit, a leading zero may be included. For example, the date 6 May may be entered either as 6MAY or 06MAY. Table 2-1 provides examples of valid SABRE date formats.

Table 2-1 Examples of SABRE Date Formats.

Date	SABRE Date Format
19 January	19JAN
3 July	3JUL or 03JUL
22 December	22DEC

When a departure date is specified in an availability entry, the date is input before the city pair, as follows:

123AUGINDDFW

This example requests availability of flights departing on 23 August. The city pair is the same as in the previous example, requesting flights from Indianapolis to Dallas-Ft. Worth. Neither example includes a departure time. If a departure time is not specified, SABRE will display flights departing around 7 A.M.

Specifying a Departure Time

Most passengers have a preference for a departure time. When a time is input, A is typed for A.M. and P for P.M. Punctuation is omitted. For example, 8:30 A.M. is input as 830A, and 11 P.M. is input as 1100P. For efficiency, the double zeros, though optional, should be omitted in even-hour times. Thus, 3 P.M. should be input as 3P. Table 2-2 provides examples of valid time formats. Note that 12N may be input for 12 noon, and 12M may be input for 12 midnight.

Table 2-2 Examples of Time Formats.

12-Hour Clock Time	SABRE Time Format
6:00 A.M.	6A or 600A
11:00 A.M.	11A or 1100A
3:30 P.M.	330P
12:00 noon	12N or 1200N
12:00 midnight	12M or 1200M

When a departure time is specified in an availability entry, the time is input after the city pair, as follows:

117APRCHIMIA10A

This example requests availability of flights departing around 10 A.M. on 17 April from the Chicago area to Miami (MIA).

The Availability Display

SABRE responds to a valid city pair availability entry with a display of flights scheduled for the specified departure date (see Figure 2-1).

The first line of the display, called the **header**, indicates the departure date and day of the week. It also indicates the origin and destination points and their time zones. As shown in Figure 2-1, Chicago local time is Central standard time (CST),

---

C L I E N T   F O C U S

Departure Time

Suppose a passenger is planning a trip from Chicago to Philadelphia. She would like to depart from O'Hare on September 13 at around 9 A.M. The data would be encoded as follows:

Departure date:	13SEP
Origin:	ORD
Destination:	PHL
Departure time:	9A

Based on this information, the following entry would be used to determine flight availability for the passenger:

113SEPORDPHL9A

The preferred departure time may be entered as 900A. For efficiency, however, it is preferable to use as few keystrokes as possible.

Figure 2-1 Example of a City Pair Availability Display.

	①	②			③			④	⑤	⑥	⑦	⑧	⑨⑩	⑪	⑫

13SEP   FRI   ORD/CST   PHL/EST‡1

#	Carrier	Flight						Pts	OTP	Dep	Arr	Acft			
1	UA	138	F4	Y4	B4	M0	Q0	ORDPHL	6	835A	1123A	767	B 0		TA
2	AA	128	F7	Y7	B0	M0	H0	ORDPHL	7	953A	1244P	72S	B 0		TA
3	US	517	F4	Y4	B4	Q4	K4	ORDPHL	8	1035A	118P	D9S	L 0		TA
4	UA	294	F4	Y4	B4	M4	Q4	ORDPHL	7	1050A	140P	727	L 0	XJ	TA
5	NW	412	F4	Y4	B4	Q4	M4	ORDDTW	7	900A	1102A	72S	0		TA
6	NW	204	F4	Y4	B4	Q4	M4	PHL	6	1215P	139P	757	S 0		TA

This display contains the following information:

① Carrier
② Flight number
③ Seat quota
④ Departure and arrival points
⑤ On-time performance
⑥ Departure time

⑦ Arrival time
⑧ Aircraft
⑨ Meal service
⑩ Stops
⑪ Frequency exceptions
⑫ Total access indicator

and Philadelphia local time is Eastern standard time (EST). The time difference is shown after the arrival point time zone. In the example, ‡1 indicates that Philadelphia local time is one hour later than Chicago local time.

The lines below the header are flight listings. Each flight listing is numbered on the left. SABRE displays a maximum of six flights in each availability screen. Let us examine the information contained in the availability display.

1. **Carrier** The first column gives the two-letter carrier code for each flight. In Figure 2-1, line 1 lists a United Airlines flight, and line 2 lists an American Airlines flight. Flights operated by USAir and Northwest are also shown in the example.

2. **Flight number** The flight number is given to the right of the carrier code. In the example, line 1 is United 138, and line 2 is American 128. The flight number may consist of one to four digits.

3. **Seat quota** To the right of the flight number are several columns consisting of a letter and a number. These columns indicate the maximum number of seats that can be sold in each class of service in one transaction. The letter indicates the class, and the number indicates the number of seats. This information is called the **seat quota**. Note that in Figure 2-1 the number of seats is always either four or zero.

The following are common classes of service available on domestic flights:

F   First class
C   Premium coach
Y   Full coach

B	Discount coach
M	Discount coach
Q	Discount coach
V	Discount coach
H	Discount coach
K	Discount coach

The classes offered on a flight depend on the carrier, the type of aircraft, the route, the airline's price strategies, and other factors.

The maximum number displayed for each class depends on the carrier's agreement with SABRE. More seats may actually be available than the number displayed. For example, on UA 138, more than four seats may be available in Y class. However, four is the maximum number that can be sold in one transaction and confirmed immediately. If more than four seats are requested, a message requesting the seats will be sent to the airline. However, the transaction may or may not be confirmed.

On UA 138, zero is displayed for M class and Q class. A zero indicates that fewer than four seats are available in each class. When a zero is displayed, the class is said to be "sold out."

4. **Departure and arrival points** To the right of the seat quota are the departure and arrival points. Note that the airport code is shown for each point. In this example, only flights departing from Chicago-O'Hare (ORD) were requested. If flights had been requested from the Chicago area, by using the city code CHI, flights departing from Midway (MDW) would also be displayed.

5. **On-time performance** The U.S. Department of Transportation (DOT) requires domestic carriers to keep statistics on the on-time performance of each flight. The **on-time performance** is the percentage of the time that the flight departs within 15 minutes of the scheduled departure time and arrives within 15 minutes of the scheduled arrival time. In the SABRE availability display, on-time performance is indicated by a digit called the **dependability factor**. A dependability factor of 6 indicates an on-time performance of about 60 percent.

If the on-time performance is not available, *N* is displayed in place of a dependability factor. An *N* may appear if the flight was recently placed in service or if the arrival time has changed by 30 minutes or more since on-time statistics were last updated.

6. **Departure time** The scheduled departure time is shown to the right of the on-time performance. In Figure 2-1, UA 138 is scheduled to depart from ORD at 8:35 A.M. local Chicago time. (As indicated in the header, Chicago is located in the Central time zone.) In this example, flights departing around 9 A.M. were requested. The first flight displayed departs 25 minutes before the specified time. SABRE searches for the first flight departing within one hour before or one hour after the specified time. Thus, in this example, SABRE begins the display with the first flight departing between 8 A.M. and 10 A.M.

7. **Arrival time** The scheduled arrival time is shown to the right of the departure time. In Figure 2-1, UA 138 is scheduled to arrive at PHL at 11:23 A.M. local Philadelphia time. (As indicated in the header, Philadelphia is located in the Eastern time zone.)

8. **Aircraft** The equipment code for each flight is shown to the right of the arrival time. According to the display in Figure 2-1, the aircraft on UA 138 is a Boeing 767, and the aircraft on AA 128 is a Boeing 727-200.

9. **Meal service** The meal service code for each flight is shown to the right of the equipment code. The following are the most common meal service codes:

B   full breakfast

V   continental breakfast

R   brunch

L   lunch

D   dinner

S   snack

If no meal code is displayed, meal service is not provided on the flight.

10. **Stops** The number to the right of the meal service code indicates the number of intermediate stops. All the flights in Figure 2-1 are nonstop flights.

11. **Frequency exceptions** *Frequency of operation* refers to the days of the week on which a flight operates. **Frequency exceptions** are days on which the flight does not operate. Any frequency exceptions are indicated to the right of the number of stops. The exception code *X* indicates the days on which the flight does not operate. Days of the week are indicated by the following letters:

M   Monday

T   Tuesday

W   Wednesday

Q   Thursday

F   Friday

J   Saturday

S   Sunday

Note that *Q* is used for Thursday, to prevent confusion with Tuesday, and *J* is used for Saturday, to prevent confusion with Sunday. In Figure 2-1, UA 294 does not operate on Saturday, as indicated by *XJ*. If no exception code is shown, the flight operates daily.

12. **Total access indicator** The code *TA*, in the last column, indicates that the SABRE total access function can be used for that flight. With total access, the number of seats actually available can be obtained directly from the carrier's reservation system. This type of display is referred to as *last-seat availability*. The total access function and last-seat availability will be discussed later in this chapter and, in more detail, in Chapter 18.

Connecting Flight Segments

In Figure 2-1, connecting flight segments are displayed in lines 5 and 6. In this example, NW 412 flies from ORD to DTW, where passengers must disembark to board NW 204, which continues on to PHL. The departure point in line 6 is omitted, indicating that it is the same as the arrival point in the previous line. The departure point of an onward connecting flight is always omitted.

When the connection is booked, two flight segments are added to the itinerary. The first segment represents NW 412 from ORD to DTW, and the second represents NW 204 from DTW to PHL.

If this connection is booked, the passenger arrives at DTW at 11:02 A.M. and boards the onward connecting flight at 12:15 P.M. All times are given in local time. Thus, the passenger has a total of 1 hour and 13 minutes to change planes in Detroit.

Connecting Segments

A passenger plans to travel from the New York metropolitan area to Los Angeles. He would like to depart on 16 June at around 4 P.M. He does not have an airport preference. The following entry is used to request city pair availability:

    116JUNNYCLAX4P

The city code *NYC* refers to all airports in the New York area. SABRE responds to the availability request as follows:

```
16JUN  THU  NYC/EST          LAX/PST-3
1  TW  901  F4  Y4  B4  Q4  M4  JFKLAX  6   410P   650P   L10  D  0      TA
2  US  621  F4  Y4  B4  Q4  M4  LGALAX  7   550P   952P   72S  D  0      TA
3  UA  165  F4  Y4  B4  Q4  M4  LGALAX  7   600P   855P   767  D  0      TA
4  CO  804  F4  Y4  B4  Q4  M4  LGALAX  8   930P  ‡139A   757  S  0      TA
5  AA  224  F7  Y7  B7  Q7  M7  JFKDFW  8   900A  1022A   D10  B  0      TA
6  AA  244  F7  Y7  B7  Q7  M7     LAX  8  1105A   132P   757  L  0      TA
```

According to the header of this display, the passenger will depart on a Thursday. New York local time is Eastern standard time, and Los Angeles local time is Pacific standard time. The time difference *–3* indicates that Los Angeles time is three hours earlier than New York time.

In this example, TW 901 departs closest to the desired departure time. Note that this flight departs from Kennedy International Airport (JFK). The flight from LaGuardia Airport (LGA) that departs closer to the desired time is US 621. American Airlines operates a connection from JFK, with DFW as the connecting point.

If the passenger selects TW 901, the nonstop flight will depart from JFK at 4:10 P.M. and arrive at LAX at 6:50 P.M. Dinner is served on the flight, and the aircraft is a Lockheed L-1011. The flight departs and arrives on time about 60 percent of the time.

Note the arrival time for CO 804 in line 4. The ‡ before the time indicates that the flight arrives the day after the departure date. Thus, CO 804 departs from LGA at 9:30 P.M. and arrives at LAX at 1:39 A.M. the next day.

Return Availability

After an availability display has been obtained, the entry code **1R** can be used to display flights for the return trip, as follows:

FORMAT   1R<Return Date><Departure Time>

EXAMPLE   1R10MAY5P

This example will display return flights on 10 May, departing at around 5 P.M. This entry can only be made after an availability display has been obtained. In the return availability display, the original city pair is reversed. Suppose flights from MEM to LAS will be displayed for the outbound segment. When return availability is requested, flights from LAS to MEM are displayed.

If the date is omitted, SABRE will display return flights for the current date. Suppose you want a display of return availability on the same date as the outbound segment. The following entry may be used to display return flights departing at around 8 P.M.:

    1R8P

Follow-up Availability Entries

After an availability display has been obtained, various follow-up entries can be used to modify the display. The following are examples of follow-up availability entries:

1*	Displays additional flights
1*11A	Changes departure time
121SEP	Changes departure date
1‡3	Moves date forward
1-3	Moves date back
1‡3*10A	Moves date forward and changes departure time
16JUN*9A	Changes departure date and time
121SEP‡DL	Changes departure date and select carrier
1*DLGA	Changes departure point
1*AFLL	Changes arrival point

Let us examine each of these follow-up entries.

Additional Flights

SABRE displays a maximum of six flights in each availability screen. However, in many cases, more than six flights exist between the specified points. The entry code *1** is used to display additional flights. Each time this entry is input, SABRE displays the next six flights for the current city pair.

Alternate Departure Time

The departure time of an existing availability display can be modified as follows:

FORMAT   1*<Alternate Time>

EXAMPLE   1*5P

This example will modify the display to list flights departing around 5 P.M.

Alternate Departure Date

The departure date can be modified as follows:

FORMAT   1<Alternate Date>

EXAMPLE   121MAY

This example will modify the display to list flights departing on 21 May.

Another method of changing the departure date is to move the date forward or back. For example, to move the date forward one day—that is, to make it one day later—the following entry is used:

    1‡1

To display availability for the same city pair three days earlier, the following entry may be used:

    1-3

When the date is moved forward or back, a new departure time can also be specified, as follows:

    1-7*10A

This example will move the date back seven days and display flights departing around 10 A.M.

When the date is modified, a carrier can be specified, as follows:

FORMAT   1<Alternate Date>‡<Carrier>

EXAMPLE   121JUL‡UA

Note that ‡ is typed before the carrier code. When this entry is input, SABRE displays only flights operated by the specified carrier on the new date.

Alternate Departure or Arrival Point

The entry code *1*D* is used to change only the departure point, as follows:

    1*DLGB

This example will change the departure point to Long Beach. The arrival point will remain the same as in the previous availability display.

The entry code *1*A* is used to change only the arrival point, as follows:

    1*AMCO

This example will change the arrival point to Orlando. The departure point will remain the same as in the previous availability display.

Original Availability

To redisplay the original availability screen, the following entry is used:

    1*OA

When this entry is input, SABRE redisplays the availability screen that was obtained before any follow-up entries were input.

Follow-up Availability

Suppose a passenger plans to travel from Seattle to Honolulu. She would like to depart on 18 September, at around 8 A.M. The following entry may be used to display availability.

118SEPSEAHNL8A

SABRE responds as follows:

18SEP	SAT		SEA/PDT				HNL/HDT-2							
1	NW	87	F4	Y0	B0	M0	Q0	SEAHNL	7	810A	1208P	747	B	0	TA
2	UA	67	F4	C0	Y0	B0	M0	SEAHNL	6	845A	1243P	D10	B	0	TA
3	DL	122	F4	Y0	B0	M0	Q0	SEALAX	8	900A	1112A	727	S	0	TA
4	DL	312	F4	Y0	B0	M0	Q0	HNL	8	1258P	350P	D10	L	0	TA
5	UA	35	F0	C0	Y0	B0	M0	SEAHNL	7	1005A	236P	747	L	1	TA

Suppose the passenger wants to travel in Y class. All the flights in this display are sold out in every class except F class, and the flight in line 5 is completely sold out. The passenger asks about flights departing later in the day. To obtain additional availability, the following entry may be used:

1*

SABRE responds by displaying additional flights for the same city pair and departure date:

18SEP	SAT		SEA/PDT				HNL/HDT-2							
1	AS	82	F4	Y4	B4	Q4	SEASFO	9	550P	740P	72S	D	0	
2	CO	3	F4	J4	Y4	B4	HNL	8	845P	1100P	D10	D	0	XWF TA
3	UA	847	F4	Y4	B4	M4	SEALAX	8	450P	655P	72S	S	0	TA
4	UA	23	F4	J4	Y4	B4	HNL	8	800P	1040P	747	D	0	TA
5	DL	712	F4	Y4	B4	M4	SEALAX	8	440P	704P	73S	S	0	TA
6	CO	1	F4	J4	Y4	B4	HNL	9	800P	1040P	747	S	0	TA

All the flights in this display are connections. Alaska 82 originates in Seattle and connects in San Francisco to Continental 3, which continues to Honolulu. United 847 connects in Los Angeles to United 23, and Delta 712 connects in Los Angeles to Continental 1.

Assume the passenger inquires about return flights. She would like to return on 26 September, departing around 1 P.M. The following entry is used to display return availability:

1R26SEP1P

(continued)

SABRE responds as follows:

```
26SEP   SUN HNL/HDT-2 SEA/PDT‡2
1 HA    22   F4 Y4 B4 M4   V4   HNLSEA 9  125P  940P  L10  L  0
2 NW    86   F4 Y4 B4 Q4   M4   HNLSEA 8  110P  929P  D10  L  0      TA
3 UA    32   F4 Y4 B4 M4   V4   HNLSEA 8 1245P  903P  D10  L  0      TA
4 DL  1560   F4 Y4 B4 M4   H4   HNLLAX 7  120P  823P  D10  L  0      TA
5 DL   951   F4 Y4 B4 M4   H4          SEA 8  941P 1159P  72S  S  0      TA
```

Observe that the city pair in this display is reversed, showing flights from Honolulu to Seattle.

Now assume the passenger inquires about alternate flights departing one day earlier at around 9 A.M. The following entry is used to change the date and time:

    1-1*9A

This entry moves the date back one day and changes the departure time to 9 A.M. The entry *125SEP*9A* would produce the same results.
SABRE responds as follows:

```
25SEP   SAT HNL/HDT-2 SEA/PDT‡2
1 DL  1552   F0 Y0 B0   Q0   V0   HNLLAX 8  915A  418P  D10  B  0      TA
2 DL  1703   F0 Y0 B0   Q0   V0          SEA 7  455P  706P  72S  D  0      TA
3 UA   812   F0 Y0 B0   M0   H0   HNLLAX 8  900A  509P  747  B  0      TA
4 UA   696   F4 Y0 B0   M0   H0          SEA 6  620P  851P  72S  D  0      TA
5 UA    32   F4 Y4 B4   M4   H0   HNLSEA 7 1235P  852P  D19  L  0      TA
```

Assume the passenger asks to review the information in the first availability display. The following entry will redisplay the original availability display:

    1*OA

SABRE responds as follows:

```
18SEP   SAT SEA/PDT     HNL/HDT-2
1 NW    87   F4 Y0 B0   M0   Q0   SEAHNL 7  810A 1208P  747  B  0      TA
2 UA    67   F4 C0 Y0   B0   M0   SEAHNL 6  845A 1243P  D10  B  0      TA
3 DL   122   F4 Y0 B0   M0   Q0   SEALAX 8  900A 1112A  727  S  0      TA
4 DL   312   F4 Y0 B0   M0   Q0          HNL 8 1258P  350P  D10  L  0      TA
5 UA    35   F0 C0 Y0   B0   M0   SEAHNL 7 1005A  236P  747  L  1      TA
```

In a city pair availability entry, various options can be used to customize the display to a client's needs or preferences. The following are examples of alternative availability entries:

124AUGPHXMIA6AATL	Specify connecting point
18MAYNYCMIA/5P	Specify arrival time
117APRORDHNL-B	Specify class of service
130JULPITPHX9A‡US	Specify carrier
19OCTSFOBOS/D	Show only direct flights

Let us examine the SABRE response to each of these entries.

Specifying a Connecting Point

A connecting point can be specified in an availability entry, as follows:

120OCTATLABQ9ADFW

This example requests connections on 20 October from ATL to ABQ that depart around 9 A.M. and connect in DFW.

A minimum connecting time can also be specified, as follows:

120OCTATLABQ9ADFW120

This example specifies a minimum connecting time of 120 minutes.

An existing availability display can also be modified to show only flights via a specified connecting point. For example, suppose the following availability entry has been input:

124APRMKEFLL10A

This entry will display all flights departing at about 10 A.M. on 24 April from Milwaukee to Fort Lauderdale. The following entry changes the display to show only connections via St. Louis:

1STL

After connecting flights have been requested, the following entry returns to the original display:

1*ORIG

Note that this entry can be made only after connections have been requested.

Specified Connection

Suppose a passenger plans to travel from PDX to PIT on 17 July. He wants to depart around 7 A.M. He would like to connect at Chicago-O'Hare, with two hours to change planes. The following entry is used to request the availability of flights that meet the client's preference:

117JULPDXPIT7AORD120

SABRE responds as follows:

17JUL	WED		PDX/PST		PIT/EST‡3										
1	NW	46	F4	Y0	B0	M0	Q0	PDXORD	7	735A	100P	72S	B	0	TA
2	US	148	F4	Y4	B4	Q4	K4	PIT	6	210P	425P	D9S	S	0	TA
3	UA	142	F4	Y4	B0	M0	V0	PDXORD	7	750A	125P	D10	B	0	TA
4	UA	124	F4	Y4	B0	M0	V0	PIT	7	215P	432P	72S	S	0	TA
5	NW	58	F4	Y4	B0	Q0	H0	PDXORD	8	530P	1103P	727	L	1	TA
6	UA	408	F4	Y4	B0	M0	V0	PIT	8	‡109A	510A	737	S	0	TA

Note that, in this display, UA 408 departs from O'Hare one day after the original departure date.

Specifying an Arrival Time

Suppose a client plans to travel from SEA to HNL on 22 October. She would like to arrive around 4 P.M. The arrival time can be specified in the availability entry as follows:

122OCTSEAHNL/4P

Note that a slash (/) is typed before the time to indicate the arrival time. SABRE responds as follows:

22OCT	THU		SEA/PST		HNL/HST-2									
1 DL	122	F4	Y4	B4	Q4	SEALAX	8	900A	1112A	727	S	0		TA
2 DL	312	F4	Y4	B4	Q4	HNL	8	1258P	350P	D10	L	0		TA
3 AS	82	F4	Y4	B4	Q4	SEASFO	9	550P	740P	72S	D	0		TA
4 CO	3	F4	J4	Y4	B4	HNL	8	845P	1100P	D10	D	0	XWF	TA

The display lists flights arriving in Honolulu closest to 4 P.M. Note, in line 4, the exception code *XWF*, indicating that CO 3 does not operate on Wednesday or Friday.

The arrival time can also be specified in a return availability entry, as follows:

1R27OCT/8P

This example requests return availability on 27 October, with arrival around 8 P.M.

Specifying a Class of Service

Suppose a passenger plans to travel on 12 December from CLE to STL. He would like to depart around 12 noon and prefers to travel in B class. The class of service can be specified in the availability entry as follows:

112DECCLESTL12N-B

Note that a hyphen (-) is typed before the class of service. SABRE responds as follows:

```
12DEC  SAT    CLE/EST    STL/CST-1
1 TW 745  B4          CLESTL  7 1250P  120P  DC9 S 0        TA
2 TW 285  B4          CLESTL  8 1015A 1050A  M80   0        TA
3 AA 149  B7          CLEORD  7 1028A 1039A  727   0        TA
4 AA 415  B7             STL  7 1117A 1212P  727   0        TA
5 TW 775  B4          CLESTL  9  845A  915A  DC9   0        TA
```

In this display, only availability in B class is shown.

The existing display can be modified to show a different class as follows:

1-Q

This entry will modify the display to show availability only in Q class. SABRE responds to this entry as follows:

```
12DEC  SAT    CLE/EST    STL/CST-1
1 TW 745  Q0          CLESTL  7 1250P  120P  DC9 S 0        TA
2 TW 285  Q4          CLESTL  8 1015A 1050A  M80   0        TA
3 AA 149  Q7          CLEORD  7 1028A 1039A  727   0        TA
4 AA 415  Q7             STL  7 1117A 1212P  727   0        TA
5 TW 775  Q0          CLESTL  9  845A  915A  DC9   0        TA
```

Specifying a Carrier

Suppose a passenger plans to travel from SEA to HNL on 18 September. He would like to depart at 9 A.M. and prefers to travel on United. The carrier can be specified in the availability display as follows:

118SEPSEAHNL9A‡UA

Note that a cross (‡) is typed before the carrier code. SABRE responds to this entry as follows:

```
18SEP  FRI     SEA/PST  HNL/HST-2
1 UA   67  F0 Y0 B0 M0 V0 SEAHNL 6   845A  1243P  D10 B  0   TA
2 UA   35  F0 Y0 B0 M0 V0 SEAHNL 7  1005A   236P  747 L  1   TA
3 UA  847  F4 Y4 B4 M4 V0 SEALAX 8   450P   655P  72S S  0   TA
4 UA   23  F4 J4 Y4 B4 V0     HNL 8   800P  1040P  747 D  0   TA
```

In this display, only flights operated by UA are shown. Some of the participating carriers include AA, AF, AS, CO, DC, IB, JL, KE, KL, LY, ML, NW, PR, SK, SR, TW, UA, and US.

Nonstop/Direct Flights

A **direct flight** is any flight that does not have a change of flight number at an intermediate connecting point. The option /D in an availability entry requests only direct flights, for example:

118SEPSEAHNL9A/D

SABRE responds as follows:

```
18SEP  FRI     SEA/PST  HNL/HST-2
1 NW   87  F0 Y0 B0 M0 Q0 SEAHNL 7   810A  1208P  747 B  0   TA
2 UA   67  F0 Y0 B0 M0 V0 SEAHNL 6   845A  1243P  D10 B  0   TA
3 UA   35  F0 Y0 B0 M0 V0 SEAHNL 7  1005A   236P  747 L  1   TA
NO MORE-1*  FOR CONX
```

The display shows only direct flights. If additional availability is requested, SABRE will display connecting flights from SEA to HNL.

Last-Seat Availability

The **total access** function is used to obtain data directly from an airline computer system. Several airlines participate in the total access program.

The seat quota in the SABRE availability display shows the maximum number of seats that may be sold in one transaction. In most cases, either four or zero is displayed for each class of service. When four is displayed, four or more seats are actually available in that class. If fewer than four seats are available in a particular class, a zero is displayed. Thus, a flight may appear to be sold out in a SABRE availability display, although one to three seats may still be available.

In this situation the total access function can be used to check availability through the airline's own reservation system. The total access display will show the actual number of seats available in each class. Such a display is referred to as *last-seat availability.*

The following format is used to change an existing availability display to a total-access display:

FORMAT   1¤<Carrier>

EXAMPLE   1¤DL

This example requests last-seat availability from the DL reservation system.

As an example, suppose you have just obtained the following availability display:

```
20NOV  SAT    ORD/CST  EWR/EST‡1
1 UA 160 F4  Y0 B0 Q0  M0 ORDEWR 9  600A   900A   72S  B  0    TA
2 AA 906 F0  Y0 B0 Q0  M0 ORDEWR 9  630A   928A   M80  B  0    TA
3 CO 310 F4  Y4 B0 H0  Q0 ORDEWR 7  915A  1104A   72S  S  0    TA
4 CO 392 F4  Y4 B0 H0  Q0 ORDEWR 7 1045A   140P   72S  L  0    TA
5 UA 638 F4  Y0 B0 Q0  M0 ORDEWR 8 1200N   254P   D10  L  0    TA
6 CO 623 F4  Y4 B4 H4  Q4 ORDEWR 8  430P   715P   72S  D  0    TA
```

As mentioned earlier in the chapter, the total access indicator *TA* signifies that availability can be obtained from the carrier's reservation system. All the carriers in this display participate in the total access program.

Suppose your client would like to travel in B class on CO 310. According to the SABRE display, the flight is sold out in B class. To check last-seat availability, you use the following entry:

1¤CO

SABRE responds as follows:

```
CO RESPONSE
 7 CO 310 F4 Y2 B0 H0 Q0 ORDEWR    915A  1104A  72S  S  0
 8 CO 392 F4 Y6 B0 H0 Q0 ORDEWR   1045A   140P  72S  L  0
 9 CO 623 F9 Y8 B5 H5 Q5 ORDEWR    430P   715P  72S  D  0
10 CO 396 F9 Y9 B9 H9 Q9 ORDEWR    650P   950P  72S  D  0   XS
```

The header indicates that this availability display was obtained from the Continental Airlines reservation system. The display shows the actual number of seats available in each class on the CO flights. Two seats are still available on CO 310.

The line numbers in a total access availability display always start with line 7 and may go as high as 16, whereas the lines in a SABRE display are always numbered from 1 to 6. A total access display will remain in the SABRE work area for approximately two minutes. After that, the display will be replaced by a normal SABRE availability display.

A total access availability display can be obtained with the original availability entry, as follows:

112JULSFOCHI10A¤UA

In this entry, (¤) is typed before the carrier code to link with the airline's reservation system.

Specific Flight Availability

Availability may be checked on a specific flight if the carrier and the flight number are known. The following format is used for this purpose:

FORMAT   1<Carrier><Flight><Class><Date><City pair>

EXAMPLE   1UA440Y10MAYLGAMIA

This example requests availability on UA 440 in Y class, departing 10MAY from LGA to MIA. Only airport codes—no city codes—may be used for the city pair in this entry. The possible responses and their meanings are as follows:

AS	Flight is available to sell.
CR	Flight is closed; seats may be requested.
CN	Flight does not operate.
CL	Flight is closed; seats may be waitlisted.
CC	Flight is closed; waitlist is closed.
NO AVAIL	Availability is not maintained for the requested carrier.

If the requested class is sold out, an availability display will appear, so that another class or flight can be selected.

Summary

The city pair availability function is used to display schedules and seat quotas for flights between specified departure and arrival points. When an availability display has been obtained, various entries can be input to change the date, time, class of service, departure point, or arrival point. A display can be customized to the preferences of the client. The total access function can be used to obtain availability directly from the reservation system of a participating carrier.

New commands included in this chapter:

110SEPORDSFO7A	Displays availability by departure time
110SEPORDSFO/4P	Displays availability by arrival time
1R12MAR2P	Displays return availability by departure time
1R12MAY/5P	Displays return availability by arrival time
1*OA	Redisplays original availability
110SEPBOSSFO7AORD	Displays availability by connecting point
110SEPBOSSFO7A-C	Displays availability by class of service
110SEPBOSSFO7A‡TW	Displays availability by carrier

118SEPSEAHNL9A/D	Displays only direct flights
1*	Displays additional flights
1*11A	Changes departure time
121SEP	Changes departure date
1+3	Moves date forward
1−3	Moves date back
1+3*10A	Moves date forward and changes departure time
16JUN*9A	Changes departure date and time
121SEP‡DL	Changes departure date and selects carrier
1STL	Specifies connecting point
1*DLGA	Changes departure point
1*AFLL	Changes arrival point
1−Q	Changes class of service
1¤CO	Changes display to total access availability
1UA189Y10MARSFOHNL	Displays specific flight availability

STUDENT REVIEW

KEY CONCEPTS AND TERMS

Identify the word or phrase for each of the following concepts:

1. The origin, the destination, and all the intermediate points in a trip.

2. One portion of an itinerary.

3. The first segment in an itinerary.

4. A point where a passenger transfers from one flight to another.

5. The first city or airport in a flight segment.

6. The second city or airport in a flight segment.

7. A departure point and an arrival point together.

8. The entry code that is used to display city pair availability.

9. In a city pair availability display, the line that indicates the departure date, and day of the week, and the time zone of each point.

10. The number of seats that can be sold in each class of service in one transaction.

11. The percentage of the time that a flight departs within 15 minutes of the scheduled departure time and arrives within 15 minutes of the scheduled arrival time.

12. Days on which a flight does not operate.

13. After an availability display has been obtained, the entry code that is used to display flights for the return trip.

14. A flight that does not have a change of flight number at an intermediate connecting point.

15. The function that is used to obtain data directly from an airline computer system.

REVIEW QUESTIONS

1. If a travel date is not specified, what flights will SABRE display?

2. What is the entry code for city pair availability?

3. What does the meal code S indicate?

4. How can the date 6 March be entered?

5. How can the time 3:00 P.M. be entered?

6. Select by letter the correct entry to display availability on 22 August from Indianapolis to Ft. Lauderdale, departing around 8:00 A.M.

   a) 22AUGINDFLL8A

   b) AUG22INDFLL8A

   c) 122AUGINDFLL8A

   d) 1AUG22INDFLL8A

7. Write the correct entry to display availability based on the following information:

   Travel date: 12 June
   City pair: New York-LaGuardia to Seattle
   Departure time: 7:00 A.M.

8. Write the correct entry to display availability based on the following information:

   Travel date: 18 September
   City pair: Chicago-O'Hare to Honolulu
   Departure time: 10:00 A.M.

9. What entry would display availability on flights from St. Louis to Pittsburgh on 6 February, departing around 3:00 P.M.?

10. When an availability display is obtained, what entry will change the departure date to 24 March?

11. What entry will change the departure date to 16 June, and also change the departure time to 11 A.M.?

12. What entry will display return availability on 19 August, departing around 4 P.M.?

13. What entry will change the departure point to MDW?

14. What entry will change the arrival point to SJC?

15. What entry will move the departure date back four days?

16. What entry will move the date forward three days?

17. What code will appear in an availability display to indicate that a flight does not operate on Wednesday?

18. After availability has been displayed for connecting flights via a specified connecting point, what entry would be input to redisplay direct flights?

19. When a normal SABRE availability display is obtained, what entry would display availability directly from the DL reservation system?

20. A client plans to travel to HNL on 22 July, departing from LAX around 7:00 A.M. Write the correct availability entry.

21. Your client wants to return in the evening on the same day, at around 6:00 P.M. Write the correct availability entry.

22. A teacher in LAX will attend a conference in New York on August 4, near the LGA airport. He would like a flight departing around 10:00 A.M. Assume your client wants to connect in ATL. Write the correct availability entry.

23. What entry will display additional availability?

24. What entry will redisplay the original availability display?

25. A geologist who travels often to SEA wants to know if space is available on AS flight 723 in first class. He will depart on 14 May from SFO. Write the correct entry to display availability on the flight.

26. A client is planning a trip between DTW and DFW. She will depart on the 23rd of January around 4:00 P.M. She asks if seats are available at an advertised discount fare (B class). Write the correct entry to display availability.

27. What entry will display availability in first class on the same flights?

28. What entry will display availability in Q class on the next day?

29. A client will be traveling from Houston to MSP on 11 March, leaving around 3:00 P.M. He would like to depart from IAH and connect via STL. Write the correct availability entry.

30. What is the shortest entry to display availability for the same city pair and date at 7:00 A.M.?

31. Assume a display shows the symbol ‡ next to the arrival time. What is the meaning?

32. What is the maximum number of seats that will be shown in each class for an AA flight?

33. What is the maximum number of seats that would be shown in each class for a flight operated by UA, TW, or DL?

34. Refer to the following display to answer a-f.

1 NW	46	F4 Y4 B0 M0 Q0	PDXORD 9	735A		100P	72S	B	0		TA
2 US	148	Y4 B4 M4 K0	PIT 8	210P		425P	D9S	S	0		TA
3 UA	142	F4 Y4 B0 Q0 V0	PDXORD 7	750A		125P	D10	B	0		TA
4 UA	124	F4 Y4 B0 Q0 V0	PIT 8	215P		432P	72S	S	0		TA
5 NW	58	F4 Y4 B4 M4 Q4	PDXORD 8	530P		1103P	727	L	1	XJ	TA
6 UA	408	F4 Y4 B4 Q4 V0	PIT 7	1210A	‡410A		737	S	0		TA

a) What flights can be used as a connection with both seats booked in Q class?

b) What time does the first leg depart from Portland?

c) What time will the passenger arrive in Pittsburgh?

d) How much time does the passenger have to change planes in Chicago?

e) When does the USAir flight arrive?

f) What meal service is provided on the flight that departs from Portland closest to 8:00 A.M.?

APPLICATIONS

Read the following scenario, and decide what should be done to satisfy the client's preferences and needs. Briefly describe how you would handle the situation, and then write the required entries.

A client is planning a trip from New York to Los Angeles. He would like to depart around 9 A.M. on 13 March. He does not have a preference for an airport, but he prefers a nonstop flight. When you display availability for the outbound segment, all the nonstop and direct flights displayed are sold out. The next display shows only connections. If your client must take a connection, he prefers to connect at Chicago-O'Hare.

He may have to postpone the departure until 15 March. If he departs on 13 March, as planned, he will return on 21 March. If he does not depart until 15 March, he will return on 24 March.

Chapter 3

Selling

Outline

Selling Air Segments

Selling From Availability

Selling a Connection

Waitlisting From Availability

Displaying the Itinerary

Selling Space on a Specified Flight

Open Segments

Passive Segments

Surface Segments

Selling From a Total Access Availability Display

Chapter Objectives

After you complete this chapter, you should be able to:

1. Sell seats from a city pair availability display.

2. Sell a connection from an availability display.

3. Sell seats on a specified flight without displaying availability.

4. Place a seat request on a carrier's waiting list.

5. Book an open segment.

6. Input a passive segment that has been booked directly with a carrier.

7. Input an ARNK segment in an air itinerary that is interrupted by surface travel.

8. Sell a guaranteed segment from a total access availability display.

PROBLEM

An actress must travel from Los Angeles to a film location in Miami. She would like to travel in first class on a flight that departs at 7 A.M., but the first-class section is sold out. A seat is available in first class on a flight departing at 10:30 A.M. The passenger prefers the earlier flight, but will take the later one if necessary.

SABRE SOLUTION

Waitlist one seat in first class on the 7:00 A.M. flight, and sell a confirmed reservation in first class on the 10:30 A.M. flight. If the waitlisted reservation is later confirmed, you can cancel the duplicate reservation. If the waitlisted segment is not confirmed, however, your client is protected by the confirmed reservation on the 10:30 A.M. departure.

In this chapter, you will learn how to sell air segments, waitlist seat requests, and input other types of segments.

Selling Air Segments

The act of booking an airline reservation is called **selling an air segment**. If the requested seats are not available, the reservations may be placed on a waitlist. If other passengers holding confirmed seats later cancel their reservations, the wait-listed seats eventually may be confirmed.

The entry code **0** is used to sell an air segment. On some SABRE keyboards, the 0 key is labeled *SEG* as a reminder that this key is used to book segments.

Selling From Availability

When availability is displayed, a segment can be sold for any flight on which seats are available in the desired class of service. **Selling from availability** is the simplest method of selling an air segment. The following format is used to sell from availability:

FORMAT   0<Seats><Class><Line number>

EXAMPLE   01Y1

This example will sell one seat in Y class from line 1 of the availability display. The line number indicates the desired flight.

In most cases, four is the maximum number of seats that may be sold in one transaction. On American Airlines flights, up to seven seats may be sold.

If you attempt to sell more than the maximum number, the reservation will not be confirmed immediately. A message requesting the seats will be sent to the carrier. If the carrier accepts the seat request, the segment will be confirmed. A response is usually received from the carrier within 24 hours.

If the class is sold out, the seats may be waitlisted. The procedure for entering a waitlisted segment will be discussed later in the chapter.

The **air segment** shows the carrier, flight number, class, departure date, day of the week, and departure and arrival airports (see Figure 3-1). The day of the week is indicated by a letter, as follows:

M   Monday
T   Tuesday
W   Wednesday
Q   Thursday
F   Friday
J   Saturday
S   Sunday

(Note that these codes are the same as those used for frequency exceptions.)

The segment status precedes the number of seats. In the segment in the following Client Focus, the status **SS** indicates that the seats are sold. The reservation will be confirmed when the transaction is ended. Normally, when an air segment is sold, the status SS is displayed if the seats are available. When the agent ends the transaction, SABRE will change the status to **HK**, indicating a confirmed reservation.

Availability

Assume you have obtained the following availability display for flights on 17 July from SFO to ORD, departing around 10 A.M.

```
17JUL FRI    SFO/PST    ORD/CST‡2
1 AA  142  F7  Y7  B7  Q7  M7  SFOORD  9  915A   305P  767  S  0  TA
2 UA  820  F4  Y4  B4  Q4  M4  SFOORD  7  1045A  440P  D10  L  0  TA
3 UA  190  F4  Y4  B4  Q4  M4  SFOORD  6  1220P  614P  727  L  0  TA
4 UA  128  F4  Y4  B4  Q4  M4  SFOORD  9  112P   715P  D10  D  0  TA
5 AA  224  F7  Y7  B7  Q7  M7  SFOORD  9  112P   715P  72S  D  0  TA
6 UA  130  F4  Y4  B4  Q4  M4  SFOORD  8  405P   955P  72S  D  0  TA
```

The passenger requests three seats in Y class on the United flight departing at 10:45 A.M. The desired flight is UA 820, in line 2. The following entry sells three seats in Y class on this flight.

    03Y2

SABRE responds as follows:

    1   UA   820Y   17JUL   F   SFOORD   SS3   1045A   440P

The response is called an air segment. Each segment is numbered based on the order in which the segments are booked. This example is segment 1, indicating that it is the first segment in the itinerary.

If the number of seats requested exceeds the seat quota, the segment will have the status NN. This code indicates that the seats will be requested from the carrier. When the transaction is ended, the status will be changed to PN, indicating that a response is required from the carrier before the reservation can be confirmed.

The status codes discussed in the preceding paragraphs are summarized in Table 3-1.

Table 3-1 Summary of Status Codes.

Status Code	Meaning	Interpretation
SS	Sold/sold	Seats will be confirmed.
HK	Have confirmed	Seats have been confirmed.
NN	Need/need	Seats will be requested from carrier.
PN	Pending need	Awaiting response from carrier.

Other segment status codes will be discussed later in this chapter and in Chapter 6.

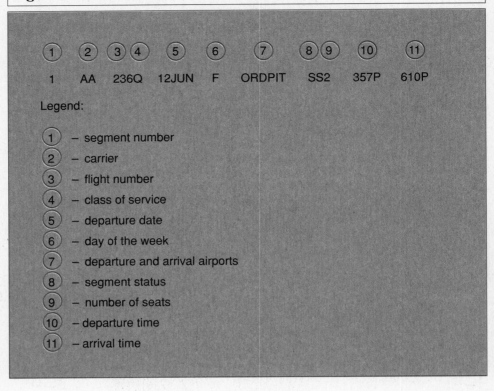

Figure 3-1 Information contained in a segment line.

① ② ③④ ⑤ ⑥ ⑦ ⑧⑨ ⑩ ⑪

1　AA　236Q　12JUN　F　ORDPIT　SS2　357P　610P

Legend:

① — segment number
② — carrier
③ — flight number
④ — class of service
⑤ — departure date
⑥ — day of the week
⑦ — departure and arrival airports
⑧ — segment status
⑨ — number of seats
⑩ — departure time
⑪ — arrival time

Selling a Connection

To sell a connection, include the class of service and line number for each leg, as follows:

02Y4Y5

This example will sell two seats in Y class from line 4 and two seats in Y class from line 5.

On most domestic connections, the class of service must be the same on all legs in order to obtain a throughfare. A **throughfare** is one fare applicable to all the legs of a connection. It is usually lower than the combined fares of the segments priced separately. In some cases, different discount classes, such as V, Q, and M, may be combined on different legs.

To determine whether different classes may be booked at a throughfare, the agent must consult the fare rules. **Fare rules** are the restrictions governing each price category, or fare basis. You will learn how to display fare rules in Chapter 8. This example will sell one seat in Y class on all legs of a connection that begins in line 2. When the short entry is used, all legs will be booked in the same class of service.

The following is a short entry for selling connecting flight segments:

01Y2*

Again, this example will sell one seat in Y class on all legs of a connection that begins in line 2. When the short entry is used, all legs will be booked in the same class of service.

CLIENT FOCUS

Connections

Assume you have obtained the following availability display:

```
03MAY   MON    ABQ/MST      TUS/MST
1  HP1257  Y4  K0  M0    ABQPHX       700A   805A   73S   0
2  HP1026  Y4  K4  M4       TUS   8  845A   920A   73S   0
3  HP 599  Y4  K4  M4    ABQPHX       840A   945A   73S   0
4  HP1027  Y4  K4  M4       TUS   8  1015A  1055A  73S   0
5  HP 399  Y4  K4  M4    ABQPHX       1200N  105P   73S   0
6  HP 594  Y4  K4  M4       TUS   8  1255P  130P   73S   0
```

This display shows three two-segment connections. Each flight segment of a connection is referred to as a leg. Your client desires one seat in K class on both legs of the connection that departs ABQ at 8:40 A.M. The following entry may be used to sell the connection:

01K3K4

Three-segment connections may be sold in the same manner, as follows:

01Y4Y5Y6

Waitlisting From Availability

Each carrier maintains waiting lists, or **waitlists**, for flights that are sold out. Passengers who desire seats on such flights are placed on a list. A separate waitlist is kept for each class of service.

The secondary code *LL* is used to waitlist seats, as follows:

02Y4LL

This example will waitlist two seats in Y class on the flight in line 4 of the availability display.

Displaying the Itinerary

When air segments have been booked, the following entry may be used to display the complete itinerary:

*I

The asterisk key (*) is labeled *DSPL* on some SABRE keyboards, as a reminder that this key is used to display information.

Waitlisting

Assume you have obtained the following availability display:

```
18NOV   MON    SFO/PST   PHX/MST‡1
1  UA 941  F4  Y0  M0  B0  V0  SFOPHX  6  1055A  1245P 727  L 0  TA
2  US 509  Y0  B0  V0  M0      SFOPHX  7  1220P   232P M80  L 0  TA
3  US 244  Y0  B0  V0  M0      SFOPHX  7   125P   332P 727  S 0  TA
4  UA 385  F4  Y0  M0  B0  V0  SFOPHX  6   140P   352P 727  S 0  TA
5  US 815  Y4  B4  V4  M4      SFOPHX  7   320P   515P M80  S 0  TA
```

Your client requests a seat in Y class on a flight departing as close to 11 A.M. as possible. All the flights except US 815 are sold out in Y class. The following entry may be used to waitlist one seat in coach on UA 941, which departs at 10:55 A.M.:

01Y1LL

SABRE responds as follows:

```
1  UA  941Y  18NOV  M  SFOPHX  LL1  1055A  1245P
```

Note the status LL, indicating that the seats will be waitlisted. When the transaction is ended, the segment status will be changed to **HL**, signifying that the space has been waitlisted.

In case the waitlisted segment is not confirmed later, a confirmed reservation should also be booked for the same routing. In this example, US 815 in line 5 has space available in Y class. The following entry may be used to book the alternate space:

01Y5

Your client's itinerary now appears as follows:

```
1  UA 941Y  18NOV M  SFOPHX  LL1  1055A  1245P
2  US 815Y  18NOV M  SFOPHX  SS1   320P   515P
```

The waitlisted segment on UA 941 is segment 1. Segment 2 is the confirmed reservation on US 815. If the waitlisted segment is later confirmed, you can cancel the USAir segment. When a waitlisted segment and a confirmed segment are booked on the same routing, the waitlisted segment should be booked first.

When the itinerary is displayed, the segments are ordered by segment number, as in the following example:

```
1 UA    53Y   12AUG   W   BOSSFO   LL1   830A   1137A
2 UA   104Y   12AUG   W   BOSDEN   SS1   700A    920A
3 UA   394Y   12AUG   W   DENSFO   SS1  1005A   1120A
4 UA    58Y   17AUG   M   SFOBOS   SS1  1010A    740P
```

In this itinerary, one passenger is waitlisted on a direct flight from BOS to SFO, and confirmed on a connection via DEN on the same date. The return flight on 17 August is a direct flight and is also confirmed.

Selling Space on a Specified Flight

Seats can often be sold on a specified flight without first displaying availability. This technique is called **direct selling**. The entry code *NN* is used to direct-sell a flight, as follows:

FORMAT   0<Carrier><Flight><Class><Date><Dep/arr points>NN<Seats>

EXAMPLE   0TW743Y12MARJFKDENNN2

This example contains the following elements:

Sell-segment entry code:	0
Carrier, flight, and class:	TW743Y
Departure date:	12MAR
Departure and arrival points:	JFKDEN
Action:	NN
Number of seats:	2

Note that the airport code must be used for a multi-airport city. The action code *NN* (need/need) is input before the number of seats.

Waitlisting Seats on a Specified Flight

To waitlist seats with a direct-sell entry, type the waitlist action code *LL* instead of *NN*. For example, assume you wish to waitlist two seats in Y class on NW 918 from MKE to MIA on 16 April. The following entry would be used:

0NW918Y16APRMKEMIALL2

SABRE responds as follows:

800A   1145A   F   SEG   1   LL   Y   HTL   CTY

Note that the segment status is LL, indicating that the seats will be placed on the carrier's waitlist.

Direct Selling

A ssume you wish to book two seats in F class on UA 599 from TPA to ORD on 27 August. The following entry would be used to direct-sell the seats:

0UA599F27AUGTPAORDNN2

SABRE responds as follows:

1020A   123P   W   SEG   1   SS   F   HTL   CTY

The response appears on the same line as the direct-sell entry and shows the flight times, day of week, segment number, segment status, and class of service. The message "HTL CTY" reminds the travel agent that SABRE can be used to book hotel reservations in the destination city.

In this case, the number of seats requested was available, as indicated by the segment status SS. If the number of seats exceeds the carrier's seat quota, the status will be NN. If the class or flight is sold out, SABRE will present an availability display so that an alternative class or flight can be selected.

Open Segments

Occasionally a passenger may book an itinerary without establishing the exact departure time for an onward or return segment. In this situation, an open segment must be booked. An **open segment** is an unspecified flight on a specified carrier.

To book an open segment, use the direct-sell format but type the word *OPEN* in place of the flight number, and use the action code *DS* (Desire Seats) before the number of seats. Technically an open segment may be input without a travel date. To price the itinerary, however, an estimated date should be included.

Passive Segments

Occasionally air space must be booked directly with a carrier by telephone, rather than through SABRE. The direct-sell format can be used to place the segment in the itinerary for the passenger's information. This type of reservation is called a **passive segment**.

To enter a passive segment, either *BK* or *GK* may be used as the action code. In the following example, *GK* is used to place the segment in the itinerary:

0DL548F22SEPDFWATLGK2

A passive segment entered with *BK* or *GK* is for information only and is entered only when a reservation is not made through SABRE.

To indicate a passive waitlisted segment, use the action code *BL* or *GL*.

Table 3-2 summarizes various action codes used in direct-sell entries. When *NN* is used to sell a segment, a message requesting the seats is transmitted to the carrier. A reply is usually received within 24 hours. If a reply is not received from the carrier within this time, the action code *IN* may be used to re-request the seat.

Open Segments

Assume that a client has already booked one seat in Y class from SFO to PIT. He would like to return on TW on 2 March, but does not yet know the exact departure time. The following entry may be used to book the open segment in Y class:

0TWOPENY2MARPITSFODS1

SABRE responds as follows:

SEG   2   OPEN   Y   2MAR   PITSFO   DS1

Note that, in this example, the outbound segment has already been booked. Thus, the open segment is segment 2.

As an example, assume an agent input the following entry to request two seats on CP 234 in Y class on 17 July from LAX to YVR:

0CP234Y17JULLAXYVRNN2

Two days later the reservation still has not been confirmed. The following entry may be used to re-request the seats:

0CP234Y17JULLAXYVRIN2

If the segment is no longer desired, the action code *IX* can be used to cancel the seat request.

Table 3-2 Action Codes Used in Direct-Sell Entries.

Code	Meaning	Action
BK	Book/confirmed	Enters a passive segment for a flight booked directly with a carrier.
BL	Book/listed	Enters a passive waitlisted segment.
DS	Desires seats	Sells an open segment.
GK	Guaranteed/confirmed	Enters a passive segment for a flight booked directly with a carrier.
GL	Guaranteed/listed	Enters a passive waitlisted segment.
IN	If not holding, need	Re-requests seats from a carrier.
IX	If holding, cancel	Cancels seats previously requested from a carrier.
LL	List/list	Books a waitlisted segment.
NN	Need/need	Requests seats from a carrier.

A **surface segment** is any segment in which the passenger will travel by a means other than air transportation. Examples of surface segments include travel by car, ship, or rail. Surface segments are not booked in an air itinerary. However, an ARNK segment is input to indicate surface travel when an air itinerary is interrupted.

ARNK is an abbreviation for "arrival unknown." Whenever the departure point of an air segment is different from the arrival point of the previous segment, an ARNK segment must be placed in the itinerary to maintain continuity.

For example, assume a client plans to travel from ORD to MIA on a CO flight. The passenger will then travel by ship from MIA to STT before boarding a return flight to ORD. The itinerary includes two air segments, as follows:

1. ORD–MIA

2. STT–ORD

The arrival point of segment 1 is MIA, but the departure point of segment 2 is STT. To maintain continuity in the itinerary, an ARNK segment must be placed between the two air segments. The ARNK segment signifies that the trip is interrupted by another form of transportation.

The following entry is used to place an ARNK segment in an itinerary:

0A

Selling From a Total Access Availability Display

Seats can be sold from a total access availability display with the normal SABRE entry. The segment will be booked directly on the airline's computer system, and the passenger's reservation will be guaranteed by the carrier.

To illustrate, assume a client desires to travel from ORD to NYC on 19 May, departing at around 8 A.M. The following entry is used to display availability:

119MAYORDNYC8A

C L I E N T F O C U S

Surface Segments

Assume a client will travel by air from MKE to DSM, but will travel by car to OMA before boarding a return flight. In this itinerary, an ARNK segment must be input after the MKE-DSM segment and before the OMA–MKE segment, as follows:

```
1  NW   47Y  01JUL  M  MKEDSM  SS2  910A  1010A
2  ARNK
3  NW  197Y  08JUL  M  OMAMKE  SS2  720P   750P
```

An ARNK segment is required whenever an air itinerary is interrupted by another form of transportation.

Assume SABRE responds as follows:

```
19MAY  TUE    ORD/CDT  NYC/EDT‡1
1 AA 430  F7  Y0  B0  Q0  M0  ORDLGA  9   700A   954A   72S  B  0    TA
2 CO 408  F4  Y0  B0  H0  Q0  ORDEWR  7   830A  1115A   72S  S  0    TA
3 TW 976  F4  Y0  B0  Q0  M0  ORDJFK  9   840A  1222P   73S  S  0    TA
4 US 450  F4  Y0  B0  Q0  M0  ORDJFK  7   900A   248P   72S  S  2    TA
5 AA 234  F7  Y7  B0  Q0  M0  ORDLGA  7  1000A   125P   72S  S  0    TA
6 UA 168  F4  Y4  B0  Q0  M0  ORDLGA  8  1000A   125P   72S  S  0    TA
```

The passenger requests one seat in Y class on the TW flight departing at 8:40 A.M. According to the SABRE display, the flight is sold out in Y class. The following entry is used to obtain last seat availability:

1¤TW

SABRE responds by redisplaying availability, using data obtained from the TW reservation system:

```
TW RESPONSE
 7 TW 976  F5  Y3  B0  Q0  M0  ORDJFK   840A  1222P   73S  S  0
 8 TW 817  F9  Y7  B2  Q0  M0  ORDJFK  1145A   440P   73S  S  1
 9 TW 746  F8  Y3  B2  Q1  M1  ORDJFK   135P   436P  L10  L  0
10 TW 806  F9  C9  Y9  B2  M0  ORDJFK   305P   649P  L10  S  0
11 TW 866  F8  Y3  B2  Q2  M0  ORDJFK   510P   922P   72S  S  1
12 TW 803  F9  Y9  B4  Q4  M4  ORDJFK  1015P  1157P   72S  S  0
```

The TW response shows three seats available in Y class on TW 976.
   The segment may be booked with the normal entry, as follows:

01Y7

This example will sell one seat in Y class on the flight in line 7. SABRE responds as follows:

```
1 TW  976Y  19MAY  T   ORDJFK  SS1  840A  1222P/TATW
```

Note that, in this segment, the code TA and the carrier code have been appended after the arrival time, indicating that the reservation is guaranteed by TW.
   A guaranteed reservation has a higher priority than a normal booking. If the flight is overbooked, passengers with guaranteed reservations will not be denied boarding.

Selling seats from a total access display is not limited to last-seat availability. The total access function can be used to obtain availability whenever the indicator *TA* appears in a flight listing. A segment may be sold from a total access availability display to obtain the best possible guarantee for a client.

According to airline statistics, 52 percent of all reservations are not fulfilled. Because a segment sold from a total access display is guaranteed by the carrier, an agent should sell from a total access display only when there is reasonable certainty that the reservation will be fulfilled. If the reservation is only tentative, or if the agent has a reason to suspect that the client's travel plans may change, the agent should book the segments through SABRE by the normal procedure.

Other factors may also affect the way an air segment is booked. In the past, SABRE subscribers were required to book a minimum number of reservations. However, a federal law enacted in 1992 now prohibits such requirements. Some carriers offer cash bonuses, called *rebates* or *commission overrides*, for booking a set number of segments through SABRE.

Summary

The act of booking an airline reservation is called *selling an air segment*. If a flight or class is sold out, the reservation may be placed on a waitlist. When availability is displayed, a segment may be sold for any flight for which seats are available in the desired class of service. If the number of seats booked exceeds the carrier's seat quota, a message requesting the reservation is transmitted to the carrier.

Seats can be sold on a specified flight without an availability display, if the carrier and flight number are known. The direct-sell entry is also used to book an open segment or to input a passive segment. Surface travel is represented in an air itinerary by an ARNK (arrival unknown) segment. When seats are sold from a total access availability display, the reservation is booked directly on the carrier's system.

New commands included in this chapter:

01Y1	Sell from availability
01Y5Y6	Sell connecting flights from availability
01Y4*	Shortcut for selling connecting flights
01Y1LL	Waitlist from availability
0TW743Y12MARJFKDENNN2	Direct-sell seats on a specified flight
0UA189Y21OCTSFOHNLLL2	Waitlist seats on a specified flight
0DLOPENY10MAYHNLSFODS2	Book an open segment
0VT41Y24JUNPPTBOBGK2	Input a passive segment
0A	Input a surface (ARNK) segment
*I	Display the itinerary

KEY CONCEPTS AND TERMS

Identify the word or phrase for each of the following concepts:

1. The act of booking an airline reservation.

2. The entry code that is used to sell an air segment.

3. When an availability display is present, the act of selling a segment on a flight for which seats are available in the desired class of service.

4. When a flight reservation has been booked, the line that shows the carrier, flight number, class, departure date, day of the week, and departure and arrival airports.

5. The status code that indicates a reservation will be confirmed when the transaction is ended.

6. The status code that is displayed if the number of seats requested exceeds the carrier's seat quota.

7. One flight segment of a connection.

8. One fare that is applied to all the legs of a connection; usually lower than the combined fares of the segments priced separately.

9. Restrictions governing each price category.

10. A list of passengers who desire seats on a flight that is sold out.

11. The secondary code used to waitlist seats.

12. After the transaction has been ended, the segment status that indicates a reservation has been waitlisted.

13. The technique of selling seats on a specified flight without displaying availability.

14. A segment on an unspecified flight operated by a specified carrier.

15. A segment representing air travel that was booked directly with a carrier rather than through SABRE.

16. A segment in which the passenger will travel by a means other than air transportation.

Answers:

1. selling an air segment; 2. 0; 3. selling from availability; 4. segment line; 5. SS; 6. NN; 7. leg; 8. through-fare; 9. fare rules; 10. waitlist; 11. LL; 12. HL; 13. direct selling; 14. open segment; 15. passive segment; 16. surface segment.

REVIEW QUESTIONS

1. Select by letter the correct entry to sell 3 seats in C class on a flight in line 2 of an availability display.

   a) 0C32

   b) 03C2

   c) 02C2

   d) 02C3

2. Refer to the following sell entry to answer a through c:

03Y2

    a) In what class is the airline space being booked?

    b) How many seats are being sold?

    c) What line number in the availability display lists the flight on which the seats will be booked?

3. Refer to the following availability display to answer a through c:

1	US 474	Y4	B0	M0	K0		MSPCLT 8	1030A	148P	73S	L 0		TA
2	DL 277	F4	Y0	B0	M0	Q0	MSPATL 8	755A	914A	727	B 0		TA
3	DL 164	F4	Y4	B0	M0	Q0	CLT 8	1112A	1205P	72S	S 0		TA
4	AA 302	F7	Y0	B0	M0	Q0	MSPORD 9	800A	912P	72S	B 0		TA
5	AA 227	F4	Y0	B0	M0	Q0	CLT 9	1115A	149P	D9S	L 0		TA

    a) What entry would sell 4 seats in Y class on the direct flight?

    b) What entry would sell 2 seats in Y class on both legs of the connection that departs at 8:00 A.M.?

    c) What entry would sell one seat in first class both legs of the connection that arrives at CLT at 12:05 P.M.?

4. Refer to the following flight segment to answer a through e.

1   QF   1Y   13JUL   W MELLHR   SS3   1330+0655

    a) In what class of service have the seats been booked?

    b) How many passengers are traveling together in the party?

    c) On what week day will the party be traveling?

    d) From what city does the flight depart?

    e) What time is the flight scheduled to arrive at the destination airport?

5. Write the correct entry to sell one seat in first class on a two-leg connection beginning in line 3.

6. Write the correct entry to sell 3 seats in B class on a two-leg connection beginning in line 2.

7. Write the direct-sell entry to sell a segment based on the following information:

Carrier/Flight:	Northwest 161
Class:	V
Travel date:	21 May
From:	Detroit
To:	Chicago-O'Hare
Number of seats:	2

8. What entry would direct-sell DL 176 in C class on 13 December, from Atlanta to Ft. Lauderdale, requesting one seat?

9. Write the correct direct-sell entry to book one seat in B class on AA 596 on 15 September, from RNO to SMF.

10. What entry would book four seats in Y class on US 438 on 5 January from Cincinnati to Newark?

11. What two-letter action code is used to waitlist seats in a direct-sell entry?

12. Select by letter the correct entry to waitlist 2 coach seats on United 816 on 12 June from Sydney to Los Angeles.

    a) 0UA816Y12JUNSYDLAXLL2

    b) 0US816Y12JUNSYDLAXNN2

    c) 0UA816Y12JUNSYDLAXPB2

    d) 0LLUA816Y12JUNSYDLAXNN22

13. Write the correct entry to waitlist one passenger in Y class on DL 3801 on 15 December from Cleveland to Milwaukee.

14. What term is used to describe a segment inserted in an itinerary to maintain continuity for pricing, when the destination of one air segment is different from the origin of the next air segment?

15. What entry will input the type of segment described in question 14 in an air itinerary?

16. Two people will travel from San Francisco to Phoenix on 19 April and would like to depart around 11 A.M. What entry would be used to display availability?

17. Refer to the following flight schedules to answer a through d:

```
1 UA 941 F4  Y0  M0  B0  V0  SFOPHX 7  1055A  1245P  727  L  0       TA
2 US 509 Y4  B4  V4  K0      SFOPHX 7  1220P   232P  M80  L  0       TA
3 US 244 Y0  B0  V0  K0      SFOPHX 8   125P   332P  727  S  0       TA
4 UA 385 F4  Y0  M0  B0  V0  SFOPHX 8   140P   352P  727  S  0       TA
5 US 815 Y4  B4  V4  K0      SFOPHX 7   320P   515P  M80  S  0  XQ   TA
```

    a) What entry will book 2 seats in V class on the USAir flight that departs at 12:20 P.M.?

    b) What meal service is provided on the above flight?

    c) What type of aircraft is used for the flight?

    d) What time will the passengers arrive in Phoenix?

18. A family of four will travel from Denver to Kahului on 22 August. They would like to depart from Denver around 8:00 A.M. What entry will display only connections via Honolulu?

19. Refer to the following partial availability display to answer questions a through e:

```
1 UA  69 F4  Y4  B4  M4  V4  DEN HNL 8   850A  235P  D10  B  0       TA
2 HA 250 F4  Y4  B4  M4          OGG 8   430P  530P  D95     0
3 CO 607 F7  Y7  B7  H7  V4  DEN HNL 8  1000A  410P  D10  L  0       TA
4 HA 706 F4  Y4  B4  M4          OGG 8   555P  622P  D95     0
```

    a) What entry will book 3 seats in M class for departure as close to 8:00 A.M. as possible?

    b) If the clients depart at 10 A.M., what time will they arrive in Maui?

    c) To arrive in Maui at 5:30 P.M., what time must they depart from Denver?

    d) How much time will your clients have to change planes in Honolulu if they take the connection in question A?

    e) What meal(s) will the passengers receive on the flight that departs at 10 A.M.?

20. **a)** Three people who travel frequently would like seats on DL 484 on 25 July in Y class, from ATL to DEN. Write the correct direct-sell entry.

b) The travelers will drive a car from DEN to SLC. What entry will show a surface segment in the itinerary?

c) For the return, the clients would like 3 seats in Y class on DL 259 on 14 August from SLC to ATL. What entry will book the reservation?

21. A client will travel from MIA to LAX on the 17th of June. She would like to depart around noon. Write the correct availability entry.

22. Refer to the following display to answer questions a and b:

1	CO	66	F0	Y0	B0	V0	MIALAX	8	1247P	243P	L10	L	0		TA
2	DL	142	F4	C0	Y0		MIALAX	7	1100A	105P	AB3	L	0		TA
3	CO	452	F4	Y4	B4	H4	MIALAX	8	207P	655P	M80	L	0		TA
4	DL	630	F0	Y0	B0	Q0	MIALAX	8	840A	1225P	L10	L	0		TA
5	CO	54	F0	Y0	B0	H0	MIALAX	7	307P	855P	M80	L	0		TA

a) Your client prefers Delta and desires to travel in business (C) class. What entry would be used to waitlist the seat?

b) If the request fails to clear the waitlist, your client will accept a seat in first class on the flight that departs around 2:00 P.M. What entry would be used to book the alternate space?

23. Write the long entry to waitlist 3 seats in Y class on UA 440 on 17 September from LGA to MIA.

24. Write the entry to book an open segment on TWA from DSM to ORD, requesting 2 seats in Y class.

25. Write the entry to place 2 seats on the waitlist for UA 214 in Y class on 22 March, from LAX to DFW.

APPLICATIONS

Read the following scenario, and decide what actions should be performed to satisfy the client's preferences and needs. Briefly describe how you would handle the situation, and then write the required entries.

Mr. Harris is planning a trip from San Francisco to Miami. The party will consist of one passenger. He would like to depart on 19 May around 9 A.M. and prefers to travel in Y class. When you display availability, the first six flights displayed are sold out in Y class. However, the next display shows seats available in Y class on a connection operated by United that is listed in lines 2 and 3. In the original availability display, a United flight in line 3 departs closest to 9 A.M.

The client will travel by ship from Miami to St. Thomas. He would like an open ticket for 8 June in Y class on United Airlines from St. Thomas to Chicago-O'Hare. He would like a flight from O'Hare to San Francisco on 12 June, departing around 6 A.M. When you display availability, an American Airlines flight in line 1 departs at 6:10 A.M. and has seats available in Y class.

After you have booked the itinerary, Mr. Harris asks you to provide him with the flight number and departure time of each flight.

Chapter 4

Passenger Name Records

Chapter Objectives

After you complete this chapter, you should be able to:

1. Identify five mandatory and three optional parts of a passenger name record (PNR).

2. Explain the type of information that is stored in the following fields: name, phone, ticketing, received-from, remarks, general facts, and address.

3. Enter data in the name, phone, ticketing, and received-from fields.

4. End the transaction or ignore a PNR.

5. Display all fields of a PNR.

PROBLEM

A client planning a vacation selects a three-segment connection from Des Moines to Lihue, Kauai, via San Francisco and Honolulu. The same connecting points will be used for the return trip. The party consists of four travelers. Your client would like to book a confirmed reservation.

SABRE SOLUTION

Book the itinerary, and then input the passengers' names, contact telephone numbers, ticketing details, and the person who requested the reservation. Review the flight information with your client, and then transmit the reservation record to the SABRE central processor.

In this chapter, you will learn how to perform these actions and build a complete passenger reservation.

Creating Passenger Name Records

As you learned in previous chapters, an airline passenger must be able to provide information about the itinerary, such as the destination, departure date, preferred departure time, number of travelers, and class of service. To obtain a reservation, the client must also provide information about the travelers, such as the passengers' names, contact telephone numbers, the ticketing date, and the person who requested the reservation. This information is referred to as *passenger data*.

The passenger data is stored with the itinerary in a passenger name record, or PNR. A PNR is created for every airline reservation. Each PNR has five mandatory parts or fields, including the itinerary. Some fields may contain multiple data items. The mandatory passenger data fields are shown in Table 4-1.

A PNR containing an itinerary and the mandatory data fields is shown in Figure 4-1. Before we examine the entry formats for inputting passenger data, let us explore how each field is used.

Name Field

The **name field** stores the names of all the passengers traveling together in the same reservation. Names are grouped together by surname, such as Jones or Smith. Each surname is referred to as a *name item*.

As an example, assume two passengers, Jack Fox and Jason Trott, will travel together on the same itinerary. Rather than creating separate reservations for each traveler, the agent can include both passengers in the same PNR. When the reservation has been completed, the tickets for both passengers can be issued from one PNR. In this example, the surnames Fox and Trott would constitute separate name items, as follows:

    1.1FOX/JACK   2.1TROTT/JASON

Each name item is numbered. In this example, Fox is name item 1, and Trott is name item 2. A secondary number in front of the surname indicates the number of passengers in that name item. In the example, each name item has one passenger.

Now assume passenger Fox will be accompanied by his wife Jill and their daughter Jane. In this case, the name items would appear as follows:

    1.3FOX/JACK/JILL MRS/JANE MISS   2.1TROTT/JASON

Name item 1 now has three passengers, as indicated by the secondary number 3 in front of the surname.

Table 4-1 Mandatory Passenger Data Fields.

Field	Data
Name	Passenger name(s)
Phone	Contact telephone number(s)
Ticketing	Ticketing details
Received-from	Person who requested the service

Figure 4-1 Example of a completed PNR.

```
    1. 1HEGARDT/E  MR
1  AA  430Y  12SEP  M  ORDEWR  HK1   700A   954A
TKT/TIME  LIMIT -
    1. TAW10SEP/
PHONES -
    1. ORD312-555-1202-A
    2. ORD312-555-3210-H
RECEIVED FROM - SEC/MARY
B4T/B4T*A47   1044/13JUL90     T2PNKD
```

A PNR may have several passengers but may have only one itinerary. All the travelers in the name field must have exactly the same itinerary. The total number of passengers in the name field must be equal to the number of seats booked in each flight segment.

A maximum of 99 passengers can be stored in the name field. However, pre-reserved seats can be assigned for a maximum of 50 passengers in one PNR.

Phone Field

Contact telephone numbers are referred to simply as phones. The travel agency phone must be included as the first item in the phone field of every PNR. The **phone field** is also used to store the passenger's business and home phones. Each telephone number in the phone field is referred to as a *phone item*. The location of each phone item is indicated by a letter, as follows:

```
PHONES-
1.SFO415-555-1009-A
2.SFO415-555-2324-B
3.SFO415-555-0927-H
```

In this example, the location code *A* indicates the agency phone, *B* indicates the passenger's business phone, and *H* indicates the passenger's home phone. Each phone item consists of the area code, the telephone number, and a location indicator. Note that SABRE displays the city code for each phone, based on the area code input for the agency phone. Each phone item is numbered. In this example, the agency phone is item 1, and the business phone is item 2.

Ticketing Field

The **ticketing field** stores details about ticketing. The **ticketing arrangement** is the date on which tickets will be issued. As an example, assume a PNR has the following data in the ticketing field:

```
TKT/TIME LIMIT-
1.TAW21SEP/
```

In this example, the ticketing code *TAW* ("tickets await writing") indicates that tickets will be issued by the agency on 21 September. On that date the PNR will appear automatically in an electronic holding area called the *ticketing queue*. By looking in the queue, the agent can determine which reservations are scheduled to be ticketed on that day. You will learn how to work with queues in Chapter 12.

Now assume tickets have already been issued. In this case, the ticketing field might appear as follows:

TKT/TIME LIMIT-
1.T-A/17SEP

In this example, the code *T-A* indicates that tickets were issued by the agency on 17 September.

In some instances, a client might desire that tickets be issued at the airport prior to departure. In such cases, the ticketing field may contain a time limit for ticketing at the airport. Other arrangements, such as a prepaid ticket advice, may also be stored in the ticketing field.

Received-From Field

The **received-from field** identifies the person who requested the service. This field is free-form—that is, the data may be input in any form—but the abbreviation *P* is often input to indicate that the passenger requested the reservation, as follows:

RECEIVED FROM - P

If the service was requested by someone other than the passenger, the person may be identified by name, by an abbreviation, such as *SEC* for a secretary or *MRS* for the passenger's wife, or by a title and surname such as *MR BROWN* or *MS CRENSHAW*.

Entering Passenger Data

An itinerary and the four mandatory data fields must be included in every PNR. In most cases, the data may be input in any order, but each item must be typed in a set format.

Each reservation is called a *transaction*. The passenger data and itinerary are assembled in the agent work area. When the PNR is complete, the agent inputs the entry to end the transaction. This action transmits the record to SABRE for storage and removes the PNR from the work area. The term *end transact* is a short way of saying to end the transaction.

If for some reason the PNR should not be stored, the reservation can be removed from the work area without being stored. This action is called ignoring the transaction.

Optional Data Fields

Besides the mandatory data fields, a passenger name record may include optional information, such as free-form remarks, service information, or the travel agency's address. The optional data fields shown in Table 4-2 are used for such types of data items.

Table 4-2 Optional Data Fields.	

Field	Information
Remarks	Free-form text
General facts	Service information
AA facts	American Airlines service information
Address	Travel agency address

Remarks Field

The **remarks field** may be used to store any free-form text. For instance, the field might be used to communicate information to other agents in the office or to remind the agent to take some future action. As an example, assume a PNR contains the following data in the remarks field:

REMARKS-1.DELIVER TICKETS

This note is a reminder to deliver the tickets to the client. Abbreviations are often used in the remarks field, but it is important to remember that other agents in the office may have occasion to consult the PNR. Therefore, the message should be clear and concise.

General Facts and AA Facts

Two fields, general facts and AA facts, are used for service information. Two types of data items may be stored in these fields: **special service requests (SSR)** and **optional service information (OSI)**. An SSR item is input to request a service not normally provided to passengers, such as special meals, wheelchair service, or assistance for a blind or deaf traveler. Each type of service has a four-letter code that is used to request the service.

   An OSI item is input to send a message to an airline regarding some aspect of a reservation. For example, an OSI item should be input to alert the airlines about young children or very important passengers. Unlike SSR entries, an OSI entry does not require specific response or action by airline personnel.

   The **general facts fields** may be used to input service information for any carrier except American Airlines. The **AA facts field** is only for SSR and OSI items directed to American Airlines.

Address Field

The **address field** is used to store the travel agency address. If a ticket or invoice is to be mailed to the passenger, the client address is stored in the remarks field.

Building a PNR

To build a PNR, the agent inputs data items into each of the passenger data fields. The PNR must contain an itinerary and information in the mandatory data fields—name, phone, ticketing, and received-from—before SABRE will store the record. Each data item is identified by a code, called the *field identifier*, which is used as the entry code. The **field identifier** indicates the PNR field where the information will be stored. Table 4-3 shows the field identifiers for the passenger data fields discussed in the preceding sections.

Table 4-3 Field Identifiers.

Identifier	Field	Field Type
-	Name	Mandatory
9	Phone	Mandatory
7	Ticketing	Mandatory
6	Received from	Mandatory
5	Remarks	Optional
3	General facts	Optional

Inputting a Name Item for One Passenger

The field identifier - is used to input name items. The following format is used to input the name item for one traveler:

FORMAT   -<Surname>/<Passenger>

EXAMPLE   -LINDBERGH/C MR

A slash (/) is typed to separate the passenger element from the surname. A separate name item is required for each surname.

SABRE will accept a name item without a title, but most airlines prefer titles. Most airlines prefer titles to be used in name entries to clarify the sex, age group, and marital or professional status of each traveler. If a title is not used, some airlines will assume the passenger is an adult male. The following **titles** are used to identify the sex, age group, and marital status of each traveler:

MR	Male, 12 years or older
MRS	Female, married
MS	Female, 12 years or older, marital status unknown
MSTR	Male, less than 12 years
MISS	Female, less than 12 years

A title may also be used to indicate professional status or military rank, as in the following examples:

DR	Medical doctor
REV	Ordained minister
PFC	Private First Class
SGT	Sergeant
LT	Lieutenant
CAPT	Captain
GEN	General

Other examples include CONGRESSMAN, SISTER (for members of religious orders), and MLLE (mademoiselle).

The passenger may be identified either by name or initial. Some airlines prefer the full given name. In most cases, however, the initial is sufficient if the passenger is traveling on a domestic itinerary. An initial requires fewer keystrokes and is not as likely to be misspelled as a full name. If the passenger will be traveling abroad, however, the full name, as shown in his or her passport, should be input. The full name should also be input if the ticket will be prepaid for pickup at a different location, such as an airport ticket counter.

Inputting Multiple Passengers in a Name Item

When multiple passengers have the same surname, the number of such passengers must be input before the surname, and a passenger element must be included for each traveler, as follows:

-2BONAPARTE/N MR/J MRS

This example will input the name item for the surname Bonaparte. Because the name item has two passengers, the number 2 is typed before the surname. The initial and a title are input for each passenger. Note that a slash is typed before each initial.

The following guidelines will help you input name items correctly and consistently:

1. Include the number of travelers for each surname. If the name item has one passenger, the number 1 is optional.
2. Verify the spelling of the surname.
3. Type a slash (/) to separate the surname from the given name or initial.

CLIENT FOCUS

Inputting Name Items

Assume a passenger, Mr. J. Caesar, will travel unaccompanied. If a name item has one passenger, the number 1 may be omitted. Thus, either of the following entries may be used to input the name item:

-CAESAR/J MR
-1CAESAR/J MR

Now suppose that Mr. Caesar will be accompanied by his wife, Mrs. L. Caesar. In this case, the number of passengers is mandatory. The following entry must be used to input the name item:

-2CAESAR/J MR/L MRS

Now assume that the passengers will be accompanied by their eight-year-old son, D. Caesar. The title *MSTR* is used to identify a male child less than 12 years of age. The name item would be input as follows:

-3CAESAR/J MR/L MRS/D MSTR

4. Identify each passenger by title. Type a space between the given name or initial and the title. A title is especially important if an initial is input, or if the name may apply to either sex.

5. Type a slash (/) to separate passengers within each surname. To enter family members, input the parents first, followed by the children in descending order of age.

The following are examples of valid name entries:

-RIVERS/L MR
-1WATERS/T MR
-2SANDS/M MR/A MRS
-4HILL/R MR/T MRS/A MSTR/T MISS
-DALE/H SGT
-2FORREST/K REV/L MRS
-3GLENN/F DR/A MRS/G MS

Passenger Reference Numbers

When a government, travel agency, or airline employee books a reservation, a passenger reference number may be input with the name item. For example, the employee ID number may be input as follows:

-SAND/K MRS*EMP60123

In this example, EMP identifies the digits as an employee ID number. An asterisk (*) is typed before the reference information. Free-form text may also be input with a name item, as follows:

-CARTER/H MR*TRAFMGR

In the example above, the abbreviation TRAFMGR indicates that the passenger, Mr. H. Carter, is a traffic manager.

When reference information is included in a name entry, any information typed after the asterisk will print on the passenger ticket.

The option 0/ may be used to prevent reference information from printing on the ticket. For example, assume you are creating a PNR for Mr. R. Robin and his 10-year-old son, Mstr. L. Robin. Suppose you desire to input the child's age in the name field for reference. The following entry will input the name item together with the reference information, but will prevent the reference information from printing on the ticket:

-2ROBIN/R MR/L MSTR*0/10YRS

AAdvantage Account Numbers

Passengers who travel frequently with American Airlines may qualify for such incentives as free travel and class upgrades. To qualify for these incentives, passengers must first join the airline's AAdvantage frequent traveler program. AAdvantage members receive mileage credits for traveling on AA flights. When the credits are accumulated, they may be redeemed for a free ticket, a class upgrade, or another award.

If an AAdvantage account number is entered in the name field, the passenger will automatically receive mileage credits for all the flight segments in the itinerary upon completing the trip. The cross (‡) is used to input the AAdvantage account number, as follows:

-SPARROW/T MR‡7654321

A passenger reference number and an AAdvantage number can be input in the same entry, as in the following example:

-SPARROW/T MR*12112‡7654321

This entry can only be used for AAdvantage numbers. Procedures for inputting account numbers for other carriers' frequent traveler programs will be discussed in Chapter 5.

Inputting Phone Items

Each phone item has three elements: the area code, the telephone number, and a location indicator. A dash (-) is input to separate the area code, the two parts of the telephone number, and the location indicator. The following location indicators are used with phone entries:

A   Agency phone

B   Business phone

H   Home or hotel phone

As an example, assume a PNR contains the following phone items:

1.LAX213-555-3409-A

2.LAX213-555-1332-B

The area code for both phones is 213. The first phone item is the agency phone, and the second item is the client's business phone. The agency phone should be input before any other phones.

The field identifier **9** is used to input phone items, as follows:

FORMAT   9<Area code>-<Phone>-<Location>

EXAMPLE   9415-222-0198-B

In the example, the location code B indicates the client's business phone. SABRE will insert the city code, as follows:

2.SFO415-222-0198-B

The phone item in this example is item 2, indicating that the agency phone was input previously. The city code is based on the area code in the agency phone item.

The preferred order for entering phone items is as follows: (1) agency phone, (2) business phone, and (3) home phone. Every PNR must contain at least one phone item. If a PNR is created by a travel agency, it must contain the agency phone.

Agency Reference. When the agency's phone is input, the name may be included for reference, as follows:

9302-555-6670-A JETSET TRAVEL

Any free-form text may be typed after the location code. Some travel agencies prefer that agents input their first names, as in the following example:

    9612-555-3949-A HEATHER

In this example, Heather is the agent who created the PNR. Each travel agency has its own policy regarding the use of agent names.

Passenger Reference. When a PNR has more than one passenger name item, the business and home phones should be identified by the applicable passenger's surname. For example, assume a PNR contains the following name items:

    1.1LEWIS/D MR   2.1CLARKE/P MR

The business phone for passenger Lewis should be input as follows:

    9713-789-3461-B LEWIS

A business phone and a home phone should be entered for all name items that have different phones. If two passengers with different surnames have the same business phone, the phone should only be entered once. If the passengers have different business phones, however, the business phone of each passenger should be input, with the appropriate passenger reference.

If family members with the same surname travel together, a title may be used to identify the business phone. For example, assume a PNR has the following name item:

    1.2WALKER/H MR/P MRS

Mr. Walker's business phone is 305-555-0218. In this case, the title *MR* should be included in the phone entry for passenger reference, as follows:

    9305-555-0218-B MR

The passenger reference in this situation prevents confusion with Mrs. Walker's business phone.

When a business or hotel phone is input, an extension number may be included, as follows:

    9301-555-4452-BX214

In this example, *X* indicates the extension number. There is no set format for inputting an extension. Thus, *EX* or *EXT* might be typed before the extension number, as in the following example of a hotel phone entry:

    9201-555-7652-HEXT1412 HILTON

When the location indicator *H* is used for a hotel phone, the hotel name is included for reference.

The maximum length of a phone item, including any optional text, is 30 characters.

Forcing the City Code When a phone item is input, SABRE inserts the city code based on the area code of the agency phone. If a contact phone is outside the local city area, the city code may be included in the phone entry.

For example, assume an agency phone in San Francisco is 415-555-9983. The agent, Karen, inputs the agency phone as follows:

9415-555-9983-A KAREN

Karen's client works in San Jose (SJC). His business phone is 408-555-2487. The contact business phone may be entered as follows:

9SJC408-555-2487-B

This entry will override the agency city code so that, when the phone field is displayed, the correct city code will be displayed for the contact business phone.

Guidelines for Phone Entries The guidelines in the following list will help you input phone items accurately and consistently. For examples of valid phone entries, see Figure 4-2.

1. Always enter the agency phone first in every PNR. Include your name or the name of your agency for reference.
2. Enter the other contact phones in the following order: business, home, and hotel (if applicable). Be sure to include the correct area code with each telephone number.
3. Include the location code after the phone.
4. Include a passenger reference after each passenger phone if there are multiple passengers with different phones in the same PNR.
5. Include the extension number, if applicable, in a business or hotel phone.
6. If the location indicator *H* is used for a hotel phone, include the hotel name for reference.

Inputting Ticketing Items

The field identifier **7** is used to input ticketing items, as follows:

FORMAT   7<Ticketing arrangement>

EXAMPLE   7TAW18MAY/

In this example, the code *TAW* is input to arrange ticketing for 18 May. In a TAW entry, a slash (/) must be typed after the date. No other characters should be typed after the slash.

Figure 4-2 Examples of Valid Phone Entries.

```
9203-555-0917-A ELIZABETH
9217-555-0091-B
9217-555-0091-B LARSEN
9602-555-2991-H
9554-555-5102-HX542 BW INN
```

The following are examples of ticketing arrangement codes:

TAW Future ticketing date
TAX Prepaid ticket advice
TAT Teleticketing request
TAV Tour ticketing
T-A Tickets issued by the agency

Ticketing Entry Guidelines The following guidelines pertain to ticketing items:

1. In a TAW entry, / must be typed at the end of the entry.
2. To place the PNR in the ticketing queue for immediate ticketing, input a TAW entry without a date.
3. The ticketing field may contain only one ticketing item.

The following are examples of valid ticketing entries:

7TAW29JUL/
7TAW/
7TAX/12APR

C L I E N T   F O C U S

Inputting Ticketing Arrangements

Assume you have created an itinerary for a client, who requests that tickets be issued on 21 June. The following entry is used to input the ticketing arrangement:

7TAW21JUN/

If the date is omitted from a TAW entry, SABRE will assume that the tickets should be issued immediately.

Now assume that, instead of having the tickets issued by the travel agency, your client would like to have the tickets issued at the airport prior to departure. The advice code *TAX* is used to indicate a prepaid ticket advice, as follows:

7TAX/10SEP

Note that, in a TAX entry, a slash (/) is typed before the date. In this example the prepaid tickets will be issued at the airport on 10 September.

Time-Limit Entries The entry code **8** is used to input a time limit as follows:

FORMAT   8<Minutes>

EXAMPLE   830

In this example, the passenger must check in at the airport counter or gate within 30 minutes before the scheduled departure time.

A time-limit entry may also apply to airport ticketing. As an example, assume a ticket must be picked up at the TWA ticket counter at STL by 2 P.M. The following entry may be used to indicate the time limit:

FORMAT   8<Airport>-<Carrier><Time limit>/<Date>

EXAMPLE   8STL-TW2P/18MAY

A dash is typed after the airport, and a slash is typed to separate the time limit and date.

Inputting Received-From Items

The field identifier **6** is used to input received-from items, as follows:

FORMAT   6<Text>

EXAMPLE   6P

In this example, the abbreviation *P* indicates that the passenger requested the service.

Redisplaying the Record

As information is entered into the various PNR fields, the data is held temporarily in the agent's work area. The following entry can be used to view all the fields:

*A

SABRE will respond by displaying any fields that contain data. The fields may be displayed at any time before the transaction is ended or ignored.

The following entry can be used to view just the itinerary:

*I

This entry will display the itinerary segments, but not any of the passenger data.

Ending the Transaction

When the PNR is complete, the agent must end transact to transmit the record to the central processor for storage. The following entry is used to end transact:

E

Received-From Items

Assume a PNR has the following name item:

1.2WEST/L MR/P MRS

Assume the reservation was received from Mrs. West. In this situation, the received-from item may be input as follows:

6MRS

In some cases, the title and surname must be used to identify the person who requested the service. For example, assume a PNR has the following name items:

1.2NORTH/K MR/L MRS   2.2SOUTH/E MR/W MRS

Assume the reservation was received from Mrs. North. The title *MRS* might refer to either Mrs. North or Mrs. South. Thus, both the title and surname must be included in the received-from item, as follows:

6MRS NORTH

A key labeled **ET** is found on some SABRE keyboards. On such keyboards the transaction can be ended either by pressing the *ET* key, or by entering the letter *E*.

When the transaction is ended, a six-character code called a **record locator** is displayed. The record locator can be used to retrieve the PNR from storage. You will learn how to retrieve a PNR by record locator in Chapter 6.

Ignoring the Transaction

If for some reason the agent does not wish to store the record, the transaction can be ignored. This action clears the work area without saving the record. To ignore a transaction, the agent types **I** and presses *Enter*.

Putting It All Together

As mentioned earlier, the PNR must contain an itinerary, as well as information in the name, phone, ticketing, and received-from fields. To illustrate, let us follow a passenger reservation from start to finish.

Mr. W. Whitman contacts his travel agent to make arrangements to travel from Memphis to Las Vegas on 12 May. He would like to depart early in the morning. The agent, Dianne, displays availability as follows:

112MAYMEMLAS

No departure time is specified, so SABRE displays flights departing around 7 A.M., as follows:

```
12MAY  TUE    MEM/CDT    LAS/MDT-1
1 DL  367  F4 Y4 B0 Q0 M0  MEMLAS  8   646A   954A   72S  B  2   TA
2 UA  217  F4 Y4 B0 Q0 M0  MEMLAS  8  1025A  1150A   72S  L  0   TA
3 AA  567  F7 Y7 B0 Q0 M0  MEMDFW  8   825A   945A   727  B  0   TA
4 AA  207  F7 Y7 B0 Q0 M0        LAS  7  1045A  1130A   72S  S  0   TA
5 UA  251  F4 Y4 B4 Q4 M4  MEMDEN  7  1025A  1155A   727  S  0   TA
6 UA  495  F4 Y4 B4 Q4 M4        LAS  6   110P   158P   72S  S  0   TA
```

Mr. Whitman tells Dianne he wants a direct flight and prefers to travel with Delta. He would also like the least expensive class of service. On 12 May, the Delta flight has seats available in F or Y class. Of these, the Y class fare is the least expensive. Dianne books the segment as follows:

01Y1

SABRE responds as follows:

```
1 DL  367Y  12MAY T   MEMLAS   SS1  646A  954A
```

In this segment, one seat will be confirmed on DL 367 in Y class on 12 May. For the return trip, Mr. Whitman would like an open ticket for 17 May. When a class of service is booked at a discount fare, open segments are often prohibited. This passenger, however, is booked at the full coach fare, so an open return is permitted. Dianne books the segment as follows:

0DLOPENY17MAYLASMEMDS1

To review the flight segments, Dianne displays the itinerary with the following entry:

*I

SABRE displays the segments as follows:

```
1 DL  367Y  12MAY T   MEMLAS   SS1  646A  954A
2 DLOPENY   17MAY S   LASMEM   DS1
```

Dianne verifies the spelling of the passenger's name and inputs the name item as follows:

-WHITMAN/W MR

Next Dianne enters the travel agency phone, as follows:

9901-555-3093-A DIANNE

She includes her name to identify herself as the agent who created the PNR. Dianne next asks the client for his business contact phone and inputs the phone as follows:

9901-555-7271-B

She also asks for his home phone and inputs the phone as follows:

9901-555-2492-H

Dianne next asks the client when he would like to have the tickets. When a ticketing date has been arranged, she inputs the ticketing item as follows:

7TAW10MAY/

To complete the PNR, Dianne enters the received-from item as follows:

6P

The abbreviation *P* indicates that the reservation was received from the passenger. To review the PNR, Dianne displays all the fields as follows:

*A

SABRE displays the entire record, as follows:

```
 1.1WHITMAN/W MR
1 DL  367Y  12MAY  T   MEMLAS   SS1  646A  954A
2 DLOPENY   17MAY  S   LASMEM   DS1
TKT/TIME LIMIT -
 1.TAW10MAY/
PHONES -
 1.MEM901-555-3093-A DIANNE
 2.MEM901-555-7271-B
 3.MEM901-555-2492-H
RECEIVED FROM-P
```

Dianne explains the itinerary to her client, verifying the carrier, flight, date, and departure time. Then she ends the transaction as follows:

E

SABRE responds as follows:

```
EOK-STGWRB
```

The response *EOK* indicates that SABRE has accepted the PNR for storage. The six-character code on the right is the record locator.

Inputting Multiple Items

The end-item key (Σ) can be used to input multiple items with one entry. On a PC keyboard, the back-slash key (\) is used to type an end-item. For instance, the following entry may be used to input two name items:

-MCGRAW/M MRΣ-HILL/L MR

Two phone items may be input as follows:

9301-555-2301-BΣ9301-555-2998-H

Items may be input to different fields as follows:

-STEINBECK/J MRΣ9415-555-2099-AΣ9415-555-7543-BΣ6P

Summary

When a flight reservation is booked, the passenger data is stored with the itinerary in a passenger name record, or PNR. The five mandatory parts of a PNR include the itinerary and the name, phone, ticketing, and received-from fields. The name field is used to store the passenger names. A separate name item is input for each surname. The agency, client business, and client home telephone numbers are stored in the phone field. Ticketing details, such as a future ticketing date, are stored in the ticketing field. The received-from field is used to store the name of the person who requested the service.

New commands included in this chapter:

-WADSWORTH/W MR	Input name item
-3BOONE/J MR/K MRS/L MISS	Input multiple passengers with the same surname
-CLARK/L MR*EMP03456	Input name item with reference number
-BARROWS/N MR‡765021	Input name item with AAdvantage account number
9415-555-2309-A	Input phone item
9213-555-4123-H MARTIN	Input phone item with passenger reference
7TAW12MAR/	Input ticketing item
830	Input time limit in minutes
8STL-TW2P/18MAY	Input time limit for airport ticketing

6P	Input received-from item
*A	Display all fields
-STEIN/K MRΣ6P	Input multiple items
E	End transaction
I	Ignore transaction

KEY CONCEPTS AND TERMS

Identify the word or phrase for each of the following concepts:

1. A record in which the computer stores passenger data and the itinerary.
2. One of the parts of a PNR that stores passenger data items.
3. The field that stores the names of all the passengers traveling together in the same reservation.
4. The field in which contact telephone numbers are stored.
5. The field in which ticketing details are stored.
6. The date on which tickets will be issued.
7. The field in which text is stored to indicate the person who requested the reservation.
8. The field in which free-form text is stored to communicate information to other agents in the office or to remind the agent to take some future action.
9. A service not normally provided to passengers, such as special meals, wheelchair service, or assistance for a blind or deaf traveler.
10. A message transmitted to an airline regarding some aspect of a reservation.
11. The field that is used to input service information for any carrier except American Airlines.
12. The field that is used to direct service information to American Airlines.
13. The field that is used to store the travel agency address.
14. A code that indicates the passenger data field where information is to be stored.
15. The field identifier that is used to input name items.
16. Abbreviations or words used in name entries to clarify the sex, age group, and marital or professional status of each traveler.
17. The field identifier that is used to input phone items.
18. A phone item code designating whether the telephone number is for a travel agency, a client's business, or a client's home or hotel.
19. The field identifier that is used to input ticketing items.
20. The entry code that is used to input a ticketing time limit.
21. The field identifier that is used to input information in the received-from field.
22. The entry to display all the fields of a PNR.
23. The entry to display only the itinerary.
24. The entry to end the transaction.
25. The entry to ignore a transaction.
26. A six-character code that is displayed when a transaction is ended and that can be used to retrieve the PNR from storage.

REVIEW QUESTIONS

1. What entry code is used to input a passenger name?

2. A passenger, Mr. T. Moorehead, will be traveling unaccompanied. What entry would be used to input the name item?

3. Mr. Arthur Clemson and his wife, Julie, will be traveling together. What entry would be used to input the name item?

4. The Lionel family is planning a vacation. The parents, William and Martha, will be traveling with their ten-year-old son, James, and six-year-old daughter, Elizabeth. Write the correct name entry.

5. Mr. Frank Steglitz will travel with his wife, Bernice, their eighteen-year-old son, Greg, and their eight-year-old daughter, Heather. Write the correct name entry for these passengers.

6. Sgt. William Chambers is traveling on furlough. Write the correct name entry.

7. Write the name entry for Reverend Arthur Coleman.

8. What title is used for an adult female passenger of unspecified marital status?

9. What title would be used for a male passenger 12 years of age or younger?

10. Dr. Charles Morris is scheduling a trip. His wife, Eleanor, and their sixteen-year-old daughter, Tina, will be accompanying him. Write the correct name entry.

11. What code is used to input a contact phone?

12. Assume you work for a travel agency with a phone number of 213 555-0067. Write the correct phone entry.

13. Suppose you are creating a PNR for a passenger whose home phone is 602 555-1632. How would you enter the phone item in the PNR?

14. Assume you are creating a PNR for a client whose business telephone is 212 555-3307. What entry would you use to input the phone item?

15. What code is used to input information to the ticketing field?

16. What entry would be input to indicate a time limit of 30 minutes for airport ticketing?

17. Write the ticketing entry to show that tickets will be written on 19 July.

18. What code is used to enter information in the received-from field?

19. What entry is used to indicate that the passenger requested his or her own flight reservations?

20. Assume you are creating a PNR for a client whose flight reservations were made by his secretary. Write the received-from entry.

21. Mr. G. Kimble and Mr. L. Stevens will travel together. Write the name entry.

22. The Swansons, a family of four, will travel on vacation. The father's initial is E. and the mother's is H. Their seven-year-old daughter, K., and four-year-old daughter, A., will accompany them. Write the name entry.

23. Assume your agency phone is 212 555-1408. Write the phone entry.

24. Assume your client's business contact phone is 212 555-7717. Write the phone entry.

25. Mr. and Mrs. Framm will travel together. Mrs. Framm placed the reservations. Write the received-from entry.

26. Assume tickets should be issued on 17 July. Write the ticketing entry.

27. Assume a client's business contact phone is 415 555-1339, and his home phone is 415 555-1727. Write the correct entry to input phone items at the same time.

28. Mr. Kronberg's reservations were made by Mr. Volker. Write the received from entry.

29. What entry will indicate a 30-minute time limit for picking up prepaid tickets at the airport?

30. Mr. L. Burrows and Mrs. C. Burrows will travel together. Mrs. Burrows requested the flight arrangements. Write the correct entry to input the name and received-from items simultaneously.

31. Mr. G. Carlson will travel to a convention. Ms. Greene requested his flight reservations. The agency phone is 305 555-9987. Write the correct entry to input the name, received-from, and agency phone items simultaneously.

32. Write the necessary entries to create a PNR for the following clients. Book the passengers in Q class on all segments. Use a separate entry for each phone item. After creating the PNR, include the entries to display the record and end the transaction.

    Mr. J. and Mrs. C. Byrd and their six-year-old daughter, R. Byrd live in Chicago. They plan to visit relatives in Denver, and then travel to Los Angeles. They will depart from Chicago-O'Hare to Denver on 12 August on AA 429. From Denver, they will depart to LAX on August 16 on AA 515. They will return from Los Angeles to Chicago-O'Hare on August 20 on AA 472. The agency phone is 312 555-5050. Mr. Byrd calls from his office to place the reservations. His business phone is 312 555-4231 and his home phone is 312 555-6879. Arrange ticketing for 24 July.

APPLICATIONS

Read the following scenario, and decide what actions should be performed to satisfy the client's preferences and needs. Briefly describe how you would handle the situation, and then write the required entries.

Mr. D. Coleman and Mrs. C. Coleman will be traveling with their six-year-old daughter, Teri. Your clients would like to travel from New York to Miami on 19 January, leaving around 9 A.M. The Colemans would like seats at a discount fare in Q class on both flights.

When you display availability for the outbound segment, the first six flights displayed are sold out in Q class. All the flights are sold out in the next display as well. To obtain the discount fare, your clients inquire about flights one day later, on 20 January, leaving around 2 P.M. In line 3, four seats are available in Q class on a Continental flight departing at 2:20 P.M. Your clients will return on 27 January, at around 3 P.M. To obtain the discount fare, the return reservations must be booked in Q or V class on the same carrier. When you display availability, the first Continental flight with seats available in Q class is in line 5.

Your agency phone is 212 555-3828. Mr. Coleman's business phone is 212 555-8172, and your clients' home phone is 212 555-0019. Mrs. Coleman, who called to make the reservations, would like to pick up the tickets on 4 December.

Chapter 5

Supplemental Data

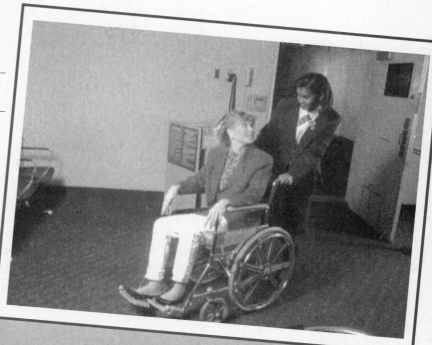

Chapter Objectives

After you complete this chapter, you should be able to:

1. Input data to the remarks and address fields.

2. Input a form of payment or a client billing address.

3. Input itinerary remarks.

4. Discuss situations requiring SSR items, and identify the codes for common service requests.

5. Input SSR items in the general facts and AA facts fields.

6. Input OSI items regarding situations about which the airline should be notified.

7. Input frequent flyer account numbers.

PROBLEM

You are making travel arrangements for two clients, Mr. and Mrs. Trainer, who will travel cross-country. Your clients will purchase the tickets by credit card. Both passengers are elderly and will require assistance with boarding and disembarking. Mrs. Trainer requires a wheelchair, although she is capable of ascending and descending stairs. Mr. Trainer is under a physician's orders to restrict his diet to low-sodium meals.

SABRE SOLUTION

Enter the credit card account number in the remarks field. Then send an OSI message to advise the airlines that the passengers are elderly. Input SSR items to request a wheelchair for Mrs. Trainer and a low-sodium meal for Mr. Trainer.

In this chapter, you will learn various uses of the remarks field and will discover how to handle situations requiring OSI and SSR items.

Supplemental Data

You will recall from Chapter 4 that, in addition to the mandatory passenger data fields, a PNR also has four optional fields, as follows:

1. address
2. remarks
3. general facts
4. AA facts

Data stored in any of these fields is referred to as **supplemental data**. The address field is used to store the agency name and address. The remarks field may be used to store any general information for the agency about the reservation. The general facts and AA facts fields are used to communicate service information to the airlines.

Inputting Remarks

Any free-form text may be stored in the remarks field. The field identifier **5** is used to input information in the field, as follows:

FORMAT   5<Text>

EXAMPLE   5ADVISE PSGR ABOUT PET TRANSPORT

Abbreviations are often used in the text portion of the entry. In the example, the word *passenger* is abbreviated *PSGR*. Other travel agents or airline personnel may need to review the PNR; therefore, the remark should be as clear as possible.

Let us examine some common situations for which remarks entries are made. Table 5-1 provides examples of remarks entries using common abbreviations.

The first example in Table 5-1 is a reminder to check the fare rules regarding the maximum stay. In this case, the client may have booked a tentative flight for the return trip but is considering staying over at the destination a few extra days.

The second example in Table 5-1 is an instruction to advise the passenger about hotels in the destination city. This remark might be directed to another agent in the office or might be entered as a reminder to the agent who created the PNR.

The third example in Table 5-1 indicates that the passenger will discuss arrangements for a rental car and hotel accommodations later. In this case, when the client booked the air itinerary, he or she may not have had time to discuss car and hotel arrangements.

The fourth example in Table 5-1 is a note that the passenger is traveling on airline business. This entry might be used for a contractor, such as a security consultant or an advertising executive.

Table 5-1 Examples of Remarks Using Common Abbreviations.

Example	Meaning
5CK RULES RE MAX STAY	Check fare rules regarding the maximum stay
5ADV PSGR RE HTLS	Advise the passenger regarding hotels
5CAR/HTL TBA	Car and hotel to be arranged
5PSGR IS TRVLNG ON A/L BUSINESS	Passenger is traveling on airline business

Remarks Entries

Assume you are creating a PNR for a client who will be traveling abroad. You have advised the passenger about documents required for international travel. The abbreviation *ADVD DOCS* is often used for this purpose, as in the following entry:

5ADVD DOCS

If a fare has been quoted to a client, but the tickets have not been purchased yet, the fare quotation may be entered in the remarks field, as in the following example:

5QTD 139.00 FARE ON 12JUL

In this example, the word *quoted* is abbreviated *QTD*.

There are no strict rules governing abbreviations in the remarks field. Keep in mind, however, that the meaning should be clear to other agents who may have occasion to review the PNR.

Most requests for airline reservations are received by telephone. Many agents prefer to obtain the client's travel plans over the phone and then book a tentative itinerary later. In such cases, the remarks field may contain numerous notes and reminders about the passenger's needs and preferences.

There is no limit on the number of remarks items that may be input in a PNR. However, the maximum length of each item is 59 characters. If a message comprises several lines of text, each line must be input as a separate item with the field identifier 5. For example, the following entries would be used to input two lines of text in the remarks field:

5MRS TATE GOES BY THE NAME DAWN HOWARD-TATE BUT

5THE NAME ON HER PASSPORT IS LEIGH DAWN HOWARD

An end-item may be used to input two or more text lines simultaneously. Remember, however, that each line must begin with the field identifier 5.

The information in the remarks field is not printed on the ticket or invoice, unless a specific code is input for that purpose.

Special Uses of the Remarks Field

The remarks field can be used for other purposes besides notes and reminders. A secondary code can be used to indicate a special purpose, such as printing text on the ticket or invoice. The secondary codes shown in Table 5-2 may be used in remarks entries.

A secondary code is typed after the field identifier 5 to perform one of the actions shown in Table 5-3.

Table 5-2 Secondary Codes for Special Uses of the Remarks Field.

Secondary Code	Purpose
-	Form of payment
/	Client address
.	Invoice remark
‡	Itinerary remark
S‡	Coded remark
H-	Historical remark
Q-	Queue instruction

Table 5-3 Effect of Secondary Codes on Remarks Entries.

Entry Code	Action
5-	Stores the form of payment to print on the ticket
5/	Stores the client address to print on the invoice
5.	Stores a remark to print on the invoice
5‡	Stores a remark to print on the itinerary
5S‡	Stores a coded remark
5H-	Stores a remark to be retained in the PNR history
5Q-	Stores a queue placement instruction

For example, if the entry code **5-** is typed before the text, the item will be stored in the remarks field, but when the ticket is issued, the text will be printed in the form-of-payment box. You will learn how to issue tickets in Chapter 10.

Let us examine the effect of each secondary code on a remarks entry.

Form of Payment

The form-of-payment box on the ticket indicates whether the ticket was purchased by cash, check, or credit card. The data to be printed in this box can be entered in the remarks field with the entry code 5-, as follows:

5-CASH	Ticket purchased by cash
5-CK	Ticket purchased by check
5-*AX4561232299990012222‡9/99	Ticket purchased by credit card

When a ticket is purchased by cash, either the word *CASH* or the code *CH000* may be input in the remarks field to print on the ticket.

If the form of payment is check, either the abbreviation *CK* or the check number may be input. If the check number is input, the option code *CH* must be typed before the number, as follows:

5-CH12214012

When a credit card account number is input as the form of payment, a two-letter code is used to identify the credit card company, or *issuer*. If an asterisk (*) is typed before the credit card code, automatic credit approval will be requested from the issuer when the ticket is printed. Automatic approval is requested in the following example:

5-*MC323456789098765‡5/95

Note that a cross (‡) is typed before the expiration date. The expiration date consists of the digits for the month and year, separated by a slash. The credit card in the example is a Mastercard expiring May 1995.

Table 5-4 provides credit card codes that are used in form of payment entries. Note that multiple codes exist for Visa and MasterCard. The exact code that will be accepted depends on the issuer and the account number. For example, *BA* is used for Visa cards issued by the Bank of America, and *VI* is used for most other issuers. When the agent attempts to issue the ticket, SABRE will respond as follows if the wrong code is input:

INVALID CC CODE

This problem can usually be solved by reentering the credit card number with a different code. In Chapter 10 you will learn how to input the form of payment when tickets are issued.

When automatic credit approval is requested, SABRE will verify the expiration date before issuing the ticket. If the card has expired, when the agent attempts to issue the ticket, SABRE will respond as follows:

INVALID EXPIRATION DATE

When a ticket is purchased with an American Express card, the client has the option of extending the payments over 12 months. Normally, purchases charged to American Express accounts must be paid within 30 days. Before requesting automatic approval, the agent should ascertain whether extended payments are preferred. If the client desires this option, the code *E may be used to request extended payments, as follows:

5-*AX4321999920501222‡6/99*E

Table 5-4 Credit Card Codes.

Code	Issuer
VI, BA	Visa
IK, MC, CA	MasterCard
AX	American Express
CB	Carte Blanche
DC	Diner's Club
DS	Discover
TP	Air travel card
AA	American Airlines travel card
AC, ER	Air Canada Enroute card

A special form-of-payment format is used for government travel requests. A **government travel request**, or **GTR**, is a document issued by a government agency to authorize a travel agency or an airline to issue a ticket. A GTR may be accepted for payment as if it were a check or a credit card slip. Like a check, each GTR has a serial number. If the GTR is made out to the travel agency, the form of payment is not entered in the PNR. If a GTR is made out to the airline, however, the serial number to print on the ticket is entered as follows:

> 5-GR‡K22349991

Client Address

The entry code **5/** is used to store in the remarks field an address to print on an invoice. For example, if a ticket will be mailed or delivered to the client, the address to print on the invoice can be entered as follows:

> 5/ABM CORP∑5/1300 N PLUM ST∑5/WICHITA KS 67226

Each line of the address is a separate remarks item. In the example, the end-item (∑) is used to input three lines simultaneously. Note that each line begins with the entry code 5/. Of course, the address lines may be entered separately, without end-items, but it is more efficient to make a single entry for the entire address.

Itinerary Remarks and Invoice Remarks

An **itinerary remark** is stored in the remarks field to print on the hard copy of the itinerary. Similarly, an **invoice remark** is a message stored in the remarks field to print on an invoice. Any information printed by a computer is referred to as hard copy. The hard copy of an itinerary shows the carrier, flight, class, times, meal service, and equipment for each flight segment. The invoice shows the client's charges and payments. You will learn how to issue an itinerary/invoice form in Chapter 10.

An itinerary or invoice remark may consist of any free-form text. The entry code **5‡** is used to input an itinerary remark, as follows:

> 5‡PLEASE RECONFIRM YOUR RETURN FLIGHT UPON ARRIVAL

The entry code **5.** is used to input an invoice remark, as follows:

> 5.THANK YOU FOR CHOOSING JETAWAY TRAVEL

The entry code **5,** may be used to input text to print in the top margin of the itinerary/invoice form, as follows:

> 5,HAVE A WONDERFUL VACATION

Historical Remarks

When a PNR is created or changed, each action performed by the agent is stored in a special record called the **PNR history**. The secondary code H- may be used to enter free-form text in the PNR history. Such remarks are called historical remarks. The maximum length of a historical remark is 35 characters. Historical remarks are not printed on the ticket, itinerary, or invoice.

The following is an example of a historical remarks entry:

> 5H-CLI STAY EXTENDED 5 DAYS

When a PNR is present, the entry code ***H** may be used to display the history.

Queue Instructions

The entry code **5Q** is used to input queue instructions. You will learn about queues and queue instructions in Chapter 12.

Address Field

The address field is used to store the travel agency's name and address. The address may be entered if items such as tour documents or car rental vouchers are to be mailed to the agency. The address may also be entered to guarantee a hotel reservation for a client. At some agencies the agency address is entered in every PNR as a matter of routine.

The entry code **W-** is used to input a travel agency address, as follows:

FORMAT   W-<Agency name>‡<Address line 1>‡<Address line 2>

EXAMPLE   W-MUNDUS TRAVEL‡1234 MAIN ST‡SANTA ROSA CA 95401

Punctuation is not necessary and in fact is best omitted. A cross (‡) is typed to separate the address lines. A minimum of two lines and a maximum of five lines may be entered in the address field. Each line may contain up to 37 characters, including spaces. The total number of characters in the field may not exceed 185 characters.

Optional Service Information

Optional service information (OSI) is advisory information about a reservation that should be communicated to an airline. For example, an OSI item might be input to alert an airline about an important passenger, such as an airline executive or foreign consul, or to indicate a passenger with a physical handicap. OSI entries are also used to communicate the ages of children, to alert the airline about elderly or first-time travelers, and to cross-reference the PNRs of passengers who will travel together on part of their trip.

OSI Entries: General Facts

The entry code **3OSI** is used to input an OSI item for any carrier except American Airlines, as follows:

FORMAT   3OSI <Carrier> <Message>

EXAMPLE   3OSI DL ELDERLY TVLR

In this example, the message is directed to Delta Airlines. The text portion of the entry is free-form.

Optional Service Information

Assume you are creating a PNR for a very important passenger, the Brazilian consul. The passenger is booked on a United flight. The following entry may be used to input the OSI item:

3OSI UA VIP BRAZILIAN CONSUL

Abbreviations are commonly used in OSI entries. In this example, the abbreviation *VIP* is used to indicate a very important passenger. There are no strict rules governing OSI messages, but consistency and clarity are important. Commonly understood abbreviations should be used, where appropriate.

If an OSI message applies to all the carriers in the itinerary, the code **YY** may be typed in place of the carrier code, as follows:

3OSI YY TRVL W/INF

The abbreviation in this example indicates that the passenger will travel with an infant. Domestic carriers do not charge fares or issue tickets for infants accompanied by a parent. However, the airline should be notified when a passenger books a reservation to travel with an infant.

Cross-Referencing PNRs If two or more parties are booked in separate PNRs, but will travel together on all or part of their itinerary, an OSI item should be input to cross-reference any PNRs. As an example, assume two passengers, Mr. J. Lyons and Mrs. P. Lamb, are booked in separate PNRs. Mr. Lyons' PNR has the following itinerary:

1	AA	300Y	12JUN	F	DFWMCO	HK1	700A	1005A
2	UA	917Y	15JUN	M	MCOMIA	HK1	1000P	1046P
3	DL	839Y	19JUN	F	MIADFW	HK1	920A	208P

Suppose Mr. Lyons will meet Mrs. Lamb in Miami and the passengers will travel together on DL 839 from Miami to Dallas. In this situation, an OSI item should be input to cross-reference the PNRs. The following entry would be input in Mr. Lyons' PNR:

3OSI DL TCP2 W/LAMB DL839Y19JUNMIADFW

The abbreviation **TCP2** means "to complete a party of two." In this case, passenger Lyons will complete a party of two with passenger Lamb on DL 839 in Y class on 19 June from MIA to DFW. As shown in this example, the flight information for the common segment must be included in the OSI item. The common segment is the flight on which the passengers will travel together.

A similar entry would also be made in Mrs. Lamb's PNR, cross-referencing it to Mr. Lyons' PNR.

The following are examples of GFAX OSI entries:

3OSI CO FIRST TIME TRAVELER
3OSI DL ELDERLY TVLR
3OSI TW TCP8 W/DURHAM NW53B18OCTMKESEA

— A YY May Be used to indicate all carriers

OSI Entries: AA Facts

The entry code **4OSI** is used to transmit an OSI message to American Airlines. Because the AA facts field applies only to American Airlines, the carrier code is omitted.

As an example, assume you are creating a PNR for a very important passenger, the governor of Arizona. Your client will travel with American Airlines. The following entry would be used to input the OSI item in the AA facts field:

4OSI VIP GOVERNOR OF ARIZONA

The text portion of the entry is free-form, and thus the following entry might also be used:

4OSI VIP GOV OF ARIZ

Entering VIP messages is a matter of discretion. However, in the view of the airlines, many VIP messages are sent unnecessarily. For example, most carriers do not wish to be notified when such celebrities as film actors, musicians, novelists, and athletes have booked reservations. In general, VIP messages should be reserved for airline executives, government leaders, and diplomats.

Name Reference If an OSI item does not apply to all the passengers in a PNR, a name reference should be included. For example, assume that a PNR contains the following name items:

1.3SCHULTZ/T MR/C MRS/D MISS   2.2GREGG/A MR/L MRS

Miss D. Schultz is six years old. The following entry would be used to notify American Airlines of the child's age:

4OSI 6 YRS-1.3

In this example, Miss D. Schultz is the third passenger in name item 1. Now assume Mrs. L. Gregg is elderly. The following entry may be used to alert American Airlines:

4OSI ELDERLY TVLR-2.2

The passenger names must be entered in the PNR before name reference may be used in an OSI item. Now let us assume that Mr. T. Schultz and Mr. A Gregg are first-time air travelers. The following entry may be used to notify American Airlines:

4OSI FIRST TIME TVLR-1.1,2.1

Note that a comma is typed to separate the name references.

In OSI entries name reference can be used only in the AA facts field, not in the general facts field.

A special service request (SSR) is transmitted to an airline to request a special service or passenger assistance. For example, an SSR item is input if a passenger requests a special meal or requires a wheelchair. SSR items are also used to request a bassinet for an infant, obtain personal assistance for an elderly or handicapped passenger, or secure approval to transport a pet. Four-letter **SSR codes** are used to request special service or assistance. For example, the code *WCHR* is used to request a wheelchair, and *BLND* is used to request assistance for a blind passenger.

As mentioned earlier, two fields are used for SSR information: general facts (GFAX) and AA facts (AFAX).

SSR Entries: General Facts

The field identifier **3** is used for the general facts field. You will recall that this field is used to transmit service information to all carriers except American Airlines. The following format is used to input an SSR item in the general facts field:

FORMAT   3<Code>-<Name reference>

EXAMPLE   3WCHR-1.1

The example requests a wheelchair for the first passenger in name item 1. For a name reference to be included in an SSR entry, the passenger name(s) must be stored in the name field.

As an example, assume a PNR has the following name items:

1.2CAESAR/J MR/L MRS   2.2BRUTUS/M MR/C MRS

The name reference for Mr. J. Caesar is 1.1, and the reference for Mrs. L. Caesar is 1.2. Similarly, the name reference for Mr. and Mrs. Brutus is 2.1 and 2.2, respectively. Suppose Mrs. Caesar is blind. The following entry may be used to request assistance from any airline except American Airlines:

3BLND-1.2

In this example, the code *BLND* is used to request assistance for a blind passenger. Now suppose Mrs. Brutus requires a wheelchair. The following entry would be used to input the SSR item in the general facts field:

3WCHR-2.2

To request a special service or assistance on a selected segment, type the segment number after the SSR code, as follows:

3WCHR2-1.2

This example will request a wheelchair for segment 2 only. The name reference 1.2 indicates the second passenger in the first name item. If the service request pertains to all passengers in the PNR or if the PNR is for one passenger, the name reference may be omitted.

For example, assume a PNR has the following name item:

1.1JAMES/J MR

The following entry may be used to request a wheelchair for all segments of the itinerary:

3WCHR

Because the segment number is omitted, the request will be transmitted to all carriers in the itinerary. Because the passenger will travel unaccompanied, name reference is not needed.

Table 5-5 provides examples of common SSR codes (other than special meals).

Wheelchair Requests Three different codes may be used to request a wheelchair. The correct code must be input to alert airline personnel about the passenger's condition. If the passenger is capable of climbing airline stairs, **WCHR** is used. If the passenger cannot climb stairs but can walk to his or her seat, **WCHS** should be used. This code instructs the airline to arrange for a passenger services agent to help the client board the aircraft. If the passenger is completely immobile and must be carried, **WCHC** must be used to request the wheelchair.

As an example, assume a PNR contains the following name items:

1.2HART/K MR/R MRS

The itinerary includes flights operated by United and TWA. Mrs. Hart will require a wheelchair on all segments. She cannot climb stairs, but after boarding the aircraft, she will be able to walk to her seat. Based on this information, the following entry would be used to input the SSR item:

3WCHS-1.2

4 for American Airlines Do Not use 3

Table 5-5 Examples of Common SSR Codes.	
AVIH	Live animal in cargo hold
BLND	Assist blind passenger
BSCT	Bassinet
BIKE	Bicycle
BULK	Bulky baggage
DEAF	Assist deaf passenger
EMER	Emergency travel
FRAG	Fragile baggage
GPST	Group seat request
LANG	Language restriction
MASS	Meet and assist
NSST	Seat requested in no-smoking section
PETC	Pet in cabin compartment
RMKS	Service remarks (followed by free-form text)
SMST	Seat requested in smoking section
UMNR	Assist unaccompanied minor
WCHR	Wheelchair (Passenger can climb stairs)
WCHS	Wheelchair (Passenger cannot climb stairs)
WCHC	Wheelchair (Passenger must be carried)

Remember that the general facts field is used for all carriers except American Airlines. If a segment number is not specified, the service will be requested for all air segments in the itinerary.

As another example, assume a PNR contains the following name items:

1.1FLOWERS/J MR 2.1CANDY/P MS

The itinerary is booked on Continental. Ms. Candy will require a wheelchair on segment 2. She is completely incapacitated and must be carried to her seat. The following entry would be used to input the SSR item:

3WCHC2-2.1

In this case, segment reference is included because the request applies only to segment 2.

Special Assistance When a reservation is made for a passenger who is blind or deaf, or who has some other type of physical restriction, an SSR item should be input to request assistance from the airline. The code *BLND* is used to obtain assistance for a passenger who is blind. The code *DEAF* is used for a passenger who is deaf. For passengers with other types of restrictions that do not require a wheelchair, e.g, such as an elderly passenger or a passenger on crutches, the code MAAS (meet and assist) may be used.

For example, assume an elderly passenger will travel unaccompanied on a United flight. The following entry may be used to request a boarding agent to meet and assist the passenger:

3MAAS-1.1

Language Restrictions SSR items should also be input to request assistance for passengers with language restrictions. The code *LANG* is used for this purpose. A description of the language restriction must be included in the entry, as follows:

3LANG/SPEAKS JAPANESE ONLY-1.1

Note that a slash is typed before the description. In this example, assistance is requested for a passenger who speaks only Japanese.

The description may consist of any free-form text, but the language restriction must be stated clearly so that the airline can provide the appropriate assistance. Note that the name reference is always input at the end of the entry. In this case, the name reference is typed after the description.

Special Meal Requests Official meal codes must be used to request meals for passengers with special dietary restrictions or preferences. Special meals are not available on all flights. When the SSR item is input, SABRE will verify whether the type of meal requested is available.

Examples of common SSR meal codes are found in Table 5-6 on page 92. The code **SPML** may be used to request a special meal for which no SSR code exists. When this code is used, a description must be included, as follows:

3SPML1/EGGLESS MEAL-1.2

Note that a slash is typed before the description. In this example, an eggless meal is requested for the second passenger in name item 1. This entry might be input for a client who has an allergy to egg products.

Meal Request

Assume a PNR has the following name item and itinerary:

```
1.2HARTPENCE/R MR/P MRS
1   DL  209Y  12JUN   W   DTWTPA   SS2   800A   1016A
2   CO  877Y  15JUN   J   TPAMCO   SS2   800A   830A
```

The availability displays indicated that meal service was provided on the Delta segment but not on the Continental segment. Mr. Hartpence is on a restricted diet and requests a low-cholesterol meal. Based on this information, the following entry may be used to input the special meal request:

```
3LCML1-1.1
```

In this example, the code *LCML* is used to request a low-cholesterol meal. The segment reference 1 indicates the Delta segment from DTW to TPA. The name reference 1.1 indicates the first passenger of name item 1.

In this case, the special meal might also be requested by omitting the segment number. Because meal service is not provided on segment 2, the entry would have no effect on the Continental segment. SABRE will not transmit special meal requests for a flight on which meal service is not provided. However, SABRE customer service representatives prefer that agents input the segment number if an SSR request pertains only to a specific segment.

SSR Entries: AA Facts

The general facts field is used for all carriers except AA. To transmit a service request for an American Airlines segment, the agent must input the SSR item in the AA facts field. The field identifier 4 is used for this purpose. For example, the following entry would be used to request a vegetarian meal for an American Airlines flight in segment 2:

```
4VGML2
```

Special meal codes for American Airlines differ slightly from those that are used for other carriers. Table 5-7 lists the types of special meals available on AA flights. Special meals are not available on all American Airlines flights.

Unaccompanied Minors

An **unaccompanied minor** is a child 11 years or younger traveling without an adult. American Airlines and most other carriers accept unaccompanied minors from 8 to 11 years old. Passengers 12 years or older are considered adults.

The code **UMNR** is used to request assistance for an unaccompanied minor. The child's age must be included in the entry, as follows:

```
3UMNR/UM08
```

Table 5-6 Example of Common SSR Meal Codes.

BBML	Baby food meal
CSML	Child meal
HNML	Hindu meal
KSML	Kosher meal
MOML	Moslem meal
LCML	Low-cholesterol meal
ORML	Oriental meal
SFML	Seafood meal
SPML	Special
VGML	Vegetarian meal

(handwritten: CHML)

Table 5-7 Special Meals Available on AA Flights.

DBML	Diabetic meal
HNML	Hindu meal
KSML	Kosher meal
LCRB	Low-carbohydrate meal
LCAL	Low-calorie meal
LOCH	Low-cholesterol meal
LSML	Low-sodium meal
VGML	Vegetarian meal

The letters **UM** are typed before the child's age. The age must consist of two digits. If the child is under 10 years of age, a zero must be typed before the age, as shown in the example just given.

If more than one unaccompanied minor is included in the same PNR, include the ages of all the passengers. For example, assume a PNR has the following name item:

1.2YOUNG/L MSTR/C MISS

Master L. Young is 9 years of age, and Miss C. Young is 8. The children will travel unaccompanied on a Delta flight. The following entry would be used to notify the airline:

3UMNR/UM09/08-1.1,1.2

The ages are typed together, separated by a slash. The name reference codes are separated by a comma. The first age input corresponds to the first name reference, the second age corresponds to the second name reference, and so forth.

In general, the same principles apply to the AA facts field. As an example, assume a 10-year-old child will travel unaccompanied on an American Airlines flight. The following entry would be used to request assistance for the unaccompanied minor:

4UMNR/UM10

In this example, name reference is omitted because the PNR has only one passenger.

In addition, the phones, addresses, and names of the responsible adults should be input by means of OSI entries. The abbreviation *CTCH* is used to indicate the "catching" parties, as follows:

3OSI DL CTCH/213 555-8124/6245 MANGROVE ST SYD-MS C THOMAS

3OSI DL CTCH/206 555-1092/812 PALM DR LAX-MR L BRENNAN

In this example, Ms. C. Thomas of Sydney is the "sender," and Mr. L. Brennan of Los Angeles is the "receiver."

Frequent Traveler Accounts

In Chapter 4, you learned how to input a passenger name with an AAdvantage account number. You will recall that members of the AAdvantage program receive mileage credits for traveling with American Airlines. These credits can be exchanged for free tickets, class upgrades, and other rewards.

Other carriers also have frequent traveler programs. For instance, the United program is called Mileage Plus, and the Continental program is called One Pass. The code FQTV is used to input a frequent traveler account number for any carrier except American Airlines. The carrier code, segment status, account number, and passenger's name all must be included in the entry.

As an example, assume Mr. A. Miles will travel on a United flight and is a member of the United Mileage Plus program. The passenger's account number is 665042. The following entry would be used to input the account number:

3FQTV UA HK/UA665042-MILES/A

In this example, the status *HK* indicates that the passenger holds a confirmed reservation on a United flight. The carrier code UA refers to the confirmed flight segment. UA is also typed before the account number, to identify the mileage program. A dash is typed before the passenger name.

In some cases, a client may receive mileage credits for flying on a different carrier. For instance, passengers who belong to the United Mileage Plus program can receive mileage credits for traveling on British Midland, and passengers who belong to the TWA Frequent Flight Bonus Program can receive credits for traveling on Alaska airlines.

To illustrate, assume Ms. J. Good will travel on an Alaska Airlines flight and would like the mileage to be credited to her TWA bonus account. The passenger's account number is 77298722. Note that a comma is typed to separate the name references.

In OSI entries name reference can be used only in the AA facts field, not in the general facts field.

Summary

Data stored in an optional field is referred to as *supplemental data*. The address field is used to store the agency name and address. The remarks field is used to store any general information about the reservation. Special uses of the remarks field include inputting the form of payment or indicating information to print on the itinerary/invoice.

The general facts (GFAX) and AA facts (AFAX) fields are used to communicate service information to the airlines. OSI entries are used to transmit messages, and SSR entries are input to send special service requirements.

New commands included in this chapter:

5ADVD DOCS	Input remarks item
5-CHECK	Input form of payment
5/MR J JONES	Input client address
5.PLEASE REMIT	Input invoice remark
5‡THANK YOU	Input itinerary remark
5S‡CK FOP	Input coded remark
5H-CHNGD HTL	Input historical remark
5Q-Q/41	Input queue remark
W-STAR TRAVEL	Input address
3WCHR-1.1	Input SSR item to general facts field
4WCHR2-1.2	Input SSR item to AA facts field
3UMNR/UM09-1.1	Input SSR item for unaccompanied minor
3OSI YY TRVL W/INF	Input OSI item to general facts field
4OSI VIP GOV OF ARIZ	Input OSI item to AA facts field

STUDENT REVIEW

KEY CONCEPTS AND TERMS

Identify the word or phrase for each of the following concepts:

1. Data stored in the address, remarks, general facts, or AA facts field.

2. The field identifier that is used to input information in the remarks field.

3. In a remarks entry, a secondary identifier that can be used to indicate a special purpose, such as printing text on the ticket or invoice.

4. The entry code used to input the form of payment.

5. The code that is used to request automatic credit approval when a credit card number is input as the form of payment.

6. The code that is typed before the expiration date when a credit card number is input as the form of payment.

7. An option code that is used to request extended payments when an American Express account number is input as the form of payment.

8. A document issued by a government agency to authorize a travel agency or an airline to issue a ticket.

9. The entry code that is used to store in the remarks field an address to print on an invoice.

10. Text that is stored in the remarks field to print on the hard copy of the itinerary.

11. Text that is stored in the remarks field to print on the passenger invoice.

12. The entry code that is used to input an itinerary remark.

13. The entry code that is used to input an invoice remark.

14. The entry code that is used to input text to print in the top margin of the itinerary/invoice form.

15. A record containing a log of each action performed by the booking agent when creating or changing a PNR.

16. Text input by an agent for storage in a PNR history.

17. The entry code that is used to input a historical remark.

18. The entry used to display a PNR history.

19. The entry code that is used to input a travel agency address.

20. The code that is typed to separate the lines of a travel agency address.

21. Four-letter codes used to request special service or assistance.

22. The field identifier that is used to input information in the general facts field.

23. A numerical code identifying a selected passenger listed in the name field.

24. The SSR code used to request wheelchair assistance if the passenger is capable of climbing airline stairs.

25. The SSR code used to request wheelchair assistance if the passenger cannot climb stairs but can walk to his or her seat.

26. The SSR code used to request wheelchair assistance if the passenger is completely immobile and must be carried.

27. The SSR code used to request a special meal for which no SSR code exists.

28. The field identifier that is used to transmit a service request for an American Airlines segment.

29. A child 11 years or younger traveling without an adult.

30. The SSR code used to request assistance for an unaccompanied minor.

31. The option code typed before the child's age in an SSR entry for an unaccompanied minor.

32. The entry code that is used in OSI entries for all carriers except American Airlines.

33. In an OSI entry, the code that is typed in place of a carrier code if the message applies to all the carriers in the itinerary.

34. An abbreviation used in OSI entries that means "to complete a party of 2."

35. The entry code that is used in an OSI entry for American Airlines segments.

Answers:

1. supplemental data; 2. 5; 3. sub-designator; 4. 5-; 5. *; 6. ‡; 7. *E; 8. government travel request (GTR); 9. 5/; 10. itinerary remark; 11. invoice remark; 12. 5‡; 13. 5-; 14. 5; 15. PNR history; 16. historical remark; 17. 5H-; 18. *H; 19. W-; 20. ‡; 21. SSR codes; 22. 3; 23. name reference; 24. WCHR; 25. WCHS; 26. WCHC; 27. SPML; 28. 4; 29. unaccompanied minor; 30. UMNR; 31. UM; 32. 3OSI; 33. YY; 34. TCP2; 35. 4OSI.

REVIEW QUESTIONS

1. What field is used to input free-form text in a PNR?

2. What entry code is used to enter information in the field in question 1?

3. Write the entry to input a reminder to mail the tickets.

4. Suppose you are booking reservations for a client who will travel to a foreign country. You have advised the passenger about documents required for international travel. What entry should be input to the remarks field?

5. Write the entry to input the following remark: QTD149.00 FARE ON 12SEP

6. Assume you quoted a fare of 89.00 on the 3rd of May. What entry would be input to note this action in the remarks field?

7. Write the entry to input the following remark to print on the itinerary: CALL FOR AIRPORT PICKUP

8. Assume you are making travel arrangements for a client who will purchase his tickets by check. Write the entry to input the form of payment.

9. Write the entry to input the form of payment as credit card account number MC3650513240402212, expiring in October, 1998.

10. Write the entry to print the following remark on the itinerary/invoice when the ticket is issued: CALL 555-2091 FOR COURTESY CAR

11. What entry code is used to send an OSI message to any carrier except American Airlines?

12. What code is used in an OSI entry to indicate all carriers in the itinerary (except AA)?

13. What entry would be used to send an OSI message to inform British Airways that a passenger is a VIP, the Japanese consul?

14. What entry code is used to send an OSI message to American Airlines?

15. What entry will notify AA that a passenger is elderly?

16. Write the correct SSR code for each of the following:

   a) Unaccompanied minor

   b) Deaf passenger

   c) Blind passenger

   d) Wheelchair (passenger can walk up stairs)

   e) Wheelchair (passenger must be carried)

   f) Wheelchair (passenger cannot climb stairs but can walk to seat)

   g) Vegetarian meal

   h) Kosher meal

   i) Seafood meal

17. Assume you are booking flight reservations for an elderly client who will require a wheelchair but is capable of ascending stairs. The passenger will travel unaccompanied on a DL flight. What entry would be input to request the wheelchair?

18. Suppose you are creating a PNR for the following clients:

   1.1FRANKS/CARL   2.2GOLDBERG/J MR/E MRS

   Mr. Goldberg requests a Kosher meal on a UA flight in segment 3. What entry would be input to request the special meal?

19. Assume you are making reservations for a client to travel on American Airlines. The passenger will be totally immobile and will require a wheelchair on all segments. What entry would be input to request the wheelchair?

20. Assume a client will travel on American Airlines and requests a wheelchair. The passenger cannot climb stairs but can walk to her seat with assistance. What entry would be input to request the wheelchair on all segments?

21. Write the entry to input the following client billing address: The address is Belltower Storage, 1822 E Industrial Dr, Los Angeles CA 90011.

22. Assume you are creating a PNR for a very important passenger, the Ethiopian ambassador, traveling on a CO flight. Write the correct entry.

23. Assume you are creating a PNR with the following passengers in the name field:

   1.2STRANTON/ERNEST MR/GRETA MRS

   Meal service is provided on all AA segments. Mrs. Stranton requests a vegetarian meal. Write the correct entry.

24. Suppose you are making flight reservations for a client who will be traveling on a United flight. Your client will travel with an infant. Write the entry to send an OSI message to the airline.

25. Assume you are creating a PNR for the following passengers:

    1.2HIGHTOWER/A MR/L MRS   2.2BARNES/C MR/C MRS

    Mrs. Barnes requires wheelchair assistance and must be carried to her seat. AA is not one of the carriers in the itinerary. What entry will request the service on all segments?

26. What entry will request a diabetic meal for a passenger who is traveling alone on an AA flight in segment 2?

27. Write the entries required to create a PNR for the following clients. Write a separate entry for each item. After booking the flights, include an entry to display the itinerary. After building the PNR, include entries to display the record and end the transaction.

    Mr. R. Glenn and Mrs. L. Glenn will travel from CVG to MIA on 17 January. The seats will be booked in M class on a flight departing around 9 A.M. When you display the schedules, the best flight appears in line 2. The passengers will return on 23 January, departing around 12 noon. The seats will be booked in the same class on the return flight. Assume the best flight is in line 4.

    Your agency phone is 614-555-1339. Mr. Glenn's business phone is 614-555-0017, and your clients' home phone is 614-555-2209. Arrange ticketing for 2 January. Mrs. Glenn is elderly. She is also recovering from an injury and requires a wheelchair for all segments. She can climb stairs with assistance. The first segment is DL 1411, and the return is AA 330. Mr. Glenn called to request the reservation.

APPLICATIONS

Read the following scenario, and decide what actions should be performed to satisfy the client's preferences and needs. Briefly describe how you would handle the situation, and then write the required entries.

Mrs. T. Elwood will travel from Portland, Oregon, to Chicago and would like to depart on 12 May around 11 a.m. She insists on arriving at O'Hare Airport. She would like to return four days later, departing around 8 a.m. She would like to book the flight reservations in F class. When you display availability for the outbound segment, an American Airlines flight in line 2 departs at 11:45 a.m. and has seats available in F class. When you display availability for the return, a Northwest Airlines flight in line 1 departs at 8:15 a.m. and has seats available in F class.

Your agency phone in SFO is 415-555-0055. Your client's business phone is 415-555-0541 and her home phone is 415-555-0901. Mrs. Elwood requested the reservation. You quoted a fare of $189.00 on 2 May. Your client would like the tickets to be issued on 10 May. She would like for you to arrange hotel accommodations later.

Mrs. Elwood is elderly. She would like a vegetarian meal on all flights on which meal service is provided. She is also disabled and would like a wheelchair for both flights. She is capable of climbing airline stairs.

Chapter 6

Modifying the Itinerary

Chapter Objectives

After you complete this chapter, you should be able to:

1. Retrieve a PNR by name; by departure date and name; by flight, departure date, origin, and name; or by record locator.

2. Display selected passenger data fields.

3. Cancel segments.

4. Cancel and rebook in the same entry.

5. Insert a segment in an existing itinerary.

6. Insert and sell in the same entry.

7. Change segment status.

PROBLEM

Your travel agency previously made flight reservations for eight passengers who plan to travel together on a round trip from Indianapolis to Ft. Lauderdale. The group decides to stay over three extra days in Ft. Lauderdale before returning. In addition, they would like to arrange a side trip to Orlando during their stay in Florida.

SABRE SOLUTION

Check availability from Ft. Lauderdale to Indianapolis for the new return date. Then cancel the return segment and rebook the best available flight on the new date. Check availability for your clients' side trip, and then insert a new segment after the Indianapolis-Ft. Lauderdale segment. Book the side trip and display the new itinerary. Then input the received-from item and end the transaction to save the changes.

In this chapter, you will learn several different techniques for retrieving PNRs and modifying the itinerary.

Retrieving PNRs

When a PNR is created and the transaction is ended, the record is transmitted to the central processor for storage. Upon request, the PNR can be retrieved from storage so that the information can be reviewed or changed.

The **display key (*)** is used to retrieve and display PNRs. A PNR can be retrieved by any of four methods:

1. by record locator
2. by name
3. by departure date and name
4. by flight, departure date, origin point, and name

Retrieving by Record Locator

You will recall from Chapter 4 that when a transaction is ended and the PNR is transmitted to the central processor for storage, SABRE displays a six-digit code called the **record locator**. The most direct method of retrieving a PNR is by record locator, as follows:

FORMAT   *<Record locator>

EXAMPLE   *SGHWQR

Some agents provide the record locator to each client as a confirmation number so that the PNR can be easily retrieved if the client inquires about the reservation later.

Retrieving by Name

The following format is used to retrieve a PNR by name:

FORMAT   *-<Surname>

EXAMPLE   *-BYRON

Only the surname is required in this entry, but the selection can be narrowed by including the first name or initial.

The agency that created the PNR is referred to as the *booking source*. A PNR can be retrieved by any of the airlines in the itinerary or by the booking source. Under most circumstances, a travel agency cannot retrieve a PNR that was created by another agency or by an airline, unless authorization is obtained from the booking source. However, SABRE subscribers can retrieve PNRs that were booked directly with American Airlines.

Retrieving a PNR created by another booking source is called ***claiming a reservation***. To claim a reservation, an agent must obtain authorization from the agency that created the PNR. For example, assume a passenger has arranged a reservation with Continental Airlines, intending to pick up the tickets at the airport. He later decides to purchase the tickets at an agency near his office. The agency is a SABRE

Retrieving by Name

Assume you previously created a PNR for Mr. S. Coleridge, who inquires about his flight reservations. The following entry may be used to retrieve the passenger's PNR:

*-COLERIDGE/S

SABRE responds by retrieving the PNR from storage and placing the record in the agent work area. The record is displayed as follows:

```
1.2COLERIDGE/S MR/M MRS
1    AA3491Y    05OCT    M    EWRBWI    HK2    800A    900A
2    AA3458Y    14OCT    W    BWIEWR    HL2    350A    450A
3    AA3433Y    14OCT    W    BWIEWR    HK2    955A    1055A
TKT/TIME LIMIT -
1.TAW30SEP/
PHONES -
1.NYC201-555-4343-A GENEVIEVE
2.NYC201-577-9767-B MR
3.NYC201-577-9767-H
REMARKS-
1.-*AX66554433220096702‡10/97
RECEIVED FROM - MR
Q9T0.Q9T0*A47 0926/24SEP90 STPFDR
```

Except for a few key differences, a PNR that is retrieved from storage appears the same as a PNR that is currently being created. However, note that, in the itinerary, segments 1 and 3 have the status **HK**. When a segment is sold, the status SS indicates that the reservation will be confirmed when the transaction is ended. When SABRE accepts an entry to end-transact, the segment status SS is changed to HK automatically.

Segment 2 has the status HL, indicating that the seats have been waitlisted. When seats are first waitlisted, the segment shows the status LL. When the transaction is ended, SABRE changes the segment status from LL to HL. In this example, the status of segment 2 is still HL, indicating that the seats have not yet been confirmed from the waitlist. When a waitlisted segment is confirmed, the seats are said to have *cleared the waitlist.*

In the phone field, the agency phone is appended by the name of the agent who created the PNR. The second phone item is appended with the title MR, identifying the phone item as Mr. Coleridge's business phone.

Note the last line of the PNR. This line was added by SABRE when the agent ended the transaction. The information in the line includes the agency pseudo city code, agent sine, creation time and date, and record locator. The pseudo city code identifies the travel agency, and the **agent sine** identifies the agent who created the PNR.

subscriber. Before the travel agent can retrieve the client's reservation, the PNR must be released by the airline. In this situation, the agent should advise the passenger to phone the booking source to have the PNR released to the agency for ticketing.

The following are some examples of PNR retrieval by surname:

*-KLINGINSMITH

*-JOSLYN/J

*-HARCOURT/T MR

The Similar-Name List Frequently, PNRs are stored for multiple passengers with the same surname. For example, several records may be stored for passengers named Smith or Jones. In this situation, when the agent attempts to retrieve the PNR, SABRE displays a **similar-name list**. This display lists the names and departure dates of PNRs for passengers with the same or similar surnames.

Each record in a similar-name list is numbered. To display a PNR from the list, the agent simply enters the number of the desired record.

As an example, assume an agency previously created a PNR for a passenger named Smith. The following entry is used to display the PNR by surname:

*-SMITH

Instead of displaying the PNR, however, SABRE displays a similar-name list, as follows:

1	SMITH/CLIFFORD	15APR	2	SMITH/JOHN	24MAR
3	SMITH/RICH	24MAR	4	SMITH/D MR	22MAR
5	SMITH/JOHN	22MAR	6	SMITH/S MRS	04APR
7	SMITH/ROY	13APR	8	SNOW/W MS	12MAY
9	SPAULDING/A MR	22MAR	10	STANS/M MS	24MAR

Assume the client in this case is Rich Smith, departing on 24 March. The desired record is item 3 of the similar-name list. The PNR can be retrieved as follows:

*3

After a record has been displayed from a similar-name list, the list can be redisplayed as follows:

*L

However, before another record can be displayed, the PNR that is currently in the agent work area must be ended or ignored.

Retrieving by Departure Date and Name

When a PNR is retrieved by name, the departure date may be included to narrow the selection, as follows:

FORMAT   *-<Departure date>-<Name>

EXAMPLE   *-26MAR-BROWNING/R

In this example, passenger R. Browning is booked on a flight departing on 26 March.

Retrieving by Flight, Date, Origin, and Name

A PNR that was created by American Airlines can be retrieved by the following format:

FORMAT   *<Flight>/<Date><Origin>-<Name>

EXAMPLE   *AA34/10AUGDFW-DUNNE

The entry in the example requests the PNR for passenger Dunne, departing on AA 34 on 10 August. This format is used to retrieve a PNR for a reservation that was booked directly with American Airlines. However, as mentioned earlier, a reservation that was booked with one agency cannot be retrieved by a different agency.

Displaying Passenger Data

When a PNR is present in the agent work area, any of the passenger data items can be displayed upon request. The display key (*) is input with a qualifying code to specify the field or item to be displayed. Table 6-1 shows entries that are used to display selected parts of the PNR. A specified passenger data field may be displayed as shown in Table 6-2.

If a PNR contains car rentals and hotel reservations in addition to air segments, each type of booking may be displayed separately, as shown in Table 6-3.

Table 6-1 Entries Used to Display Selected PNR Elements.

*A	Display all fields
*B	Display reserved seat and boarding pass information
*H	Display history
*I	Display itinerary
*P	Display passenger data fields
*-	Display form of payment
*/	Display client address
*‡	Display itinerary remarks
*.	Display invoice remarks

Displaying Passenger Data

Assume a PNR is currently in your work area. To display only the passenger data fields, the following entry may be used:

*P

SABRE responds by displaying the name, ticketing, phone, remarks, and received-from fields:

```
1.2COLERIDGE/S MR/M MRS
TKT/TIME LIMIT -
1.TAW30SEP/
PHONES -
1.NYC201-555-4343-A GENEVIEVE
2.NYC201-577-9767-B MR
3.NYC201-577-9767-H
REMARKS-
1.-*AX66554433220096702‡10/97
RECEIVED FROM - MR
```

To display only the itinerary, the following entry may be used:

*I

SABRE responds as follows:

```
1   AA3491Y   05OCT   M   EWRBWI   HK2   800A    900A
2   AA3458Y   14OCT   W   BWIEWR   HL2   350A    450A
3   AA3433Y   14OCT   W   BWIEWR   HK2   955A   1055A
```

To display only the form of payment, the following entry may be used:

*_

(continued)

Canceling Segments

On occasion, a segment that was previously booked in a PNR itinerary must be canceled. For example, the client's travel plans might change, or a duplicate reservation might occur if a waitlisted segment is confirmed. The entry code X is used to cancel segments, as follows:

FORMAT   X<Segment number>

EXAMPLE   X1

SABRE responds as follows:

1.-*AX66554433220096702‡10/97

To display all of the record, the following entry may be used:

*A

SABRE responds as follows:

```
1.2COLERIDGE/S MR/M MRS
1   AA3491Y   05OCT   M   EWRBWI   HK2   800A    900A
2   AA3458Y   14OCT   W   BWIEWR   HL2   350A    450A
3   AA3433Y   14OCT   W   BWIEWR   HK2   955A    1055A
TKT/TIME LIMIT -
1.TAW30SEP/
PHONES -
1.NYC201-555-4343-A GENEVIEVE
2.NYC201-577-9767-B MR
3.NYC201-577-9767-H
REMARKS-
1.-*AX66554433220096702#10/97
RECEIVED FROM - MR
Q9T0.Q9T0*A47 0926/24SEP90 STPFDR
```

While the PNR remains in the agent work area, all or part of the record may be redisplayed as desired.

Table 6-2 Entries Used to Display Specified PNR Fields.

*N	Display name field
*P3	Display general facts field
*P4	Display AA facts field
*P5	Display remarks field
*P6	Display received from field
*P7	Display ticketing field
*P9	Display phone field
*PAD	Display address field

Table 6-3	Entries Used to Display Specific Types of Segments.

-*IA	Display air segments only
*IC	Display car segments only
*IH	Display hotel segments only

The example will cancel segment 1. When a segment is canceled, SABRE responds as follows:

NEXT REPLACES 1

The response indicates that if a new segment is sold, it will replace the segment that was canceled. In this case, if a new segment is booked, it will become segment 1.

If a new segment is not booked, the itinerary must be redisplayed to reset the order. For example, assume an itinerary has the following segments:

1	US	203Y	12JUN	F	BOSMDT	HK1	950A	1102A
2	US	102Y	17JUN	Q	MDTBOS	HL1	1259P	201P
3	US	70Y	17JUN	Q	MDTBOS	HK1	940P	1044P

In this example, the passenger is confirmed on US 203 in Y class from Boston to Harrisburg. On the return trip, the client is waitlisted on US 102 and confirmed on US 70, which departs several hours later. Let us say the passenger decides definitely to depart on the 9:40 P.M. flight. The following entry would be used to cancel the waitlisted segment.

X2

SABRE responds as follows:

NEXT REPLACES 2

The response indicates that the next segment that is sold will become segment 2. However, in this case, a new segment will not be booked. Thus, the itinerary now consists of segments 1 and 3. To reset the order, the agent must redisplay the itinerary as follows:

*I

When SABRE displays the itinerary, the segments are reordered as follows:

```
1 US 203Y  12JUN  F  BOSMDT  HK1 950A  1102A
2 US  70Y  17JUN  Q  MDTBOS  HK1 940P  1044P
```

The confirmed segment on US 70, which was previously segment 3, is now segment 2. When a segment is canceled and a new segment is not booked, the itinerary is always reordered when the segments are redisplayed.

Whenever a PNR is created or changed, the received-from item must be input. Assume the change was received from the passenger. With the end-item key, the following entry may be used to input the received-from item and end-transact:

6PΣE

In this example, the abbreviation *P* indicates that the change was received from the passenger.

Canceling and Rebooking

Now let us examine what happens when an existing segment is canceled and a new segment is sold. Assume a PNR has the following itinerary:

| 1 | DL | 930Q | 17FEB | W | CVGPIT | HK2 | 707A | 800A |
| 2 | DL | 1021Q | 21FEB | S | PITCVG | HK2 | 500P | 555P |

In this example, two passengers are confirmed on Delta Airlines on a round trip from Cincinnati to Pittsburgh. Let us say the clients decide to depart from Cincinnati later in the day. To handle this situation, the agent would cancel the outbound segment and rebook a new flight at a later departure time. However, before canceling the segment, the agent should check availability to be certain the desired class and flight can be sold. In addition, the agent should check the fare rules. It is important to remember that with many discount classes a penalty may apply if any changes are made after the reservation has been ticketed. For illustration, let us say tickets have not been issued and the departure date can be changed if the clients stay over Saturday night and travel in the same class on both segments.

Assume the passengers prefer to depart around 3 P.M. The agent displays availability for the same city pair and date but requests a new departure time as follows:

117FEBCVGPIT3P

Assume SABRE responds as follows:

```
17FEB   WED   CVG/EST   PIT/EST
1 DL 908  F4 Y4 B4 M4 Q4   CVGPIT  9   242P   335P   D9S 0        TA
2 US 246  Y4 B4 M4 Q4 K4   CVGPIT  9   250P   344P   B11 0   X6   TA
3 US 970  F4 B4 M4 Q4 K4   CVGPIT  9   250P   344P   D9S 0        TA
4 US 132  F4 B4 M4 Q4 K4   CVGPIT  8   755P   846P   D9S 0        TA
5 DL1050  F4 Y4 B4 M4 Q4   CVGPIT  9   817P   910P   D9S 0        TA
```

The clients select the Delta flight departing at 2:42 P.M. Seats are still available in Q class. In the itinerary, the flight to be canceled is segment 1. The following entry is used to cancel the segment:

X1

SABRE responds as follows:

NEXT REPLACES 1

The next air segment that is sold will become segment 1. The following entry may now be used to sell the new segment:

02Q1

Note that the same number of seats must be booked on all segments of the itinerary. SABRE responds as follows:

> DL   908Q   17FEB   W   CVGPIT   SS2   242P   335P

Next, the agent redisplays the itinerary to reset the order:

*|

SABRE displays the revised itinerary, as follows:

> 1 DL 908Q   17FEB   W   CVGPIT   SS2   242P   335P
> 2 DL1021Q   21FEB   S   PITCVG   HK2   500P   555P

Assume the change was received from the clients' secretary, Ms. Peterson. The following entry is used to input the received-from item and end-transact:

6MS PETERSONΣE

Note that, in this example, the agent checked availability before canceling the outbound segment and selling the new segment. If the outbound segment had been canceled first, the clients would have been unprotected if the desired space was not available.

For instance, assume the agent cancels segment 1 and then displays availability on 17 February from CVG to PIT, departing around 5:00 P.M. Let us say the display shows that all discount coach fares are completely sold out on this date. Because the outbound segment has already been canceled, the clients cannot travel in Q class on the return segment.

To protect a client from losing confirmed space, an agent should not cancel an existing reservation without first determining that the desired flight and class are available.

Canceling and Rebooking With One Entry

The **cross (‡)** can be used to cancel and rebook with one entry, as follows:

X1‡02Q1

A direct-sell entry can be used to rebook a canceled segment, as follows:

X3‡0UA1268Q2OCTSEASFONN2

This example will cancel segment 3 and rebook UA 1268 in Q class on 2 October from SEA to SFO, requesting 2 seats. The direct-sell format should be used only if there is a reasonable certainty that the segment can be rebooked in the desired flight and class. If the requested flight or class is sold out, the segment will remain canceled, but an availability screen will be displayed.

Rebooking the Same Flight and Class

To rebook the same flight and class on a different date, the following short entry may be used:

FORMAT   X<Segment>‡00<Date>

EXAMPLE   X1‡0025OCT

This example will cancel segment 1 of an itinerary and rebook the same flight on 25 October.

Canceling Multiple Segments

To cancel multiple segments with one entry, type a slash (/) to separate the segment numbers, as follows:

X1/3

This example cancels segments 1 and 3 of an itinerary. SABRE responds as follows:

NEXT REPLACES 1

When multiple segments are canceled, the next segment that is sold will replace the first segment specified.

To cancel a range of consecutive segments, type a dash (-) between the first and last segments in the range, as follows:

X1-4

This example will cancel segments 1, 2, 3, and 4 of an existing itinerary. Of course, the entry X1/2/3/4 can be used instead.

Canceling an Itinerary

To cancel an entire itinerary, the following entry may be used:

XI

To cancel only the air segments in an itinerary, the following entry may be used:

XIA

The entry code / is used to insert a new air segment in an existing itinerary, as follows:

FORMAT   /<Segment to follow>

EXAMPLE   /2

In this example, a new segment will be inserted after segment 2. SABRE will respond as follows:

NEXT FOLLOWS 2

The next segment that is sold will follow segment 2 and thus will become segment 3. After the segments have been inserted, the itinerary must be redisplayed to reset the order.

As an example, assume a PNR has the following itinerary:

1	NW	51B	24FEB	T	DTWLAX	HK2	945A	1046A
2	NW	330B	07MAR	T	LAXDTW	HK2	805A	314P

The passengers decide to take a side trip to San Francisco from 3 March to 5 March. They would like to depart from Los Angeles around 10 A.M. First, the agent displays availability, as follows:

03MARLAXSFO10A

SABRE responds as follows:

```
03MAR  TUE    LAX/PST   SFO/PST
1 AA 607  Y7 B7 M7 V7  Q7 LAXSFO  9   900A 1007A 73S 0        TA
2 US1939  Y4 B4 M4 V4  K4 LAXSFO  8   929A 1042A 146 0        TA
3 US  49  Y4 B4 M4 V4  K4 LAXSFO  9   930A 1035A M80 0  X67   TA
4 AA 259  Y7 B7 M7 V7  Q7 LAXSFO  8   955A 1104A 73S 0        TA
5 UA1566  F4 Y4 B4 M4  H4 LAXSFO  9   955A 1106A 73S 0        TA
6 US1923  Y4 B4 M4 V4  K4 LAXSFO  9  1000A 1112A D9S 0        TA
```

Assume the passengers select the USAir flight departing at 10 A.M. and qualify for a discount fare in B class. The side trip should follow the outbound segment in the existing itinerary. The following entry is used to insert a new segment after segment 1:

/1

SABRE responds as follows:

NEXT FOLLOWS 1

The next segment that is sold will become segment 2 when the order is reset. The agent now inputs the following entry to sell the LAX-SFO segment:

02B6

SABRE displays the segment as follows:

```
US1923B    03MAR T  LAXSFO SS2 1000A    1112A
```

If another segment is sold, it will follow this segment. If the itinerary is redisplayed, however, the order will be reset. In this case, a return segment from SFO to LAX must be booked before the order is reset. Therefore, the agent next displays return availability. Assume the passengers desire to return on 5 March around 5 P.M. The following entry is used to display return availability:

1R5MAR5P

SABRE displays the return flights for the side trip as follows:

```
05MAR THU   SFO/PST   LAX/PST
1 US 454 Y4 B4 M4 V4 K4  LAXSFO 9    400P    459P  146 0          TA
2 AA 126 Y7 B7 M7 V7 Q7  LAXSFO 9    400P    508P  73S 0          TA
3 UA1121 F4 Y4 B4 M4 V4  LAXSFO 9    400P    516P  73S 0          TA
4 US  60 Y4 B4 M4 V4 K4  LAXSFO 8    430P    531P  M80 0          TA
5 CO  37 F4 Y4 B4 M4 V4  LAXSFO 7    430P    535P  D10 0    X6    TA
6 AA 718 Y7 B7 M7 V7 Q7  LAXSFO 9    500P    616P  146 0          TA
```

Assume that the discount fare in B class requires the return flight to be booked on the same carrier and in the same class of service as the outbound segment. The clients select the USAir flight departing at 4:30 P.M. The following entry may be used to book the flight:

02B4

SABRE displays the segment as follows:

```
US    60B  05MAR J  SFOLAX SS2  430P    531P
```

Next, the agent redisplays the itinerary to reset the order, as follows:

*I

CSS - Change Segment Status -

SABRE displays the reordered air segments as follows:

```
1 NW  51B   24FEB   T   DTWLAX    HK2   945P    1046P
2 US1923B   03MAR   T   LAXSFO    SS2   1000A   1112A
3 US  60B   05MAR   J   SFOLAX    SS2   430P    531P
4 NW 330B   07MAR   T   LAXDTW    HK2   805A    314P
```

Note that the new segments are now numbered 2 and 3. The LAX-DTW segment, which was formerly segment 2, is now segment 4.

To insert a new segment as the first segment in the itinerary, insert after segment zero, as follows:

/0

Remember to redisplay the itinerary and enter the received-from item before ending the transaction.

Inserting and Selling

To insert and sell in the same entry, type a slash after the segment number and before the entry to sell, as follows:

/0/02B6

The direct-sell entry may also be used in this format, as follows:

/0/0CO252Y23OCTSFODENNN2

However, unless there is a reasonable certainty that the desired flight and class will be available, the agent should check availability before attempting to sell a new segment.

Changing Segment Status

When a waitlisted segment is confirmed, SABRE changes the segment status from HL (have listed) to KL (confirmed from list). When this situation occurs, the agent must change the segment status to HK before the ticket can be issued.

Normally, the agent first contacts the passenger to confirm the reservation. If the passenger accepts the confirmed segment, the agent changes the segment status from KL to HK.

The entry code . is used to change segment status, as follows:

FORMAT   .<Segment><Status>

EXAMPLE   .1HK

The example will change the status of segment 1 to HK.

Changing Segments

Assume a PNR has the following name item and itinerary:

```
1.2KEATS/J MR/L MRS
1   US   244Y   13APR   T   PHLBOS   KL2   1010A   1116A
2   US   290Y   13APR   T   PHLBOS   HK2   325P    431P
```

In this example, the clients preferred to depart at mid morning and travel in Y class, but the desired flight and class were sold out. Therefore, the agent booked a waitlisted segment for US 244 and sold a confirmed segment departing later in the day. Segment 1 has now cleared the waitlist, as indicated by the status KL.

After notifying the client, the agent changes the segment status to HK, as follows:

```
.1HK
```

Each time a PNR is changed or updated, a received-from item should be input. Assume the agent notified Mrs. Keats about the status change. The following entry may be used to input the received-from item and end-transact:

```
6MRSΣE
```

Other segment status codes besides KL also require the agent to take action. See Table 6-4 for examples of various segment status codes that may appear in an itinerary after seats have been requested, waitlisted, or confirmed.

Handling Status Changes

Some segment status codes do not require any action. However, the following situations require the agent to notify the passenger and change the segment status.

Confirmed Seat Requests

Most flights in an availability display show a seat quota of either four or zero in each class of service. If fewer than four seats are available, zero is displayed. If four or more seats are available to sell, four is displayed. If an agent attempts to sell more than four seats, the segment will have the status NN. When the transaction is ended, a message requesting the seats is transmitted to the carrier. Until a reply is received from the carrier, the segment will have the status HN, NN, or PN.

If the space is confirmed by the carrier, the segment status will be changed to KK. The PNR will be placed in an electronic holding area called the *confirmation queue*. Each business day, the agent can look in the queue to see which PNRs have itineraries with confirmed seat requests. You will learn how to work with queues in Chapter 12.

When a segment has the status KK, the agent must change the segment status to HK before the ticket can be issued.

Table 6-4 SABRE Segment Status Codes.

Code	Meaning	Action
DL	Deferred from waitlist	Cancel the segment and book a new waitlisted segment.
DS	Desires seats	No action is required.
HK	Holding confirmed status	No action is required.
HL	Holding waitlisted status	No action is required.
HN	Have requested	No action is required.
KK	Confirmed by carrier	Notify the client and change the segment status to HK.
KL	Confirmed from waitlist	Notify the client and change the segment status to HK.
NO	No action	Cancel the segment and sell alternative flight.
PN	Pending need	No action is required. After 24 hours, change the status to IN to re-request.
SB	Standby passenger	No action is required.
SC	Schedule change	Notify the client and change the status to HK.
UC	Unable to confirm	Cancel the segment and sell an alternative flight.
UN	Unable to sell	Cancel the segment and sell an alternative flight.
US	Unable to sell	To waitlist, change the status to HL. Otherwise, cancel the segment and sell an alternative flight.
UU	Unable/unable	To waitlist, change the status to HL. Otherwise, cancel the segment and sell an alternative flight.
WK	Was confirmed	Cancel the segment and confirm the suggested alternative (SC) segment.
WL	Was waitlisted	Cancel the segment.

To illustrate, assume an agent desires to sell six seats in Y class on AS 2525 from the following availability display:

```
22JUN   MON   SLC/MST   BOI/MST
1 DL1455 F4 Y4 B4 M4 Q4 V4 SLCBOI 9 1115A  1216P   72S  S  0    TA
2 AS2525 F4 Y4 B4 V4 Q4 H4 SLCBOI 9  155P   350P  SWM  S  1
3 AS2558 F4 Y4 B4 V4 Q4 H4 SLCBOI 9  205P   345P  SWM  S  1
4 AS2542 F4 Y4 B4 V4 Q4 H4 SLCBOI 8  400P   520P  SWM  S  0
5 DL1639 F4 Y4 B4 M4 Q4 V4 SLCBOI 8  510P   611P   73S  S  0    TA
6 DL1485 F4 Y4 B4 M4 Q4 V4 SLCBOI 9  930P  1031P   72S  S  0    TA
```

The following entry may be used to book the segment:

06Y2

SABRE responds as follows:

```
1 AS2525Y   22JUN  M  SLCBOI  NN6   155P    350P
```

Because more than four seats were requested, the segment has the status NN. When the agent ends the transaction, a message requesting the seats is transmitted to Alaska Airlines.

When the agent retrieves the PNR two days later, the itinerary appears as follows:

```
1 AS2525Y   22JUN  M  SLCBOI  KK6   155P    350P
```

The status **KK** indicates that the seat request was confirmed by the carrier. To acknowledge the reservation, the agent changes the segment status to HK, as follows:

.1HK

To finish, the agent inputs the received-from item and ends the transaction.

If a segment has the status PN, no action is required for 24 hours. If a reply is not received from the carrier within this time, however, the seats may be re-requested with the action code IN, as follows:

.1IN

The status IN will cause another seat request to be transmitted to the carrier.

Declined Seat Requests

On occasion, space requested from a carrier in an NN segment may be declined, either because of a schedule change or because the flight is completely sold out. When a seat request is declined, the segment may have one of the following status codes:

UC   Unable to confirm
US   Unable to sell
UU   Unable/unable

If the status is UC, the agent must cancel the segment and book an alternative flight. If the status is US or UU, however, the agent can waitlist the segment by changing the status to HL. If the passenger does not wish to be waitlisted on the flight, the agent should cancel the segment and book an alternative flight.

As an example, assume an itinerary has the following segment:

1 AC 790 20 MAY W LAXYYZ US5 105P 825P

In this example, five seats were requested on an Air Canada flight. However, the carrier was unable to confirm the space, as indicated by the status US. The clients would like to be waitlisted on the flight. The following entry would be used to change the segment status:

.1HL

An alternative flight should also be booked to protect the passengers in case the waitlisted segment is not confirmed.

Schedule Changes

If a segment has been affected by a schedule change, or if a flight has ceased to operate, the segment may have one of the status codes found in Table 6-5.

If a previously confirmed segment has any of the status codes in Table 6-5, the agent must cancel the segment and book an alternative flight.

When an American Airlines flight is affected by a schedule change, SABRE may *protect the client* by recommending an alternative segment. The original segment will have the status WK (was confirmed) or WL (was waitlisted). The alternative segment will appear in the itinerary with the status **SC** (schedule change). When a segment has this status, the agent should notify the client immediately about the schedule change. If the passenger accepts the alternative segment, the agent then would change the segment status from SC to HK to secure the reservation, and cancel the WK or WL segment. If the client declines the alternative segment, the agent would cancel both segments and book a different flight.

To illustrate, assume an itinerary has the following segment:

1 AA4243Y 30 MAR F MKEORD SS1 540A 620A

When the transaction is ended, SABRE changes the segment status from SS to HK. If the PNR is then redisplayed, the itinerary appears as follows:

```
1 AA4243Y   30MAR  F  MKEORD  HK1   540A    620A
```

Now let us assume that, before the departure date a schedule change occurs and AA 4243 no longer operates on Friday. When the PNR is retrieved and the itinerary displayed, the segment appears as follows:

```
1 AA4243Y   30MAR  F  MKEORD  WK1   540A    620A
1 AA4224Y   30MAR  F  MKEORD  SC1   734A    814A
```

The segment status WK indicates that AA 4243 will not operate. However, the client has been protected on AA 4224, as indicated by the status SC in segment 2. Assume the client accepts the alternative flight. The agent secures the reservation by changing the segment status from SC to HK, as follows:

.2HK

Table 6-5 SABRE Status Codes Used for Schedule Changes.

UC	Unable to confirm
UN	Unable to sell
US	Unable to sell
UU	Unable/unable
WK	Was confirmed
WL	Was waitlisted
YK	Cancel confirmed segment

The agent uses the following entry to cancel the WK segment:

X1

Next, the agent redisplays the itinerary to reset the order, as follows:

*I

SABRE now displays only the confirmed segment:

```
1 AA4224Y  30MAR  F  MKEORD  HK1  734A  814A
```

When one or more American Airlines flights are affected by a schedule change, the following entry may be used to change the status of all the alternative segments:

.HKALL

This entry will change the SC segments to HK and also cancel any WK segments in the itinerary.

.3/4 HK

Summary

A PNR can be retrieved by any of four methods: by record locator; by name; by departure date and name; or by flight, departure date, origin point, and name. If PNRs are stored for more than one passenger with the same surname, a similar-name list is displayed. When a PNR is in the agent work area, any of the passenger data items can be displayed upon request.

The entry code, X, is used to cancel segments, and the code / is used to insert segments. A segment can be canceled and rebooked in the same entry, by means of the cross key (‡). A segment can be inserted and sold in the same entry, by means of the slash key (/).

When a waitlisted segment is confirmed, SABRE changes the segment status from HL to KL. When a segment with the status NN is confirmed, the status changes to KK. The CSS key (.) is used to change segment status.

New commands included in this chapter:

*-BYRON	Retrieves a PNR by name
*-10MAY-BYRON	Retrieves a PNR by date and name
*AA412/10MAY-BYRON	Retrieves a PNR by carrier, flight, date and name
*SFDFWQ	Retrieves a PNR by record locator
*3	Displays a PNR from the similar-name list
*L	Redisplays the similar-name list
*A	Displays all fields
*B	Displays reserved seat/boarding pass information
*H	Displays history
*I	Displays itinerary
*P	Displays passenger data fields
*-	Displays form of payment
*/	Displays client address
*‡	Displays itinerary remarks
*.	Displays invoice remarks
*N	Displays name field
*P3	Displays general facts field
*P4	Displays AA facts field
*P5	Displays remarks field
*P6	Displays received-from field
*P7	Displays ticketing field
*P9	Displays phone field
*PAD	Displays address field
*IA	Displays air segments only
*IC	Displays car segments only
*IH	Displays hotel segments only
X1	Cancels a segment
X1/3/5	Cancels a series of segments
X2-5	Cancels a range of segments
X1‡01Y2	Cancels a segment and sells a new segment
X1‡0012MAY	Changes the departure date of a segment
/1	Inserts after a segment
/1/01Y1	Inserts and sells with one entry
.1HK	Changes a segment status

KEY CONCEPTS AND TERMS

Identify the word or phrase for each of the following concepts:

1. The key that is used to retrieve and display PNRs.
2. The entry code that is used to retrieve a PNR by its record locator.
3. The entry code that is used to retrieve a PNR by the passenger's surname.
4. In a PNR that has been retrieved from storage, the segment status of a confirmed flight reservation.
5. In a PNR that has been retrieved from storage, the segment status of a waitlisted flight reservation.
6. In the last line of a retrieved PNR, a code identifying the agent who created the PNR.
7. Retrieving a PNR created by another booking source.
8. A display of the names and departure dates of PNRs that have the same or similar surnames.
9. The data required to retrieve a PNR for a reservation that was booked directly with American Airlines.
10. The entry code that is used to cancel segments.
11. The key that is used to cancel and rebook with one entry.
12. The entry to cancel the entire itinerary.
13. The entry to cancel only the air segments in an itinerary.
14. The entry code that is used to insert a new air segment in an itinerary.
15. The key that is used to insert and sell a flight segment with one entry.
16. The entry code that is used to change segment status.
17. In a retrieved PNR, the segment status of a confirmed flight reservation that previously had the status HN, NN, or PN.
18. In a PNR affected by a schedule change, the segment status of an alternative segment recommended by the carrier.

Answers:

1. display (*); 2. *; 3. -; 4. HK; 5. HL; 6. agent sine; 7. claiming a reservation; 8. similar-name list; 9. the flight, the date, the origin, and the passenger's surname; 10. X; 11. cross (‡); 12. XI; 13. XIA; 14. /; 15. /; 16. .; 17. KK; 18. SC.

REVIEW QUESTIONS

1. Write the correct entry to retrieve the PNR for passenger Templeton.
2. Your agency previously booked flight reservations for passenger Greene. Write the entry to retrieve the client's PNR.
3. Write the correct entry to retrieve the PNR for passenger Norman.
4. Write the correct entry to retrieve the PNR for R. Hurt.
5. Write the correct entry to retrieve the PNR for Mrs. L. Silverstein, using all the information available.
6. Your agency previously booked flight reservations for passenger Mr. F. Brodervic. Write the entry to retrieve the client's PNR, using all the information available.

7. Write the entry to retrieve the PNR for passenger Thiessen, departing on 12 August. Include the date in the entry.

8. Passenger Broderick will depart on 17 July. Write the entry to retrieve the PNR by date and name.

9. Passenger Kleinman will depart on AA 2784 on 18 June. Write the correct entry to retrieve the PNR by flight, date, and name.

10. Write the entry to retrieve the PNR for record locator STKJPH.

11. Write the correct entry to display all fields of a PNR, including the itinerary.

12. Which entry will display only the itinerary?

13. Which entry will display only the passenger data fields?

14. Write the entry to display the AA facts field.

15. Write the entry to display the general facts field.

16. Which entry will display only the phone field?

17. Write the entry to display only the name field.

18. Write the entry to display the PNR for passenger Lee, departing on the 13th of June.

19. Assume SABRE responds to the entry in question 18 as follows:

1	LEE/ARNOLD	13JUN	2	LEE/BARRY	13JUN
3	LEE/B MR	13JUN	4	LEE/RICHARD	13JUN
5	LEE/TERI MRS	13JUN	6	LEIGH/LOIS MS	13JUN

    Assume your client is Mr. Richard Lee. Which entry would be used to display the PNR?

20. Assume you wish to display a PNR with the record locator number VB73QK. What entry would you use?

21. What code is used to cancel an air segment in a passenger itinerary?

22. What entry would cancel the third segment in an itinerary?

23. What entry would cancel the return segment of a two-segment round trip?

24. What entry would cancel the outbound segment in a round trip itinerary?

25. What entry would you use to cancel the entire itinerary in a PNR?

26. Assume two clients are waitlisted on a flight in segment 1 and confirmed in segment 2. The waitlisted flight fails to clear the waitlist. Write the correct entry to cancel the waitlisted segment.

27. Which entry would cancel the waitlisted segment in question 6 and rebook the same flight and class on 15 June?

28. Which entry would be used to cancel segments 1, 3, and 7 in an itinerary?

29. Refer to the following itinerary to answer questions a through f:

1	CO	201Y	10OCT	M	LGAMIA	HK1	850A	1110A
2	CO	141Y	10OCT	M	LGAMIA	HK1	1245P	330P
3	CO	932Y	15OCT	J	MIAMSY	HK1	245P	335P
4	CO	876Y	18OCT	T	MSYLGA	HK1	1040A	205P

    a) What entry would cancel the New Orleans-New York segment and rebook CO 667 in Y class on the same date?

    b) What entry would cancel the Miami-New Orleans segment and rebook the same flight and class on 20 October?

    c) What entry would cancel both New York-Miami segments without rebooking?

    d) What entry would cancel only the afternoon flight from New York to Miami, without rebooking?

     e)   What entry would cancel all segments except the New York-Miami morning flight?

     f)   What entry would cancel the entire itinerary?

30. What key is used to insert a new segment in an itinerary?

31. Write the entry to insert after segment 2.

32. Write the entry to insert after segment 1.

33. Write the entry to insert a new segment as segment 1.

34. Write the entry to insert an ARNK segment after segment 5.

35. Write the correct entry to insert after segment 3 and sell 2 seats in B class on TW 718 on 19 January from CVG to JFK.

36. When a segment has cleared the waitlist, what status code is displayed?

37. When a request for more than four seats has been confirmed by a carrier other than American Airlines, what status code is displayed?

38. When a confirmed segment has been canceled because of an AA schedule change, what status code appears in the previously booked segment?

39. Write the entry to change the status of segment 5 to HK.

40. What action should be taken if the status code SC appears in a segment?

APPLICATIONS

Read the following scenario, and decide what actions should be performed to satisfy the client's preferences and needs. Briefly describe how you would handle the situation, and then write the required entries.

Mr. Hughes contacts you regarding the status of his flight reservations. The PNR is displayed as follows:

```
1.1HUGHES/P MR
1    UA    417Y    12APR    DTWORD    HK1    713A    713A
2    UA    465Y    12APR    DTWORD    HK1    1201P   1201P
3    UA    402Y    15APR    ORDMIA    HK1    835A    1155A
4    UA    715Y    20APR    MIAORD    HK1    710A    915A
5    AA    508Y    21APR    ORDDTW    WK1    133P    313P
6    AA    608Y    21APR    ORDDTW    SC1    402P    542P
TKT/TIME LIMIT -
1.TAW7APR/
PHONES -
1.CHI312-555-7721-A
2.CHI312-555-1432-B
RECEIVED FROM - P
```

Your client prefers the early morning departure from Detroit to Chicago and accepts the alternative flight for the Chicago–Detroit journey.

Mr. Hughes would like to arrange a side trip from Miami to Orlando. He would like to depart on 18 April around 8 A.M. When you display availability, a United flight in line 1 departs at 7:40 A.M. and has seats available in Y class. He will return from Orlando to Miami by motorcoach.

Chapter 7

Changing, Reducing, and Dividing

Outline

Changing Passenger Data

Dividing a PNR

Reducing the Number in the Party

Chapter Objectives

After you complete this chapter, you should be able to:

1. Delete or change data in a passenger data field.

2. Reduce the number in a party.

3. Divide a PNR.

PROBLEM

Your agency previously booked a round-trip itinerary for Mr. Crenshaw, Ms. Lawson, and Ms. Bloomfield to travel together from Atlanta to Detroit. Ms. Bloomfield's plans have changed, and she will not be able to make the trip. Ms. Lawson will depart as scheduled, but Mr. Crenshaw has decided to depart one day later. The passengers will travel together on the return flight.

SABRE SOLUTION

First, reduce the party to two passengers, and then delete the data items pertaining to Ms. Bloomfield. Then divide the PNR to create a separate record for Ms. Lawson. Make the changes to Mr. Crenshaw's itinerary, and cross-reference the PNRs.

In this chapter, you will learn how to delete or change passenger data, reduce the number in a party, and divide a PNR.

Information stored in the passenger data fields of an existing PNR can be deleted or changed while the PNR is in the agent work area. The change code (¤) is used for this purpose.

Deleting a Data Item

The following format is used to delete a data item:

FORMAT   <Field><Item>¤

EXAMPLE   -2¤

This entry would delete the second name item from a displayed PNR.
Assume a PNR has the following phone items:

1.BOS617-555-4542-A RACHEL
2.BOS617-555-1191-B
3.BOS617-555-2052-H

The following entry can be used to delete the home phone:

93¤

In this case, *9* identifies the phone field, and *3* indicates the third phone item.
If the specified field has only one data item, the item number *1* may be omitted, as in the following example:

7¤

This entry would be used to delete the ticketing item in a PNR with one item in the ticketing field.
If a name item consists of multiple passengers, name reference may be used to delete a passenger within the name item. For example, assume a PNR has the following name field:

1.2HICKORY/N MR/M MRS   2.2WHITING/K MR/Y MRS

Assume Mrs. Y. Whiting, the second passenger in name item 2, has decided not to travel. The following entry may be used to delete the passenger:

-2.2¤

This example would delete the second passenger in name item 2 without affecting any other passengers in the name item.
Other examples of entries to delete data items are shown in Table 7-1.

Changing Data Items

To change the information in a passenger data field, input the new data after the change code ¤, as follows:

FORMAT   <Field><Item>¤<New data>

Table 7-1 Examples of Entries Deleting Data Items.

Entry	Action
92¤	Deletes the second phone item
-¤	Deletes the name item in a PNR with one surname
55¤	Deletes the fifth line of the remarks field

EXAMPLE   -1¤JOHNSON/H MR

This example above would change the first name item in a displayed PNR. Other examples of entries to change data items in a PNR are shown in Table 7-2.

─ *C L I E N T   F O C U S* ─

Changing Passenger Data Fields

Let us examine some typical situations requiring changes to the passenger data fields. Assume a PNR has the following name items:

1.2HOFFMAN/G MR/R MRS   2.2CARLISLE/A MR/K MRS

Let us say that the second surname is misspelled and the correct spelling is *Carlysle*. The following entry is used to change the name item:

-2¤2CARLYSLE/A MR/K MRS

If the PNR has only one name item, the item number *1* may be omitted, as in the following example:

-¤SANDERS/C MR

To change only the first name or initial in a name item, include the name reference. For example, assume a PNR has the following name item:

1.1MORRIS/P MR/S MRS/J MISS

Let us say that the third passenger in the name item is Miss G. Morris. In this case, the initial was input incorrectly. The following entry may be used to correct the name item:

-1.3¤G MISS

The name reference *1.3* indicates the third passenger in name item 1. When a name reference is input to change the first name or initial, the surname must be omitted.

Other Name Change Entries Besides names, other information can also be added to or changed in the name field. For example, assume a PNR has the following name field:

> 1.1PULLMAN/T MR   2.1FRANKS/J MR

The following entry would be used to add Mr. Pullman's AAdvantage account number to the name field:

> -1¤‡7765443

Reducing the Number in the Party

No matter how many travelers are booked in a PNR, the number of passengers in the name field must be equal to the number of seats in the itinerary. For example, assume a PNR has the following name field and itinerary:

```
1.4HILL/G MR/H MRS/T MS/P MISS
1 UA 201V   14JAN   W   DENHNL   HK4   930A   1235P
2 UA 812V   28JAN   W   HNLDEN   HK4   845A   903P
```

In this case, the name field has four passengers, and four seats are booked in the itinerary. However, suppose the clients' travel plans have changed, and Ms. T. Hill will not make the trip. If the name field is changed to three passengers, the PNR will have more seats than passengers. One solution to this problem might be to cancel the entire itinerary and rebook three seats on each segment. However, the clients will be unprotected if the same flight or class is not available on each segment.

A preferable—and simpler—solution is to reduce the number in the party. The *New # key* (,) is used for this purpose, as follows:

FORMAT   ,<New number in the party>

EXAMPLE   ,3

Reducing a Party

Assume the following PNR has been retrieved from storage and is in the agent work area:

```
1.3MCGRAW/M MR/H MRS/A MS
1   DL   555Y   12JUL   W   ATLPHL   HK3   1215P   159P
2   TW   393Y   18JUL   T   PHLBOS   HK3   517P    621P
3   TW   325Y   25JUL   T   BOSPHL   HK3   903A    1005A
4   DL   588Y   25JUL   T   PHLATL   HK3   1100A   1250P
TKT/TIME LIMIT - TAW10JUL/
PHONES -
1. ATL404-555-0075-A
2. ATL404-555-9822-B MR
3. ATL404-555-2767-H
RECEIVED FROM - MRS
```

In this example, three passengers are booked in the itinerary. Let us say that one passenger, Ms. A. McGraw, has decided not to travel. The following entry may be used to reduce the number in the party:

```
,2
```

SABRE responds as follows:

```
PARTY NOW 2 STARTING AT 1 NO ACT ON AUX
```

The response indicates that the party now consists of two passengers, starting at segment 1. No action has been taken on any auxiliary segments, such as car or hotel segments. The agent displays the itinerary to review the change:

```
*I
```

SABRE displays the segments, as follows:

```
1   DL   555Y   12JUL   W   ATLPHL   HK2   1215P   159P
2   TW   393Y   18JUL   T   PHLBOS   HK2   517P    621P
3   TW   325Y   25JUL   T   BOSPHL   HK2   903A    1005A
4   DL   588Y   25JUL   T   PHLATL   HK2   1100A   1250P
```

The itinerary now shows two seats booked in each segment. However, the name field still has three passengers. Ms. A. McGraw is the third passenger in name item 1. The following entry may be used to delete her name from the name field:

```
-1.3¤
```

If the name field is redisplayed, it will now appear as follows:

```
1.2MCGRAW/M MR/H MRS
```

The previous example would reduce the number of passengers to three. When this entry is input, SABRE will change the number of seats in each air segment. However, the agent must also change the name field and any other passenger data fields that are affected by the action.

The *New #* key can only be used to reduce, but not increase, the number of seats in an itinerary. To increase the number of seats, you must cancel and rebook the entire itinerary.

Dividing a PNR

If a PNR has multiple passengers and one or more travelers wish to change their itinerary, the PNR can be divided. When a PNR is divided, a separate record is created for the travelers whose travel plans have changed.

The entry code **D** is used to divide a PNR that has been retrieved from storage and is in the agent work area, as follows:

FORMAT D<Name item>

EXAMPLE D2

The example above will divide the passengers in name item 2 from the PNR and create a new record for them. The new PNR will be displayed automatically. The entry code **F** is then used to file the new PNR.

The following steps are required to divide a PNR:

1. Retrieve the existing PNR.

2. Divide out the passengers who desire to change their itinerary. A new PNR will be created automatically.

3. Input the received-from item and file the record to save the new PNR. The original PNR will be displayed automatically.

4. Input the received-from item and end-transact to save the changes to the original PNR.

5. Retrieve the new PNR and change the itinerary to meet the client's needs. Then cross-reference the PNR to the original PNR and end-transact.

6. Retrieve the original PNR and cross-reference it to the new PNR. Then end-transact.

To illustrate, assume the following PNR has been retrieved from storage and is in the agent work area:

```
  1.1MCDONNELL/R MR      2.1DOUGLAS/C MR
1 UA  81Y  19APR  M  LAXSFO  HK2  200P   310P
2 UA 525Y  23APR  F  SFOLAX  HK2  755P   905P
TKT/TIME LIMIT -
1.TAW29MAR/
PHONES -
1.LAX213-555-5250-A   PENELOPE
2.LAX213-555-7738-B
3.LAX213-555-7738-H   MCDONNELL
4.LAX213-555-7738-H   DOUGLAS
RECEIVED FROM - MS KLEIN
```

In this example, Mr. McDonnell and Mr. Douglas are booked on a round-trip itinerary. However, Mr. Douglas has now decided to return to Los Angeles one day earlier. The following entry is used to divide the party:

D2

In this case, it is Mr. Douglas who desires to change his itinerary. Therefore, name item 2 is divided from the PNR. SABRE creates a new record for Mr. Douglas. The new PNR is displayed automatically, as follows:

```
  1.1DOUGLAS/C  MR
1 UA  81Y  19APR  M  LAXSFO  HK1  200P   310P
2 UA 525Y  23APR  F  SFOLAX  HK1  755P   905P
TKT/TIME LIMIT -
1.TAW29MAR/
PHONES -
1.LAX213-555-5250-A   PENELOPE
2.LAX213-555-7738-B
3.LAX213-555-7738-H   MCDONNELL
4.LAX213-555-7738-H   DOUGLAS
REMARKS -
1.SPLIT  PTY/Q9X0*31   1419/2APR - ASGLGP
RECEIVED FROM  - MS KLEIN
```

In the new PNR, only the divided passenger, Mr. C. Douglas, is shown in the name field. The correct number of seats is shown in the itinerary. SABRE has added a text item called a **split-party remark** in the remarks field. The text includes the agency's pseudo city code, the time and date on which the PNR was divided, and the record locator of the original PNR.

As a safeguard, the PNR should be saved before any changes are made. To save a record created as a result of dividing a PNR, the entry code **F** must be used. On some SABRE keyboards, a key labeled **FILE** is used for this purpose.

Assume the change was received from the client's secretary, Ms. Klein. The following entry can be used to input the received-from item and file the new PNR:

    6MS KLEINΣF

When the record is filed, the original PNR is redisplayed automatically, as follows:

```
RECORD FILED
 1.1MCDONNELL/R MR
1 UA  81Y  19APR  M  LAXSFO  HK1  200P  310P
2 UA  525Y  23APR  F  SFOLAX  HK1  755P  905P
TKT/TIME LIMIT -
1.TAW29MAR/
PHONES -
1.LAX213-555-5250-A    PENELOPE
2.LAX213-555-7738-B
3.LAX213-555-7738-H    MCDONNELL
4.LAX213-555-7738-H    DOUGLAS
REMARKS -
1.SPLIT  PTY/Q9X0*31   1419/2APR90 - SKVDQN
RECEIVED FROM -  MS KLEIN
```

Note that only passenger McDonnell is shown in the name field, and one seat is booked in the itinerary. A split-party remark has also been added to the remarks field. The following entry can be used to input the received-from item and end-transact:

    6MS KLEINΣE

Note that *F* (file) is input to store the new PNR, but *E* (end-transact) is input to store the original PNR.

The next step is to retrieve the new PNR for passenger Douglas, so that the desired changes can be made to the itinerary. The following entry may be used:

    *-DOUGLAS

The PNR is displayed as follows:

```
 1.1DOUGLAS/C MR
1 UA  81Y  19APR  M  LAXSFO  HK1  200P    310P
2 UA 525Y  23APR  F  SFOLAX  HK1  755P    905P
TKT/TIME LIMIT -
1.TAW29MAR/
PHONES -
1.LAX213-555-5250-A    PENELOPE
2.LAX213-555-7738-B
3.LAX213-555-7738-H    MCDONNELL
4.LAX213-555-7738-H    DOUGLAS
REMARKS -
1.SPLIT  PTY/Q9X0*31   1419/2APR-ASGLGP
RECEIVED FROM - MS KLEIN
```

The client will return from San Francisco one day earlier than he originally planned. Assume you are reasonably certain that the same flight and class are available on 22 April. Using the format for rebooking the same flight and class on a new date, the following entry may be used to modify the itinerary:

X2‡0022APR

When the itinerary is redisplayed, it will now appear as follows:

```
1 UA  81Y   19APR  M  LAXSFO  HK1  200P  310P
2 UA 525Y   22APR  Q  SFOLAX  SS1  755P  905P
```

The home phone for Mr. McDonnell is not needed in this PNR. The following entry may be used to delete the phone item:

93¤

Before the PNR is stored, an **OSI** item should be input to cross-reference this record to the original PNR for passenger McDonnell. The passengers will travel together on the outbound flight. Therefore, the following entry would be used to cross-reference the PNRs:

3OSI UA TCP2 W/MCDONNELL UA81Y19APRLAXSFO

No further changes are required. The agent inputs the received-from item and ends the transaction, as follows:

6MS KLEINΣE

Although *F* was input to file the record when it was created, *E* must be input to end transact after the PNR has been retrieved from storage.

The original PNR for passenger McDonnell should also be retrieved and cross-referenced to the new PNR for passenger Douglas. You use the following entry to retrieve the record:

*-MCDONNELL

The PNR is displayed as follows:

```
 1.1MCDONNELL/R  MR
1 UA  81Y  19APR  M  LAXSFO  HK1  200P   310P
2 UA 525Y  23APR  F  SFOLAX  HK1  755P   905P
TKT/TIME LIMIT -
1.TAW29MAR/
PHONES -
1.LAX213-555-5250-A    PENELOPE
2.LAX213-555-7738-B
3.LAX213-555-7738-H    MCDONNELL
4.LAX213-555-7738-H    DOUGLAS
REMARKS -
1.SPLIT  PTY/Q9X0*31   1419/2APR90- SKVDQN
RECEIVED FROM - MS KLEIN
```

The home phone for Mr. Douglas is not needed in this PNR. The following entry may be used to delete the phone item:

94¤

Before the PNR is stored, it should be cross-referenced to the new PNR for passenger Douglas, as follows:

3OSI UA TCP2 W/DOUGLAS UA81Y19APRLAXSFO

The following entry may now be used to input the received-from item and end-transact:

6MS KLEINΣE

Dividing by Name Reference

To divide a selected passenger within a name item, include the name reference, as follows:

D1.3

This example will divide out the third passenger in name item 1 but will have no effect on other passengers within that name item.

To illustrate, assume a PNR contains the following name item:

1.3LEONARD/J MR/R MRS/C MSTR

Let us say that Mrs. R. Leonard would like to change her itinerary. The following entry may be used to divide the PNR:

D1.2

The name reference *1.2* indicates the second passenger in name item 1.

Dividing Multiple Passengers

To divide multiple passengers, type an asterisk (*) to separate the names. For example, to divide the passengers in name items 1 and 3, the following entry may be used:

D1*3

Name reference may also be included in this entry. To illustrate, assume a PNR contains the following name items:

1.2GUERRERA/J MR/S MRS   2.2LOPEZ/H MR/L MRS

Assume that Mrs. S. Guerrera and Mrs. L. Lopez wish to change their itinerary. The following entry may be used to divide the PNR:

D1.2*2.2

When a PNR is divided, any supplemental information in the name field, such as an AAdvantage number or employee number, will be placed in the name field of the new PNR.

Dividing a Range of Passengers

To divide consecutive passengers within a name item, type a dash (-) between the first and last passengers in the range. For example, to divide name items 1.3, 1.4, and 1.5, the following entry may be used:

D1.3-1.5

To illustrate, assume a PNR has the following name items:

1.1JONES/R MR   2.1HALD/E MR   3.1BRAUN/F MR   4.1CROWELL/LMR

Let us say that Mr. Hald, Mr. Braun, and Mr. Crowell wish to change their itinerary. The following entry may be used to divide the PNR.

D2-4

Summary

Information stored in a passenger data field can be deleted or changed by means of the change code (¤). When a party is reduced, SABRE changes the number of seats in each air segment. The name field and any other passenger data fields that are affected by the action must also be changed. If a PNR has multiple passengers and one or more travelers wish to change their itinerary, the PNR can be divided. When a PNR is divided, a separate record is created for the travelers whose travel plans have changed. The entry code *F* is used to file the new record.

New commands included in this chapter:

92¤	Deletes the second phone item
-¤	Deletes the name item in a PNR with one surname
55¤	Deletes the fifth line of the remarks field
92¤612-555-3499-B	Changes phone item 2
52¤-CK	Changes the second line of the remarks field
7¤TAW18JUL/	Changes the ticketing item in a PNR with one item in the ticketing field
-3¤2LEE/K MR/C MRS	Changes the surname in name item 3
-2.2¤P MRS	Changes the initial and title of the second passenger in name item 2
,2	Reduces the number in a party
D3	Divides a party by surname
D1.2	Divides a party by name item
D1.2*2.2	Divides multiple passengers from a party
D2.2-2.4	Divides a range of passengers

STUDENT REVIEW

KEY CONCEPTS AND TERMS

Identify the word, phrase, or symbol for each of the following concepts:

1. The code that is used to delete or change information in a passenger data field.
2. The information that is typed before the change code when one data item of a multiple-item field is deleted or changed.
3. The code that is used to reduce the number in a party.
4. The entry code used to divide a PNR that has been retrieved from storage.
5. The entry code or key that is used to store a record created by dividing a PNR.

6. The type of entry that is input to cross-reference the original PNR with a new PNR created by dividing a party.

7. In a PNR created by dividing a party, text inserted by SABRE that shows the agency's pseudo city code, the time and date when the PNR was divided, and the record locator of the original PNR.

8. The character that is typed to separate the name references when multiple passengers are divided from a PNR.

9. The character that is typed to separate the name references when a range of passengers are divided from a PNR.

Answers:

1. ⨯; 2. item number; 3. .; 4. D; 5. F or FILE; 6. OSI; 7. split-party remark; 8. *; 9. -.

REVIEW QUESTIONS

1. What code is used to change information stored in a passenger data field?

2. Write the correct entry to change the second name item to Ms. R. Whitehead.

3. Write the correct entry to change the first name item to show Mr. G., Mrs. G., and Miss J. Heilman as the passengers.

4. Write the entry to delete the second name item.

5. Write the entry to change the second phone item to a business number of 602-555-1006.

6. Write the entry to change the third phone item to a home number of 312-555-9445.

7. What entry would delete the third phone item?

8. What entry would delete the seventh remark?

9. Assume the third item in the remarks field should read as follows:

QTD119.00 FARE/16JUN

What entry could you use to change the remark?

10. What entry would change the ticketing field to arrange ticketing on 18 September?

11. What code is used to reduce the party?

12. Write the correct entry to reduce the party to one.

13. Write the correct entry to reduce the party to three.

14. What entry will reduce the party to two?

15. Assume a PNR has the following names:

1.1BRADLEY/FRANK   2.1SIMON/FRED   3.1PARKER/THOMAS

Mr. Simon decides to stay behind. Write the correct entry to reduce the party.

16. What entry will delete only Mr. Simon from the name field in question 15?

17. Assume a PNR has the following names:

1.2GREENE/CHARLES/EDNA MRS

If Mrs. Greene decides not to travel, what entry will be used to reduce the party?

18. What entry would you use to change the name field in question 17?

19. Assume a PNR has the following names:

1.3MURRAY/ROY/MAY MRS/TIMOTHY MSTR
2.1HEFLER/ANTHONY MSTR

If Mrs. Murray decides not to travel, what entry would be used to reduce the party?

20. What entry would you use to change the name field in question 19?

21. What code is used to divide a passenger from the PNR?

22. What code is used to file a divided PNR?

23. Assume a PNR has the following passengers in the name field:

1.1MERITT/R MR   2.1GOULD/F MS

What entry would divide Ms. Gould from the PNR?

24. Assume a PNR has the following passengers:

1.1SIMPSON/A MR   2.1CRENSHAW/K MS   3.1LEE/M MS

If Ms. Lee changes her itinerary, what entry would be used to divide the PNR?

25. Assume a PNR has the following passengers:

2.5SIMMS/H MR/G MRS/L MSTR/A MISS/L MISS

If Mrs. G. Simms changes her itinerary, what entry would be used to divide the PNR?

26. Assume a PNR has the following passengers:

1.2FORREST/A MR/T MRS   2.2MERTZ/D MR/L MRS

Mrs. Forrest and Mrs. Mertz would like to depart a few days later and take a side trip. What entry would be used to divide this PNR?

27. Assume a PNR has the following passengers:

1.4MCNAMARA/F MR/G MRS/L MS/W MS

Mrs. McNamara and her children have decided to depart three days later. What entry will you use to divide this PNR?

28. After a PNR has been divided, what entry is used to store the new record?

29. After a PNR has been divided, what entry would be used to store the original record and, in the same entry, indicate that the change was received from the passenger?

30. Indicate whether the following statement is true or false: It is not necessary to end the transaction after dividing a PNR and filing the new record.

Refer to the following PNR to answer questions 31 through 40:

```
1.2ABELMAN/L MR/F MRS  2.2HOFFMEYER/A MR/C MRS  3.1LEE/C MS
1  DL  199M  24AUG  M  DFWSAN  HK5  1108A  1201P
2  DL  1914Q  30AUG  W  SANDFW  HK5  1120A  410P
TKT/TIME LIMIT-
1.TAW22AUG/
PHONES -
1.DFW214-555-3221-A
2.DFW214-555-5550-H ABELMAN
3.DFW214-555-5667-H HOFFMEYER
4.DFW214-555-1122-H LEE
REMARKS
1.-CK
RECEIVED FROM - MR ABELMAN
```

31. If one of the passengers is unable to make the trip, what entry would be used to reduce the party?

32. If Mr. R. Gamble travels in place of Ms. Lee, what entry can be used to change the name field?

33. If Mr. Gamble's home phone is 214-555-1818, what entry can be used to change the phone field?

34. Assume Mrs. Hoffmeyer's initial is K, not C. What entry will correct her name item?

35. What entry would delete Ms. Lee's phone number?

36. Assume your clients want to pick up their tickets one week before departure. Write the entry to change the ticketing field.

37. If the Hoffmeyers decide to take a different itinerary, what entry would be used to divide the PNR?

38. If only Mrs. Hoffmeyer takes a different itinerary, what entry can be used to divide the PNR?

39. If the Hoffmeyers and Ms. Lee all take a different itinerary, what entry would be used to divide the PNR?

40. If the Hoffmeyers decide not to travel, what entry would be used to reduce the number in the party?

APPLICATIONS

Read the following scenario, and decide what actions should be performed to satisfy the client's preferences and needs. Briefly describe how you would handle the situation, and then write the required entries.

Mrs. Thomas contacts you to change her flight reservations. The PNR is displayed as follows:

```
1.2THOMAS/L MRS/H MS
1  NW  737V  12MAR  F  MKEMEM  HK2  140P  310P
2  NW  730V  19MAR  F  MEMMKE  HK2  350P  552P
TKT/TIME LIMIT -
1.TAW15FEB/
PHONES -
1.MKE414-555-0399-A
2.MKE414-555-1863-B MRS
2.MKE414-555-0091-H
REMARKS -
1.-CK
RECEIVED FROM - MRS
```

Mrs. Thomas's daughter, Heather, will not depart until 15 March but will return on 19 March as planned. Assume you are able to rebook the same flight and class on the new departure date. Mrs. Thomas has a new business phone, 414-555-1736. Your client now plans to purchase the tickets by credit card. The account number is IK3234009816525552, and the card expires November 1998.

Chapter 8

Fare Displays

Outline

Basic Concepts

Fare Types

Fare Quotes

Alternative Fare Quote Entries

Modifying a Fare Quote Display

Fare Shopper Displays

Displaying a Fare Quote From Availability

International Fare Quotes

Fare Rules

Chapter Objectives

After you complete this chapter, you should be able to:

1. Display and interpret a fare quote for a specified carrier.

2. Display a fare quote for a specific fare type or fare basis.

3. Modify an existing fare quote display.

4. Display fare rules from a fare quote display and interpret those rules.

5. Display rules for a specified fare basis and carrier.

PROBLEM

A client inquires about fares for a round trip from Chicago to Seattle. She asks which carrier has the lowest fares. She plans to depart ten days from the current date and will stay five days in Seattle.

SABRE SOLUTION

Display a fare shopper display from Chicago to Seattle on the desired departure date. The check the fare rules to determine whether the client qualifies for a discount fare.

In this chapter, you will learn how to display fares for a specified carrier, compare competitive fares of different carriers, and display fare restrictions.

Two types of fares can be displayed: domestic and international. **Domestic fares** apply to travel between points in the United States, Canada, Mexico, the Caribbean, and Bermuda. If either point in a city pair is outside these countries, **international fares** apply.

Displaying and interpreting fares requires an understanding of three basic concepts: class of service, fare basis, and fare rules. The following discussion may be either an introduction or a review, depending on the student's previous studies or experience.

Class of Service

The fare level is indicated by the **class of service**. The class is also called the *booking code* or booking class. On domestic airlines, the two basic classes are first class and coach. First, or F, class is the most expensive class of service. On international carriers, first class may be called *premium* or *P class*, and full coach, or Y, class may be called *economy* or *standard class*. Many domestic and international carriers offer a premium coach, or C, class, which is less expensive than first class but more expensive than coach. Depending on the carrier, this third class of service may be called *business, club, connoisseur,* or *ambassador class.*

Various discounted coach fares, called **restricted** or **inventory fares**, are also offered. Passengers who travel at a discounted coach fare receive the same level of service as other coach passengers, but the fares have various restrictions. For example, the ticket must be purchased a preset number of days before departure, and the itinerary must originate and terminate at the same point. Often, the outbound and return segments must be booked on the same carrier. Other restrictions, such as a minimum stay, a Saturday stayover, and penalties for cancellation or changes, may also apply. Discounted coach classes include B, M, Q, V, K, H, and L.

Fare Basis

A **fare basis** is a price category determined by the class of service and such factors as destination, season, day of the week, one-way or round-trip travel, advance purchase, and length of stay. Each fare basis has a primary code and one or more secondary codes. For instance, the BAP7 fare basis applies to travel in B class and requires the ticket to be purchased at least seven days prior to departure. The primary code *B* specifies the class of service, and the secondary code *AP7* indicates the advance-purchase requirement. In most cases, but not all, the primary code is the same as the booking code.

The fare basis may consist of a primary code by itself. For example, F is the fare basis for the first-class fare, and Y is the fare basis for the full coach fare. Different primary codes may be used for the same class of service, depending on the carrier. For example, C class on TWA is the same as J class on Japan Airlines. Various primary codes are used for discounted coach travel, including B, M, Q, V, H, and L. Table 8-1 provides examples of primary fare codes.

Secondary codes indicate such restrictions as an advance-purchase requirement, a penalty for canceling or changing the itinerary, and a departure on a specified day of the week. Table 8-2 provides examples of common secondary fare codes.

Numbers are often used in the fare basis to indicate days of the week. For instance, the fare basis *Y3* may indicate a coach fare that is valid only for departure on Wednesday. A day restriction may also be indicated by one or two letters, such as *W* for Wednesday, or *TU* for Tuesday. For instance, the fare basis *BTU* refers to a discount coach fare valid only for departure on Tuesday. Numbers may also be used to indicate an advance-purchase requirement. For example, *BAP21* indicates a discount coach fare that must be purchased 21 days prior to departure.

Table 8-1 Examples of Primary Fare Codes.

Code	Primary Fare
F	First class
P	Premium class
A	Discounted first class
C	Business or club class
Y	Coach or economy class
S	Standard class
B	Discounted coach class
M	Discounted coach class
Q	Discounted coach class
V	Discounted coach class

Table 8-2 Examples of Common Secondary Fare Codes.

Code	Secondary Fare
AP	Advance purchase
E	Excursion fare (valid for a circle trip only) or exception
G	Group fare
H	High or peak period
L	Low or off period
M	Military discount
NR	Nonrefundable
IT	Inclusive tour fare
N	Discounted for travel at night
PE	Penalty for cancelation or change
R	Round-trip fare (not valid for one-way travel)
W	Weekend departure required
X	Exception (not valid on a specified day)

Table 8-3 provides examples of various fare basis codes that might appear in a fare display. The examples in Table 8-3 represent only a small percentage of the fare bases that appear in SABRE fare displays. Fares and fare basis codes constantly change. To book a segment at a particular fare basis, the agent must use the correct booking code. For example, to obtain the QE7RT fare basis, the agent must book the passenger in Q class.

Fare Rules

The booking code, the valid dates for travel or ticketing, and any restrictions that apply to a particular fare basis are set forth in the **fare rules**. The main types of restrictions apply to advance purchase, ticketing, minimum and maximum stay, penalties for canceling or changing the itinerary, combinability, and routing. If an **advance-purchase rule** applies, the ticket must be purchased a set number of days prior to departure. The most common advance purchase requirements are 3, 14, 21, and 30 days. If a **ticketing rule** applies, the ticket must be purchased within

Table 8-3 Examples of Fare Basis Codes.

Code	Fare Basis
F	First class
C	Premium coach or business class
Y	Unrestricted coach fare
Y2	Coach fare/Tuesday departure required
QAP3	Discount coach/3-day advance purchase required
VE7NR	Discount coach/excursion/7-day advance purchase/nonrefundable
BTUWETH	Discount coach/departure on Tuesday, Wednesday, or Thursday required
BAP21PE50	Discount coach/21-day advance purchase/50% penalty for cancellation or change
MLX16	Discount coach/low period/not valid for departure on Monday or Saturday
MAP14	Discount coach/14-day advance purchase
QE7RT	Discount coach/excursion/7-day advance purchase/round trip required

a predefined period of time after the reservation is made, or by a specified date. A **combinability rule** determines whether a particular booking code or fare basis can be combined with other booking codes or fare bases. Fare rules will be examined in greater depth later in this chapter.

Fare Types

In the SABRE system, fares are classified by type. The full fare for first class, premium coach, and regular coach are referred to as **normal fares**. Restricted discount fares requiring round-trip travel are classified as **excursion fares**. Some carriers also offer discounted fares for children 12 years old or younger; those carriers have two additional fare types: adult fares and child fares. Other fare types include military, government, senior citizen, and youth categories. However, not all fare types are offered by each carrier. For example, as of this writing, American Airlines does not offer child, military, or senior citizen fares.

Fare Quotes

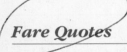

A **fare quote** is a display of fares for a specified carrier, listed from most expensive to least expensive. The entry code **FQ** is used to obtain a fare quote, as follows:

FORMAT   FQ<City pair><Departure date>-<Carrier>

EXAMPLE   FQSFOMIA13JUL-CO

This example will display a fare quote for travel from SFO to MIA on 13 July on Continental Airlines. This entry will display only normal, full adult fares. If the date is omitted, fares are displayed for the current date.

A different fare type may be requested as follows:

FQSFOMIA13JULNLX-CO

Table 8-4 Fare Type Codes (FTCs) Used in Fare Quote Entries.

Code	Fare Type	Code	Fare Type
NLX	Adult normal/excursion fares	EX	Adult excursion fares only
NEC	Child normal/excursion fares	YM	Military fares
NLC	Normal adult/child fares	IT	Tour adult fares
EXC	Excursion adult/child fares	ITC	Tour adult/child fares
NXC	Normal/excursion adult/child fares	PM	Promotional fares
CHX	Child excursion fares only	YZ	Youth standby fares
GVT	Government fares	SC	Senior fares
GRP	Group fares	ARP	American Association of Retired Persons fares
CH	Child fares only		

In this example, the fare type *NLX* refers to normal and excursion fares. Thus, SABRE will display both full and discounted fares. If a fare type is not specified, only normal, full-price adult fares will be displayed. Table 8-4 provides examples of fare type codes (FTCs) used in fare quote entries.

To illustrate, assume a client will travel from LAX to DFW on 13 July. She prefers Delta Air Lines and requests the lowest available fare. The fare type code *NLX* will obtain normal and excursion fares. Based on this information, the following entry may be used to obtain a fare quote:

FQLAXDFW13JULNLX-DL

SABRE responds as follows:

```
ORG-LAX  DST-DFW  TRIP-OUTBOUND CXR-DL    13JUL    USD
AA CO NW UA
     QTE  F/B      BK  FARE     EFF   EXP   TKT   AP  MIN/MAX RTG
01    -   F        F X 607.00    -     -     -     -    -/-    96
02    -   FN       FNX 430.00    -     -     -     -    -/-    96
03  23MR Y         Y X 410.00    -     -     -     -    -/-    96
04    -   KXE3     K X 258.00  21MY    -     -     3   SUN/-   96
05    -   KWE3     K X 308.00  21MY    -     -     3   SUN/-   96
06    -   QAP7P25  Q R 378.00  21MY    -   14MY    7   SUN/-   96
07    -   BAP7P50  B R 344.00  21MY    -     -     7   SUN/-   96
08    -   MAP7NR   M R 338.00  21MY    -     -     7   SUN/-   96
09    -   BWAP21NR B R 338.00  21MY    -     -    21   SUN/-   96
10    -   MAP21NR  M R 334.00    -     -   14MY   21    -/-    96
11    -   QAP21NR  Q R 328.00    -     -     -    21   SUN/-   96
     96 ABQ DEN ELP FAT LAS MKC OKC PHX RNO SAN SJC SLC SMF TUL
```

The information that appears above the fare lines is called the header and gives the origin and destination. The fares in this example apply to outbound travel on Delta Air Lines for departure on 13 July. The currency on which the fares are based is also shown in the header. In this case, all fares are quoted in U.S. dollars (*USD*). The second line of the header lists other carriers who service the same route. In this example, fares are also available from American, Continental, Northwest, and United from LAX to DFW. (See Figure 8-1.)

Each fare line in the fare quote display is numbered on the left. The line number can be used to display the fare rules. The quote date column (*QTE*) shows the first date on which the fare may be quoted to a client. For example, the fare in line 3 may not be quoted to a client until 23 March.

The fare basis (*F/B*) and booking code (*BK*) are shown for each fare. For example, the fare in line 6 has the fare basis *QAP7P25*, and the booking code *Q* would be used to sell a segment at this fare. The letter to the right of the booking code is called the *fare application*. (See Figure 8-2.)

The fare application *X* indicates a one-way fare that is valid for one-way or round-trip travel. If the fare is used in a round-trip itinerary, the round-trip fare is calculated by multiplying the fare by 2. For example, if the fare in line 3 is used for one-way travel, the one-way fare would be $410. If the fare is used for a round trip, the round-trip fare would be $820.

The fare application *R* indicates a fare that is valid only for round-trip travel, not for one-way. For example, the round-trip fare in line 6 is $378, but a one-way ticket cannot be issued at a fare of $189, half of this fare basis.

The fare application *O* indicates a fare that is valid only for one-way travel and cannot be used in a round trip.

If an effective date, expiration date, or ticketing date applies, it is shown in the *EFF, EXP,* or *TKT* column, respectively. (See Figure 8-3.) For example, the fare in line 6 is valid for travel on or after 21 May, and the ticket must be purchased by 14 May.

If a fare has an advance-purchase requirement, the number of days is given in the *AP* column. For example, the fare in line 5 requires the ticket to be purchased 3 days before departure. If a minimum or maximum stay is required, the information is shown in the *MIN/MAX* column. In this example, to obtain the fare in line 4, the

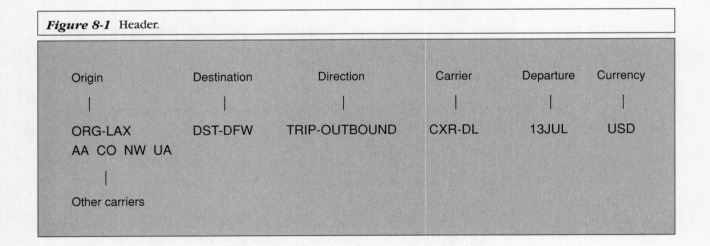

Figure 8-1 Header.

Origin	Destination	Direction	Carrier	Departure	Currency
|	|	|	|	|	|
ORG-LAX	DST-DFW	TRIP-OUTBOUND	CXR-DL	13JUL	USD
AA CO NW UA					
|					
Other carriers					

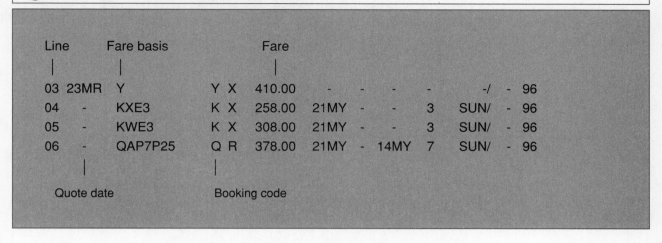

Figure 8-2 Quote Date, Fare Basis, and Booking Code.

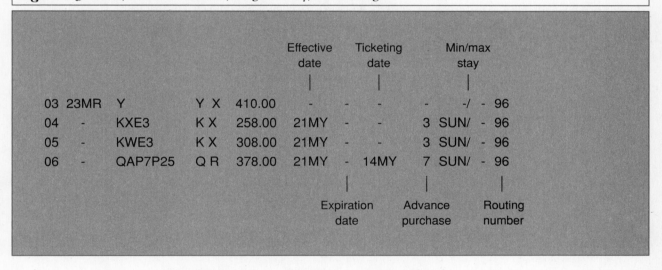

Figure 8-3 Dates, Advance Purchase, Length of Stay, and Routing.

passenger must stay over until the first Sunday after the departure date. In other words, a Saturday stayover is required.

The column on the far right in Figure 8-3 gives the routing number. The permitted routing for each fare appears at the bottom of the display. In this example, routing 96 lists 14 different connecting points that may be used between LAX and DFW.

The abbreviations in the SABRE fare quote display are interpreted in Table 8-5. In the date columns, months are abbreviated as shown in Table 8-6.

Alternative Fare Quote Entries

The ticketing date may be specified in a fare quote entry, as follows:

FQ14AUGDFWLAX14SEPNLX-AA

The ticketing date is typed before the city pair. In the example above, the ticket will be issued by 14 August, but the client will depart on 14 September.

Table 8-5 Abbreviations in Fare Quote Display.

Abbreviation	Interpretation
ORG	Origin
DST	Destination
TRIP	Direction
CXR	Other carriers offering fares on this route
QTE	Quote date (the first date the fare may be offered)
F/B	Fare basis code
BK	Booking code. The fare application is shown to the right of the booking code, as follows:
	X One-way fare (must be doubled for round-trip fare)
	R Round-trip fare (valid for round-trip travel only)
	O One-way fare only (not valid for round-trip travel)
FARE	Fare amount, including tax where applicable
EFF	Effective date (the first date travel may commence)
EXP	Expiration date (the last date travel may commence)
	* Indicates travel must be completed by that date.
	‡‡ means to consult the applicable fare rule.
TKT	Ticketing date (last date tickets may be issued)
AP	Advance-purchase requirement (days)
	‡‡ means to consult the applicable fare rule.
MIN/MAX	Minimum and maximum stay
RTG	Routing number

Table 8-6 Abbreviations for Months in Date Columns.

JA	January	FE	February	MR	March
AP	April	MY	May	JN	June
JL	July	AU	August	SE	September
OC	October	NO	November	DE	December

Various secondary codes can also be used to obtain an alternative fare quote display. The following are examples of secondary codes used in fare quote entries:

‡Q   Specified fare basis

‡B   Specified booking code

-*J   Joint fares

Specifying a Fare Basis

The secondary code ‡**Q** may be used to specify a fare basis for a fare quote display, as follows:

FQATLLAX9APR-CO‡QVAP7

This example requests the VAP7 fare basis for travel on CO.

Specifying a Booking Code

The secondary code ‡B may be used to specify a booking code or class, as follows:

FQATLIND9APR-DL‡BM

This example requests fares in M class for travel on DL.

Joint Fares

A *joint fare* is a single fare, or throughfare, for a connection involving different carriers. The secondary code -*J is used to request joint fares, as follows:

FQSFOZRH13FEB-*J‡ALL

In this example, the option code ‡ALL is also input, to specify all carriers that offer joint fares. To specify a carrier, input the carrier code, as in the following example:

FQSFOZRH13FEB-*J‡UA

This entry requests joint fares with UA and other carriers. The option code *X* may be input to specify a connecting point, as follows:

FQSFOZRH13FEB-*JXLON‡ALL

This entry requests joint fares offered by all carriers, using LON as the connecting point. The above example will display joint fares for connections from San Francisco to Zurich.

When a joint fare entry is input, a carrier can be specified for each segment of the connection. For example, assume an agent wishes to check whether joint fares are offered by United and Swissair from San Francisco to Zurich. The following entry can be used to determine whether joint fares exist:

FQSFOZRH13FEB-*J1UA2SR

The resulting fares will apply to connections from San Francisco to Zurich, with the passenger connecting from United to Swissair.

Modifying a Fare Quote Display

When a fare quote is displayed, the entry code *FQ** can be used to modify the display. For example, the following entry will change the display to a fare quote for departure on 24 June:

FQ*24JUN

This entry will display fares for the same city pair and carrier as in the existing display, based on the new departure date.

The following entry may be used to request a different fare type:

FQ*EXC

This example will change the fare type in an existing fare quote to excursion/ child fares.

Whereas a fare quote gives fares for a specific airline, a **fare shopper display** gives competitive fares for all carriers, listed from least expensive to most expensive. The entry code **FS** is used to obtain a fare shopper display, as follows:

FORMAT   FS<City pair><Departure date><Fare type>

EXAMPLE   FSATLSLC21JULEX

This example will display excursion fares (*EX*). If the departure date is omitted, fares will be displayed for the current date. If the fare type code is omitted, both normal and excursion fares (*NLX*) will be displayed.

To illustrate, assume a passenger will travel from Atlanta to Salt Lake City. He plans to depart on 21 July and would like the lowest available fare. To display normal and excursion fares offered by all carriers, the following entry may be used:

FSATLSLC21JUL

Because no fare type is specified, normal and excursion fares (*NLX*) will be displayed. SABRE responds as follows:

```
ATLSLC        21JUL                        USD
AA    0/ 0/ 5  DL  4/1/ 9 TW     0/ 2/ 0    UA   0/ 0/ 5
NW    0/ 0/ 3
F/B           O/W      R/T   CXS          EFF    EXP    TKT
QHAP21NR              212.00  NW           21MY   12JL   24MR
VHAP21NR              212.00  NW           21MY   12JL   24MR
KHLE21RT              212.00  TW            -      -      -
KXE21RT               232.00  TW            -      -      -
MHHE70                388.00  AA            -      -     24MR
QHHE70                392.00  AA            -      -     24MR
MRA2X                 412.00  NW            -      -     24MR
QA3           282.00  564.00  DL            -      -      -
YN            353.00  706.00  DL            -      -      -
Y             409.00  818.00  AA TW UA      -      -     24MR
FN            461.00  922.00  DL            -      -      -
F             536.00 1072.00  AA TW UA      -      -     24MR
```

This example is shortened for illustration. An actual fare shopper display would cover several pages of this book. The following entries are used to scroll the display:

MD   move down

MU   move up

MT   move to the top

MB   move to the bottom

The top of the display is the first character of the first line. The bottom of the display is the last character of the last line.

The first header line shows the city pair, departure date, and currency. The next two lines show the number of nonstop, direct, and connecting flights operated by each carrier. For example, AA does not operate any nonstop or direct flights, but operates five connections. Delta operates four nonstop flights, one direct flight, and nine connections. (See Figure 8-4.)

Note that the lines in the fare shopper display are not numbered. The fare basis code appears first in each listing. The one-way (*O/W*) and round-trip (*R/T*) fare is given for each fare basis. If a one-way fare is not shown, the fare is valid only for round-trip travel. The carrier codes in the *CXS* column indicate the airlines that offer each fare basis and fare.

In Figure 8-5, the QHAP21NR fare basis offered by Northwest is not valid for one-way travel. Thus, only a round-trip fare is displayed. The remaining columns of the fare shopper display show the effective date (*EFF*), expiration date (*EXP*), and last ticketing date (*TKT*).

In this example, the QHEP21NR fare basis is effective on 21 May and expires on 12 July. To obtain this fare, the ticket must be purchased by 24 March.

Displaying a Fare Quote From Availability

The entry code *FQL* can be used to obtain a fare quote from a city pair availability display, as follows:

FORMAT   FQL<Line><Fare type>

EXAMPLE   FQL3NLX

This example will display a fare quote for the carrier in line 3 of an existing availability display. The fare type code *NLX* requests normal and excursion fares. If the fare type is omitted, only normal adult fares will be displayed.

To illustrate, assume a client inquires about availability and fares from Atlanta to Denver for travel on 21 April, departing around 8 A.M. The following entry may be used to display availability:

121APRATLDEN8A

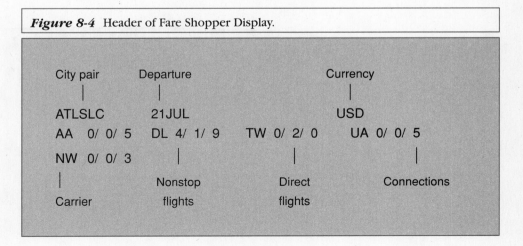

Figure 8-4 Header of Fare Shopper Display.

Figure 8-5 Sample Fare Shopper Fare Basis Display.

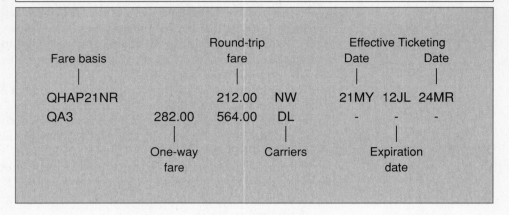

SABRE responds as follows:

```
21APR  TUE    ATL/EST   DEN/MST-2
1 DL 587 F4 Y4 Q4 M4 V4 ATLDEN 7   900A  1010A  767  B  0   TA
2 UA 255 F4 Y4 B4 M4 Q4 ATLDEN 8   910A  1010A  727  B  0   TA
3 CO1247 F4 Y4 Q4 B4 H4 ATLDEN 6   955A  1111A  72S  S  0   TA
4 DL 705 F4 Y4 Q4 M4 V4 ATLDEN 8  1210P   120P  727  L  0   TA
5 UA 593 F4 Y4 B4 M4 Q4 ATLDEN 7   235P   333P  727  S  0   TA
6 DL 711 F4 Y4 Q4 M4 V4 ATLDEN 7   320P   430P  757  S  0   TA
```

Assume the passenger prefers Continental and requests the lowest excursion fare. The following entry may be used to display a fare quote:

FQL3EX

In this example, Continental is the carrier in line 3. The fare type code *EX* is input to display excursion fares.

SABRE responds as follows:

```
ORG-ATL  DST-ENW  TRIP-OUTBOUND  CXR-CO     13JUL             USD
AA DL NW UA
      QTE  F/B      BK  FARE      EFF   EXP  TKT   AP  MIN/MAX  RTG
01     -   F        F X 669.00    -     -    -     -   -/-      2
02     -   Y        Y X 477.00    -     -    -     -   -/-      2
03     -   Y3       Y X 419.00    -    31AU  -     -   -/-      2
04     -   QE30     Q R 549.00    -    31AU  -     3   SUN/7    2
05     -   BE70     B R 498.00    -    31AU  -     7   SUN/14   2
06     -   HLE21NR  H R 429.00    -     -    -    21   SUN/30   2
       2  CHI CLE DSM IND LIT MSP OKC TUL
```

The example display is shortened, for the purposes of illustration.

To obtain a fare quote from an availability display, the agent must make the fare quote entry within 30 minutes after displaying availability.

International Fare Quotes

Besides fares for domestic travel, SABRE can also quote international fares for travel originating in the United States, Canada, Mexico, or the Caribbean. Many international fares are joint fares offered by a U.S. airline and a foreign carrier. For example, as of this writing, joint fares are available from Seattle to Amsterdam on Northwest and KLM. The passenger would travel on Northwest from Seattle to Minneapolis and then transfer to a KLM flight to Amsterdam. Instead of purchasing separate tickets for each portion of the trip, the passenger would pay a single joint fare for the entire itinerary.

When an international fare quote is requested, city codes should be used, rather than airport codes. If the origin or destination is a foreign point, joint fares will be included in the display.

The format for international fares is exactly the same as the format for domestic fares. As an example, assume a client will travel from Los Angeles to Tokyo on 12 August and prefers Japan Airlines. The agent uses the following entry to display a fare quote:

FQLAXTYO12AUG-JL

SABRE responds as follows:

```
ORG-LAX  DST-TYO      TRIP-OUTBOUND        CXR-JL    12AUG  USD
**  AA CI CP  KE NW POR RS SQ TG TW UA
TAX NOT INC  IN  TTL- ITT/OTHER TAXES  MAY   APPLY
  QTE    F/B        BK    FARE    EFF   EXP  TKT  AP  MIN/MAX  RTG
  01    - F         P X   1370.00  -     -    -    -    -/-     1
  02    - Y         C X    689.00  -     -    -    -    -/-     1
  03    - Y02       C X    410.00  -     -    -    -    -/-     1
   1 MPM - 6000
```

Because a fare type was not specified, only normal adult fares are displayed. The international fare quote includes some additional information not displayed in a domestic fare quote. Note the third header line, indicating that tax is not included in the total fare but that international transportation tax and other taxes may be assessed. Passengers who depart from the United States to a foreign point are required to pay an **international transportation tax** of $6. However, neither this tax nor passenger facility charges (PFCs) are included in the fare quote display.

In a domestic fare quote, U.S. transportation tax is included in all fares. As of this writing, the domestic tax is 10 percent of the base fare. For example, a total fare of $352 includes a base fare of $320 and a tax of $32. However, U.S. transportation tax does not apply to international travel and is, therefore, not included in an international fare quote.

Note the routing at the bottom of the display. The abbreviation *MPM* refers to the maximum permitted mileage. International fares may be based either on mileage or on routing. If a fare is based on mileage, the passenger may be routed via any intermediate points between the origin and destination, as long as the maximum permitted mileage is not exceeded. If the fare is based on routing, only the specified intermediate points may be used.

In this example, the maximum permitted mileage between Los Angeles and Tokyo is 6,000 miles.

Fare Rules

The booking code, valid dates, and restrictions that pertain to a particular fare basis are set forth in the fare rules. When a fare quote is displayed, the entry code **RD** may be used to obtain a rules display, as follows:

FORMAT   RD<Line Number>

EXAMPLE   RD5

This example will display the rules for the fare basis in line 5 of a displayed fare quote.

To illustrate, assume the following partial fare quote is displayed:

ORGGSO		DST-LAX	TRIP-OUTBOUND		CXR-UA			24OCT	USD	
AA CO DL NW										
	QTE	F/B	BK	FARE	EFF	EXP	TKT	AP	MIN/MAX	RTG
01	-	F	F X	830.00	-	-	-	-	-/-	96
02	23MR	Y	Y X	469.00	-	-	-	-	-/-	96
03	-	QXE3P25	B R	508.00	-	-	-	2	SUN/-	96
04	-	MXE7P50	B R	462.00	-	-	-	2	SUN/-	96
05	-	VXE7NR	B R	448.00	-	-	-	2	SUN/-	96
06	-	BXE21NR	B R	389.00	-	-	-	2	SUN/-	96

Let us say the client inquires about the fare in line 6. To obtain a rules display for this fare basis, the following entry may be used:

RD6

SABRE responds as follows:

```
ORIGIN-GSO DST-LAX     CXR-UA     TRVL DATE - 24OCT
RULES FOR FARE BASIS-BXE21NR          RT   FARE   RULE   4165 - ATP
FEE ON CHG/REFUND
01 BK CODE     -B-
02 PENALTY     -NONCHANGEABLE/NONREFUNDABLE. 100 PERCENT
               PENALTY APPLIES FOR CHANGES/CANCELLATION OF TKTD
               ITINERARIES
03RES/TKTG     -RES MUST BE MADE NO LATER THAN 21 DAYS BEFORE
               DPTR FROM ORIGIN. TKT MUST BE PURCHASED NO LATER THAN
               21 DAYS BEFORE DPTR FROM ORIGIN OR 1 DAY AFTER RES IS
               MADE, WHICHEVER COMES FIRST.
04 MIN STAY    -RETURN TRVL IS VALID ON THE 1ST SUN AFTER
               12:01 A.M. MEASURED FROM DPTR FROM ORIGIN TO DPTR FROM
               LAST STOPOVER POINT.
05 MAX STAY    -RETURN TRVL MUST COMMENCE NO LATER THAN 30
               DAYS MEASURED FROM DPTR FROM ORIGIN TO DPTR FROM
               LAST STOPOVER POINT.
06 DAY/TIME    -TRVL IS VALID FROM 12:00 N MON THRU 12:00 N
               THU
```

The first header line shows the origin, destination, carrier, and travel date. The second line gives the fare basis and indicates that it is a round-trip fare. The rule reference number is also shown. The third header line indicates that a fee applies if a change or refund is made after the ticket is issued.

The rules display consists of several categories. Note that each category has an item number and a heading. Each heading is followed by an explanation of the rule. In this example, category 01 indicates the booking code. To obtain this fare basis, the itinerary must be booked in B class.

Penalty information is given in category 02. In this example, a 100 percent penalty is assessed for change or cancellation of any portion of the itinerary after ticketing.

The advance purchase requirement is indicated in category 03, which governs reservations and ticketing. In this example, the reservation must be made and ticketed at least 21 days before departure. Once a reservation has been made, the ticket must be purchased within one day.

The minimum and maximum stay are indicated in categories 04 and 05, respectively. In this example, the passenger is prohibited from returning until the first Sunday after the departure date. In other words, a Saturday stayover is required. The maximum stay is 30 days.

Category 06 indicates the day/time restriction. The fare basis in the example is valid only for midweek departures. The first flight in the itinerary must depart between noon Monday and noon Thursday.

Scrolling the Rules Display

If the rules display has too many lines to display at one time, the entries *MU, MD, MT,* and *MB* can be used to scroll the display. For example, just as in a fare quote display, the entry **MD** is used to "move down," as follows:

MD

SABRE displays the next screen of the rules display, as follows:

```
12 TKT/ISSUE    -PTA ALLOWED BUT DOES NOT SATISFY TKTG
                 REQUIREMENTS.
17 COMBINE      -CIRCLE/ONE JAW TRIPS ARE PERMITTED.  OPEN JAW
                 IS VALID IF THE MILEAGE BTWN THE OPEN JAW POINTS IS
                 EQUAL TO/LESS THAN THE MILEAGE OF THE SHORTEST FLOWN
                 SGMT.
18 OPEN RTN     -TICKETS MAY NOT BE ISSUED WITH OPEN RETURN.
19 REFUNDS      -SVC CHARGE MAY APPLY-SEE PENALTY.
22 CO-TERM      -THE FOLLOWING GROUPS OF CITIES ARE CONSIDERED
                 TO BE THE SAME POINT. WAS - BWI. MIA -  FLL. NYC -
                 EWR. LAX -  ONT -  BUR  -  SNA. SFO  -  OAK  -  SJC.
```

To redisplay the previous screen, the following entry may be used:

MU

This entry commands SABRE to "move up."

Fare Rules Categories

The categories in a rules display may vary, depending on the fare basis and carrier. However, a specific category always has the same item number and heading. Any of the categories in Table 8-6 may appear in a rules display.

Table 8-6 Categories in a Rules Display.

Number and Heading	Category
01 BK CODE	Booking code (used to book the fare)
02 PENALTY	Cancellation or rebooking penalty
03 RES/TKT	Reservation and ticketing data requirements
04 MIN STAY	Minimum stay requirements
05 MAX STAY	Maximum stay requirements
06 DAY/TIME	Valid days of the week and departure times
07 SEASON	Season for which fare is valid
08 BLACKOUTS	Dates on which fare is not valid
09 EFF/EXP	Effective date/Expiration date
10 FLT APPL	Valid flights
11 STOPOVERS	Stopovers allowed
12 TKT/ISSUE	Type of ticketing permitted
13 SURCHGS	Surcharges that may be applied
14 DISCOUNTS	Discounts that may be applied
15 REROUTE	Rules governing changes in routing
16 TRANSFERS	Rules governing ticket transfers
17 COMBINE	Rules governing combined fares
18 OPEN RTN	Rules governing open return segments
19 REFUNDS	Rules governing refunds
20 STANDBY	Rules governing standby travel
21 SPCL PROV	Special provisions
22 CO-TERM	Other points which may be substituted
23 INTL CONST	International fare construction rules
24 MISC	Miscellaneous rules and restrictions

Displaying a Rules Menu

The secondary code *M can be used to display a menu of rule categories. When the menu is displayed, categories can be selected by item number. To illustrate, assume the following partial fare quote is displayed:

```
ORG-ANC    DST-SFO   TRIP-OUTBOUND    CXRS-AS   12JUL   USD
UA  NW
    QTE F/B    BK  FARE    EFF  EXP  TKT   AP  MIN/MAX RTG
01   -  Y      Y X 252.00   -    -    -    -    -/-     2
02   -  BE3    B R 224.00   -    -    -    3    -/-     2
03   -  QE14   Q R 196.00   -    -    -   14    -/-     2
04   -  ME14   M R 196.00   -    -    -   14    -/-     2
05   -  VE21   V R 182.00   -    -    -   21    -/-     2
     2 PDX SEA RNO
```

Assume the client inquires about the BE3 fare basis. The following entry is used to display a rules menu:

RD2*M

The *BE3* fare basis is in line 2 of the fare quote. The secondary code *M* will display a rules menu, as follows:

```
                          RULES MENU
    01 BK CODE      02 PENALTY      03 RES/TKTG     04 MIN STAY
    05 MAX STAY     06 DAY/TIME     07 SEASON       08 BLACKOUTS
    09 EFF/EXP      10 FLT APPL     11 STOPOVERS    12 TKT ISSUE
    13 SURCHGS      14 DISCOUNTS    15 REROUTE      16 TRANSFERS
    17 COMBINE      18 OPEN RTN     19 REFUNDS      20 STANDBY
    21 SPCL PROV    22 CO-TERM      23 INTL CONST   24 MISC
```

Each category in the rules menu has an item number. The entry code *RD** is used to display a category from the menu. For example, assume you want to check the effective and expiration dates. The following entry may be used to display the category:

RD*9

In the rules menu, the category pertaining to effective and expiration dates is item 9.

One or more categories may apply to a particular fare basis. However, a given category always has the same item number, no matter how many categories are displayed.

Displaying Fare Rules Without a Fare Quote

The following format is used to display fare rules without a fare quote:

FORMAT   RD<City pair><Departure date><Fare basis>-<Carrier>

EXAMPLE   RDSFOBOS10MAYQAP7-TW

This example will display the rules for the QAP7 fare basis for travel on TWA from SFO to BOS on 10 May.

The secondary code *M* can be used to display the rules menu, as follows:

RDORDSEA22JUNVLE70NR-DL*M

The fare level is indicated by the class of service. On domestic airlines, the two basic classes are first class and coach. Various discounted coach fares, called restricted or inventory fares, are also offered. A fare basis is a price category determined by the class of service and such factors as destination, season, day of the week, one-way or round-trip travel, advance purchase, and length of stay. Each fare basis has a primary code and one or more secondary codes.

A fare quote is a display of fares for a specified carrier, listed from most expensive to least expensive. The entry code *FQ* is used to obtain fare quotes. A ticketing date, booking code, or fare basis may be specified when a fare quote is requested. The entry code *FQL* can be used to obtain a fare quote from a city pair availability display. Whereas a fare quote gives fares for a specific airline, a fare shopper display gives competitive fares for all carriers, listed from least expensive to most expensive. The entry code *FS* is used to obtain a fare shopper display.

The booking code, valid dates, and restrictions that pertain to a particular fare basis are set forth in the fare rules. When a fare quote is displayed, the entry code *RD* may be used to obtain a rules display. The secondary code **M* can be used to display a menu of rule categories.

New commands included in this chapter:

FQSFOMIA13JUL-CO	Displays a fare quote by carrier
FQLAXDFW13JULEX-DL	Displays a fare quote by fare category and carrier
FQ14AUGDFWLAX14SEPNLX-AA	Displays a fare quote by ticketing date, fare category, and carrier
FQATLLAX9APR-CO‡QVAP7	Displays a fare quote by carrier and fare basis
FQATLIND9APR-DL‡BV	Displays a fare quote by carrier and booking code
FQSFOZRH13FEB-*J‡ALL	Displays joint fares
FQSFOZRH13FEB-*J1UA2SR	Displays joint fares by specified carriers
FQ*24JUN	Changes the date of a fare quote
FQ*EXC	Changes the fare category
FSATLSLC21JULEX	Displays competitive fares from lowest to highest for all carriers
FQL3NLX	Displays a fare quote from an availability display
RD5	Displays fare rules from a fare quote
RD2*M	Displays a menu of fare rules
RDORDSEA8AUGVA7NR-DL*M	Displays fare rules menu without a fare quote

KEY CONCEPTS AND TERMS

Identify the word, phrase, or symbol for each of the following concepts:

1. Fares that apply to travel between points in the United States, Canada, Mexico, the Caribbean, and Bermuda.

2. Fares that apply when the origin or destination point is outside the United States, Canada, Mexico, the Caribbean, and Bermuda.

3. A code indicating the overall fare level for air travel.

4. Discounted coach fares subject to restrictions.

5. A price category determined by the class of service and factors such as destination, season, day of the week, one-way or round-trip travel, advance purchase, and length of stay.

6. Text that describes the booking code, the valid dates for travel or ticketing, and any restrictions that apply to a particular fare basis.

7. Rules requiring the ticket to be purchased a set number of days prior to departure.

8. Rules requiring the ticket to be purchased within a predefined period of time after the reservation is made, or by a specified date.

9. Rules determining whether a particular booking code or fare basis can be combined with other booking codes or fare bases.

10. Restricted discount fares requiring round-trip travel.

11. A display of fares for a specified carrier, listed from most expensive to least expensive.

12. The entry code that is used to display a fare quote.

13. The secondary code that is used to specify a fare basis for a fare quote display.

14. The secondary code that is used to specify a booking code or class.

15. The secondary code that is used to request joint fares.

16. A display of competitive fares for all carriers, listed from least expensive to most expensive.

17. The entry code that is used to display competitive fares for all carriers.

18. The entry code that is used to obtain a fare quote from a city pair availability display.

19. A tax imposed on passengers who depart from the United States to a foreign point.

20. The entry code that is used to display fare rules.

21. The entry to scroll down a fare quote display or a rules display.

22. The entry to scroll up.

23. In a rules display entry, the secondary code used to display a menu of rule categories.

Answers:

1. domestic fares; 2. international fares; 3. class of service; 4. restricted or inventory fares; 5. fare basis; 6. fare rules; 7. advance-purchase rules; 8. ticketing rules; 9. combinability rules; 10. excursion fares; 11. fare quote; 12. FQ; 13. ‡Q; 14. ‡B; 15. *J; 16. fare shopper display; 17. FS; 18. FQL; 19. international transportation tax; 20. RD; 21. MD; 22. MU; 23. *M.

REVIEW QUESTIONS

Write the correct entry for each of the following fare requests.

1. A client requests adult excursion fares for travel from ATL to LAX on 13 June. He prefers CO.

2. A client would like to know normal and excursion fares for travel on 15 October from MSP to SEA on any airline.

3. A client will travel from PHL to STL on 5 May and would like an excursion fare for himself and his 5-year-old son. He prefers TWA.

4. A passenger will travel from SLC to BOI on 10 April. He would like a military fare on TWA.

5. An adult will travel with her 3-year-old daughter from BTR to LAS on 24 March. She would like the lowest fare on any airline.

6. An adult will travel from LAX to ICT on 2 April. She would like an excursion fare on United.

7. A client requests excursion adult fares on CO from SAN to HNL, for travel on 21 September.

8. A client requests excursion fares on any airline for travel on 3 June from GSO to MCO.

9. A client will travel on 23 May from DEN to BNA and would like the YJE1 fare basis on CO.

10. A client requests the least expensive fare on AA. She will travel on 31 March from DFW to ANC.

Refer to the following fare display to answer questions 11 through 15:

```
FQSYDLAX12JANNLX-QF
ORG-SYD DST-LAX TRIP-OUTBOUND CXR-QF 13JUL  AUD
AA CO CP NZ NZ UA UT
```

QTE	F/B	BK	FARE	EFF	EXP	TKT	AP	MIN/MAX	RTG
01 -	P	P X	3670.58	-	-	-	-	-/ -	4001
02 -	Y	Y X	2043.27	-	-	-	-	-/ -	4001
03 -	YHE	Y R	1423.60	-	-	-	14	-/ -	4001
04 -	TK200	T R	1552.67	-	-	-	++	7/6M	4001
05 -	J	J X	2509.77	-	-	-	-	-/ -	4001
06 -	J2	J X	1949.97	-	-	-	-	-/ -	4001

```
 4001 MPM-  8997   PA-  VIA THE PACIFIC
```

11. What fare category is displayed?

12. What carrier's fares are displayed?

13. What is the fare basis for the 1423.60 return-trip fare?

14. What is the advance purchase requirement for the fare in question 13?

15. What entry would display the rules for the TK200 fare?

Write the correct entry for each of the following fare requests:

16. A client requests adult excursion fares for travel from PHX to BOS on 13 June. He prefers TWA.

17. Mrs. Smythe would like to know normal and excursion fares for travel on 15 October from ORD to MIA on any airline.

18. Mr. Jackson will travel from LAX to ATL on 5 May and would like an excursion fare for himself and his 5-year-old son. He prefers United.

19. Capt. Meyers will travel from CSP to PHX on 10 April. He would like a military fare on Continental.

20. Mrs. Farnhurst will accompany her 7-year-old son from SAN to PHL on 24 March. She prefers HP.

21. A client requests excursion adult fares on TWA from Newark to Kansas City, for travel on 21 September.

22. Mr. Ware will travel on 23 May from PHX to HVN and would like the QLEX7 fare basis advertised by TWA.

23. Mrs. Thompson inquires about normal and excursion fares offered by all airlines for travel on 31 March from SFO to DEN.

24. Write the entry to display a menu of fare rules for the fare basis in line 7 of a fare quote.

25. Ticket issuance is item 12 of the rules menu. Write the entry to display this rule.

APPLICATIONS

Read the following scenario, and decide what actions should be performed to satisfy the client's preferences and needs. Briefly describe how you would handle the situation, and then write the required entries.

Mr. and Mrs. Harrison would like to travel from Des Moines to Las Vegas on 21 March, departing around 8 A.M. They would like the least expensive excursion fare on Continental. When you obtain a fare quote, they inquire about fares offered by other carriers. According to the display, United offers fares for the same city pair. In the United fare quote, the lowest fare displayed is the VA21NR fare in line 1. Your clients inquire about the restrictions for this fare.

Your clients would like to book the reservation in the appropriate class to obtain the lowest fare on United. When you display availability, the first six flights are sold out in the requested class, but in the next display a United flight in line 3 has seats available at the desired fare. The passengers will return on 26 March, leaving around 9 A.M. When you display availability, a United flight in line 5 has seats available in the desired class. The passengers' first names are Frank and Tina. Your agency phone is 515-555-5000. Mr. Harrison's business phone is 515-555-5210, and the clients' home phone is 305-555-3656. Mr. Harrison requested the reservation.

Chapter 9

Itinerary Pricing

Outline

The Pricing Function

Forcing a Connection

Specifying a Future Ticketing Date

Specifying a Fare Basis

The Bargain Finder Entry

Future Pricing

Chapter Objectives

After you complete this chapter, you should be able to:

1. Determine the total ticket price for a booked air itinerary.

2. Use secondary codes to override the passenger type, booking code, fare basis, or ticketing date.

3. Store price information in the PNR.

PROBLEM

A PNR for two passengers has an itinerary with six air segments, including a three-segment connection. Four segments are booked in V class, and four are booked in M class. The client would like to know the total fare for both passengers.

SABRE SOLUTION

Use the itinerary pricing function to compute the total fare.

In this chapter, you will learn how to price a complete itinerary or selected segments, passengers, or passenger types.

The **itinerary pricing** function is used to determine the total ticket price for an itinerary. The **ticket price** is the total fare, including tax, for all segments. When an itinerary is priced, any rules, such as an advance purchase requirement, or fare applications, such as a throughfare for a connecting flight, are applied. SABRE can be used to price most domestic itineraries, as well as many international itineraries.

The entry code **WP** is used to price a displayed itinerary for all passengers in the PNR. A secondary code may be input to obtain an alternative price. However, let us first examine what happens when the entry WP is used by itself to price an itinerary.

Assume the following PNR is in the agent work area:

```
1.1JEFFERSON/T MR        2.1ADAMS/J MR
1 TW  94V  06APR  M  ABQSTL  SS2 1000A     108P
2 TW 105V  10APR  F  STLABQ  SS2 620P      753P
TKT/TIME LIMIT -
1.TAW4MAR/
PHONES -
1.ABQ808-822-6154-A    MARTHA
2.ABQ808-643-0097-B
RECEIVED FROM - MR JEFFERSON
```

Assume that Mr. Jefferson would like to know the total price for both passengers. The following entry may be used to price the itinerary:

```
WP
```

SABRE responds as follows:

```
06APR  DEPARTURE DATE-LAST DAY TO PURCHASE  16MAR
  2-   160.00        16.00        176.00  VE21NR
       320.00        32.00        352.00  TTL
2-ADT
6APR ABQ TW STL80.00VE21NR TW ABQ80.00VE21NR 160.00  END
FEE ON CHG/REFUND
```

In the first line, SABRE indicates the last date on which tickets may be purchased to obtain the fare. In this example, the passengers will depart on 6 April, but to obtain the indicated price, they must purchase their tickets by 16 March.

In the next line, SABRE indicates the number of passengers that have been priced, followed by the base fare, tax, and total fare for each passenger. (See Figure 9-1.) The fare basis is shown to the right of the total fare. U.S. transportation tax applies to domestic itineraries.

In this example, the base fare for each passenger is $160, and the transportation tax is $16. Thus, the total fare for each passenger is $176 for the VE21NR fare basis.

The second line of the price display gives the total base fare, total tax, and total fare for all the passengers priced.

Figure 9-1 First Line of Price Display.

Number of passengers

Tax

Total fare per passenger

2- 160.00   16.00   176.00   VE21NR

Base fare

Fare basis

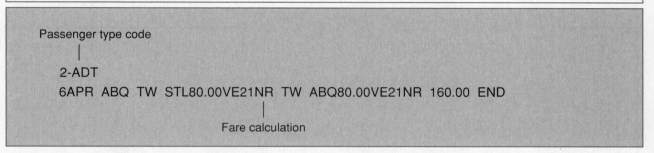

Figure 9-2 Passenger Type Code.

Passenger type code

2-ADT
6APR ABQ TW STL80.00VE21NR TW ABQ80.00VE21NR 160.00 END

Fare calculation

Below the price, SABRE shows a number followed by a **passenger type code (PTC)**. (See Figure 9-2.) This information represents the number of passengers priced at each PTC. A PTC indicates whether a passenger is an adult, a child, a military passenger, a senior citizen, or an adult standby passenger. In this example, the code *ADT* indicates that two passengers were priced at the adult fare. More will be said about passenger type codes later in this chapter.

The **fare calculation** line itemizes the base fare by segment and carrier. When the tickets are issued, this information will be printed in the fare calculation box on each ticket. Taxes are not included in the fare calculation.

The first item in the fare calculation is the departure date from the origin point. In this example, the passengers will depart on 6 April. The carrier for each flight segment is shown between the departure and arrival points. The base fare and fare basis code for each passenger are shown after the arrival point. In this example, TW is the carrier between ABQ and STL. The base fare for this segment is $80, and the fare basis is VE21NR. TW is also the carrier for the next segment, which terminates at ABQ. The base fare and fare basis are $80 and VE21NR, respectively, the same as for the first segment. The total base fare for each passenger is shown at the end of the fare calculation line. The last line of the display indicates that a fee will be assessed for cancellation or change after ticketing.

SABRE can price itineraries with up to 99 passengers in the name field and up to 24 air segments. When an itinerary is priced, SABRE attempts to determine whether an excursion fare may be used for any segment.

Passenger Type Codes

A passenger type code (PTC) may be input in a pricing entry to specify an alternative fare type. For example, the code *CHD* may be input to specify child fares. Children from two to 12 years of age may qualify for a discounted fare on some carriers. However, not all carriers offer child fares, and in many cases, adult excursion fares are priced lower than child fares.

Other PTCs may be used to price an itinerary for military passengers (*MIL*), senior citizens (*SCR*), and adult stand-by passengers (*ASB*). The PTCs used in itinerary pricing entries are listed in Table 9-1.

Itineraries cannot be priced for every PTC. Some domestic carriers no longer offer child, military, or senior citizen fares.

When a PTC is input in a pricing entry, SABRE calculates the price based on the appropriate fare type. For example, if *CHD* is input, the itinerary will be priced using child fares, if available.

To specify a passenger type, the secondary code **P** must be typed before the PTC, as follows:

WPPSCR

This example requests a price based on senior citizen fares.

CLIENT FOCUS

Pricing with Passenger Type Codes

To price a party using both adult and child fares, the appropriate PTC must be input for each member of the party. To illustrate, assume a PNR has the following name field and itinerary:

```
1.4TRAVIS/C MR/L MRS/C MSTR/A MISS
1   TW   582Y   09JAN   F   STLMIA   SS4   940A   113P
2   TW   499Y   19JAN   S   MIASTL   SS4   315P   456P
```

Assume Master C. Travis and Miss A. Travis qualify for a discounted child fare. However, Mr. and Mrs. Travis should be priced at the adult fare. In this case, the agent must price two passengers using adult fares and two passengers using child fares, as follows:

WPP2ADT/2CHD

If a PTC is omitted, only adult fares will be used to price the itinerary. The code *CHD* may be combined only with *ADT* or *ITB*. No other combinations are permitted.

If one passenger is to be priced at a specified PTC, the number *1* may be omitted, as follows:

WPPADT/CHD

In this example, one passenger will be priced using adult fares, and one will be priced using child fares. Both of the examples above assume that child fares are offered by the carrier.

Table 9-1 Passenger Type Codes (PTCs).

Code	Interpretation
ADT	Adult
ASB	Adult standby
CHD	Child (2-11)
C09	Child (including age)
CMP	Companion
CLG	Clergy
CSB	Clergy standby
CVN	Convention
FFY	Frequent flyer
FDT	Family plan adult
ACC	Family plan accompanying adult
F10	Family plan child (including age)
GTR	Government transportation
GCF	Government contract
MDP	Military dependent
MIL	Military
MLD	Military stationed in U.S.
SCB	Senior citizen standby
SCR	Senior citizen
STU	Student
ITB	Individual inclusive tour basing
ITC	Child's tour basing
YSB	Youth standby
YTH	Youth
ARP	American Association of Retired Persons

Pricing Selected Segments

The secondary code **S** is used to price selected segments of a displayed itinerary, as follows:

WPS3/4

This example will price only segments 3 and 4. No other segments will be priced. To illustrate, assume a PNR has the following itinerary:

```
1 AA 3489Y   11NOV   W   EWRBWI   SS2   800A  900A
2 AA  433Y   13NOV   F   BWIBNA   SS2   827A  915A
3 AA  941Y   17NOV   T   BNAMCO   SS2   945A 1223P
4 DL  344Y   22NOV   S   MCOLGA   SS2  1200N  214P
```

Assume the client requests the price of the Delta flight from Orlando to New York. The following entry will price only the requested segment:

WPS4

SABRE responds as follows:

```
      2-   280.00    28.00   308.00  Y
           560.00    56.00   616.00  TTL
   2-ADT
   22NOV  MCO  DL  NYC280.00Y  280.00  END
```

If a PNR contains two segments with the same routing, one segment must be selected when the itinerary is priced. For example, assume a PNR has the following itinerary:

```
1 UA   183Y   05JUL   M   PDXHNL   LL1   915A   205P
2 UA   183C   05JUL   M   PDXHNL   SS1   915A   205P
3 UA   184Y   19JUL   M   HNLPDX   SS1   945A   ‡824A
```

In this example, two segments are booked for the outbound trip from Portland to Honolulu. The client desired space in Y class on UA 183, but the flight was sold out in Y class. Thus, the passenger was waitlisted in Y class and confirmed in C class on the same flight. To price the itinerary, the agent must select one of the segments from PDX to HNL. The following entry will price only the Y class segments:

WPS1/3

The Y class segments are segments 1 and 3. SABRE responds as follows:

```
      1-       440.00    44.00   484.00  Y
               440.00    44.00   484.00  TTL
   1-ADT
   05JUL  PDX  UA HNL220.00Y  UA HNL220.00Y     440.00 END
```

Pricing Selected Passengers

The secondary code **N** is used to price an itinerary for selected passengers in a PNR, as follows:

WPN1.1

This example will price only the first passenger in name item 1.

Pricing Selected Passengers

Assume a PNR has the following name field and itinerary:

```
1.2KNUTZ/R MR/L MRS       2.2BOLTZ/E MR/F MRS
1   AA   622Y   01JUN   S   LAXDFW   SS4   722A   1202P
2   AA   333Y   15JUN   S   DFWLAX   SS4   1107A   1205P
```

Let us say Mrs. Boltz requests the price of her ticket only. The following entry may be used to price the itinerary for the selected passenger:

WPN2.2

Now assume the client requests the price for both Mrs. Knutz and Mrs. Boltz. The following entry may be used to price the itinerary for the selected passengers:

WPN1.2/2.2

Note that a slash is typed to separate the name references. The secondary code N is typed only before the first name reference.

Forcing a Connection

[handwritten margin note: Make the entry to Price this itinerary using a through-fare]

When an itinerary includes a valid connection with a connecting time of four hours or less, the itinerary is priced based on the throughfare. However, in rare instances, a connection has connecting time of more than four hours. In such cases, SABRE will price each leg of the connection as a separate flight. To force SABRE to use a throughfare, the secondary code **X,** may be used, as follows:

WPX2

In this example, segment 2 will be priced as a connecting flight. To illustrate, assume a PNR has the following itinerary:

```
1  AA   265Y   31MAY   S   DTWORD   SS2   700A   758A
2  AA   73Y    31MAY   S   ORDOGG   SS2   1130A  440P
3  AA   72Y    10JUN   W   OGGDTW   SS2   338P   ‡845A
```

In this example, the passengers will depart on AA 265 from Detroit and connect at Chicago-O'Hare to AA 73 to Kahului. However, the connecting time in Chicago exceeds four hours. To price the itinerary using a throughfare from DTW to OGG, the following entry may be used:

WPX1

In this example, segment 1 will be priced as a connecting flight. SABRE responds as follows:

```
   2-    540.00  54.00   594.00   Y
        1080.00 108.00  1188.00   TTL
2-ADT
31MAY DTT   AA  X/CHI AA OGG260.00Y AA DTT280.00Y
540.00 END
```

Look closely at the fare calculation line. Only city codes are used. The *X/* before the arrival point of the first segment indicates that Chicago is a connecting point. In this case, the throughfare and fare basis are shown after the destination point, OGG.

Specifying a Future Ticketing Date

A future ticketing date may be specified in a pricing entry to take advantage of an anticipated fare change. The secondary code **B** is used to indicate a future ticketing date, as follows:

WPB18SEP

In this example, the itinerary will be priced based on a ticketing date of 18 September.

Assume a PNR has the following itinerary:

```
1   AA   492Y   14APR   T   EWRDFW   SS1   742A   1014A
1   AA   240Y   18MAY   S   DFWEWR   SS1   755P   1138P
```

Assume a fare change will occur on 2 March. To price an itinerary for ticketing on 27 March, the following entry may be used:

WPB27MAR

This entry will price the itinerary using the fares that are valid for ticketing on 27 March.

Specifying a Fare Basis

The secondary code **Q** is used to specify a fare basis, as follows:

WPQVAP21

This example will price a displayed itinerary using the VAP21 fare basis. Assume a PNR has the following itinerary:

```
1   UA   411V   08APR   W   CLTDEN   SS2   700P   825P
2   UA   356V   12JUN   S   DENCLT   SS2   1120A  410P
```

The passengers in this example are booked in V class. The following entry may be used to price the itinerary at the ME70 fare basis:

    WPQME70

This entry will price both segments at the specified fare basis. If desired, a selected segment can be priced at a specified fare basis, as follows:

    WPS1*QME70

This entry will price only segment 1 at the ME70 fare basis. An asterisk is typed after the segment, and the secondary code Q is typed before the fare basis code.

Multiple segments can be priced using different fare basis codes. For instance, the following entry will price segment 1 at the ME70 fare basis and segment 2 at the KAP7 fare basis:

    WPS1*QME70‡S2*QKAP7

Observe that a cross (‡) is typed to separate the first segment and fare basis from the second segment and fare basis. The secondary code Q is typed before each fare basis.

Pricing an itinerary at a specified fare basis is referred to as *command pricing* or *phase 3.5 pricing*.

The Bargain Finder Entry

The bargain finder entry **WPNC** is used to price an itinerary at the lowest available fare. When this entry is used, SABRE searches for the lowest applicable fare for each segment booked. To illustrate, assume a PNR has the following itinerary:

```
1 AA    67Y   18FEB   M   DTWLAX   SS2    930A 1105A
2 AA    96Y   22FEB   F   LAXDTW   SS2   1200P  700P
```

The bargain finder entry may be used to obtain the lowest available price, as follows:

    WPNC

SABRE responds as follows:

```
18FEB  DEPARTURE DATE--LAST DAY  TO PURCHASE  4FEB
    2-   203.70    16.30   220.00 VAP14
         407.40    32.60   440.00 TTL
2-ADT
18FEB  DTW AA  LAX101.85VAP14  AA DTW101.85VAP14
203.70 END
CHANGE BOOKING CLASS - 1V 2V
```

In this case, a lower fare was located for both segments, based on the VAP14 fare basis. At the bottom of the display, SABRE indicates the segments to rebook and the booking code to use for each segment. In this example, segments 1 and 2 should be changed to V class to obtain the lowest available fare for each segment.

Changing the Class

The entry code **WC** may be used to change the class of service after a WPNC entry has been input. For example, to change segment 1 to V class, the following entry may be used:

WC1V

Multiple segments can be changed in the same entry, as follows:

WC1V/2V

A slash is typed to separate the first segment and class from the second segment and class.

A variation of the bargain finder entry, *WPNCB*, can be used to obtain the lowest price and, at the same time, rebook the applicable segments in the appropriate class.

For example, assume a PNR has the following itinerary:

```
1   AA   840Y   10FEB   T   DFWTPA   SS2   100P   359P
2   AA   229Y   16FEB   M   TPADFW   SS2   141P   302P
```

The following entry may be used to price and rebook the itinerary at the lowest fare for each segment:

WPNCB

SABRE responds as follows:

```
10FEB  DEPARTURE DATE--LAST DAY TO PURCHASE 27JAN
    2-  200.00    20.00  220.00  QHE70
        400.00    40.00  440.00  TTL
2-ADT
10FEB  DFW AA TPA100.00QHE70   AA DFW100.00QHE70
200.00 END
1 AA  840Q  10FEB  T  DFWTPA    SS2  100P  359P
2 AA  229Q  16FEB  M  TPADFW    SS2  141P  302P
```

In this case, SABRE located a lower fare for each segment and then rebooked the segments in Q class to obtain the fare.

The bargain finder entry may be used with name or segment selection codes, as in the following examples:

WPNCB+S1/3   (Price and rebook segments 1 and 3)
WPNCB+N1.1/1.2   (Price and rebook name items 1.1 and 1.2)

The entry code **FP** is used to store price instructions for ticketing on a future date. Whereas the *WP* entry merely calculates the price, *FP* calculates the price and stores the information in the PNR.

As an example, assume the following itinerary is in the agent work area:

```
1 TW   94Y   08APR  W  ABQSTL   SS2   1000A  108P
2 TW  105Y   12APR  S  STLABQ   SS2    620P  753P
```

The following entry will price the itinerary and store the price instructions for ticketing:

FP

SABRE responds as follows:

```
            2-     230.00    23.00   253.00  Y
                   460.00    46.00   506.00  TTL
2-ADT
8APR  ABQ  TW STL115.00Y TW  ABQ115.00Y 230.00 END
```

The response is the same as for a *WP* entry. However, the price information has been stored in the PNR, in a field called the *ticketing instructions field*. When the tickets are issued, the information in the ticketing instructions field will be used to price the itinerary.

Many of the secondary codes that are used in *WP* entries may also be used to future-price an itinerary. (See Table 9-2.)

Besides the secondary codes in Table 9-2, other codes may also be used in a future pricing entry—to specify the issuing carrier, enter the agency commission, or indicate a tour number.

Storing the Issuing Carrier

When a ticket is issued, the name of the issuing airline is printed in the upper left corner of the ticket. Normally, the issuing airline is the first carrier in the itinerary. However, the secondary code **A** can be used to specify a different issuing carrier, as follows:

FPAUA

This example will cause *United Airlines* to be printed in the issuing-carrier box when the ticket is printed.

Table 9-2 Examples of Future Pricing Entries.

Code	Interpretation
FPP2ADT/2CHD	Future-prices by passenger type
FPS1/3	Future-prices selected segments
FPX2	Future-prices with a forced connection
FPN1.2/2.2	Future-prices for selected passengers

Storing the Agency Commission

The travel agency commission may be input, either as a dollar amount or as a percentage, by means of the following secondary codes:

K   Commission amount

KP   Commission percentage

For example, to indicate a commission of $31.20, the following entry is used:

FPK31.20

Dollar signs may not be used in the entry. The exact amount, including decimals, must be entered. This example will cause *31.20* be printed in the commission box when the ticket is issued.

To indicate a percentage, the following entry is used:

FPK10

The percent sign may not be typed in the entry. This example will cause *10* to be printed in the commission box when the ticket is issued.

Storing a Tour Number

The secondary code **U** may be input to print a tour number on the ticket, as in the following example:

FPUIT1234AA

In this example, the tour number IT1234AA will be printed on the ticket.

Secondary action codes may be entered in any desired order. Multiple codes may be combined in the same entry with a cross (‡), as follows:

FPADL‡P2ADT/CHD‡KP11

This example will store DL as the issuing carrier. The itinerary will be priced for two adults and one child. An agency commission of 11 percent will be stored along with the price instructions.

Summary

The pricing function is used to determine the total ticket price for an itinerary. When an itinerary is priced, any rules, such as an advance purchase requirement, or fare applications, such as a throughfare for a connecting flight, are applied. The entry code WP is used to price a displayed itinerary for all passengers in the PNR. A secondary code may be input to obtain an alternative price.

A passenger type code (PTC) may be input in a pricing entry to specify an alternative fare type. To specify a passenger type, the secondary code P must be typed before the PTC.

If a PNR contains two segments with the same routing, one segment must be selected when the itinerary is priced.

The bargain finder entry WPNC is used to price an itinerary at the lowest available fare. A variation, WPNCB, is used to obtain the lowest price and rebook the applicable segments in the appropriate class. The entry code FP is used to store price instructions for ticketing on a future date.

New commands included in this chapter:

WP	Prices a displayed itinerary
WPPSCR	Prices an itinerary by passenger type
WPP2ADT/2CHD	Prices an itinerary using multiple passenger types
WPS3/4	Prices specified segments
WPN1.1/2.1	Prices specified passengers by name item
WPX2	Prices an itinerary using throughfares
WPB18SEP	Prices an itinerary by a specified future ticketing date
WPQVAP21	Prices an itinerary by fare basis
WPS1*QE70‡S2*QAP7	Prices an itinerary by segment and fare basis
WPNC	Prices an itinerary at the lowest available fare
WPNCB	Prices and rebooks an itinerary at the lowest fare
WC1V/2V	Rebooks an itinerary by segment and class
FP	Stores pricing instructions for ticketing
FPP2ADT/2CHD	Future-prices by passenger type
FPS1/3	Future-prices selected segments
FPX2	Future-prices with a forced connection
FPN1.2/2.2	Future-prices selected passengers
FPAUA	Stores the issuing airline
FPKP10	Stores the agency commission
FPUIT1234AA	Stores a tour code

KEY CONCEPTS AND TERMS

Identify the word, phrase, or symbol for each of the following concepts:

1. The function that is used to determine the total ticket price for an itinerary.

2. The total fare, including tax, for all segments.

3. The entry code that is used to price a displayed itinerary.

4. In a price display, the line that itemizes the base fare by segment and carrier.

5. A code indicating whether the passenger is an adult, a child, a military passenger, a senior citizen, or an adult stand-by passenger.

6. The secondary code that is used to price an itinerary with a passenger type code.

7. The secondary code that is used to price selected segments of a displayed itinerary.

8. The secondary code that is used to price an itinerary for selected passengers in the name field.

9. The secondary code that is used to price an itinerary using a throughfare for connecting flights in which the connecting time exceeds 4 hours.

10. The secondary code that is used to price an itinerary based on a future ticketing date.

11. The secondary code that is used to price an itinerary at a specified fare basis.

12. The entry to price an itinerary at the lowest available fare.

13. The entry code that is used to change the class of service after a bargain finder entry has been input.

14. The entry code that is used to store price instructions for ticketing on a future date.

15. The secondary code that is used to specify the issuing airline in a future pricing entry.

16. The secondary code that is used to input the travel agency commission.

17. The secondary code that is input to print a tour number on the ticket.

Answers:

1. itinerary pricing; 2. ticket price; 3. WP; 4. fare calculation; 5. passenger type code (PTC); 6. P; 7. S; 8. N; 9. X; 10. B; 11. Q; 12. WPNC; 13. WC; 14. FP; 15. A; 16. K or KP; 17. U.

REVIEW QUESTIONS

1. Write the entry to price an entire itinerary at the normal adult fare for all passengers.

2. Write the entry to price segments 1, 3, and 5 only.

3. Write the entry to price an itinerary using the throughfare for a connection exceeding 4 hours that occurs at segment 5.

4. Write the entry to price segment 1 at the VE1 fare basis.

5. Write the entry to price an itinerary at the QLE21NR fare basis.

6. Write the entry to price an itinerary at the lowest available fare.

7. Write the entry to price segment 4 only.

8. Write the entry to price only the second passenger in the first name item.

9. Write the entry to price segment 2 at the ME60 fare basis.

10. Write the entry to price an itinerary for name item 1.1 at an adult fare and name item 1.2 for a five-year-old child.

Refer to the following name field and itinerary to answer questions 11 through 17:

```
1.2HART/J MR/D MRS     2.3JENKINS/R MR/M MRS/B MSTR
1   DL   702Y   13SEP   F   LAXCVG   HK5   800A   104P
2   DL   404Y   13SEP   F   CVGBOS   HK5   230P   605P
3   DL   311Y   16SEP   M   BOSDFW   HK5   800A   1005A
4   DL   713Y   16SEP   M   DFWLAX   HK5   400P   411P
```

11. What entry would price an itinerary for the Harts only?

12. What entry would price the entire reservation for all passengers?

13. What entry will price only the Boston-Dallas and Dallas-Los Angeles segments?

14. What entry will store pricing instructions and enter a check as the form of payment?

15. What entry will price an itinerary at the HLE60 fare basis?

16. What entry would price the itinerary only for Mr. Hart, using a military fare?

17. What entry would price the itinerary for Master B. Jenkins using child fares?

18. What entry will both price and rebook an itinerary at the lowest available fare?

19. After pricing an itinerary at the lowest fare without rebooking, what entry would be used to change segment 2 to Q class and segment 5 to M class?

20. What entry will store pricing instructions, indicating 10 percent as the commission and CO as the issuing airline?

APPLICATIONS

Read the following scenario, and decide what actions should be performed to satisfy the client's preferences and needs. Briefly describe how you would handle the situation, and then write the required entries.

Mr. and Mrs. Bee will accompany their friends, Mr. and Mrs. Stone, on a trip. Their PNR has the following name field and itinerary:

```
1.2BEE/R MR/K MRS     2.2STONE/J MR/F MRS
1   UA   53Q    12AUG   BOSSFO   HL4   830A    1137A
2   UA   104M   12AUG   BOSDEN   HK4   700A    920A
3   UA   394M   12AUG   DENSFO   HK4   1005A   1120A
4   UA   58Q    17AUG   SFOBOS   HK4   1010A   740P
```

Mr. and Mrs. Bee would like to know how much their tickets will cost, excluding the price for Mr. and Mrs. Stone, if the waitlisted segment is confirmed. Mrs. Stone asks how much the tickets will cost for the entire party if the waitlisted segment is not confirmed. Mr. Bee wants to be certain that the reservations are booked at the lowest available fare.

Chapter 10

Issuing Tickets
and Invoices

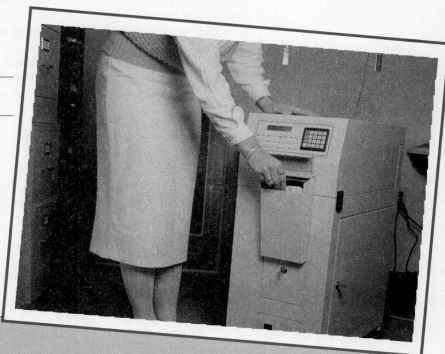

Outline

Automated Tickets   Issuing Invoices

Secondary Codes   Issuing an Automated Ticket and Boarding Pass (ATB)

Accounting Lines

Chapter Objectives

After you complete this chapter, you should be able to:

1. Initialize a ticket printer.

2. Issue tickets from a retrieved PNR.

3. Issue an automated ticket with boarding pass (ATB).

4. Assign ticket numbers.

5. Issue an itinerary/invoice.

PROBLEM

Your agency previously created a PNR for Mr. and Mrs. Tower. When the reservation was made, ticketing was arranged for 17 March. On 12 March, the clients arrive to purchase the tickets. They would also like to receive a printed itinerary.

SABRE SOLUTION

Retrieve the clients' PNR, and then issue the tickets with an itinerary/invoice.

In this chapter, you will learn how to initialize the ticket printer, issue tickets, and print itineraries and boarding passes.

To sell tickets on behalf of a domestic airline, a travel agency must first apply for and receive approval from an accrediting body. In the U.S., approval may be given by an airline or by Airlines Reporting Corporation (ARC), which is jointly owned by the major domestic airlines.

Airline tickets re issued on a standard form. A ticket may be written by hand or printed by computer with a ticket printer. A ticket that is issued by computer is called a *machine ticket*. Most tickets that are issued by travel agencies are printed on ticket forms provided by ARC.

Ticket forms issued by ARC are referred to as **ticket stock**. Each ticket has a form number and a serial number, which, together, make up the ticket or document number. When blank ticket stock is provided to an agency by ARC or by an airline, the serial numbers are recorded as a control in the event of loss or theft.

Figure 10-1 shows an example of blank ARC ticket stock. On the sample ticket form, the serial number appears in the upper right corner.

Initializing the Ticket Printer

Before tickets can be issued, the ticket printer must be initialized with the following entry:

FORMAT   W*TK<Printer Code>

EXAMPLE   W*TK776543

The code *TK* indicates that standard ARC ticket stock will be used. Each ticket printer has a unique six-digit code that identifies the travel agency and printer.

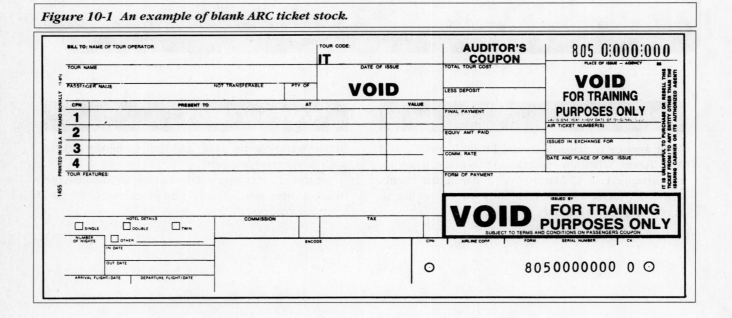

Figure 10-1 An example of blank ARC ticket stock.

Ticket Issuance

After the ticket printer has been initialized, the entry **W‡** can be used to issue tickets from a retrieved PNR. If the issuing airline and the commission were stored previously in the ticketing instructions field, tickets may be issued as follows:

W‡

SABRE will display the total fare amount and print a ticket for each passenger in the PNR. SABRE will respond as follows:

```
OK      293.00
        FARE AMOUNT
```

After the tickets have been issued for all passengers in the PNR, SABRE will change the ticketing field to indicate the pseudo city code, duty code, agent sine, and date of issue. For SABRE to update the ticketing field, the PNR must be ended, not ignored.

Figure 10-2 shows an example of a ticket generated by SABRE.

Secondary Codes

You will recall from Chapter 9 that the future pricing entry *FP* may be used to store the issuing airline and agency commission along with the pricing instructions for ticketing. This data is stored in the PNR in the ticketing instructions field. When the tickets are issued, the issuing airline will be printed in the *issuing carrier* box, and the agency commission will be printed in the *commission* box, as shown in Figure 10-2.

However, if the issuing airline and commission were not previously stored, the information may be input in the ticket entry, using the secondary codes A and KP, as follows:

W‡ACO‡KP10

Figure 10-2 Sample of a SABRE-Generated Ticket.

PASSENGER TICKET AND BAGGAGE CHECK   SUBJECT TO CONDITIONS CONTAINED IN THIS TICKET
ISSUED BY   CONJUNCTION TICKETS   **9999 | 000 | 299**

ENDORSEMENTS/RESTRICTIONS AMERICAN AIRLINES   ORIGIN
CHANGE SUBJECT TO FEE   ARC AGENT COUPON   DESTINATION PHX/PHX   **VOID**
                          DATE OF ISSUE
                                                                                           FOR TRAINING
PASSENGER NAME _____ NOT TRANSFERABLE ___   ISSUED IN EXCHANGE FOR   PURPOSES ONLY
EARHART/MARY   04DEC

_XO_ _FROM_   CARRIER FLIGHT CLASS DATE   TIME   STATUS FARE BASIS/TKT DESIGNATOR   NOT VALID BEFORE NOT VALID AFTER ALLOW
   TO PHOENIX   AA   316   B   08DEC 900A   OK   BAP3
X TO DALLAS FT WORTH   AA   874   B   08DEC 104P   OK   BAP3
O TO RICHMOND   AA   95   B   12DEC 103P   OK   BAP3
X TO DALLAS FT WORTH   AA   813   B   12DEC 410P   OK   BAP3
      PHOENIX
FARE   FARE CALCULATION
EQUIV FARE PD 410.00   04DEC PHX AA-XDFW AA RIC205.00 AA-XDFW AA PHX 205.00
TAX   TL410.00
TAX   41.00
TOTAL   451.00 FORM OF PAYMENT
                CHECK   APPROVAL CODE   TOUR CODE

A/L AGT. INFO.   001 9999000299   4   _AIRLINE_ CK _____ COMMISSION _____ TAX _____ COMM RATE
CONTROL NO

The code **A** is typed before the issuing airline, and **KP** is typed before the commission percentage. In this example, *Continental Airlines* will be printed in the issuing carrier box, and *10* will be printed in the commission box.

Other secondary codes may also be input when tickets are issued—to ticket only selected passengers or segments or to input a passenger type code for pricing.

Ticketing Selected Passengers

The secondary code **N** is used to ticket only selected passengers in a PNR, as follows:

W‡N1.2

This example will ticket only the second passenger in name item 1.

C L I E N T   F O C U S

Issuing Tickets for Selected Passengers

Assume a PNR has the following name field:

1.2FRANKLIN/T MR/C MRS 2.2CARLSON/P MR/F MRS

The following entry may be used to issue tickets for Mr. Carlson without ticketing any other passengers in the PNR.

W‡N2.1

A zero may be used to indicate all passengers in a name item. For example, the following entry will ticket both Mr. and Mrs. Carlson, without ticketing any other passengers:

W‡N2.0

To ticket multiple passengers in different name items, type a slash to separate the name references, as follows:

W‡N1.2/2.2

In the example above, Mrs. Franklin and Mrs. Carlson would be ticketed, but not Mr. Franklin or Mr. Carlson.

All these examples assume that the issuing carrier and agency commission are stored in the ticketing instructions field. If this data was not input previously, the data may be included in the ticket entry, as follows:

W‡ACO‡KP10‡N1.2/2.2

If name selection was stored previously in the ticketing instructions field, it does not have to be input again when the tickets are issued.

Ticketing Selected Segments

The secondary code **S** is used to ticket selected segments in the itinerary, as follows;

    W‡S1/2

This example will issue tickets for segments 1 and 2 only. To illustrate, assume a PNR has the following itinerary:

```
1 US   486Y   11NOV   W   TPACLE   HK1    235P  453P
2 TW   691Y   15NOV   S   CLESTL   HK1    940A 1010A
3 TW   600Y   18NOV   W   STLTPA   HK1   1005A  121P
```

Assume the client requests a ticket just for the USAir flight. The following entry will ticket only the requested segment:

    W‡S1

In this example, the USAir flight is segment 1. No other segments will be ticketed. If necessary, the issuing airline and the commission can be included in the same entry, as follows:

    W‡AUS‡KP10‡S1

If segment selection is already stored in the ticketing instructions field, it does not have to be input again when tickets are issued.

Ticketing With Passenger Type Codes

To specify a passenger type for pricing, the secondary code **P** may be input, as follows:

    W‡PSCR

When this entry is made, the ticket will be priced using senior citizen fares for all passengers in the PNR.

To ticket a party using both adult and child fares, the agent must input the appropriate PTC for each member of the party.

Form-of-Payment Option

If the form of payment was not input previously in the remarks field, it can be included in the ticket entry with the secondary code **F.** For example, if the tickets will be purchased by check, the following entry may be used to issue tickets:

    W‡FCK

When this entry is input, *CK* will be printed in the *form-of-payment* box on the ticket.

Ticketing With Passenger Type Codes

Assume a PNR has the following name field:

1.3THOMAS/V MR/S MRS/T MISS

Assume Miss T. Thomas qualifies for a discounted child fare. However, Mr. and Mrs. Thomas should be priced at the adult fare. In this case, the agent must price two passengers using adult fares and one passenger using child fare, as follows:

W‡P2ADT/CHD

If a PTC is omitted, only adult fares will be used to price the itinerary when the ticket is issued. The code CHD may be combined only with ADT or ITB. No other combinations are permitted.

If the issuing airline and the commission were not input previously with an FP entry, the data can be included in the ticket entry, as follows:

W‡ADL‡P2ADT/CHD‡KP10

If PTCs were input previously, when price instructions were stored, they do not have to be input again when tickets are issued.

A credit card account number is input as follows:

W‡FAX5003212654052232‡9-96

Note that this entry is slightly different from the one that is used when the form of payment is entered in the remarks field. In a ticket entry, the month and year of the expiration date are separated by a dash. (In a remarks entry, the month and year are separated by a slash.) The secondary code F is typed before the credit card code to indicate the form of payment.

The issuing airline and commission may also be included, as follows:

W‡AUS‡FVI4250667210092244‡5-99‡KP10

Other Secondary Codes

The secondary code **ED** is used to input information to print in the *endorsements/restrictions* box, as follows:

W‡EDNON REFUNDABLE

This example will issue tickets and print *NON REFUNDABLE* in the *endorsements/restrictions* box.

The secondary code **Q** may be used to specify a fare basis, as follows:

W‡QVAP21

This example will issue tickets, using the VAP21 fare basis to price the itinerary.
The secondary code **ET** is used for exchange tickets. The data is input as follows:

W‡ET017794576541/123/29NOV95SFO

The information in this entry is broken down as follows:

Ticket entry/exchange ticket:	W‡ET
Ticket number:	017794576541
Ticket coupon number(s):	/123
Ticket issue date and city:	/29NOV95SFO

When this entry is used, the ticket number, coupon numbers, issue date, and issue location of the exchanged or refunded ticket will be printed in the *issued-in-exchange-for* box.

Table 10-1 lists secondary codes that can be used in a ticket entry.

Guidelines for Issuing Tickets

Observe the following guidelines for issuing tickets:

1. The PNR must be ended and then retrieved from storage before tickets can be issued. To ticket a newly created PNR, the entry *ER* can be used to end-transact and redisplay the PNR.

Table 10-1 Secondary Codes for Ticket Entry.

Code	Interpretation
P	Passenger type
S	Segment selection
X	Forced connection
N	Name selection
A	Validating airline
KP	Commission percentage
K	Commission amount
T	Tour number
ED	Endorsement information
ET	Exchanged ticket information
F	Form of payment
TE	Tax exempt override
EX	Excursion ticketing on open segments
Q	Command pricing
E	Print equivalent amount paid
V	Valid dates

ER - End and Retrieve

2. If the form of payment is not stored in the remarks field, use the secondary code *F* to indicate the form of payment when issuing the ticket.

3. If the issuing airline is not specified, SABRE will use the first carrier in the itinerary as the issuing airline. To specify a different issuing airline, use the secondary code *A* when issuing the ticket.

4. For accurate accounting, the commission must be printed on every ticket issued by a travel agency. If the commission was not input previously with an *FP* entry, use the secondary code *KP* to indicate the commission percent (or *K* to indicate a dollar amount).

To ensure proper accounting, some agencies include the issuing airline and the commission in the W‡ entry each time a ticket is issued.

Accounting Lines

An invoice is a document that summarizes charges and payments. A ticket invoice shows the total ticket price and any client payments made by cash, check, or credit card. If full payment is not made at the time of ticketing, the balance due—the amount owed by the client—is also shown on the invoice.

After a prepaid or hand ticket has been issued, certain accounting data must be added to the PNR so that an invoice can be printed. The data that is required to print an invoice is called the **accounting line**. The following format is used to add data to the PNR accounting line:

FORMAT AC/<AL>/<Tkt>/P/<Pct>/<BaseFare>/<Tax>/<Appln>/<FOP>/<Nbr>/<Tariff basis>

EXAMPLE AC/AA/9002543986/P10/212.96/17.04/PER/CK/1/D

The entry code for inputting data to the accounting line is *AC*. The remainder of the entry consists of the following items.

1. Issuing airline (AL)
2. Ticket number (Tkt)
3. Commission percentage (Pct)
4. Base fare, excluding tax (BF)
5. Tax
6. Fare application (Appln)
7. Form of payment (FOP)
8. Number of documents (Nbr)
9. Tariff basis (T/B)
10. Optional data

Let us examine each part of the entry separately.

Issuing Airline. This portion of the entry states the carrier code for the airline used to validate the ticket. Normally, the issuing airline is the carrier in the first segment of the itinerary.

EXAMPLE   /AA/

Ticket Number. This portion of the accounting line shows the ticket number. If conjunction tickets were issued, only the first ticket number is required.

EXAMPLE   /30039871928/

Commission. This part of the accounting line is used for the agency commission. The code P is used to indicate the percentage. If a dollar amount is entered, an alpha code is not used.

EXAMPLES   /P10/   /23.00/

Base Fare. This part of the accounting line indicates the total base fare, including service charges but excluding tax. The decimals (cents if the currency is USD) must be included.

EXAMPLE   /212.96/

Tax. The total tax amount is entered after the base fare. Decimals must be included.

EXAMPLE   /17.04/

Fare Application. The fare application may be one of the following:

/ONE/   Total amount for one passenger
/PER/   Total amount per passenger in a group
/ALL/   Total amount for all passengers in a group

Form of payment. The form of payment is entered in the accounting line as follows:

/CK/   Check
/CA/   Cash
/CC/   Credit Card

When *ONE* appears in the fare application portion of the entry, the passenger name must follow the form of payment.

EXAMPLE   /ONE/CK SMITH J/

If the form of payment is a credit card, the account number and the cardholder name must follow the code /CC.

EXAMPLE   /CCAX998765540091878 SMITH J/

Number of Documents. This part of the accounting line indicates the number of documents to be issued.

EXAMPLE /1/

Tariff Basis. The tariff basis consists of a single letter and may be one of the following:

D   Domestic tariff

F   Foreign tariff

T   Transborder (Mexico or Canada)

Optional Data. Besides the foregoing mandatory information, optional data may be added to the entry as free-form text.

Issuing Invoices

After an accounting line has been stored, an invoice can be generated as follows:

FORMAT   DIN<Secondary code>

EXAMPLE   DIN

If a secondary code is not included, as in the example above, an invoice will be printed for all passengers and segments in the PNR.

The following secondary codes may be used in an invoice entry:

N   Name selection

S   Segment selection

A   Accounting line selection

The following are examples of invoice entries:

DIN‡N1.1/2.1   Issues invoice with name selection

DIN‡S1/3-5   Issues invoice with segment selection

DIN‡A12   Issues invoice with accounting line selection

Accounting line selection is required if any accounting data for auxiliary segments, such as hotel or car segments, has been stored in the accounting line.

To request a separate invoice to be printed for each name item in the PNR, the following entry may be used:

DIN‡NIALL

Issuing an Automated Ticket and Boarding Pass (ATB)

Many agencies have the capability of issuing automated tickets and boarding passes for flights of selected carriers. Not all SABRE subscribers have this capability.

Special ticket stock, called **automated ticket/boarding pass (ATB) stock**, is used to print a ticket and boarding pass on the same document. When an ATB ticket is generated, the ticket number, the issuing airline, and a check digit (used for inventory control) are printed at the bottom of each coupon and boarding pass. A ticket printed on ATB stock is commonly referred to as a *card ticket*. A separate card is printed for each flight coupon and for the auditor's coupon and passenger receipt.

ATB ticket stock does not have a preprinted ticket number. ARC assigns ticket numbers to each CRS, for use on ATB stock. The numbers that are assigned to SABRE are referred to as the *AA Common Pool*. Before ATB tickets can be printed, the agency must request a block of ticket numbers.

The following entry is used to request a block of ticket numbers from the AA Common Pool:

FORMAT   DTB><Number of Tickets>

EXAMPLE   DTB200

This example requests 200 consecutive ticket numbers for use with ATB tickets and boarding passes. A maximum of 250 ticket numbers may be requested at one time. Ticket numbers are assigned in consecutive order.

Preparing the ATB Printer

To print ATB-type documents, the ATB printer must be prepared, or readied. The following steps must be taken:

1. Initialize the ATB Printer.

FORMAT   W*AT<Printer Code>

EXAMPLE   W*AT7D5502

2. Specify the Number of ATB Forms to Be Used. (The maximum number is 999.)

FORMAT   DB<Printer Code>/<Number of Forms>

EXAMPLE   DB7D5502/50

3. Display the Remaining Quantity of SABRE-Assigned Ticket Numbers.

FORMAT   DQB

Issuing ATB Documents

After the ATB printer has been readied, the desired ATB documents can be generated. ATB documents can be printed in the following combinations:

1. Ticket only
2. Boarding pass only
3. Ticket and boarding pass

Issuing a Ticket Only. Any standard ticketing entry can be used to issue tickets without a boarding pass. For example, the following entry will generate an ATB ticket:

W‡KP10‡ABA

In this example, *10* will be printed in the commission box and *BA* will be printed in the issued-by box. All secondary codes pertaining to ticket entries, including agency commission, issuing carrier, and pricing options, apply to ATB tickets.

Issuing a Boarding Pass Only. The following entry can be used to issue a boarding pass only:

4GA‡BP

The entry code *4G* is for seat assignment. (Seat assignment will be discussed in Chapter 11.) The secondary code *A* refers to all segments, and *BP* is used to generate boarding passes. When this entry is made, SABRE will generate a boarding pass for each applicable flight. Boarding passes are not available from all carriers. The ticket stock used for ATB tickets is also used for boarding passes.

Issuing a Ticket and a Boarding Pass. To issue a ticket with a boarding pass on ATB stock, the following entry can be used:

FORMAT   W‡<Secondary Option Code>‡BP

EXAMPLE   W‡KP10‡BP

In this example, *10* will be printed in the commission box. The second code *BP* is used to generate boarding passes.

Summary

Before tickets can be issued, the ticket printer must be initialized. After the ticket printer has been initialized, the entry *W‡* can be used to issue tickets from a retrieved PNR. If the issuing airline and commission were not stored previously in the ticketing instructions field, secondary codes may be input to print this information on the ticket. Qualifiers may also be used to ticket selected segments or passengers and to specify the passenger types. If the form of payment was not input previously in the remarks field, it can be included in the ticket entry with the secondary code *F.* Information may also be included to print in the endorsements or ticket-exchange box.

If a prepaid or hand ticket is issued, accounting data must be added to the PNR so that an invoice can be printed. After an accounting line has been stored, an invoice can be generated.

ATB stock is used to print a ticket and boarding pass on the same document. Before ATB tickets can be printed, the agency must request a block of ticket numbers.

New commands included in this chapter:

W‡	Issues a ticket from a displayed PNR
W‡ACO‡KP10	Issues a ticket with issuing airline and commission
W‡N1.2/2.2	Tickets selected passengers by name item
W‡S1/2	Tickets selected segments
W‡PSCR	Issues a ticket for specified passenger type
W‡FCK	Issues a ticket with form of payment
W‡EDNON REFUNDABLE	Issues a ticket with endorsement information
W‡QVAP21	Issues a ticket with a specified fare basis
W‡ET017794576541..	Issues a ticket with exchange information
AC/AA/9002543986..	Enters an accounting line for a prepaid or hand ticket
DIN	Issues an invoice only
DIN‡N1.1/2.1	Issues an invoice with name selection
DIN‡S1/3-5	Issues an invoice with segment selection
DIN‡A12	Issues an invoice with accounting line selection
DTB200	Requests a ticket block
W*AT7D5502	Initializes an ATB ticket printer
DB7D5502/99	Specifies the number of ATB forms
DQB	Displays the remaining ticket inventory
4GA‡BP	Issues a boarding pass only
W‡KP10‡BP	Issues a ticket and boarding pass

STUDENT REVIEW

KEY CONCEPTS AND TERMS

Identify the word, phrase, or symbol for each of the following concepts:

1. Ticket forms issued to travel agencies by Airlines Reporting Corporation.
2. The entry code that is used to issue tickets from a retrieved PNR.
3. The secondary code that is used to specify the issuing airline.
4. The secondary code that is used to input the travel agency commission.
5. The secondary code that is used to ticket only selected passengers in a PNR.
6. The secondary code that is used to ticket selected segments of an itinerary.
7. The secondary code that is used to include passenger type codes in an entry to issue tickets.
8. The secondary code that is used to input the form of payment in an entry to issue tickets.
9. The secondary code that is used to specify a fare basis in a ticket entry.
10. The secondary code that is used to input information to be printed in the endorsements/restrictions box.
11. The secondary code that is used to input exchanged ticket information.

12. Data required to print a ticket invoice.

13. The entry code that is used to print an invoice.

14. Special ticket stock used to print a ticket and boarding pass.

Answers:

REVIEW QUESTIONS

1. Write the entry to issue tickets for all passengers from a displayed PNR.

2. What entry would issue tickets for name items 2 and 3 only?

3. Write the entry to issue tickets for segments 1, 3, and 5 only.

4. What entry would be used to issue a ticket for passenger name 2.2 for segment 2 only?

5. Write the entry to issue tickets and indicate a check as the form of payment.

6. Write the entry to issue tickets and indicate that the ticket is nonrefundable.

7. Write the entry to issue tickets, indicating CO as the issuing airline and 10 percent as the commission.

8. Write the entry to issue tickets, indicating AA as the issuing airline; 10 percent as the commission; and credit card AX6003242498761234, expiring October 1998, as the form of payment.

9. What entry would be used to issue a ticket, use military fares to price the itinerary, and override the passenger type in the PNR?

10. What entry would issue a ticket using the VA21NR fare basis to price the itinerary?

11. Which secondary code is used to input ticket exchange information?

12. Which secondary code is used to input information to print in the endorsements/restrictions box?

13. Which entry code is used to input an accounting line so that an invoice can be printed for a hand ticket?

14. Write the entry to issue an invoice from a displayed PNR.

15. What entry would be used to issue an invoice for name item 3 only?

16. Write the entry to request a block of 200 consecutive ticket numbers from the AA common pool.

17. Write the entry to issue a ticket and a boarding pass, specifying a 10 percent commission.

18. What entry would be used to issue only a boarding pass?

19. Write the entry to issue an invoice for all passengers for segments 3 and 5 only.

20. What entry would be used to issue tickets, indicating UA as the issuing airline, 10 percent as the commission, and a check as the form of payment?

Refer to the following name field and itinerary to answer questions 21 through 30:

```
1.2GREEN/K MR/P MRS    2.2GRAY/H MR/B MRS
1   TW   443Y   22APR   F   PHLLAX   HK4   625A   1046A
2   AA   759Y   25APR   M   LAXSFO   HK4   800A   907A
3   US   34Y    01MAY   S   SFOPHL   KH4   800A   506P
```

21. What entry would issue tickets for all segments for Mr. and Mrs. Gray only, indicating a 10-percent commission?

22. What entry would issue tickets for all passengers for the American Airlines segment only, indicating a 10 percent commission and payment by check?

23. What entry would issue tickets for the TWA and USAir segments for Mr. and Mrs. Green only, indicating a 10 percent commission?

24. What entry would issue tickets for all passengers, indicating AA as the issuing airline, 10 percent as the commission, and cash as the form of payment?

25. What entry would ticket Mr. and Mrs. Gray only, using senior fares to override the passenger types in the PNR?

26. What entry would ticket Mr. Green and Mr. Gray only, using the YE7 fare basis to price the itinerary?

27. What entry would issue only an itinerary/invoice for all passengers?

28. What entry would issue tickets and boarding passes?

29. What entry would issue only a boarding pass?

30. What entry would ticket the entire itinerary for all passengers?

APPLICATIONS

Read the following scenario and decide what actions should be performed to satisfy the client's preferences and needs. Briefly describe how you would handle the situation, and then write the required entries.

Your agency previously made flight reservations for Mr. and Mrs. Benson and their friends, Mr. and Mrs. Honeywell. Their PNR appears as follows:

```
1.2BENSON/R MR/K MRS    2.2HONEYWELL/J MR/F MRS
1   UA   53Q   12AUG   F   BOSSFO   HK4   830A    1137A
2   UA   58Q   17AUG   W   SFOBOS   HK4   1010A   740P
TKT/TIME LIMIT -
1.TAW3AUG/
PHONES -
1.BOS617-555-4003-A
2.BOS617-555-3354-B MR BENSON
3.BOS617-555-0101-B MR HONEYWELL
RECEIVED FROM = MR BENSON
```

Mr. and Mrs. Honeywell would like to purchase their tickets by credit card. The account number is AX62241098334714345, and the card will expire December 1998.

Chapter 11

Seat Assignments

Outline

Prereserved Seats	Canceling Seat Assignments
Seat Availability Maps	Off-Line Seat Requests

Chapter Objectives

After you complete this chapter, you should be able to:

1. Identify passenger seating by location and zone.

2. Request automatic seat assignment on participating carriers.

3. Assign specific seats by row and letter.

4. Display and interpret seat maps.

5. Cancel or change advance seat assignments.

PROBLEM

You are arranging flight reservations for a passenger who requests a prereserved seat. Your client would like a window seat and prefers to sit as close to the front of the cabin as possible.

SABRE SOLUTION

Display a seat availability map for the flight, and select a seat that meets the passenger's requirements.

In this chapter, you will learn how to request automatic seat assignment, assign specific seats, and display seat maps.

Before boarding a flight, a passenger receives a **seat assignment**, indicating the row and seat to be occupied by the passenger. Normally, the seat assignment is obtained from a ticket agent at the airline counter or from a boarding agent at the boarding gate. If a ticket is purchased from a travel agency, however, an advance seat assignment can often be obtained. An advance seat assignment is called a **prereserved seat**.

SABRE can be used to assign prereserved seats on flights operated by various participating carriers. On many flights, advance boarding passes can be issued for the prereserved seats. On American Airlines flights, seats can be reserved up to 331 days before departure. Table 11-1 gives examples of domestic carriers that provide advance seat assignment through SABRE. The period during which advance seat assignment can be made is different for each of the carriers listed.

Seat Location

Most clients have a preference for a particular seat location. Seat location is referred to by a one-letter code. Depending on the aircraft configuration, various location codes may be used. Table 11-2 provides examples of location codes.

Smoking Zones

On flights within the continental United States, cigarette, pipe, or cigar smoking is not permitted anywhere on the aircraft. On most international flights, however, cigarette smoking is permitted in designated seats. On those flights, seat assignment may be requested in one of two zones: the **smoking section** or the **no-smoking section**. Cigarette smoking is permitted only in the smoking section. The code *N* refers to the no-smoking section, and *S* refers to the smoking section.

Automatic Seat Assignment

The entry code **4G** is used to request automatic seat assignment on a confirmed flight segment. The zone and location codes are combined as follows:

FORMAT   4G<Segment>/<Zone and location>

EXAMPLE   4G2/NW

Table 11-1 Domestic Carriers That Provide Advance Seat Assignment.

CO	Continental	TW	TWA
DL	Delta	UA	United
NW	Northwest	US	USAir

Table 11-2 Aircraft Seat Location Codes.

A	Aisle	L	Left side of the aircraft
W	Window	R	Right side of the aircraft
X	Opposite sides of the aisle	J	Upper deck (747 aircraft only)
C	Business class		

Before the entry is input, a PNR must be in the agent's work area, and the passenger must hold a confirmed reservation on the specified segment. This example requests a prereserved seat on segment 2. The code *NW* indicates a no-smoking seat by a window. When the entry is input, SABRE will search for an available no-smoking window seat. If one is found, SABRE will make the seat assignment automatically. On no-smoking flights, the zone code *N* is optional and may be omitted.

When automatic seat assignment is requested, SABRE attempts to assign the best available seat based on the client's preferences and to distribute the weight of the passengers uniformly over the aircraft. If a PNR has more than one passenger, SABRE attempts to assign adjacent seats, with one seat in the specified location. If the requested location or zone is not available, a seat availability map will be displayed. Seat maps will be discussed later in this chapter.

In each of the Client Focus boxes, the zone *N* could have been included to specify a no-smoking seat. However, because smoking is not permitted on any domestic flight, a no-smoking seat will always be assigned, even if zone *S* is specified.

— *C L I E N T   F O C U S* —

Automatic Seat Assignment

Assume a PNR has the following name field and itinerary:

```
1.1WYATT/T MR
1  UA  626Y  10APR  M  DSMORD  SS1  540P    648P
2  KL  614M  11APR  T  ORDAMS  SS1  905P    ‡1145A
```

Assume the passenger requests an aisle seat on the United flight. The following entry is used to request automatic seat assignment:

```
4G1/A
```

In this example, an aisle seat will be assigned on segment 1. SABRE responds as follows:

```
DONE   FLT   UA   626Y   10APRDSMORD   REQUESTED
```

The response indicates the carrier, flight, class of service, departure date, and city pair. The text on the right indicates that advance seat assignment has been requested from the carrier.

When prereserved seats are requested, the code **HRQ** ("have requested seats") is added to the flight segment. Mr. Wyatt's itinerary would now appear as follows:

```
1  UA 626Y  10APR  M  DSMORD  SS1  540P    648P   HRQ
2  KL 614M  11APR  T  ORDAMS  SS1  905P  ‡1145A
```

Note that a prereserved seat was not requested on the KLM flight. When a seat assignment is received from United, the code HRQ will be changed to **HRS** ("holds reserved seats"). On American Airlines flights, the seat assignment may be obtained immediately.

Prereserved Seats for Multiple Passengers

Assume a PNR has the following name field and itinerary:

```
1.2WILLIAMS/O MR/J MRS
1   AA   527Y   16JUN   T   CLTDFW   HK2   856A   1029A
2   MX   785Y   16JUN   T   DFWACA   HK2   200P    340P
```

Assume your clients request a window seat on the American Airlines flight. The following entry may be used to request advance seat assignment:

```
4G1/W
```

SABRE responds as follows:

```
24A   AA   527Y16JUNCLTDFW   N   NOSMOKE FLT   WILLIAMS/O
24B   AA   527Y16JUNCLTDFW   N   NOSMOKE FLT   WILLIAMS/J
```

SABRE made the seat assignment immediately. A separate response is displayed for each passenger. In this case, SABRE has assigned adjacent seats in row 24. Passenger O. Williams holds seat 24A, and passenger J. Williams holds seat 24B. When the itinerary is redisplayed, the segments will appear as follows:

```
1   AA   527Y   16JUN   T   CLTDFW   HK2   856A   1029A   HRS
2   MX   785Y   16JUN   T   DFWACA   HK2   200P    340P
```

The code *HRS* has already been added to the American Airlines segment, indicating that the passenger holds a prereserved seat.

Assigning Seats on Multiple Segments

Seat assignments can be requested for multiple segments in the same entry, as follows:

```
4G1,3,5/A
```

A comma (,) is typed to separate the segment numbers. This example requests an aisle seat on segments 1, 3, and 5.

If the itinerary has fewer than six confirmed segments, the secondary code *A* may be used to request prereserved seats on all segments, as follows:

```
4GA/W
```

This example requests a window seat on all segments for which advance seat assignments are available. However, if the itinerary consists of more than five confirmed segments, a separate segment specification must be input for each segment.

Assigning a Specific Seat

A specific seat can be assigned by row and letter, as follows:

    4G1/14C

This example will attempt to assign seat 14C on the flight in segment 1. Adjacent seats can be assigned in the same entry, as follows:

    4G1/14ABC

This example will attempt to assign seats 14A, 14B, and 14C on the flight in segment 1. Note that the location and zone are not input when specific seats are assigned.

To determine if a specific seat is available, a seat availability map can be displayed.

Seat Availability Maps

A **seat availability map** shows the status of all the seats on a particular flight. The seating arrangement depends on the configuration of the aircraft. For example, seats on 727 aircraft are arranged on both sides of a single aisle, whereas on wide-body aircraft such as a Boeing 747 or McDonnell Douglas DC-10, several center seats may be located between two aisles.

If an itinerary is in the agent work area, the following format can be used to display a seat availability map for an American Airlines flight:

FORMAT   4G<Segment>*

EXAMPLE   4G2*

This example requests a seat availability map for segment 2. To request the smoking or no-smoking zone on an international flight, the following entries may be used:

4G2*-AS	Displays the smoking zone only
4G2*-AN	Displays the no-smoking zone only
4G2*-AC	Displays the entire cabin

A seat availability map is displayed for the class of service booked in the flight segment. For example, if the passenger is booked in first class, the map for the first-class cabin will be displayed. If the passenger is booked in any coach class, such as Y, B, V, M, or Q class, the map for the coach cabin will be displayed.

To illustrate, assume a PNR has the following itinerary:

1	AA	580Y	14AUG	F	DFWORD	SS1	708A	918A
2	AA	823Y	23AUG	S	ORDDFW	SS1	450P	659P

The following entry may be used to display the seat map for segment 1:

    4G1*

SABRE responds as follows:

```
      11 AU   BU   **   .UH  .U   .U   .U   GUH  **   .U   .U
      12 .    /    **   .    /    E    F    /    **   /    .
X     13 .    B    **   C    D    E    F    .    **   H    .
      14 /    B    **   C    D    E    F    G    **   H    .
      15 .    B    **   C    D    E    F    /    **   H    J
W     16 .    B    **   .    .    .    .    .    **   H    J    W
W     17 A    B    **   C    D    E    F    G    **   H    J    W
W     18 A    B    **   C    D    E    F    G    **   H    J    W
W     19 A    B    **   C    D    E    F    G    **   H    J    W
W     20 A    B    **   C    D    E    F    G    **   H    J    W
W     21 A    B    **   C    D    E    F    G    **   H    J    W
W     22 A    B    **   C    D    E    F    G    **   H    J    W
W     23 A    B    **   C    D    E    F    G    **   H    J    W
W     24 .    B    **   C    D    E    F    G    **   H    J    W
W     25 A    B    **   C    D    E    F    G    **   H    J    W
W     26 A    B    **   C    D    E    F    G    **   H    J    W
W     27 A    B    **   C    D    E    F    G    **   H    J    W
W     28 A    B    **   C    D    E    F    G    **   H    J    W
W     29 A    B    **   C    D    E    F    G    **   H    J    W
W     30 A    B    **   C    D    E    F    G    **   H    J    W
      31 A    B    **   C    D    E    F    G    **   H    J
      32 A    B    **   C    D    E    F    G    **   H    J
      33 /    /    **   /    /    /    /    /    **   /    /
```

In this example, the aircraft is a McDonnell Douglas DC-10. In the seat availability map, each row is numbered, starting at the front, or forward section, of the cabin. Aisles are indicated by ** (no-smoking) or - - (smoking). If a seat is available for advance seat assignment, the seat letter is displayed. For example, seat 24B is indicated in row 24 by the letter *B*.

If a seat has already been reserved, a dot (.) is displayed instead of the seat letter. The slashes indicate seats that have been blocked out for group sales or that are located in the buffer zone between the smoking and no-smoking sections. To assign any of these seats, the agent must obtain permission from the airline. Table 11-3 gives examples of seat map codes.

The locations of the wings are indicated by the code **W**. In these rows, the wing partially obstructs the passengers' view of the ground. On larger aircraft, seats in the rows between the wings are more susceptible to turbulence.

The emergency exits are indicated by the code **X**. Under federal regulations, a window seat next to an emergency exit may not be assigned unless the passenger is capable of assisting the flight crew in an emergency. The passenger must be capable of opening the aircraft door and willing to help the flight crew evacuate passengers from the plane.

Table 11-3 Seat Map Codes.	

.	Reserved seat
/	Buffer zone or blocked seat
U	Undesirable
H	Handicapped passengers
M	Mobility restricted
B	Bulkhead locations
X	Emergency exits
W	Wing locations

A seat with undesirable characteristics is indicated by the code **U**. For example, the seat may not recline, or it may have an obstructed view of the movie screen. The code **M** indicates seats that have restricted mobility. Passengers in these seats have limited leg room or less freedom or movement. Such seats should be assigned only to unaccompanied minors, to infants, or to elderly or pregnant passengers.

Seats located by a bulkhead are indicated by the code **B**. These seats do not have space in overhead compartments for passengers to store their carry-on items.

The code **H** indicates seats that are suitable for passengers with medical handicaps.

When a seat map is displayed, the agent can assign a specific seat based on the client's preferences and needs. For instance, assume the client desires a window seat as close as possible to the front of the cabin. Seats that are indicated by a dot have already been reserved. Thus, the window seat that is nearest the front is seat 15J, on the right side of the aircraft. The agent uses the following entry to assign the seat:

4G1/15J

SABRE responds as follows:

15J AA 580Y14AUGDFWORD N NOSMOKE FLT SMITH/L MS

Displaying a Seat Map by Flight Number

If an air itinerary is not present, the following format may be used to display a seat map on a specified flight:

FORMAT 4G*<Carrier><Flight><Class><Date><City pair>

EXAMPLE 4G*AA241Y5MAYLGALAX

This example will display the seat map for AA 241 in Y class on 5 May from LGA to LAX.

To display seat maps for other carriers besides American Airlines, the agent must use the total access function to link with the carriers' reservation systems. Total access will be discussed in detail in Chapter 18.

Displaying Prereserved Seat Data

As mentioned earlier, when prereserved seats are requested, the code *HRQ* is added to the flight segment. When a seat assignment is received from the carrier, the code is changed to *HRS*, indicating that the passengers hold reserved seats.

The entry *B is used to display the prereserved seat data.

Canceling Seat Assignments

Canceling an itinerary segment also cancels the seat assignment. It is possible, however, to cancel only the seat assignment without affecting the confirmed segment. To cancel an assigned seat, the entry code **4GX** is used as follows:

FORMAT   4GX<Segment>/<Seat Number>

EXAMPLE   4GX1/23B

This entry cancels previously assigned seat 23B on segment 1, permitting a different seat to be assigned.

— C L I E N T F O C U S —

Prereserved Seat Data

The following is the itinerary for passenger Wyatt, for whom advance seat assignment was requested earlier in the chapter.

```
1   UA   626Y   10APR   M   DSMORD   SS1   540P    648P   HRS
2   KL   614M   11APR   T   ORDAMS   SS1   905P   ‡1145A
```

Assume the PNR has been retrieved from storage, and the itinerary is displayed as above. Note that the United segment is now tagged with the code *HRS*, indicating that an advance seat assignment has been received from the carrier. The following entry would be used to display the seat data:

```
*B
```

SABRE responds as follows:

```
1   UA   626Y   10APR   DSMORD   KK   12C   N   1.1   WYATT
```

Note the status *KK*, indicating that the seat assignment has been confirmed by the carrier. In this example, seat 12C has been assigned.

If an airline does not permit agents to make advance seat assignments through SABRE, an SSR item may be input to request a seat reservation. For example, the following entry may be used to request an aisle seat in the smoking section:

3SMST/AISLE

The SSR codes **NSST** (no-smoking section seat) and **SMST** (smoking section seat) are used in SSR entries. The location should be indicated in the text portion of the entry, as illustrated in the example.

An SSR seat request does not guarantee that the carrier will prereserve the seats.

Summary

SABRE can assign prereserved seats on flights operated by various carriers, up to 331 days before departure. The entry code *4G* is used to request automatic seat assignment on a confirmed flight segment.

On flights within the continental United States, cigarette, pipe, or cigar smoking is not permitted anywhere on the aircraft. On most international flights, however, cigarette smoking is permitted in designated seats.

A seat availability map shows the status of all the seats on a particular flight. When a seat map is displayed, the agent can assign a specific seat based on the client's preferences and needs.

When prereserved seats are requested, the code *HRQ* is added to the flight segment. When a seat assignment is received from the carrier, the code is changed to *HRS*, indicating that the passengers hold reserved seats.

If an airline does not permit agents to make advance seat assignment through SABRE, an SSR item may be input to request a seat reservation.

New commands included in this chapter:

4G2/NW	Requests automatic seat assignment by segment
4G1,3,5/NA	Requests automatic seat assignment on multiple segments
4GA/NW	Requests automatic seat assignment on all segments
4G1/14C	Assigns a specific seat
4G1/14ABC	Assigns multiple adjacent seats
4G2*	Displays a seat map from an itinerary
4G*AA241Y5MAYLGALAX-AN	Displays a seat map without an air itinerary
*B	Displays prereserved seat data
4GX1/23B	Cancels a seat assignment

KEY CONCEPTS AND TERMS

Identify the word, phrase, or symbol for each of the following concepts:

1. A record of the row and seat to be occupied by a passenger on each flight segment.
2. An advance seat assignment.
3. The zone in which cigarette smoking is permitted on designated smoking flights.
4. The zone in which cigarette smoking is not permitted.
5. The entry code that is used to request automatic seat assignment on a confirmed flight segment.
6. The code that is added to a flight segment when prereserved seats have been requested but have not yet been confirmed.
7. The code in a flight segment that indicates prereserved seats have been confirmed.
8. A display showing the status of all the seats on a particular flight.
9. The code in a seat availability map indicating a seat that has been reserved.
10. The code in a seat availability map indicating the location of a wing.
11. The code in a seat availability map indicating the location of an emergency exit.
12. The code in a seat availability map indicating a seat with undesirable characteristics.
13. The code in a seat availability map indicating a seat with restricted mobility.
14. The entry code that is used to display a seat map for a specific flight, if an air itinerary is not present.
15. The entry to display prereserved seat data stored in a PNR.
16. The entry code that is used to cancel a seat assignment.
17. The SSR code that is used to request a no-smoking seat from an airline that does not offer advance seat assignment through SABRE.
18. The SSR code that is used to request a smoking section seat from a nonparticipating carrier.

Answers:

1. seat assignment; 2. prereserved seat; 3. smoking section; 4. no-smoking section; 5. 4G; 6. HRQ; 7. HRS; 8. seat availability map; 9. .; 10. W; 11. X; 12. U; 13. M; 14. 4G*; 15. *B; 16. 4GX; 17. NSST; 18. SMST.

REVIEW QUESTIONS

1. Write the correct seat zone and location code for each of the following:
   a. No-smoking section, aisle seat
   b. Smoking section, window seat
   c. Smoking section, aisle seat
   d. No-smoking section, window seat

2. Indicate whether each of the following statements is true or false:

    a. Reserved seats are available from Sabre for AA flights only.

    b. A seat assignment cannot be changed or canceled without canceling the air segment.

    c. Seats can be assigned automatically or by a specific seat number.

    d. Smoking is permitted on domestic flights of four hours or more.

3. Write the entry to request an aisle seat in the smoking section for all segments.

4. What entry would cancel assigned seat 12J on segment 4?

5. Write the entry to request a window seat in the no-smoking section on segment 1.

6. Write the entry to request an aisle seat in the smoking section on all segments.

7. Write the entry to request seats on opposite sides of the aisle in the no-smoking section on all segments.

8. Write the entry to assign seat A in row 23 on segment 3.

9. Write the entry to assign seats D, E, and F in row 14 on segment 2.

10. Write the entry to display the seat map for a flight in segment 2.

Refer to the following name field and itinerary to answer questions 11–16:

```
1.2PARKER/T MR/J MRS
1   AA   369V   12JUN   W   LGADFW   HK2   759A   1040A
2   MX   731V   13JUN   Q   DFWMEX   HK2   835P   1055P
3   CO   144Y   19JUN   W   MEXLGA   HK2   700A   325P
```

11. Assume your clients prefer a window seat. What entry would request automatic seat assignment in the no-smoking section on the American Airlines flight?

12. What entry would request advance assignment of an aisle seat in the no-smoking section on the Continental flight?

13. What entry would request seat assignment in the no-smoking section on all segments?

14. What entry would display the seat map for the American Airlines flight?

15. If the itinerary were not present, what entry would be used to display the seat map for the American Airlines flight in this itinerary?

16. Assume seats D and E in row 26 are available on the American Airlines flight. What entry would be used to assign the seats?

Refer to the following partial seat map to answer questions 17–20.

```
      12  A  /  **  .  /  E  F  /  **  /  J
      13  A  B  **  C  D  E  F  .  **  H  J
      14  /  B  **  C  D  E  F  G  **  H  J
      15  .  B  **  C  D  E  F  /  **  H  J
  W   16  .  B  **  .  .  .  .  .  **  H  J  W
  W   17  A  B  **  C  D  E  F  G  **  H  J  W
  W   18  A  B  **  C  D  E  F  G  **  H  J  W
```

17. What type of seat is 13C: window, aisle, or center?

18. What does a dot (.) indicate?

19. What rows are over the wing in this partial display?

20. How many seats are in the center section of each row on this aircraft?

APPLICATION

Read the following scenario, and decide what actions should be performed to satisfy the client's preferences and needs. Briefly describe how you would handle the situation, and then write the required entries.

Your agency previously made flight reservations for Mr. and Mrs. Shore. In their PNR, the name field and itinerary appear as follows:

```
1.2SHORE/C MR/K MRS
1  AA  73Y  12MAR  J  ORDHNL  HK2  1130A  316P
2  UA   2Y  22MAR  T  HNLORD  HK2   415P  +510A
```

The passengers request prereserved seats in the no-smoking section on both flights. They would like to sit as close to the front of the cabin as possible and prefer one seat to be by a window. When you display the seat map on the American Airlines flight, seats J and K in row 12 are available.

Chapter 12

Queues

Outline

The SABRE Queue Program

Queue Counts

Accessing Records in a Queue

Placing PNRs on Queue

Continuous Queue Ticketing

Emptying a Queue

Chapter Objectives

After you complete this chapter, you should be able to:

1. Explain the purpose and use of agency queues.
2. Obtain a record count, either for all queues or for a selected queue.
3. Sign in to a queue.
4. Remove, end, or ignore records in a queue.
5. Route records to a designated queue.
6. Initiate queue ticketing.

PROBLEM

In several PNRs, passengers requested seats on flights that were sold out, and the reservations were waitlisted. Now you would like to know which PNRs, if any, have flight segments that have been confirmed from the waitlist.

SABRE SOLUTION

First, obtain a record count of queue 3, which contains waitlist confirmations received within the last 24 hours. Then sign in to the queue, and begin processing the records.

In this chapter, you will learn how to obtain queue counts, work a queue, and place a PNR on queue.

The SABRE Queue Program

The term *queue* is derived from the French word meaning "a waiting line." In France, a line of people waiting at a theater box office, or a row of boats tethered at a dock, is referred to as a *queue*. In data processing, a queue is an organized sequence of records that can be accessed in consecutive order.

To visualize a queue, imagine a stack of papers sitting in an in-basket. The paper on top is the first record in the queue. If the sheet is removed, another sheet of paper is exposed. Records are accessed in a computer queue in the same way—one after another—until the queue is empty.

The SABRE queue program is called *AAquarius*. Each queue has a unique number that identifies its function. All the records in a given queue have some common trait. For instance, all the PNRs in queue 3 have segments that have cleared the waitlist within the past 24 hours, and all the PNRs in queue 5 have itineraries affected by airline schedule changes.

Table 12-1 lists SABRE queues and their functions.

Most queues contain PNRs that require some sort of action. For example, the PNRs in queue 3 require the segment status to be updated, and the PNRs in queue 9 have TAW ticketing arrangements for the current date.

A record that awaits attention or action in a queue is said to be **on queue**. Accessing the records in a queue is referred to as **working a queue**.

Not all queues contain PNRs. Three queues, called **message queues**, provide the agency with an electronic mailbox system by which agents can leave text messages on the computer for other agents in the office.

Queue Counts

A **queue count** is a summary of the messages or records currently on queue. The entry code **QC** is used to obtain a queue count, as follows:

FORMAT   QC/<Queue number>

EXAMPLE   QC/3

This example requests a record count for queue 3, which is used for waitlist clearances. SABRE responds as follows:

```
1044/18MAY   B4TO
PNR/Q030     4
```

The first line of the response indicates the time and date of the queue count and the pseudo city code of the agency where the count was requested. The second line gives the number of records on queue. In this example, queue 3 has four records on queue.

To obtain a message and record count for all the queues used by the agency, omit the queue number, as follows:

QC/

Table 12-1 Various SABRE Queues With Functions.

NUMBER	QUEUE	FUNCTION
GEN	General messages	General communications
SVR	Supervisory messages	Telex messages, supervisory advice
NOT	Notification messages	Notifications from SABRE
LMC	Left message to contact	PNRs suspended from original queue for preset interval
UTR	Unable to reach	PNRs suspended from original queue after preset interval
0	Basic PNR/urgent	PNRs requiring urgent action (within 24 hours)
1	Basic PNR/nonurgent	PNRs requiring nonurgent action
2	Car/hotel confirmations	Confirmation numbers for car and hotel reservations
3	Waitlist clearance	PNRs that have cleared the waitlist within the past 24 hours (urgent)
5	OA schedule change	Schedule changes for airlines other than AA
9	TAW	All priceable PNRs are placed in this queue on the date specified in the TAW entry. (Unpriceable PNRs are placed in queue 19.)
10	Ticket suspense	"Suspends" a queue for a time-limit option date. Used for TAX, tour orders, etc.
11	Airline rated PNRs	PNRs containing responses from carriers regarding fare quotes
12	Large party	All PNRs containing 10 or more passengers booked on carriers other than AA are placed in this queue
13	Special meals/services	PNRs with special meal or miscellaneous service requests (e.g. WCHR) on off-line carriers
14	Tour desk response	PNRs with tour confirmations
15	Reserved seats (AA)	
16	AA schedule change	PNRs with itineraries affected by AA schedule changes
17	AA schedule change	(Beyond 17 days)
18	Waitlist confirmation	(KL—beyond 24 hours)
19	Default queue	Unpriceable PNRs
20	Assigned-special	
21	Unable to invoice	PNRs with incomplete accounting lines
22	Corporate travel policy	Modified by AA
23	No-show PNRs (AA)	PNRs for passengers who did not check in for AA flights
24	OA boarding pass	PNRs with confirmed seats on carriers other than AA, for boarding pass issuance
25	Boarding pass (unable)	PNRs with seat requests that cannot be confirmed by carriers other than AA
26	Tour time limit	
27	Rejected BP	Boarding passes that SABRE is unable to print
28	Group/Corporate PNRs	(KK)
29	EAASY SABRE	PNRs for subscribers of the EAASY SABRE program

SABRE responds as follows:

```
GEN ......17        5 .......19
SVR........2        9 .......27
UTR........6        17 .......2
LMC .......1        23 .......1
TOTAL MESSAGES ...........19
TOTAL SPECIAL................7
TOTAL PNRS.................49
```

The response gives the number of messages or records assigned to each queue, along with a summary of the items in the message queues, special queues, and record queues. In the example, 19 messages are contained in the general and supervisory message queues. The general message queue is indicated by **GEN**, and the supervisory message queue by **SVR**.

Seven records are assigned to the special queues—the UTR and LMC queues. The purpose of these queues is discussed later in this chapter. In this queue count, 49 PNRs require special handling in the record queues.

To obtain a queue count of the UTR or LMC queue, the first letter of the queue name is input, as follows:

QC/U   Counts the PNRs in the UTR queue

QC/L   Counts the PNRs in the LTR queue

Multiple record counts may be requested as follows:

QC/1/5   Counts the PNRs in queues 1 and 5

QC/1-5   Counts the PNRs in queues 1, 2, 3, 4, and 5

A slash is typed to separate multiple queue numbers, and a dash is typed to define a range of consecutive queue numbers.

To obtain a queue count from a branch office, the pseudo city code must be included, as follows:

QC/B4T0   Requests a record count for all queues at branch office B4T0

QC/B4T0/B4R0   Requests a record count for all queues at branch offices B4T0 and B4R0

QC/B4T03   Requests a record count at branch office B4T0 for queue 3

Accessing Records in a Queue

To access the records in a queue, the agent must sign in to the queue. The entry code **Q** is used to sign in to a queue, as follows:

FORMAT   Q/<Queue number>

EXAMPLE   Q/3

When the agent has signed in to the queue, the first record is displayed automatically. In this example, the first record in queue 3 will be displayed.

To sign in to a queue at a branch office, the pseudo city code must be input before the queue number, as follows:

Q/B4T09

This example will access the records in queue 9 at branch office B4T0.

Working a Queue

When an agent signs in to a record queue, the first PNR is displayed automatically. When the agent ends the transaction, the PNR is removed from the queue, and the next PNR on queue is displayed. If the transaction is ignored, the PNR is moved to the end of the queue.

While the agent is signed in to a queue, no other PNRs can be accessed except the records that are on queue. To perform other duties, the agent must exit from the queue. When the agent exits, the last PNR that was displayed remains in the work area until the transaction is ended or ignored.

While the agent is working a queue, the queue number can be displayed with the entry *Q, as follows:

*Q

To remove the current PNR from the queue when no action has been taken, the agent can use the entry **QR**, as follows:

QR

When the queue is worked, certain commands can be used to exit the queue. See Table 12-2 for those commands.

When a transaction is ended, the next PNR on queue is displayed automatically. The PNR that was displayed previously is removed from the queue. If a transaction is ignored, the PNR is placed at the back of the queue but is not removed from the queue.

If the client cannot be contacted to confirm a reservation, the agent may place the record on the **UTR** (unable-to-reach) queue. If a message has been left for the client to call back, the agent may place the PNR on the **LMC** (left-message-to-contact) queue. These special queues are used to suspend a PNR for a set time interval. When the interval has expired, the PNR will reappear at the front of the queue from which it was originally suspended.

For example, assume an agent is working queue 3 and is unable to contact a client to confirm a waitlist clearance. The agent places the PNR on the UTR queue. After 15 minutes, the PNR reappears at the front of queue 3.

Table 12-2 Queue Exit Commands.

Commands	Exit Functions
QXR	Exits from the queue and removes the last PNR from the work area
QXE	Exits from the queue and ends the transaction
QXI	Exits from the queue and ignores the transaction
QXU	Exits from the queue and places the PNR in the UTR queue
QXL	Exits from the queue and places the PNR in the LMC queue

Working a Queue

Assume an agent desires to work queue 18, which contains waitlist clearances for flights departing beyond 24 hours. Before the agent signs in to the queue, a queue count may be obtained as follows:

    QC/18

SABRE responds as follows:

    1044/18MAY   B4T0
    PNR/Q18   3

In this case, three PNRs have segments that were confirmed from the waitlist. Next, the agent signs in to the queue, as follows:

    Q/18

The first PNR in the queue is displayed automatically, as follows:

    CFM TO PSGR
    1.2BARKER/H MR/M MRS
    1 DL 818Y 13APR   M   PHLBOS   KL2   1010A   1116A
    2 DL 390Y 14APR   T   PHLBOS   HK2   1250P   149P
    3 US 969Y 17APR   F   BOSPHL   HK2   645A   755A
    TKT/TIME LIMIT -
    1.TAW5APR/
    PHONES-
    1.PHL215-555-7676-A MARTHA
    2.PHL215-555-3003-B MR
    3.PHL215-555-2541-H
    RECEIVED FROM - MR
    Q9T0.Q9T0*A47 0915/15SEP9-   AFQTWE

(continued)

The time intervals for the UTR and LTR queues can be set by the agency. In most cases, the UTR queue is set to suspend a PNR for 15 minutes; the LMC for 24 hours.

The following entries are used to place a displayed PNR in one of the special queues:

QU   Places the displayed PNR in the UTR queue

QL   Places the displayed PNR in the LMC queue

A message is displayed above the PNR, instructing the agent to confirm the itinerary to the passengers, Mr. and Mrs. Barker. This message is called a *prefatory instruction*. In this itinerary, the passengers were originally waitlisted on DL 818 departing on 13 April and confirmed on DL 390 on the following day. Segment 1 has cleared the waitlist, as indicated by the status *KL*. After reconfirming the reservation with Mrs. Barker, the agent changes the segment status to *HK*, as follows:

.1HK

The duplicate reservation on 14 April is no longer needed. The agent cancels the segment, as follows:

X2

The agent then redisplays the itinerary to reset the order:

*I

SABRE responds as follows:

```
1  DL  818Y  13APR  M  PHLBOS  HK2  1010A  1116A
3  US  969Y  17APR  F  BOSPHL  HK2   645A   755A
```

The agent now inputs the received-from item and ends the transaction as follows:

6MRSΣE

When a PNR is placed in the UTR or LMC queue, the next PNR in the queue is displayed automatically.

The following entry is used to end the current transaction and exit the queue:

QXE

When this entry is made, the displayed PNR will be removed from the queue. If no action is desired on the displayed PNR, the following entry may be used to ignore the current PNR and exit the queue:

QXI

When this entry is made, the PNR will remain on queue, but will be placed at the back of the queue.

If all the records in a queue are removed, the agent is signed out of the queue automatically.

Some records, such as PNRs with waitlist clearances or schedule changes, are placed on queue automatically by SABRE. The agent can also place a PNR on queue for special handling. Each agency has several queues that it can use for its own purposes.

To illustrate, assume a client contacts a travel agent to obtain reservations. The agent writes down the information and promises to call the client back with the arrangements. After checking availability, the agent books a confirmed reservation to ensure that a particular flight and class will be available on the desired departure date. The agent then contacts the client and explains the flight arrangements. If the tentative reservation is acceptable, the agent simply returns the PNR to storage. If the client does not like the arrangements, the agent can rebook the itinerary or cancel the reservation.

Tentative reservations are often placed on queue to remind the agent to contact the clients to confirm the space. Each business day, the agent signs in to that queue to begin making client call-backs.

When a PNR is placed on queue, a prefatory instruction should be included to advise the agent who works the queue. In the Client Focus earlier in this chapter, the prefatory instruction *CFM TO PSGR* was displayed above the first PNR in the queue. Various other messages can also be displayed, depending on the situation. A **prefatory instruction code**, or **PIC**, is used to specify the message.

The following format is used to place a PNR on queue:

FORMAT   QP/<Queue number>/<PIC>

EXAMPLE   QP/34/11

In this example, the PNR that is currently displayed will be placed on queue 34. The prefatory instruction code 11 specifies the message that will be displayed when an agent works the queue. In this case, the message *SEE REMARKS* will be displayed with the PNR, instructing the agent to consult the remarks field for detailed advice or instructions. See Table 12-3 for a list of prefatory instruction codes along with the message each code generates.

Continuous Queue Ticketing

Queue 9, called the **TAW queue**, holds PNRs that have ticketing arrangements for the current date. In this queue, the ticketing field of each PNR has a TAW item with today's date. For example, on 12 April, the ticketing field of each PNR in the queue will appear as follows:

TKT/TIME LIMIT -
1. TAW12APR/

The **continuous queue ticketing** function can be used to issue tickets for the PNRs. The following entry is used to initiate continuous queue ticketing:

FORMAT   QLT/<Queue number>

EXAMPLE   QLT/9

Table 12-3 Prefatory Instruction Codes With Messages.

PIC	Message	Meaning	PIC	Message	Meaning
1	CFM TO PSGR	Confirm reservation to passenger	45	MSG ACTN RQD	Message action required
2	UTR or LMC	Unable to reach, or left message to contact	46	CK ITIN	Check itinerary
3	-UNTKTD PTA-	Unticketed prepaid ticket advice	49	NEED MAN NBR	PNR needs man number
4	COMPUTE RATE	Ticket rate must be computed	50	PENDING ACTION	PNR pending action
5	ADV FLIFO	Advise client of flight information	52	RECREATE TKT	Recreate ticket
6	ASC	Advise client of schedule change	54	AGT ACTN RQD	Agent action required
7	TA	Ticketing arrangement	58	CNCL HTL	Cancel hotel segment
10	-CNI PTA-	Contact and issue PTA	59	RQST FNL PMT	Request final payment
11	SEE REMARKS	Instructions may be found in remarks field	60	NEED HOTEL	Need hotel confirmation
12	CFM FRM LIST	Confirm from waitlist	65	NEED SEAT	Need seat confirmation
14	FUFB	Follow up for business	67	AUX-SEG-CNCLD	Auxiliary segment canceled
15	GRP	Group PNR	68	HARDCOPY	Hard copy (print out)
16	SEE FACTS	See AFAX/GFAX fields for handling	74	ADV DOCS	Advise of documents needed
18	SPCL MEAL	Special meal request	81	ND BDG PASS	Need boarding pass
20	SEAT CNTRL	Seat control	82	ND INV/ITIN	Need invoice/itinerary
21	SEE PTA SRMK	See PTA special remark	83	CK DK NBR	Check DK number
24	AAIRPASS PNR	PNR for AAirpass traveler	84	CONF NR RTN	Confirmation number returned
27	-FLT CNLD-	Flight canceled	86	REBOOK HRS	Rebook prereserved seat
30	SKDCHG CKOUT	Schedule change; check out itinerary	89	CK ADV NBR	Check AAdvantage number
33	FARE CHG	Fare change	120	SEE HISTORY	Display PNR history
34	CORRECT ITIN	Correct the itinerary	123	ST OUT ZN	Seat out of zone
37	SSR ACTN RQD	SSR action requested	124	ND SEAT	Need seat
41	UNA TKT	Unable to ticket	125	ST CLS CHG	Seat class change
42	CK ACCT DATA	Check accounting data	126	SEAT UNAVL	Seat unavailable
			128	RUSH RATE	Rush rate request
			131	NEED CAR	Need car rental
			132	NEED LIMO	Need limousine
			133	RUSH TKT	Rush ticket
			135	NN PHASE IV	Need phase IV ticket record

SABRE can print up to 80 tickets at one time. If pricing information was not input previously with an FP entry, SABRE will price all passengers and segments using full adult fares. If pricing information was input previously in the ticketing instruction field, the FP data will be used to price the ticket for each passenger.

To initiate queue ticketing at a branch office, the agent must include the pseudo city code, as follows:

QLT/B4R0/9

After the last PNR has been ticketed, the status message *INACTIVE* is displayed, indicating that the TAW queue is now empty.

Prefatory Instruction Code

Assume the following PNR was created to make a tentative reservation for a client:

```
1.4EVANS/K MR/F MRS/B MSTR/H MISS
1   CO4189V   17JUL   F   BUFMCO   HK4    900A    114P
2   CO4154V   26JUL   S   MCOBUF   HK4   1245P    441P
TKT/TIME LIMIT -
1.TAW22JUN/
PHONES -
1.BUF716-555-0092-A
2.BUF716-555-8761-B
3.BUF716-555-3222-H
REMARKS -
1.-CK
2.CHECK FOR A HOTEL NEAR DISNEY WORLD
3.CLIENTS PREFER HOLIDAY INN OR RAMADA
RECEIVED FROM - MR
```

Instructions regarding hotel accommodations have been entered in the remarks field. Assume that, in this office, queue 41 is assigned to an agent who handles leisure accommodations. The following entry may be used to place the PNR on queue:

```
QP/41/11
```

The prefatory instruction code 11 will cause the message *SEE REMARKS* to be displayed when the queue is worked.

Ticketing Recap

A ticketing recap is a summary of PNRs processed by SABRE during continuous queue ticketing. The secondary code *D* is input to request a ticketing recap, as follows:

```
QLT/D/9
```

The ticketing recap is displayed as follows:

```
001.  TEMPLETON/A........QZYQOP
002.  MASON/L ............ZB7TRE
003.  HOROWITZ/S .........RTCEWE
```

The display shows the name and record locator number of each PNR that was ticketed. A recap can only be requested when the status message *INACTIVE* is displayed, signifying that all the PNRs in the TAW queue have been ticketed.

Halting Queue Ticketing

The following format can be used to halt continuous queue ticketing:

FORMAT   QLT/STOP/<Queue number>

EXAMPLE   QLT/STOP/9

If a PNR is still being processed when this entry is made, any tickets that have not yet been issued for that PNR will be printed before ticketing is halted.

To halt queue ticketing at a branch office, the pseudo city code must be input, as follows:

QLT/STOP/B4R0/9

Emptying a Queue

Emptying a queue by removing all the records is called *zapping the queue*. The following entry is used to zap a queue:

FORMAT   QZAP/<Queue number>

EXAMPLE   QZAP/32

This example will empty queue 32 without processing any of the records. The PNRs will be removed from the queue but will remain in storage. The records can then be retrieved by normal means—for example, by passenger name or record locator.

To empty a queue at a branch office, the pseudo city code must be input, as follows:

QZAP/B4R032

Summary

The SABRE queue program is called AAquarius. Each queue has a unique number that identifies its function. All the records in a given queue have some common trait, such as a waitlist confirmation, a schedule change, or a special meal request. A queue count is a summary of the messages or records currently on queue.

To access the records in a queue, the agent must sign in to the queue. When the agent has signed in to the queue, the first record is displayed automatically. When the transaction is ended, the PNR is removed from the queue, and the next PNR on queue is displayed. If the transaction is ignored, the PNR is moved to the end of the queue. If the client cannot be contacted to confirm a reservation, the record may be placed on the UTR or LMC queue for a preset interval.

Some records, such as PNRs with waitlist clearances or schedule changes, are placed on queue automatically. The agent can also place a PNR on queue for special handling.

New commands included in this chapter:

QC/3	Displays a queue count by queue number
QC/	Displays a queue count for all queues
QC/U	Displays a queue count for the UTR queue
QC/L	Displays a queue count for the LMC queue
QC/1/5	Displays a count for a series of queues
QC/1-5	Displays a count for a range of queues
QC/B4T0	Displays a queue count at a branch office
Q/3	Accesses a queue by queue number
Q/B4T09	Accesses a queue at a branch office
*Q	Displays the current queue number
QR	Removes the current PNR from the queue
QXR	Exits from the queue and removes the last PNR
QXE	Exits from the queue and ends the transaction
QXI	Exits from the queue and ignores the transaction
QXU	Exits from the queue and places the PNR in the UTR queue
QXL	Exits from the queue and places the PNR in the LMC queue
QP/34/11	Places a PNR on queue with a prefatory instruction
QLT/9	Initiates continuous queue ticketing
QLT/B4R0/9	Initiates continuous queue ticketing at a branch office
QLT/D/9	Displays a ticketing recap
QLT/STOP/9	Halts continuous queue ticketing
QZAP/32	Empties a queue

STUDENT REVIEW

KEY CONCEPTS AND TERMS

Identify the word, phrase, or symbol for each of the following concepts:

1. A term describing a record that awaits attention or action in a queue.
2. Accessing the records in a specific queue.
3. A queue in which agents can leave text messages for other agents in the office.
4. A summary of the messages or records currently on queue.
5. The entry code that is used to obtain a summary of records on queue.
6. In a queue count, the code that indicates the general message queue.
7. The code that indicates the supervisory message queue.
8. The entry code that is used to sign in to a queue.
9. The entry to display the current queue number.
10. The entry to remove the current record from the queue.
11. The queue on which a PNR can be placed if the client cannot be contacted to confirm a reservation.
12. The queue on which a PNR can be placed if a message has been left for the client to call back.

13. The entry to suspend a PNR for a short interval, usually 15 minutes.

14. The entry to suspend a PNR for an extended interval, usually 24 hours.

15. The entry to end the transaction and exit the queue.

16. The entry to ignore the current PNR and exit the queue.

17. A code input when a PNR is placed on queue, specifying a message to be displayed when the queue is accessed and the record is displayed.

18. The entry code that is used to place a PNR on queue.

19. The queue that holds PNRs with ticketing arrangements for the current date.

20. The function used to issue tickets for all PNRs with ticketing arrangements for the current date.

21. The entry code that is used to initiate ticketing of all PNRs with ticketing arrangements for the current date.

22. The entry code that is used to remove all the records from a queue.

Answers:

1. on queue; 2. working a queue; 3. message queue; 4. queue count; 5. QC; 6. GEN; 7. SVR; 8. Q; 9. *Q;10. QR; 11. UTR; 12. LMC; 13. QU; 14. QL; 15. QXE; 16. QXI; 17. prefatory instruction code (PIC); 18. QP; 19. TAW queue (queue 9); 20. continuous queue ticketing; 21. QLT; 22. QZAP.

REVIEW QUESTIONS

1. Explain the use of the SVR queue.

2. Explain the use of the GEN queue.

3. In what situation would a PNR be placed in the LMC queue?

4. What do the initials UTR mean?

5. In which queue would an agent find PNRs with waitlist confirmations?

6. Which queue contains PNRs with TAW ticketing arrangements for the current date?

7. What entry code is used to obtain a count of records or messages in a queue?

8. What entry code is used to sign in to a queue?

9. When an agent signs in to a queue, what is displayed?

10. What entry is used to sign out of a queue and end the transaction?

11. What entry code would be used to obtain a queue count of queue 9 at a branch office with the pseudo city code W3R0?

12. What entry will place the current PNR in the UTR queue?

13. What entry is used to sign out of a queue and ignore the transaction?

14. What entry is used to remove a PNR from the current queue?

15. What entry is input to place the current PNR at the back of the queue?

16. Write the entry to display a queue count for all queues.

17. Write the entry to display a queue count for queue 18.

18. Write the entry to access queue 18.

19. Write the entry to place a PNR on queue 35 with prefatory instruction 11.

20. Write the entry to exit from the queue and ignore the last record displayed.

21. What entry will access the records in queue 40?

22. Write the entry to ticket all the records in queue 9.

23. Write the entry to display a ticketing recap for queue 9.

24. Write the entry to remove all records from queue 38.

To answer questions 25 through 30, assume your branch office (pseudo city) code is Z9T0.

25. Write the entry to obtain a queue count for all queues.

26. Write the entry to display a queue count for queue 9.

27. Write the entry to ticket all the records in queue 9.

28. Write the entry to sign in to queue 44.

29. What entry would be used to interrupt queue ticketing?

30. When queue ticketing has been completed, what entry can be input to display a ticketing recap?

APPLICATIONS

Read the following scenario, and decide what actions should be performed to satisfy the client's preferences and needs. Briefly describe how you would handle the situation, and then write the required entries.

Assume you want to process the records in the queue for American Airlines schedule changes. After obtaining a record count, you begin processing the records. The first PNR in the queue has the following itinerary:

1	AA	931Y	12SEP	S	CLEMSY	WK2	841A	1114A
2	AA	361Y	12SEP	S	CLEMSY	SC2	112P	339P
3	AA	346Y	19SEP	S	MSYCLE	HK2	424P	851P

The client accepts the alternative space. The next PNR in the queue has the following itinerary:

1	AA	931Y	12SEP	S	CLEMSY	WK4	841A	1114A
2	AA	361Y	12SEP	S	CLEMSY	SC4	112P	339P
3	DL	546Y	17SEP	F	MSYMCO	HK4	320P	538P
4	CO	336Y	30SEP	M	MCOCLE	HK4	752P	1004P

You are unable to contact the clients, but have left a message to contact you regarding the reservation.

The next PNR in the queue does not have an itinerary and does not need to remain in the queue. While the next record is displayed, a client contacts you to make a new reservation.

Chapter 13

Client Profiles

Chapter Objectives

After you complete this chapter, you should be able to:

1. Explain the purpose and use of client profiles.

2. Display a primary or secondary STAR.

3. Transfer mandatory data from a STAR to a PNR.

4. Transfer selected optional data.

PROBLEM

Your agency handles all the travel arrangements for Ultratech, a large electronics firm. Many of the company's employees travel frequently.

SABRE SOLUTION

When an Ultratech employee requests a reservation, use the STAR function to retrieve the client profile, and then transfer the passenger data items to the PNR.

In this chapter, you will learn how to display client profiles, transfer data items, and create or update a profile.

A **client profile** is a computer record that contains passenger data items for a frequent traveler. Passenger data can be transferred from a client profile to facilitate the creation of a PNR. For example, assume a travel agency makes all the travel arrangements for a large corporation, Diverse Products, Inc. To aid in building PNRs for this client, the agency creates a client profile containing the business contact phone, company billing address, and various other data items. When an employee of Diverse Products requests a reservation, the agent retrieves the client profile, and then moves the applicable data items into the PNR.

SABRE refers to a client profile as a **Special Traveler Account Record** or **STAR**. A STAR may be stored on one of two levels. A **level-1 STAR** contains data for a primary client, such as a company, government agency, or school district. A **level-2 STAR** contains data for a passenger associated with a level-l STAR. For example, a corporation would have a level-1 STAR, but each employee would have a level-2 STAR. A level-1 STAR may have any number of associated level-2 STARS.

Displaying a STAR

Each STAR has an identification code, called the *STAR ID code*. The ID code of a level-1 STAR may consist of up to 25 alphanumeric characters. The ID code may not contain a slash. The entry code **N*** is used to display a STAR, as follows:

FORMAT   N*<ID code>

EXAMPLE   N*ABM

This example will display the level-l STAR that has the ID code *ABM*.
The line code may be one of the following:

S   Subject line
P   Priority information
A   Always used
O   Optional data
N   Never used
R   Restricted

The line coded *S* is called the **subject line** and contains the account name. A line coded *P* is called a **priority line** and contains important information but is not used in a PNR.

The codes *A* and *O* indicate lines that contain passenger data items. If a line is coded **A**, the item is a mandatory item that should always be transferred to the PNR. If a line is coded **O**, the item is an optional item that may or may not be transferred to the PNR, depending on the situation.

If a line is coded **N**, the data is informational only and is never transferred to the PNR. A line coded *R* contains restricted data and is also for informational purposes only.

Displaying a STAR

Assume an agent is creating a PNR for an employee of Sample Stars, Inc. The company has a client profile with the ID code *SAMPLE*. The following entry is used to display the STAR:

    N*SAMPLE

The STAR is displayed as follows:

    STAR   SAMPLE
    0S   SAMPLE STARS INC
    1A   9702-555-1234-A
    2A   9702-555-5432-B
    3A   5/SAMPLE STARS INC
    4A   5/2001 ODYSSEY BLVD
    5A   5/LAS VEGAS NV 89001
    6A   W-DISCOVERY TRAVEL‡1234 BUCKHORN ST‡LAS VEGAS NV 89001
    7O   5-*IK518717171213191‡9/99
    8O   5-CK
    9N   **AUTH TO BK - ALICE OR CHRIS**

The header indicates the STAR ID code. Each of the remaining lines has a line number and a one-letter code. Line 0 has the code *S*, indicating the account name. The other lines have the code *A*, *O*, or *N*.

In this example, the STAR contains the agency phone, the client business phone, the client billing address, the agency address, and two optional form-of-payment entries. The one-letter code indicates the type of data in each line.

Determining a STAR ID Code

To determine a STAR ID code, a list of codes can be displayed, using the first letter or number. The entry code *NLIST* is used to list STAR ID codes, as follows:

FORMAT   NLIST/<Initial>

EXAMPLE   NLIST/S

This example requests all STAR ID codes with the initial *S*. SABRE responds as follows:

```
LEVEL 1 STARIDS
         1 SAS
         2 SAMPLE
  *      3 SEABORN
  *      4 SENTRY
         5 STP
  * HAS LEVEL 2 STARS
       5 LEVEL 1 STARS
```

The header indicates that the display is for level-1 STARs. An asterisk indicates that level-2 STARs exist. When an ID list has been obtained, a STAR can be displayed from the list, as follows:

FORMAT   N*<Line>

EXAMPLE   N*2

This example will display the STAR in the second line of the ID list. In this case, the STAR with the ID code *SAMPLE* would be displayed.

Displaying a Level-2 STAR

The following format is used to display a level-2 STAR:

FORMAT   N*<Level 1 ID code>-<Level 2 ID code>

EXAMPLE   N*ABM-SMITH

In this example, the level-1 STAR has the ID code *ABM*, and the level-2 STAR has the ID code *SMITH*. The level-2 ID code may consist of up to 12 characters. This entry will display the profiles for both ABM and SMITH, so that the data items can be transferred to the PNR.

Moving Data Lines

The following entry will move all the data lines coded *A* from a displayed STAR to a PNR:

NM

One or more **O lines** can also be moved, as follows:

NM8

Displaying a Level-2 STAR

Assume an agency handles all the travel arrangements for Aerospace Dynamics, which has a level-1 STAR with the ID code *AERO*. The company's officers, sales representatives, and managers all have separate level-2 STARs. The vice president, Jill Cogwheel, requests flight reservations for a business trip. The passenger has a level-2 STAR with the ID code *COGWHEEL*. The following entry is input to display the level-2 STAR:

N*AERO-COGWHEEL

SABRE responds as follows:

STAR	AERO
0S	AEROSPACE DYNAMICS
1P	. 2ND LEVELS
2A	9602-555-9930-A
3A	9602-555-0312-B
4A	5/AEROSPACE DYNAMICS
5A	5/11310 N CACTUS
6A	5/PHOENIX AZ 85038
7A	W-PRESTIGE TRAVEL‡225 N CENTRAL AVE‡PHOENIX AZ 85004
8O	5-*VI3042300912129176‡9/99
9O	5-CK
STAR	
0S	COGWHEEL/J
10A	-COGWHEEL/J MS
11A	9602-555-9821-H
12N	REQUEST NO-SMOKING AISLE SEAT

The level-1 STAR for Aerospace Dynamics contains the agency phone, business contact phone, client billing address, agency address, and two optional form-of-payment entries. The level-2 STAR for J. Cogwheel contains the passenger name and home phone. Line 12N is informational only. In this example, all the passenger data items are mandatory, except the form-of-payment in lines 8 and 9.

This example will transfer all the mandatory lines along with optional line 8. The mandatory lines are coded *A* in the STAR display, and the optional lines are coded *O*. If an optional line is not specified, only the mandatory lines will be transferred to the PNR.

Moving Data Lines

Assume an agent is creating a PNR for Mrs. M. Hubbard, who owns a small business, Mother's Cupboards. To determine the Star ID, the agent displays a list of ID codes with the initial *M*, as follows:

NLIST/M

SABRE displays the requested ID codes as follows:

```
LEVEL 1 STARIDS
*          1  MCI
*          2  MOON
           3  MOTHERS
*          4  MOUNT
*          5  MTA
*          6  MTOC
* HAS LEVEL 2 STARS
           6  LEVEL 1 STARS
```

The ID code *MOTHERS* is listed in line 3. The following entry may be used to display the level-1 STAR:

N*MOTHERS

or

N*3

The STAR is displayed as follows:

```
STAR       MOTHERS
  0S       MOTHERS CUPBOARDS
  1A       -HUBBARD/M MRS
  2A       9213-555-5544-A
  3A       9213-555-2002-B
  4O       5-CK
  5O       5-*AX6024119822126022‡6/99
  6N       BOOK ZD FOR CAR RENTALS
```

(continued)

This level-1 STAR contains the passenger name, the agency phone, the business contact phone, and two optional form-of-payment items. Assume the client will purchase the ticket by check. The following entry is used to transfer the desired data items to the PNR:

NM4

Line 4 is specified so that the correct form-of-payment item will be transferred along with the mandatory items. SABRE responds as follows:

-HUBBARD/M MRS
9213-555-5544-A
9213-555-2002-B
5-CK
*
DATA DERIVED FROM P LINES
01 USE ZD FOR CAR RENTALS

The asterisk indicates that the passenger data items have been accepted. For emphasis, the information in the priority line is repeated. Assume the agent redisplays the record, as follows:

*A

The passenger data fields now appear as follows:

1.1HUBBARD/M MRS
PHONES -
1.LAX213-555-5544-A
2.LAX213-555-2002-B
REMARKS-
1.-CK

Selecting Multiple Optional Lines

An end-item (Σ) may be used to transfer multiple optional lines, as follows:

NM7Σ9

This example will transfer optional lines 7 and 9 along with the mandatory lines.

As an example, assume the following STAR is displayed:

```
STAR  SPRATT
   OS  JACK SPRATT
   1A  9817-555-9187-A
   2A  9817-555-7621-B
   30  -SPRATT/J MR
   40  -2SPRATT/J MR/A MRS
   50  5-CK
   60  5-CASH
   70  6MR SPRATT
   80  6MRS SPRATT
```

The agent is creating a PNR for Mr. and Mrs. Spratt, who will purchase the tickets with cash. The reservation was received from Mr. Spratt.

In this case, the agency phone and the business contact phone are mandatory items. However, the applicable name item, form of payment, and received-from item must be selected from the optional lines. The name item for Mr. and Mrs. Spratt is line 4, the form-of-payment entry for cash is line 6, and the received-from item for Mr. Spratt is line 7. Based on this information, the following entry is used to transfer the data to the PNR:

NM4Σ6Σ7

Excluding Mandatory Lines

The secondary code **X** can be used to prevent a line that is coded *A* from transferring to the PNR. For example, the following entry will transfer all mandatory lines except line 2:

NMX2

An end-item may be used to exclude multiple lines, as follows:

NMX2ΣX3

This example will transfer all lines that are coded *A*, except lines 2 and 3. Note that *X* is typed before each line number to be excluded.

An end-item may also be used to exclude a mandatory line and specify an optional line, as follows:

NMX2Σ5

This example will transfer all lines that are coded *A*, except line 2, and will also transfer optional line 5.

Universal STARs

Besides storing passenger data items for frequent travelers, STARs are also used by the SABRE customer service department to communicate information to SABRE subscribers. A STAR that is used for this purpose is called a **Universal STAR**. An index of Universal STARs may be displayed with the following entry:

N*/VL

In the index, Universal STARs are listed by category number and title. See Table 13-1 for examples of various categories and titles.

The following format is used to display an index of Universal STARS for a particular category:

FORMAT   N*VL/CA\<Category number>

EXAMPLE   N*VL/CA14

This example requests the index for category 14, Ferry Services. SABRE responds as follows:

```
1.ADRIATIC              2.CALEDONIAN
3.EUROPEAN FERRIES      4.NORTH SEA
5.P AND O               6.SCOTTISH
7.SMYRIL
```

Table 13-1   Examples of Category Numbers and Titles for Universal STARs.

Category Number	Category Title
1	Airport Ground Transportation
2	Tours
7	Business Forms Suppliers
14	Ferry Services
15	Foreign Currency Service
17	Functional and Operational Information
19	Handicapped Traveler Information
25	Limousines
27	Notices and Bulletins
29	Office Equipment
41	Restaurants
45	SABRE Travel Guide
48	Ski Conditions
49	Theatre and Events Tickets
59	Weekend Specials
74	AAdvantage Program
78	American Eagle Commuter
82	Family Plan

Note that each topic in the index has an item number.

An index may also be obtained by initial, as follows:

FORMAT   N*VL/AN<Initial>

EXAMPLE   N*VL/ANB

The initial is the first letter of the ID code. This example requests an index of Universal STARs with the initial *B*. SABRE responds as follows:

```
         CATEGORY 2      TOURS
1.BOURNES BRITAIN
         CATEGORY 41     RESTAURANTS
2.BENTLEYS OF PICCADILLY
         CATEGORY 45     SABRE TRAVEL GUIDE
3.BAHAMAS               4.BARBUDA
5.BELGIUM               6.BERMUDA
7.BFL                   8.BHM
9.BNA                   10.BOS
```

This display lists the topics for each category. To display a Universal STAR from the index, the following format is used:

FORMAT   N*/<Item number>

EXAMPLE   N*/5

This example requests topic 5.

Summary

A Client profile is a computer record that contains passenger data items for a frequent traveler. Passenger data can be transferred from a client profile to facilitate the creation of a PNR. SABRE refers to client profiles as *Special Traveler's Account Records* or *STARs*. A level-1 STAR contains data for a primary client, such as a company, a government agency, or a school district. A level-2 STAR contains data on the passenger level.

The mandatory lines in a STAR are coded *A*, and the optional lines are coded *O*. If an optional line is not specified, only the mandatory lines will be transferred to a PNR. Besides storing passenger data items for frequent travelers, Universal STARs are also used to communicate information to SABRE subscribers.

Displaying a Category Index

Assume the following category index is displayed for topics with the initial *H*:

```
           CATEGORY 2        TOURS
    1.HOLIDAY TOURS OF CALIF
           CATEGORY 14       FERRY SERVICES
    2.HYDROFOIL EXPRESS
           CATEGORY 17       FUNCTIONAL-OPERATIONAL INFO
    3.HOTELGD
```

SABRE format and policy changes appear in category 17, Functional and Operational Information. This category should be consulted periodically to keep abreast of new agent procedures. In this example, topic 3 indicates a change in the SABRE hotel program. The following entry would be used to display the topic:

N*/3

SABRE responds as follows:

```
        ** UNIVERSAL STAR **
   U STAR ID - HOTELGD
   0S  HOTEL GUARANTEE/DEPOSIT CHANGE
   1N  .
   2N  . NEW HOTEL GUARANTEE AND DEPOSIT FORMATS
   3N  .
   4N  EFFECTIVE TODAY, JUNE 12, NEW HOTEL
   5N  GUARANTEE FORMAT MAY NOW BE USED
   6N  /THE PREVIOUS ENTRIES ARE NO LONGER VALID/
   7N  .
   8N  - - - - AGENCY NAME AND ADDRESS - - - -
   9N  GUARANTEE- GT
  10N  . . . /GT-ABC TRAVEL 1510 EVENT ST DENVER CO 89680
  11N  IF THE NAME AND ADDRESS IS THE SAME AS IN THE. . .W-
  12N  FIELD OF THE PNR, JUST ENTER. . . /GT- OR /GDPSTT-
```

This Universal STAR was created by SABRE to notify agents about a change in the procedure for guaranteeing a hotel reservation.

New commands included in this chapter:

N*ABM	Displays a level-1 STAR
NLIST/S	Lists STAR ID codes by initial
N*2	Displays a level-1 STAR from the list
N*ABM-SMITH	Displays a level-2 STAR
NM	Transfers all A lines to a PNR
NM8∑11	Transfers all A lines and specified O lines
NMX2	Excludes a specified A line
NMX2∑X3	Excludes multiple A lines
NMX2∑5	Excludes an A line and specifies an O line
N*/VL	Displays the index of Universal STARs
N*VL/ANB	Displays the Universal STAR index by initial
N*VL/CA14	Displays an index from a category list
N*/5	Displays a specified item from the index

STUDENT REVIEW

KEY CONCEPTS AND TERMS

Identify the word, phrase, or symbol for each of the following concepts:

1. A computer record that contains passenger data items for a frequent traveler.
2. The name for which STAR is an acronym.
3. A STAR that contains data for a primary client, such as a company, government agency, or school district.
4. A STAR that contains data for a passenger associated with another STAR containing data for a primary client.
5. The entry code that is used to display a STAR.
6. The line in a STAR that is coded *S* and contains the account name.
7. A line that is coded *P* and contains important information but is not used in a PNR.
8. The code in a STAR that indicates a mandatory item that should always be transferred to a PNR.
9. The code in a STAR that indicates an optional data item.
10. The code that indicates an informational line that is never transferred from a STAR to a PNR.
11. The entry code that is used to list STAR ID codes.
12. The entry to move all mandatory data items from a displayed STAR to a PNR.
13. The type of lines that can be moved along with mandatory data items from a STAR to a PNR.
14. The secondary code that is used to prevent a mandatory item from transferring to a PNR.

15. A STAR created by the SABRE customer service department to communicate information to subscribers.

REVIEW QUESTIONS

1. What is the maximum number of characters that a STAR ID code may contain?
2. Indicate whether the following statement is true or false: A STAR ID code may contain both letters and numbers.
3. What entry code is used to display a STAR?
4. What entry would be used to display a list of STAR ID codes with the initial *B*?
5. Write the entry to retrieve a level 1 STAR with the ID code *UNISYS*.
6. Write the entry to display a level 2 STAR for passenger Harman who works for PACTEL.
7. In a displayed STAR, what code identifies mandatory data that is always transferred to a PNR?
8. What code identifies optional data that may or may not be transferred, depending on the situation?
9. What code identifies data that is informational only and is never transferred to a PNR?
10. What code identifies the line in a STAR in which the account name appears?
11. Write the entry to transfer the mandatory data lines from a displayed STAR.
12. Write the entry to transfer all mandatory lines along with optional line 8 from a STAR.
13. Write the entry to transfer the mandatory lines and optional lines 7, 9, and 11.
14. Write the entry to transfer the mandatory lines and optional lines 4 through 7.
15. What entry would transfer all mandatory lines except line 3?
16. Write the entry to transfer all mandatory lines except lines 3 and 6.
17. Write the entry to transfer all mandatory lines except line 4 but including optional line 7.
18. Which entry code would be used to transfer all mandatory lines except line 2?
19. Write the entry to display a list of Universal STARs.
20. Make the entry to display item 3 from a Universal STAR index.
21. Assume a passenger, Mr. Pullman, is employed by New Century Publishing, which has a level 1 STAR with the ID code *NEWCENT*. What entry would be used to display the level 1 STAR?
22. If the agent is uncertain of the exact ID code, what entry can be input to display a list of STAR ID codes with the initial *N*?

23. Assume SABRE displays the following list of ID codes:

LEVEL 1 STARIDS

*	1	NATPUB
*	2	NBC
	3	NEIMANN
*	4	NETCO
*	5	NEWCENT
*	6	NORELCO
	7	NORTH

What entry can be used to display the level 1 STAR in question 21 by item number?

24. Write the entry to display the level 2 STAR in question 21.

Refer to the following STAR to answer questions 25 through 28:

STAR	NEW CENT
0S	NEW CENTURY PUBLISHING
1P	. 2ND LEVELS
2A	9212-555-9475-A
3A	9212-555-8762-B
STAR	
0S	PULLMAN/P
4A	-PULLMAN/P MR
5A	9212-555-3230-H
6O	5-CK
7O	5-*AX3002998012127654‡9/98

25. What entry would transfer only the agency, business, and home phone items, and the name item?

26. What entry would transfer all the phone items, the name item, and the credit card form of payment?

27. What entry would transfer all the mandatory items except the home phone?

28. Assume that the client will pay by check and that the business phone has changed since the STAR was created. Write the correct entry to transfer the appropriate items but exclude the business phone.

29. Assume a passenger, Ms. Nagelmachers, is employed by Transcontinental Railroad Corporation, which has a level 1 STAR with the ID code TRANSRAIL. Write the entry to display the level 2 STAR for this passenger.

30. Write the entry to display a Universal STAR index for category 41.

APPLICATIONS

Read the following scenario, and decide what actions should be performed to satisfy the client's preferences and needs. Briefly describe how you would handle the situation, and then write the required entries.

Ms. Peterson is the sales manager for Optimum Value Corporation. She would like to travel from Chicago to Charlotte on 17 October, leaving around 9 A.M. She is a member of the United Mileage Plus program. When you display availability, you see that United flight in line 1 departs at 7:45 A.M. and has seats available in Y class.

Ms. Peterson will rent a car in Charlotte and drive to Greensboro. She will be returning to Chicago from Greensboro on 22 October, departing around 2 P.M. When you display availability, you see that a United flight in line 5 departs at 4:35 P.M. and has seats available in Y class.

Your agency has a level 1 STAR for Optimum Value Corporation, with the ID code *OPTIVAL*. Ms. Peterson's surname is the ID code for a level 2 STAR. The client profile is displayed as follows:

```
STAR    OPTIVAL
  0S    OPTIMUM VALUE CORP
  1P    . 2ND LEVELS
  2A    9312-555-0022-A
  3A    9312-555-6456-B
  4O    6MR KLEINMAN
STAR
  0S    PETERSON/K
  4A    -PETERSON/K MS
  5A    9312-555-4404-H
  6O    5-CK
  7O    5-*VI4244662372930301‡10/98
  8O    6P
```

The ticket will be charged to the passenger's credit card, and the reservation was received from Ms. Peterson.

Chapter 14

Hotel Reservations

Outline

The ShAArp Plus System	Hotel Reference Points
Displaying a Hotel Index	Modifying Hotel Segments
Date Availability	Direct Bookings
Hotel Descriptions	Canceling Hotel Segments
Selling Hotel Space	Displaying Hotel Codes

Chapter Objectives

After you complete this chapter, you should be able to:

1. Display and interpret a hotel index for a specified city.

2. Display a hotel index by rate category, bedding type, or location.

3. Display hotel availability with or without an air itinerary.

4. Display hotel reference points.

5. Display a hotel description.

6. Sell a hotel segment from a description.

7. Input guarantee and deposit information in a hotel segment.

8. Modify an existing hotel segment.

9. Input a direct hotel booking.

10. Cancel hotel space.

PROBLEM

You are making travel arrangements for a client whose itinerary includes four cities. She would like to arrange hotel accommodations near the airport in each city. She prefers Marriott and would like a corporate rate.

SABRE SOLUTION

Display hotel availability in each city for the client's arrival and departure dates, specifying the airport area. Request Marriott properties, specify corporate rates, and sell a hotel segment in each city.

In this chapter, you will learn how to display a hotel index, obtain hotel availability, list reference points, display a property description, and sell, modify, or cancel a hotel segment.

The ShAArp Plus System

The SABRE hotel reservation system is named ShAArp Plus. Each hotel vendor represented in the system is identified by a two-letter code, called the **chain code**. For example, *HI* refers to the Holiday Inn chain, and *IC* refers to the Inter-Continental chain. See Table 14-1 for a list of major hotel vendors that participate in the ShAArp Plus system. Independent properties are represented by referral organizations, such as Best Western (BW) or Utell International (UI).

The following entry can be used to display a complete list of hotel vendors and chain codes:

DU*/HTL

Room Types and Rates

At most properties, room rates vary based on the room category and bedding. The following codes are commonly used to indicate various room categories:

Code	Room Categories
A	Deluxe room
B	Superior room
C	Standard room
D	Discounted rate
P	Promotional rate
S	Suite

Table 14-1 Examples of Hotel Participants.

Chain Code	Hotel Chain
BW	Best Western
DI	Days Inn
HH	Hilton (domestic)
HL	Hilton (international)
HI	Holiday Inn
HJ	Howard Johnson
HY	Hyatt
IC	Inter-Continental
MC	Marriott
RA	Ramada
SI	Sheridan
TL	Travelodge
UI	Utell International

A **bedding code** is used with the room category to indicate the number and size of beds. For instance, *1K* refers to a room with one king bed, and *2Q* refers to a room with two queen beds. The following are examples of common bedding codes:

Bedding Code	Bedding
1K	One king bed
1Q	One queen bed
2Q	Two queen beds
2D	Two double beds
1D	One double bed
2T	Two twin beds

The codes for the room category and the bedding are combined to indicate the **room type**. For example, *A1K* refers to a deluxe room with one king bed, and *B2D* refers to a superior room with two double beds.

The following are examples of common rate categories:

Rate Codes	Rate Categories
RAC	Rack rates
COR	Corporate rates
GOV	Government rates
MIL	Military rates
WKD	Weekend rates
SPL	Special rates
IND	Industry rate

Other category codes may also appear, depending on the property or chain. **Rack rates** are the normal room rates that are offered to the general public. Other categories indicate discounted rates that are offered to special groups or are designed to offset periods of low demand. Some rate categories may require a deposit or guarantee. The following codes are used to indicate guarantee policies:

Code	Guarantee Policy
G	Guarantee required
D	Deposit required
4	4 P.M. hold
6	6 P.M. hold

Displaying a Hotel Index

A **hotel index** is a list of participating hotels in a specified city. (The index lists all participating properties but does not give availability information.) The entry code **HOT** is used to display a hotel index. If an itinerary is present, the following entry may be used to display a hotel index:

FORMAT   HOT<Segment>

EXAMPLE   HOT2

This example requests an index of hotels in the arrival point of segment 2.

To illustrate, assume a PNR has the following itinerary:

```
1  UA  319Q  22JUN  F  BWISFO  HK3   820A  1200P
2  UA  486Q  29JUN  F  SFOBWI  HK3  1215P   908P
```

The client inquires about hotels in San Francisco. The following entry may be used to display a hotel index:

HOT1

In this example, SFO is the arrival point in segment 1. SABRE responds as follows:

```
QUALIFIERS-NONE
HOTELS IN SFO                                    LOCATION DIS/DIR/TRAN
1 JA13253 CARLTON               -C 1075 SUTTER STREET   -15N O
    58.00  RAC  TUR
2 HI 2304 GOLDEN GATE           -C SAN FRANCISCO, CA  -14N L
    83.00  COR  RAC  TUR
3 HI 2303 HI FISHERMANS WHARF   -C SAN FRANCISCO, CA -15N O
    72.00  COR  RAC  TUR
```

Each hotel listing is identified by a line item number. The first line of each listing gives the chain code, property code, and property name.

The location is indicated by a one-letter code. In the example, the code C indicates the city center. The location indicator may be one of the following:

Code	Location
C	City center
A	Airport
R	Resort
S	Suburban

The location indicator is followed by the property address.

The alphanumeric code following the address is called the mileage/direction indicator and shows the distance and direction of the property from the airport. In the example, 15N indicates that the property is 15 miles north of the airport.

The one-letter code at the end of the line indicates the type of transportation that is available. The transportation code may be one of the following:

Code	Transportation
H	Hotel courtesy car
L	Limousine service
P	Public transportation
O	Other

The transportation code O (other) indicates that clients must arrange their own transportation.

The second line of each listing gives the minimum rate and rate categories offered by the property. In this example, the lowest rate offered by the property in line 1 is $58 per night. The rate category RAC refers to rack rates, and TUR refers to tour rates.

Displaying a Hotel Index by City

If an air itinerary is not in the agent work area, a hotel index can be displayed by city, as follows:

FORMAT   HOT<City>

EXAMPLE   HOTSFO

This example requests the hotel index for San Francisco.
A location may be specified as follows:

    HOTSFO/A

A slash is typed before the location indicator. This example requests properties near the airport. Other location indicators, such as *C* (city center) or *R* (resort area), may also be requested when a hotel index is displayed. For example, the following entry may be used to request a hotel index for Honolulu, specifying the resort area:

    HOTHNL/R

A vendor may also be specified, as in the following entry:

    HOTATL/MC

This example requests a hotel index for Atlanta and specifies the Marriott chain.
Secondary codes called **qualifiers** may be used to narrow the selection in a hotel index. For example, the qualifier *RC* is used to specify a rate category, as follows:

    HOTORD/RC-C

In this example, the category code *C* specifies corporate rates. The following rate categories may be requested:

Code	Category
C	Corporate
G	Government
W	Weekend
V	Convention
F	Family plan
M	Military
P	Promotional
S	Senior citizen
T	Tour/package

Other qualifiers may be used to specify properties with a particular type of room location, a maximum rate, particular bedding, or a maximum distance from the airport.

The qualifier **L** is used to specify properties with a particular room location, as follows:

HOTMIA/L-OF

This example will display only properties with oceanfront rooms. The following are examples of room location codes:

Code	Room Location
OF	Oceanfront
PS	Poolside
SV	Sea view

The qualifier **R** is used to specify a maximum rate, as follows:

HOTLAX/R-100

This example will display only properties that offer rates of $100 per night or less. The bedding type can also be specified, as follows:

HOTGSO/1K

In this example, the bedding code *1K* specifies properties that offer rooms with one king bed.

The qualifier **D** may be used to specify the maximum distance from the airport. For example, the following entry will display only properties within 10 miles of Chicago-O'Hare:

HOTORD/D-10

Multiple qualifiers may be combined in the same entry. For example, assume a client who will travel to Seattle prefers a Hilton property in the city center and requests corporate rates. The following entry will request a display of only hotels that meet this client's requirements:

HOTSEA/HH/C/RC-C

The following are examples of hotel index entries:

HOTMIA/R-75	Displays the hotel index for Miami with a specified maximum rate
HOTORD/MC/2Q	Displays the hotel index for Chicago with a specified chain and bedding type
HOTHNL/L-OF/R-150/2Q	Displays the hotel index for Honolulu with a specified room location, maximum rate, and bedding type

A hotel index lists participating properties in a specified city, but does not indicate the properties, rooms, or rates that are available for a particular date range. If an air itinerary is present, the following format can be used to display date availability:

FORMAT HOT<Segment>

EXAMPLE HOT2

When this entry is input, SABRE will display hotel availability for the arrival point and date of segment 2. The default is one night and one adult per room. If the stay will exceed one night, the number of nights and the number of adults must be specified, as follows:

HOT1/3NT2

This example will display availability for the date and arrival city of segment 1 for a three-night stay with two adults per room.

If an air itinerary is not present, the city, arrival date, number of nights, and number of adults must be included, as follows:

HOTSFO/20NOV-3NT2

This entry will display hotel availability in San Francisco for arrival on 20 November for a three-night stay with two adults per room. Note that, in this entry, the number of adults is mandatory.

When date availability is requested, SABRE responds as follows:

```
1  BW 2515 BW CAPRI HOTEL PLAZA          -C  DENVER CO DWTN  -12 O
   32.00      RAC COR
2  DY 8119 DY DENVER SOUTH-TECH  CTR     -C  ENGLEWOOD CO    -21 O
   59.00      RAC COR
3  HI  3319 HI  DOWNTOWN                 -C  15TH & GLENARM  -18 H
   65.00      RAC COR
4  MC 6623 MC RESIDENCE INN DTWN         -C  2777 E ZUNI     -20 O
   49.00      RAC COR
5  HI  9307 HI  EMBASSY SUITES SE        -C  HAMPDEN AVE     -23 O
   80.00      RAC COR GVT
```

Although the **date availability** display appears similar to a hotel index, it shows only those rate categories that are available during the specified date range.

To display date availability, the check-out date may be input in lieu of the number of nights, as follows:

HOTLHR/10SEP-17SEP2

This example requests hotel availability in London, for arrival on 10 September and departure on 17 September, with two adults per room. For a multi-airport city, the code for the arrival airport should be input, to obtain the correct mileage/direction data.

The optional qualifiers that are used with hotel index entries can also be included in an availability entry. For example, assume a client plans to travel to Maui, Hawaii, arriving 2 November and departing 7 November. He prefers the Hilton chain but would like a maximum rate of $100. He desires an oceanfront room with two queen beds. Based on this information, the following entry may be used to display hotel availability:

HOTOGG/2NOV-7NOV2/HH/R-100/L-OF/2Q

Multiple qualifiers should be input in the order of the client's preference. For example, if a specified chain is more important than the type of bedding, the chain should be input first.

Hotel Descriptions

Information about each property is contained in a detailed record called a **hotel description**. The entry code **HOD** is used to display descriptions. When date availability is displayed, a description can be displayed for a selected property, as follows:

FORMAT   HOD*<Line>

EXAMPLE   HOD*1

This example would display the description for the property in line 1.

To illustrate, assume an agent has obtained the following date availability display:

```
1 BW 7722 BW CIVIC CENTER INN          -C  SAN FRANCISCO CA   -19  O
         46.00   RAC COR
2 MC 9894 MC SAN FRANCISCO             -C  SAN FRANCISCO CA   -18  C
         172.00 RAC COR
3 HY 5523 HY REG SAN FRANCISCO         -C  EMBARCADERO CTR    -16  C
         175.00 RAC COR   WKD
4 HI  2024 HI  UNION SQUARE            -C  SAN FRANCISCO      -15  O
         165.00 RAC COR
5 HI  1808 HI  FISHERMANS WHARF        -C  BAYSHORE BLVD      -24  O
         46.00   RAC COR
```

Let us say the client inquires about the San Francisco Marriott. The following entry may be used to display the description:

HOD*2

In this example, the Marriott is listed in line 2. The description is displayed as follows:

```
MC SAN FRANCISCO MARRIOTT
1280 COLUMBUS AVE
SAN FRANCISCO CA 91433
FONE 415-362-5500
RATES-           A1K    A2Q    B2D    C1K
        RAC      245.00 245.00 205.00 185.00
        COR 6    185.00 185.00
        GOV 6                  172.00
EXTRAS/OPTS- RA .00 RC .00 CR .00 EX 20.00 FAM-Y MEAL-N TAX-B
TRANSPORTATION- COURTESY CAR    TAXI    CAR RENTAL
POLICY- FAMILY PLAN--CHILDREN UNDER 13 YRS NO CHG IN SAME RM AS
    PARENTS.
    6PM HOLD UNLESS GTD BY 1NT DEPOSIT. CANCEL 24 HRS BEFR
    ARRIVAL.              CREDIT CARDS--VI, MC, AX, DC
FACILITIES- 841 ROOMS, RESTAURANTS, COCKTAIL LOUNGES, INDOOR
    POOL, IN-HOUSE MOVIES, GIFT SHOP, MEETING & BANQUET ROOMS
SERVICES- BABYSITTING, LAUNDRY, VALET, ROOM SERVICE, PARKING
    GARAGE
```

The description contains the following information:

1. **Name, address, and telephone** The full property name, mailing address, and contact telephone number appear at the top of each description.

2. **Rates** A rate grid is displayed in the first screen of each hotel description. The room types are listed across the top of the grid, and the rate categories are listed in the column on the left.

3. **Extras and options** This section of the description provides information about room options, guest plans, and bed taxes. Room options are indicated by the following codes:

   RA   Rollaway bed for an adult

   RC   Rollaway bed for a child

   CR   Crib

   EX   Extra adult

In the description, the charge is indicated next to each option code. In the example, guests are not charged for a rollaway or a crib, but a $20 charge applies for each extra adult. The extra-adult charge is incurred if a room is occupied by more than two adults. At some hotels, a third guest may be assessed both a rollaway bed charge and an extra-adult charge.

Depending on the property, two types of guest plans may be available: a family plan and a meal plan. A **family plan** permits one to three children to stay in the same room as a parent at no charge. However, the applicable charges may be assessed for any rollaway beds that are required. A **meal plan** includes one to three daily meals in the room rate. The following are the most common types of meal plans:

American plan	Includes three daily meals
Modified American plan	Includes full breakfast and dinner
Continental plan	Includes continental breakfast
Bermuda plan	Includes full breakfast
European plan	Does not include any meals

In the example display, a family plan is available, but not a meal plan. A bed tax is assessed on the room rate. Bed taxes, also called *value-added* or *tourist taxes*, are usually levied by a local government, such as a city or a county, to raise money for the local tourism industry.

4. **Transportation** The type of transportation is described in this section. In the example, a hotel courtesy car is available. Other recommended transportation includes taxicab or rental car.

5. **Policy** The hotel's reservation policies are described in this section. In the example, children under 13 years of age qualify for the family plan. A 6 P.M. hold applies unless a one-night deposit is paid. Under this arrangement, a reservation is held until 6:00 P.M. on the check-in date but will be canceled if the client fails to check in by that time. If a deposit is paid, the reservation will be held for late arrival. If the client does not check in, however, the deposit will be forfeited. A credit card may be used to guarantee a reservation.

6. **Facilities** This section of the description gives the number of rooms and lists such guest facilities as a restaurant, lounge, swimming pool, and meeting rooms.

7. **Services** This section lists such guest services as laundry, valet, and parking.

Each property has a unique identification code. The following entry may be used to obtain a description using the identification code, or **property number**:

HOD7724

In this example, the property number is 7724.

Displaying Chain Policy Information

Policy information for a specified chain can be obtained as follows:

HODHI

This example will display policy information for the Holiday Inn chain. The **chain description** is a summary of policies regarding deposits, refunds, extra guests, guest plans, credit card acceptance, and so forth.

When a hotel description is displayed, the following format may be used to sell a hotel reservation:

FORMAT   0<Number of rooms><Room code><Rate category>

EXAMPLE   01C1KRAC

This example will book one room of type C1K at the rack rate.

CLIENT FOCUS

Selling Hotel Space

Assume a hotel description is displayed with the following rate grid:

RATES-		A1K	A2D	B1K	B2D	C2D
	RAC 6	210.00	198.00	185.00	185.00	175.00
	COR 6					162.00
	WKD G				150.00	135.00

Let us say the client needs rooms for three travelers and would like the $162 corporate rate. According to the rate grid, the corporate rate is valid for a standard room with two double beds. One adult will occupy each room. Based on this information, the following entry is used to book the rooms:

03C2DCOR

When a hotel segment is sold, SABRE responds as follows:

2 HHL HY SS3 SFO IN12MAR-OUT17MAR 5NT 5523 HYATT REGENCY
3C2D-1/162.00USD/AGT04662245/SI-CF/

Hotel segments appear in the same itinerary as flight segments. Each hotel segment is labeled **HHL** and includes the chain code, segment status, number of rooms, and hotel city. The hotel in this example is part of the Hyatt chain. The segment status *SS3* indicates that a reservation is confirmed for three rooms.

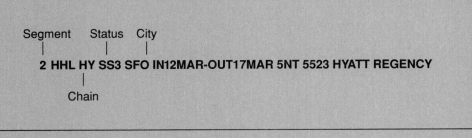

(continued)

The check-in and check-out dates, number of nights, property number, and property name are also shown in the hotel segment. In this example, the client will arrive on 12 March and depart on 17 March. The property code is 5523, and the name is the Hyatt Regency.

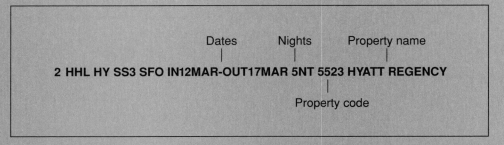

The second line of the segment indicates the number of rooms, the room type, and the number of adults per room. The rate, currency, and booking source are also shown. The **booking source** is indicated by the agent ARC or IATA number.

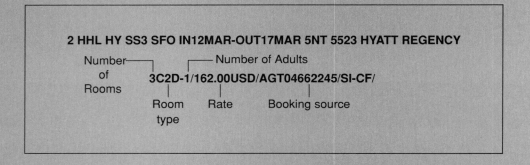

When the transaction is ended, a message will be transmitted to notify the hotel about the reservation. The hotel will then send back a confirmation number to be appended to the hotel segment in the service information (SI) field. The code CF identifies the confirmation number.

Guarantee Information

Some properties require all reservations to be guaranteed, whereas others require a guarantee only to hold a room for late arrival. If a guarantee is required, the secondary code /G is used to indicate the deposit or guarantee information, as follows:

01B2QRAC/GDPST

This example indicates that a deposit will be sent to the hotel to guarantee the reservation. If a credit card is used to guarantee a reservation, the information is input as follows:

01B2QRAC/GAX3002543100219989EXP 10 99-POWELL

In this example, *AX* indicates an American Express card. Note that **EXP** is typed before the expiration date. In the date, only the digits for the month and the last two digits of the year are typed, separated by a space. A space is also typed before the year. The credit card in this example is an American Express card, expiring October, 1999. The cardholder's surname, preceded by a dash is input after the expiration date.

The following codes are used for other means of guaranteeing a hotel reservation:

Code	Guarantee Method
GT	Travel agency address
GC	Company address
GH	Client home address
GCR	Corporate number
GAGT	Travel agency ARC/IATA number

For example, if the agency address has been stored in the address field, the following entry will guarantee the reservation with the travel agency address:

01A1KRAC/GT

Likewise, if the company address has been stored in the remarks field, the following entry will guarantee the reservation with the company address:

01A1KRAC/GC

If a reservation is guaranteed with an address, the addressee will be billed for a one-night stay if the client does not check in. For example, if a reservation is guaranteed with a travel agency address, the agency will be billed. Policies regarding guarantees and deposits vary depending on the property. Some hotels accept only a cash deposit or a credit card to guarantee a reservation.

Room Options

When a hotel segment is sold, a room option such as a rollaway bed or a crib can be requested as follows:

FORMAT   <Basic Entry>/<Option>-<Number>

EXAMPLE   01A1KRAC/EX-1

A dash (-) is typed after the option and before the number. This example indicates that one extra guest will occupy the room. If an adult rollaway bed is also required, the following entry is input:

01A1KRAC/EX-1/RA-1

Displaying Hotel Segments

The following entry is used to display just the hotel segments in an itinerary:

*IH

To illustrate, assume a PNR has the following itinerary:

1 UA 205Y 10SEP Q MIASFO HK1 710A 1110A
2 HHL HI HK1 SFO IN10SEP-1NT HI CROWNE PLAZA SFO AIRPT
   1A1KRAC-1/129.00USD/AGT098761234

The entry *IH will display only the hotel segment, as follows:

2 HHL HI HK1 SFO IN10SEP-1NT HI CROWNE PLAZA SFO AIRPT
   1A1KRAC-1/129.00USD/AGT098761234

Although just one segment is displayed, the segment number remains the same as if the entire itinerary had been displayed.

Hotel Reference Points

Often, a client may desire a property located near a particular site or attraction. For instance, a client may wish to stay near an amusement park, a sports arena, or a museum. The entry code **HCC** may be used to display hotel reference points, as follows:

FORMAT HCC<State>*<Initial>

EXAMPLE HCCUT*M

This example would display reference points in Utah with the initial *M*. Note that the two-letter state code is input to specify the state in which the reference point is located.

If the name of the reference point is already known, the following entry can be used to obtain a hotel index without displaying the list:

FORMAT HOT<State>-<Reference point>

EXAMPLE HOTAZ-GRAND CANYON

This example requests a hotel index for Arizona, with the Grand Canyon as a reference point. When the index is displayed, the mileage/direction indicator will refer to the specified reference point. For instance, assume an agent has displayed a hotel

Hotel Reference Points

Assume a client will travel to New York and would like to stay at a hotel near Broome Industrial Park. However, the client is unsure of the correct spelling of the reference point. The following entry will display a list of reference points with the initial *B*:

    HCCNY*B

SABRE responds as follows

    1 NY   BGM-BINGHAMPTON
    2 NY   BUF-BUFFALO
    3 NY   BROOME INDUSTRIAL PARK
    4 NY   BROTHERHOOD WINERY
    5 NY   BASEBALL HALL OF FAME
    6 NY   BELMONT PARK RACE TRACK

Each reference point has an item number, which can be used to display a hotel index. For example, the following entry would display the hotel index for Broome Industrial Park:

    HOT*3

Note that the display key (*) is typed before the line number.

index for Louisiana with Bourbon Street as the reference point. The client expresses an interest in the following property:

    6 HI 2972 HI FRENCH QUARTER -C NEW ORLEANS LA -1S O

In this example, the mileage/direction indicator *1S* signifies that the property is one mile south of Bourbon Street.

Foreign Reference Points

To display reference points in foreign countries, the entry code **HCCC** is used, as follows:

FORMAT   HCCC/<Country>*<Initial>

EXAMPLE   HCCC/NO*S

This example will display reference points in Norway beginning with the initial *S*. One to four letters may be typed after the asterisk. When this entry is input, SABRE will respond as follows:

```
1  NO  SKE-SKIEN
2  NO  SVJ-SVOLVAER
3  NO  SOG-SOGNDAL
4  NO  SSJ-SANDNESSJOEN
5  NO  SKN-STOKMARKNES
6  NO  SVG-STAVANGER
7  NO  SDN-SANDANE
```

Modifying Hotel Segments

The entry code **HOM** is used to modify an existing hotel reservation, as follows:

FORMAT   HOM<Segment><Field>/<New Data>

EXAMPLE   HOM2R/1A1K-1

In this example, the code **R** indicates the room information field. This entry would modify a hotel reservation in segment 2 to change the room type to A1K with one adult. The number of adults must be entered even if the number is unchanged.

Direct Bookings

If a hotel reservation is not booked through SABRE, the hotel segment can still be entered in the itinerary for reference. For instance, an agent might telephone a hotel reservation center to book a reservation at a particular property. In this case, the following format must be used to enter the direct booking in the itinerary:

FORMAT   0HHTAAHK<Rooms><City><In-out>/<Prop.>/<Type>/<Rate>/<Guar. info.>/ SI<Address and phone>/CF-<Conf. number>

EXAMPLE   0HHTAAHK1BOSIN20APR-OUT21APR/COLONNADE HOTEL/DBLB/65.00/ G-DPST/SI-120 HUNTINGTON AVE‡BOSTON MA 02116‡FONE 617-424-7000/CF-1295TG

In this example, a reservation was booked for one room at a property in Boston. The client will arrive on 20 April and depart on 21 April. The property name is the Colonnade Hotel, and a double room has been confirmed. The room rate is 65.00, and a deposit will be sent to the property to guarantee the reservation. In this example, the property address and phone are input with the secondary code */SI*, and the

Modifying a Hotel Segment

Assume an agent wishes to change a hotel reservation in segment 4. The client previously booked two rooms at the B2D rate, with two adults per room. Two of the guests have now canceled their reservations, and the client desires to change the reservation to two rooms at the B1D rate, with one adult per room. Based on this information, the following entry is used to modify the hotel segment:

    HOM4R/2B1D-1

The code **O** is used to add or modify a room option field, as follows:

    HOM2O/EX-1/RA-1

This entry indicates one extra guest and requests one adult rollaway bed. The existing reservation is segment 2.

The code **D** is used to modify the date field, as follows:

    HOM5D/10MAY-15MAY

This entry would change the arrival and departure dates of a hotel reservation in segment 5.

verbal confirmation number is input with */CF*. The supplementary information (SI) and confirmation (CF) fields are optional.

The following room type codes are commonly used in direct hotel segments:

Code	Room Type
SGLB	Single room with bath
DBLB	Double room with bath
QUAD	Quadruple room
TRPB	Triple room with bath
TWNB	Twin with bath

One of the following rate categories may be input instead of the rate:

Code	Rate Range
MAXR	Maximum rate
MODR	Moderate rate
MINR	Minimum rate

Canceling Hotel Segments

To cancel a hotel reservation booked through SABRE, the agent simply cancels the corresponding segment in the itinerary. For example, assume a PNR has the following itinerary:

```
1 UA 205Y 10SEP Q MIASFO HK1 710A 1110A
2 HHL HI HK1 SRO IN10SEP-1NT HI CROWNE PLAZA SFO AIRPT
  1A1KRAC-1/129.00USD/AGT098761234
```

In this case, the hotel reservation is segment 2. The following entry can be used to cancel only the hotel segment:

```
X2
```

If a reservation was booked directly with the hotel and then entered in the PNR itinerary, a CSS entry must be made after the reservation has been canceled. The status/action code *XK* is used for this purpose, as in the following example:

```
.2XK
```

This entry will change the status of segment 2 to XK, instructing SABRE to remove the direct booking from the itinerary. Note that this entry will remove the passive hotel segment from the itinerary but will not transmit the information to the vendor. The agent must contact the property directly to cancel the reservation.

Displaying Hotel Codes

The following entries can be used to display various codes used in the ShAArp Plus system:

DU*/HTL/VENDOR	Displays hotel chain codes
Y/HHL	Displays participating hotels
Y/HHL/NBR	Displays participating hotels with rate guarantee information
DU*HTL/TYPE	Displays room type codes
T/HHL/Q<Chain>	Displays policies for a specific chain
HCC<State name>	Displays two-letter state code
HCC<State code>	Displays state name
HCCC/<Country name>	Displays two-letter country code
HCCC/<Country code>	Displays country name

Summary

The SABRE hotel reservation system is named ShAArp Plus. Each hotel vendor represented in the system is identified by a two-letter chain code. The entry code *HOT* is used to display an index of participating hotels in a specified city. Optional qualifiers may be used to specify a location, a vendor, a rate category, properties with a particular type of room location, a maximum rate, a bedding type, or a maximum distance from the airport. Whereas a hotel index lists participating properties in a specified city, a date availability display indicates the properties, rooms, and rates that are available for a particular date range.

Information about each property is contained in a detailed record called a *hotel description*. The entry code *HOD* is used to display descriptions. When a hotel description is displayed, a hotel segment can be sold by room type and category. Some properties require that a reservation be guaranteed. A guarantee may also be required to hold a reservation for late arrival. When a hotel segment is sold, a room option such as a rollaway bed or a crib can be requested. If a hotel reservation is not booked through SABRE, the hotel segment can still be entered in the itinerary for reference.

New commands included in this chapter:

HOT2	Displays a hotel index by segment
HOTSFO	Displays a hotel index by city
HOTSFO/A	Displays a hotel index by city and location
HOTORD/RC-C	Displays a hotel index by city and rate category
HOTMIA/R-75	Displays a hotel index by maximum rate
HOTORD/MC/2Q	Displays a hotel by arrival airport, specified chain, and bedding type
HOTSFO/20NOV-3NT2	Displays date availability by city
HCCUT*M	Displays reference points by state and initial
HOT*3	Displays a hotel index from a list of reference points
HOTAZ-GRAND CANYON	Displays a hotel index by reference point
HCCC/NO*S	Displays reference points by country and initial
HOD*1	Displays a hotel description from a hotel index or an availability display
HOD7724	Displays a hotel description by property number
HODHI	Displays a chain policy description
01C1KRAC	Sells a hotel segment from a description
01B2QRAC/GDPST	Sells a hotel segment with guarantee information
01A1KWKD/EX-1	Sells a hotel segment with room option
HOM4R/2B1D-1	Modifies room information in a hotel segment
HOM2O/EX-1/RA-1	Modifies room options in a hotel segment
HOM5D/10MAY-15MAY	Modifies date information in a hotel segment
OHHTAAHK1...	Inputs a direct booking
X2	Cancels a hotel segment
.2XK	Deletes a direct booking
DU*/HTL/VENDOR	Displays hotel chain codes
Y/HHL	Displays participating hotels

KEY CONCEPTS AND TERMS

Identify the work, phrase, or symbol for each of the following concepts:

1. A two-letter code identifying a participating hotel vendor.

2. The entry to display hotel vendors and chain codes.

3. A code that indicates the number and size of beds provided at a specific room rate.

4. A code consisting of the room category and bedding codes for a specific rate.

5. The normal room rates that are offered by a hotel to the general public.

6. A list of participating hotels in a specified city.

7. The entry code that is used to display a hotel index or hotel availability.

8. In a hotel index, the alphanumeric code that shows the distance and direction of the property from the airport.

9. The one-letter code at the end of each listing in a hotel index.

10. Secondary codes used to narrow the selection in a hotel index display.

11. The secondary code that is used to specify properties with a particular room location.

12. The secondary code that is used to specify a maximum rate.

13. The secondary code that is used to specify the maximum distance from the airport.

14. A hotel listing showing only those rate categories that are available during a specified date range.

15. A detailed record of facilities, policies, guest plans, and other information about a specific property.

16. The entry code that is used to display detailed information about a specific property.

17. A policy permitting one to three children to stay in the same room as a parent at no additional charge.

18. An arrangement in which one to three daily meals are included in the room rate.

19. A summary of chain policies regarding deposits, refunds, extra guests, family plans, credit card acceptance, and so forth.

20. The entry code that is used to sell a hotel segment.

21. The part of a hotel segment that shows the travel agent's ARC or IATA number.

22. The secondary code that is used to indicate deposit or guarantee information when a hotel segment is sold.

23. When a credit card number is input to guarantee a hotel reservation, the code that is typed before the expiration date.

24. The entry used to display only the hotel segments in an itinerary.

25. The entry code that is used to display hotel reference points.

26. The entry code that is used to modify an existing hotel reservation.

27. In an entry to modify a hotel segment, the secondary code that is used to change room information.

28. The secondary code that is used to change the room option field.

29. The secondary code that is used to change date information.

REVIEW QUESTIONS

1. What entry code is used to display a hotel index?

2. Write the entry to display a hotel index for Salt Lake City.

3. Which entry would be used to display a hotel index after segment 2 of a displayed itinerary?

4. Write the entry to display an index of hotels near the Tampa airport.

5. Write the entry to display a hotel index for Phoenix, specifying the Best Western chain.

6. Write the entry to display a hotel index for Chicago, for arrival at O'Hare airport, specifying a maximum rate of $90.

7. Write the entry to display an index of hotels that offer corporate rates in St. Louis.

8. A client who will travel to Cincinnati prefers Marriott and would like a property in the city center area. She will arrive on 17 July and stay 3 nights. The room will be occupied by one adult. Write the entry to display a hotel index based on this client's needs.

9. A client who will travel to New York prefers Best Western and will arrive at LaGuardia airport. He would like a maximum rate of $125 and a room with one king bed. Write the entry to display hotel availability after segment 2 based on this client's needs.

10. A client who will travel to Los Angeles prefers Holiday Inn. He would like a corporate rate and wants to stay near the airport. Write the entry to display hotel availability after segment 3 for two nights and one adult per room.

11. A client who will travel to Philadelphia prefers Hilton. She would like a corporate rate of $100 or less, and wants to stay in the city center area. Write the entry to display hotel availability after segment 1 for two nights and one adult per room.

12. Write the entry to display a list of hotel reference points in Illinois (IL) with the initial *C*.

13. Write the entry to display a list of reference points in Australia (AU) with the initial *K*.

14. When a list of reference points is displayed, what entry can be used to display an index for the reference point in line 6?

15. What entry would be used to display a hotel index for Los Angeles with Disneyland as a reference point?

16. A client will arrive in Miami on 12 February and depart on 16 February. Write the entry to display date availability for one adult.

17. Two adults will arrive in Boise on 24 June and stay six nights. Write the entry to display date availability.

18. Two adults will arrive in Greensboro on 8 August and stay three nights. They would like a maximum rate of $75 and a room with two queen beds. Write the entry to display date availability.

19. A client will arrive at Kennedy airport in New York on 12 October and depart on 17 October. He prefers the Marriott chain and would like a corporate rate. Write the entry to display date availability for one adult.

20. Two adults will arrive in Honolulu on 2 March and stay five nights. They would like an oceanfront room with one king bed and a maximum rate of $150. Write the entry to display date availability.

21. When hotel availability is displayed, what entry will display a description of the property in line 2?

22. Write the entry to display the hotel description for property number 5402.

23. Assume a client asks what credit cards are accepted by the Marriott chain. What entry can be used to display a policy description?

24. What is the correct room type code for a superior room with two queen beds?

25. What is the meaning of the room type code *A1K*?

26. What room type code refers to a standard room with two double beds?

27. What is the meaning of the room type code *S2K*?

28. What room type code would indicate a standard room with two twin beds?

29. What is the meaning of the rate category code *TUR*?

30. What rate category code refers to a hotel's standard rates offered to the general public?

31. What type of rates are represented by the category code *COR*?

32. What rate code refers to weekend rates?

33. When a hotel description is displayed, what entry will sell a hotel segment for one room of type B2Q at the rack rate?

34. Assume a description is displayed. A client would like to book three rooms of type C1D at the corporate rate. The reservation will be guaranteed by a credit card, AX6002876110092442, expiring November 1998. The cardholder's surname is Franklin. Write the correct entry to sell the hotel segment.

35. Write the entry to sell one room of type B1Q at the weekend rate from a displayed description. An adult rollaway bed will be required for an extra guest.

36. Write the entry to sell one room of type A1K at the rack rate. A deposit will be sent to the property to guarantee the reservation.

37. Write the entry to sell, from a displayed description, one room of type S2K at the tour rate. A crib will be required. The room will not be guaranteed for late arrival.

38. Assume a description is displayed. A client would like to book one room of type A1K at the rack rate. The reservation will be guaranteed by her credit card, IK3323987622387191, expiring December 1998. The cardholder's surname is Jenkins. Write the correct entry to sell the hotel segment.

39. Write the entry to sell, from a displayed description, one room of type C2T at the weekend rate. Assume that a deposit or guarantee is not required.

40. Write the entry to sell, from a displayed description, one room of type B2D at the corporate rate. A child's rollaway bed is requested. A deposit will be sent to guarantee the reservation.

Refer to the following hotel segment to answer questions 41–48:

3 HHL HH HK3 BWI IN22JUN-4NT HH TOWERS 3B2QCOR-1/99.00USD/
AGT098761234/CF-2327665

41. What is the segment number of this reservation?

42. With which chain is the reservation booked?

43. On what date will the clients check out of the hotel?

44. How many rooms are booked?

45. Which rate category has been used to determine the rate?

46. Assume two additional rooms will be required. Write the correct entry to modify the hotel segment.

47. Assume the clients will stay five nights. Write the correct entry to modify the reservation.

48. What entry would be used to cancel the hotel reservation without affecting other segments in the itinerary?

49. What entry is used to display chain codes?

50. What entry would be used to modify a hotel reservation in segment 4 to request a rollaway bed for a child?

APPLICATIONS

Read the following scenario, and decide what actions should be performed to satisfy the client's preferences and needs. Briefly describe how you would handle the situation, and then write the required entries.

Several employees of Electro-Dyne Corporation will travel from Pittsburgh to attend a conference in Denver. They will depart on 21 May around 10 A.M. When you display availability, your clients select a flight in line 3. They will return on 25 May around 3 P.M. When you display availability, your clients select a flight in line 2. They will travel in Q class on both segments.

The passengers' names are Mr. G. Clark, Mr. L. Park, Mr. A. Shark, Ms. F. Bark, Ms. H. Stark, and Ms. V. Lark. The agency phone is 412-555-2001, and the clients' business phone is 412-555-7777. The reservation was received from Mr. Clark.

The passengers will need hotel accommodations in Denver. They will arrive on 21 May and stay four nights. Each room will be occupied by one adult. Your clients would like a hotel near the city center. The hotel availability display appears as follows:

```
1 BW 2515 BW  CAPRI HOTEL PLAZA         -C DENVER CO DWTN -12 O
       32.00   RAC COR
2 DY 8119 DY  DENVER SOUTH-TECH CTR -C ENGLEWOOD CO   -21 O
       59.00   RAC COR
3 HI 3319 HI  DOWNTOWN                 -C 15TH & GLENARM -18 H
       65.00   RAC COR
4 MC 6623 MC  RESIDENCE INN DTWN       -C 2777 E ZUNI    -20 O
       49.00   RAC COR
5 HI 9307 HI  EMBASSY SUITES SE        -C HAMPDEN AVE    -23 O
       80.00   RAC COR GVT
```

The Embassy Suites is close to the conference site. In the property description, the rate grid appears as follows:

RATES-	A1K	A2Q	B1K	B2Q	C2D
RAC G	135.00	135.00	110.00	110.00	95.00
COR 6			95.00		80.00
GVT G			85.00		75.00

Your clients would like six rooms at the lowest available corporate rate. The reservation will be guaranteed by credit card account AX300019285555, expiring October 1998. The cardholder's surname is Clark.

Chapter 15

Car Rentals

Outline

Car Vendor Codes   Selling Car Segments

Car Type Codes   Modifying Car Segments

Basic Car Availability   Displaying Vendor Policies

Rate Displays

Chapter Objectives

After you complete this chapter, you should be able to:

1. Identify common car type codes.
2. Display car availability by segment.
3. Display car availability by pickup date and city.
4. Book a car rental from a car availability display.
5. Obtain a car rental rate quotation.
6. Display an index of car rental outlets for a designated vendor in a designated city.
7. Alter the rate display to change the car type, date, location, or vendor.
8. Display competitive prices in a rate shopper display.
9. Book a car rental from a rate quotation.
10. Enter optional data in a car rental booking.
11. Modify a car segment.
12. Display vendor policies and information.

PROBLEM

You are making travel arrangements for a client planning a ski trip to Innsbruck. He would like to rent a car at the airport for pickup on arrival and wants to know what company offers the lowest daily rate for a station wagon with a ski rack.

SABRE SOLUTION

Display car availability at the airport in INN, then obtain a rate quote for a station wagon. Book the car rental and request a ski rack.

In this chapter, you will learn how to display car availability and rates, display vendor policies, and sell, modify, or cancel a car segment.

Car Vendor Codes

Any type of rental vehicle that can be booked through a CRS may be referred to as a *car*. The SABRE car rental system is named *Cars Plus*.

Car vendors that participate in the Cars Plus system are identified by two-letter **vendor codes**. For instance, *ZE* refers to the Hertz chain, and *ZD* refers to the Budget chain. When a car rental is booked, both the car type and the vendor code must be specified. See Table 15-1 for examples of major car rental vendors that permit reservations to be booked through SABRE.

The entry **Y/CAR** can be used to display the car vendor table, as follows:

```
Y/CAR
```

The car vendor table is a complete list of vendor codes for participating car companies.

Car Type Codes

To facilitate airline, hotel, car rental, and other types of bookings, the major computer reservation systems have adopted a coding system known as **Standard Interline Passenger Procedures (SIPP)**. The SIPP codes enable airline reservation systems to exchange data with airlines, hotel chains, and car rental chains.

Table 15-1 Sample Car Rental Vendor Codes.

Code	Vendor
AI	American International
AJ	Ajax
AL	Alamo
ED	Eurodollar
EP	Europcar
FR	Freedom
HO	Holiday
RW	Rent-a-Wreck
TR	Tropical
ZC	Econo Car
ZE	Hertz
ZI	Avis
ZL	National
ZN	General
ZR	Dollar
ZT	Thrifty
ZS	Sears
ZD	Budget

SIPP **car type** codes are composed of the following elements:

1. vehicle class (size)
2. body type
3. automatic or manual shift
4. air conditioning

Each element is represented by a one-letter code as shown in Table 15-2. The elements may be combined to indicate a particular car type. For instance, **ECAR** signifies an economy car with two or four doors, automatic shift, and air conditioning. See Table 15-3 for the most common car types offered by major car rental chains.

The car types ECAR, CCAR, ICAR, and SCAR may be abbreviated to the first two letters. For example, *ECAR* may be abbreviated to *EC*.

Table 15-2 SIPP Car Type Elements.

SIZE	TYPE	SHIFT	A.C.
E economy	B car/2 door	A automatic	R yes
C compact	C car/2 or 4 door	M manual	N no
I intermediate	D car/4 door		
S standard	L limousine		
F full size	V van		
L luxury	T convertible		
M mini	S Sports car		
P premium	F 4-wheel drive		
X special	X special		
	W wagon		
	P pickup		
	J all-terrain vehicle		
	K truck		
	R recreational vehicle		

Table 15-3 Common Car Types Available Through Car Rental Chains.

ECAR	Economy car/automatic shift/air conditioning
ECMR	Economy car/manual shift/air conditioning
CCAR	Compact car/automatic shift/air conditioning
ICAR	Intermediate car/automatic shift/ air conditioning
SCAR	Standard car/automatic shift/air conditioning
SWAR	Standard wagon/automatic shift/air conditioning
FCAR	Full-size car/automatic shift/air conditioning
PCAR	Premium car/ automatic shift/air conditioning
LCAR	Luxury car/ automatic shift/air conditioning
XXAR	Special request/automatic shift/air conditioning

The following codes can be used to indicate all vehicles of a particular type:

ACAR   All cars

AVAN   All vans

ASPT   All sports cars

AWGN   All station wagons

ALMO   All limousines

ACNV   All convertibles

AFWD   All 4-wheel drive vehicles

A complete list of car type codes can be displayed with the following entry:

DU*/CAR/TYPE

Basic Car Availability

The **car availability** function is used to display vendors and car types for a specified city and date. The entry code **CAR** is used to display basic car availability. If an itinerary is present, basic car availability can be displayed for any arrival point as follows:

FORMAT   CAR<Segment to follow>

EXAMPLE   CAR2

This example requests basic car availability in the arrival point of segment 2.

The date on which a rental car will be picked up is called the **pickup date**, and the city where the car will be obtained is called the **pickup point**. When car availability is obtained from an air segment, the pickup date and point are derived from the departure date and arrival point of specified segment. If an air itinerary does not exist, or if the pickup date and point differ from the arrival information in the itinerary, the date and city must be specified as follows:

FORMAT   CAR<Pickup date><Pickup point>

EXAMPLE   CAR10MAYSFO

To illustrate, assume a client inquires about rental cars for pickup on August 22 in Minneapolis. The following entry can be used to display car availability:

CAR22AUGMSP

Rate Displays

A basic car availability display shows available vendors and car types without rate information. Two entry codes may be used to display availability with rates:

CQ   Car rate quote

CF   Car fare shopper

Basic Car Availability

Assume a PNR has the following itinerary:

```
1  TW  330Y  16DEC  T  STLMIA  HK1   515P   808P
2  TW  512Y  20DEC  J  MIASTL  HK1  1030A   352P
```

The client inquires about rental car availability in Miami after the outbound segment. The agent uses the following entry to display car availability:

```
CAR1
```

SABRE responds as follows:

MIA MIAMI   16DEC

	ECMN	ECAR	CCAR	ICAR	SCAR	LCAR	FCAR	PCAR	SWAR
ZI AVIS	NN	CL	NN	SS	CL	NN	NN	SS	NN
ZD-BUDGET	SS	CL	SS	SS	NN	NN	—	NN	NN
ZR-DOLLAR	NN	SS	NN	SS	SS	SS	—	—	—
ZE-HERTZ	CL	CL	CL	NN	SS	SS	NN	NN	NN
ZL-NATIONAL	SS	NN	SS	NN	SS	SS	—	—	NN
HO PAYLESS	SS	CL	NN	SS	CL	NN	NN	SS	NN
ZS-SEARS	SS	CL	SS	SS	NN	NN	—	NN	NN
AI-AMER INTL	SS	SS	SS	SS	SS	SS	—	—	NN
AL-ALAMO	CL	CL	SS	SS	SS	SS	NN	NN	NN

The carriers are listed on the left. Each column corresponds to a car type. The status **SS** indicates that the car type is available to sell. The following status codes may appear in a car availability display:

SS   Available to sell (Sell/Sell)

NN   On request only (Send "need" message)

CL   Not available (closed)

—   Not offered

The entry code **CQ** is used to request the rates offered by a specified vendor. To obtain a rate quote, the pickup date, drop-off date, pickup time, and drop-off time are required. If an air itinerary is present, the following format can be used to obtain a rate quote:

FORMAT   CQ<Arrival segment>/<Departure segment>-<Vendor>

EXAMPLE   CQ2/3-ZD

This example will display rates offered by Budget (ZD) for the arrival point of segment 2. The pickup date and time will be obtained from segment 2, and the drop-off date and time will be obtained from segment 3.

To display a rate quote without an air itinerary, the following format may be used:

FORMAT   CQ<Vendor><City>/<Pickup date>-<Drop-off date>/<Pickup time>-<Drop-off time>

EXAMPLE   CQZILAX/10MAY-15MAY/2P-10A

This example will display rates for Avis in Los Angeles. The vehicle will be picked up on 10 May at 2:00 P.M. and returned on 15 May at 10:00 A.M. Note that a slash is typed before the pickup date and after the drop-off date.

A car type can be specified as follows:

    CQZILAX/10MAY-15MAY/2P-10A/CC

This entry requests car rates for compact cars (CC).

A **rate plan** can be specified, as follows:

    CQZILAX/10MAY-15MAY/2P-10A/SC/W

In this example, the code *W* specifies weekly rates. The following rate plans can be requested:

Code	Rate Plans
D	Daily rates
W	Weekly rates
M	Monthly rates
E	Weekend rates

If a rate plan is not specified, daily rates will be displayed.

A rate category may also be specified, as follows:

    CQZILAX/10MAY-15MAY/2P-10A/SC/P

In this entry, promotional rates are requested. If a rate category is not specified, standard rates will be displayed. The following rate categories can be requested:

Code	Rate Category
S or STD	Standard
P or PRO	Promotional
A or ASC	Association
G or GOV	Government
I or IND	Industry
C or COR	Corporate
U or CNU	Consortium
B or BUS	Business
C or CNV	Convention
P or PKG	Package
C or CRE	Credential

Rate Displays

A ssume a PNR has the following itinerary:

```
1  UA  709Y  22MAR  T  PVDLAX  HK1  715A   1214P
2  UA  560Y  25MAR  F  LAXPVD  HK1  1030A  801P
```

The client inquires about rental car rates offered by Hertz in Los Angeles. The following entry can be used to display the rate quote:

CQ1/2-ZE

A car type may be specified as follows:

CQ1/2-ZE/SC

In this example, the abbreviation *SC* is used to specify standard-sized cars. If a car type is not specified, SABRE will display rates for a limited selection of car types.

Either the one-letter code or the three-letter code may be used to specify a rate category. The rate categories are defined as follows:

Standard rates are a vendor's normal unrestricted rates.

Promotional rates have specific restrictions, such as an advance reservation requirement or a minimum rental period.

Association rates are available to selected groups, such as the American Association of Retired Persons or the American Automobile Association.

Government rates are discounted rates that have been negotiated with a government branch or agency.

Industry rates are discounted rates offered to individuals employed in the travel industry, such as travel agents and airline personnel.

Corporate rates are discounted rates that have been negotiated with a corporation.

Consortium rates are discounted rates offered to travel consortiums.

Business rates are discounted rates offered to business travelers who do not qualify for a corporate rate.

Convention rates are discounted rates offered to attendees of a convention or conference.

Package rates are offered in conjunction with other travel products, such as hotel accommodations or a cruise.

Credential rates require the client to present a specified form of identification, such as a coupon or a voucher.

Rate Quote

Assume a client requests the rates for standard-sized cars offered by Budget in Atlanta. He will pick up the vehicle on 11 January at 3 P.M. and return it on 13 January at 4 P.M. Based on this information, the following entry is used to obtain a rate quote:

CQZDATL/11JAN-13JAN/3P-4P/SC

In this example, a rate plan is not specified. Thus, daily rates will be displayed. SABRE will respond with the following car rate quote display:

```
1BUDGET  ATLANTA - ON    IN TERMINAL STD THRU 12FEB
HOURS - 24 HOURS 7 DAYS
*********************************************************************************

4S * WEEKEND RATE APPLIES FOR PICKUP 600A FRIDAY
        .TYPE    ST    DAILY    MILES    CHG    R
01G     SCAR     S     52.00    UNL      .00    -
02G     SCAR1    C     49.00    UNL      .00    D
03G     SCAR     S     46.00    300      .25    -
04G     SCAR1    N     42.00    UNL      .00    -

-----------------------------------------------------------------------------------
D- 1 DAY ADVANCE
E- 7 DAY ADVANCE
```

Each line of the display is numbered. The code *G* after the line number indicates that the rate is guaranteed. The car type is indicated in the "Type" column. The availability status is indicated by a one-letter code. The status **S** indicates that the car type is available to sell, **N** indicates that the car type is available on a request basis only, and **C** indicates that the car type is not available.

The mileage allowance appears in the "Miles" column, and the mileage charge is displayed in the "Chg" column. In line 3, the rate includes a mileage allowance of 300 miles, and a charge of $0.25 is assessed for excess mileage. However, the rate in line 4 has an unlimited mileage allowance; thus, no mileage charge is indicated.

The column labeled "R" is used to indicate any applicable rules. The codes in this column refer to the rules at the bottom of the display. In this example, the rate in line 2 requires a one-day advance reservation.

Off-Airport Locations

A pickup location other than an airport outlet is called an **off-airport location**. The entry code **CQL** is used to list off-airport offices, as follows:

CQLZEATL

This example will list Hertz locations in Atlanta. SABRE will respond as follows:

```
1  ATL   HERTZ   ATLANTA - ON              IN-TERMINAL
2  C10   HERTZ   202 COURTLAND ST. NE      NON-AIRPORT
3  C17   HERTZ   MARRIOTT MARQUIS          NON-AIRPORT
4  C15   HERTZ   246 PERIMETER CENTER      NON-AIRPORT
5  C21   HERTZ   MARRIOTT HOTEL I-75 NW    NON-AIRPORT
6  C12   HERTZ   4711 BEST RD              NON-AIRPORT
```

Each location has a line number and is identified by a three-digit code. An area can be specified as follows:

CQLZEATL/C

In this example, the indicator *C* requests locations in the city center area. Other area indicators include *R* (resort) and *S* (suburban).

When a vendor location list is displayed, a rate quote may be obtained as follows:

FORMAT   CQ*<Line>/<Pickup date>-<Drop-off date>/<Pickup time>-<Drop-off time>

EXAMPLE   CQ*3/10SEP-14SEP/2P-11A

This example requests a rate quote for the location in line 3. In this example, the rates for pickup at the Marriott Marquis hotel will be displayed.

The three-digit location code can be used to obtain a rate quote without displaying the location list, as follows:

FORMAT   CQ<Vendor><Pickup point><Pickup location>-<Drop-off point><Drop-off location>/<Dates>/<Times>

EXAMPLE   CQZEATLC17-ATLC17/16SEP-19SEP/11A-10A

In this example, the vehicle will be picked up in Atlanta at location C17 and will be returned at the same location.

Modifying a Rate Display

An existing rate quote can be modified to display a different car type, rate, pickup date, or location. The entry code **CQ*** is used to redisplay or modify a rate quote, as follows:

CQ*	Redisplays the current rate quote
CQ*SC	Changes the car type to SC
CQ*ALL	Redisplays the rate quote for all car types
CQ*C01	Changes the outlet location to C01
CQ*ZL	Changes the vendor to ZL
CQ*/9A	Changes pickup time
CQ*-6P	Changes drop-off time
CQ*/9A-6P	Changes pickup and drop-off times
CQ*/22MAY-27MAY	Changes pickup and drop-off dates

Rate Shopper Displays

A **rate shopper display** gives the lowest available rates offered by all participating vendors in a specified market. The rates are listed from least expensive to most expensive. The entry code **CF** is used to obtain a fare shopper display. As with a vendor rate quote, the pickup date, the pickup time, the drop-off date, and the drop-off time are required. If an air itinerary is present, a rate shopper display can be obtained from a flight segment, as follows:

CF1/2

This example will display low-to-high rates for the arrival point of segment 1, obtaining the pickup date and time from segment 1 and the drop-off date and time from segment 2.

A car type may be specified as follows:

CF1/2/CC

In this example, the car type *CC* is used to request the rates for compact cars. SABRE will respond with the following display:

```
*******************************************************************
          CAR CO   ST   DAILY   MILE   CHG   LOCN   CAT   TYPE
   01G  HO HOLIDAY  S   25.00   UNL    .00   OFF    S     CCMR
   02G  TR THRIFTY  C   29.00   UNL    .00   OFF    S     CCAR
   03G  ZD BUDGET   N   32.00   UNL    .00   IN     P     CCAR
   04G  ZR DOLLAR   S   35.00   UNL    .00   IN     S     CCAR
   05G  ZI AVIS     S   39.00   100    .35   IN     S     CCAR
   06G  ZE HERTZ    N   43.00   100    .35   IN     S     CCAR
```

Each line of the rate shopper display is numbered. The display shows the vendor code and name, availability status, daily rate, mileage allowance, mileage charge, location, rate category, and car type. In this example, the lowest rate is offered by Holiday at an off-airport location. This rate is the standard rate for a compact car with two or four doors, manual shift, and air conditioning.

If an itinerary is not present, or if the pickup date and time differ from the arrival information in the itinerary, the pickup point must be specified, along with the rental dates and times, as follows:

CFMIA/12JUL-16JUL/10A-9A/SC

The following secondary codes may be used to obtain a rate shopper display:

UN   Unlimited mileage

FM   Free miles

TM   Time and mileage

For example, the following entry requests only those rates that include unlimited mileage:

CFMIA/12JUL-16JUL/10A-9A//SC/UN

A vendor rate quote can be displayed from a rate shopper display as follows:

CF*3

This example will display a rate quote for the vendor in line 3 of the rate shopper display.

Rules Displays

When a rate shopper display has been obtained, the rules governing each rate can be displayed as follows:

FORMAT   CF*R<Line>

EXAMPLE   CF*R1

This example will display the rules for the rate in line 1 of the rate shopper display. The rules display appears as follows:

```
DATE OF PICKUP        - 22MAR        - TUESDAY
DATE OF RETURN        - 27MAR        - SUNDAY
RATE                  - USD    39.99    100F    .10      DAILY
XTRA DAY/HOUR         - USD XD          XH 7.99    10F
ADVANCE BOOKING       - 1DAY
MINIMUM DAYS          - 1
MAXIMUM DAYS          - 14
PICKUP AFTER          - 0600
RETURN  BY            - 2400
OVERNIGHT REQUIRED    - MONDAY
RATE  CODE            - SUPDAY
```

The entry code **0C** is used to sell a car segment. When car rental rates are displayed, the following format can be used to sell a car segment:

FORMAT   0C<Line>

EXAMPLE   0C1

This example will book a car rental at the rate in line 1 of the rate display. This entry can be used to sell a reservation from either a rate quote or a rate shopper display.
   To illustrate, assume a PNR has the following itinerary:

```
1 DL1195Q   21MAR J  BOSABQ  HK1 815A   205P
2 DL1123Q   24MAR T  ABQDFW  HK1 500A   728A
3 DL1654    24MAR T  DFWBOS  HK1 922A   205P
```

The following entry will display a rate quote for intermediate-sized cars offered by Avis in Albuquerque:

CQ1/2-ZI/IC

The pickup date and time are obtained from segment 1, and the drop-off date and time are obtained from segment 2. SABRE responds as follows:

```
1AVIS ALBUQUERQUE  -  ON     IN TERMINAL STD SAT   21MAR
HOURS- 24 HOURS 7 DAYS
*********************************************************
        .TYPE  ST      DAILY    MILES  CHG    R
01G     ICAR   S       54.00    UNL    .00    -
02G     ICAR1  S       39.75    100    .25    -
```

Assume the client would like the $54.00 daily rate with unlimited mileage. The following entry can be used to book the car rental:

0C1

In this example, the desired rate is in line 1 of the display. Note the code *G* after the line number, signifying that the rate is guaranteed.
   The following is an example of a car segment:

```
3 CAR ZI  21MAR  J  SSI   ABQ/24MAR/ICAR/BS-4665545/CF-
```

In this example, the car reservation is the third segment in the itinerary. The car segment shows the vendor and the pickup date and day of the week (see Figure 15-1). The segment status *SS1* indicates that a reservation will be confirmed for one vehicle.

The pickup point, drop-off date, and car type are also shown. The booking source (BS) is identified by the agency ARC/IATA number. When the transaction is ended, a message will be transmitted to notify the vendor about the booking. The vendor will send back a confirmation number, which will be appended to the car segment in the CF field.

To book more than one car, include the number of cars as follows:

0C1‡2

This example will book two cars from line 1 of a rate display.

Optional Data

Optional data may be included in a car sell entry as follows:

0C1/ID-1233456

In this example, the secondary code *ID* is used to input an identification number, such as a Hertz #1 Club account or a frequent traveler number.

The following are other secondary codes that may be used to input optional data:

Secondary Codes	Optional Data
ARR-	Arrival information
W-	Written confirmation
CD-	Corporate discount number
RT-	Rate input by agent (not guaranteed)
IR-	Itinerary remarks
PH-	Outlet phone number
SI-	Service information

Modifying Car Segments

The entry code **CM** is used to modify an existing car segment, as follows:

FORMAT CM<Segment>/<Field>-<Data>

EXAMPLE CM3/CF-77049872001

Figure 15-1 Sample Car Segment Display.

```
              Vendor    Day of week      Drop-off date
                |           |               |
   3   CAR   ZI   21MAR   J   SS1   ABQ/24MAR/ICAR/BS/-4665545/CF-
                     |                          |
                 Pickup date                 Car type
```

This example will add a confirmation number to a car reservation in segment 3. The field identifier *CF* is used to input the confirmation number. This procedure might be required if a car segment was not booked through SABRE and a verbal confirmation number was received by telephone.

Other field identifiers that may be used to modify car segments are shown in Table 15-4.

The following are examples of car modification entries:

CM2/PD-18JUL	Changes the pickup date of segment 2
CM3/BS-98076543	Adds the booking source to segment 3
CM2/PD-23MAR/CT-ECAR/CD-99869002	Changes the pickup date and car type, and adds a corporate discount number to segment 2

Displaying Vendor Policies

The entry code **CP*** is used to display vendor policies, as follows:

FORMAT   CP*<Car company><City>

EXAMPLE   CP*ZESFO

This example will display policies for Hertz in San Francisco. SABRE will respond as follows:

```
HERTZ        --      SAN FRANCISCO AIRPORT        --      IN-TERMINAL
ADDRS-SAN FRANCISCO INTERNATIONAL AIRPORT
        19982 AIRPORT BLVD
        BURLINGAME, CA 94128
PHONE-*415-555-1001-AIRPORT OPERATIONS/NO
        RESERVATIONS
        415-555-4321-UA TERMINAL COUNTER
        415-555-3003-INTERNATIONAL TERMINAL
HOURS-EVERY DAY FROM  0630AM  TO  1200MIDNITE
INSUR-OPTIONAL  ON ALL TYPES EXCEPT LCAR/PSAR
PAI   -PERSONAL ACCIDENT INSURANCE 7.95/DAY
CDW  -COLLISION DAMAGE WAIVER 7.95/DAY
GAS   -TANKS SHOULD BE RETURNED FULL.  OTHERWISE, A
        LOCALLY DETERMINED CHARGE WILL BE ADDED TO
        THE FINAL BILL.
```

Table 15-4 Field Identifiers Used to Modify Car Segments.

PD	Pickup date	CT	Car type
RD	Return date	CD	Corporate discount number
DO	Drop-off city	SI	Service information
PUP	Pickup location	ARR	Arrival time
PH	Phone number	ID	Customer I.D. number
DOC	Drop-off charge	BS	Booking source

The following codes can be used to display only a specified category:

PH	Phone
H	Hours
I	Insurance
PA	Personal accident insurance
CD	Collision damage waiver
TA	Taxes
G	Gasoline allowance/charges
EX	Express return
S	Shuttle (airport transportation)
PY	Payment policies
V	Valid credit cards
CO	Commissions
EQ	Equipment
O	Other
D	Drop-off points allowed
M	Makes of vehicles
R	Rules
F	Facts

For example, the following entry will display only the vendor phone number and the hours of operation for Avis in San Francisco:

CP*ZISFO/PH/H

The category code consists of either one or two alpha characters.

While a specified category is being displayed, the following entry can be used to display the entire policy record:

CP*

Summary

Car rental companies that participate in the Cars Plus system are identified by two-letter vendor codes. SIPP codes for rental cars are based on the vehicle class, body type, automatic or manual shift, and air conditioning. The car types ECAR, CCAR, ICAR, and SCAR may be abbreviated using the first two letters.

The car availability function is used to display vendors and car types for a specified city and date. When car availability is obtained from an air segment, the pickup date and point are derived from the departure date and arrival point of a specified segment. If an air itinerary does not exist, or if the pickup date and point differ from the arrival information in the itinerary, the date and city must be specified.

Two entry codes may be used to display availability with rates: *CQ* for car rate quotes and *CF* for car fare shopper displays. A pickup location other than an airport outlet is called an *off-airport location*. An existing rate quote can be modified to display a different car type, rate, pickup date, or location. Car segments can be sold from a rate display by line number. When a rate shopper display has been obtained, the rules governing each rate can be displayed by item number. Vendor policies can also be displayed.

New commands included in this chapter:

Y/CAR	Displays the car vendor table
CAR2	Displays car availability by segment
CAR10MAYSFO	Displays car availability by date and city
CQ1/2-ZE/IC	Displays a rate quote by segment reference, vendor, and car type
CQZILAX/10MAY-15MAY/ 2P-10A/SC/W	Displays a car rate quote by vendor, city, pickup and drop-off dates, pickup and drop-off times, car type, and rate plan
CQLZEATL	Displays vendor locations by city
CQ*3/10SEP-14SEP/ 2P-11A	Displays a rate quote from a location index
CQZEATLC17-ATLC17/ 16SEP-19SEP/ 11A-10A	Displays a rate quote by pickup and drop-off location
CQ*	Redisplays the current rate quote
CQ*SC	Changes the car type
CQ*ALL	Redisplays the rate quote for all car types
CQ*C01	Changes the outlet location
CQ*ZL	Changes the vendor
CQ*/9A	Changes the pickup time
CQ*-6P	Changes the drop-off time
CQ*/9A-6P	Changes pickup and drop-off times
CQ*/22MAY-27MAY	Changes pickup and drop-off dates
CF1/2/CC	Displays a rate shopper display by segment reference and car type

CFMIA/12JUL-14JUL/ 10A-9A/EC/E	Displays a rate shopper display by city, pickup and drop-off dates, pickup and drop-off times, car type, and rate plan
CF*2	Displays a rate quote from a rate shopper display
CF*R1	Displays car rules from a rate shopper display
0C1	Sells a car segment from a rate display
0C1‡3	Books multiple cars from a rate display
0C1/ID-1233456	Sells a car segment with optional data
CM3/CF-77049872001	Adds the confirmation number to an existing car segment
CM2/PD-18JUL	Changes the pickup date of a car segment
CM3/BS-98076543	Adds the booking source to a car segment
CM2/CT-ECAR	Changes the car type in a car segment

STUDENT REVIEW

KEY CONCEPTS AND TERMS

Identify the word, phrase, or symbol for each of the following concepts:

1. A two-letter code identifying a car rental vendor.
2. The entry to display the car vendor table.
3. A standard coding system for the CRS industry, enabling airline reservation systems to exchange data with airlines, hotel chains, and car rental chains.
4. A code identifying the vehicle class, body type, type of shift, and availability of air conditioning.
5. The function that is used to display vendors and car types for a specified city and date.
6. The entry code that is used to display car availability.
7. The status code in a car availability display that indicates a car type is available to sell.
8. The date on which a rental car will be obtained by the driver.
9. The city where a rental car will be obtained.
10. The entry code that is used to request rates of a specific car vendor.
11. Adjusted rates for daily, weekly, monthly, and weekend rentals.
12. A car vendor's normal unrestricted rates.
13. Rates that have specific restrictions, such as an advance reservation requirement or a minimum rental period.
14. Discounted rates that have been negotiated with a corporation.
15. Rates that are offered in conjunction with other travel products, such as hotel

accommodations or a cruise.

16. The code in a rate quote display that indicates a car type is available on a request basis only.

17. The code that indicates a car type is not available.

18. A pickup location other than an airport outlet.

19. The entry code that is used to list locations other than airport outlets.

20. The entry code that is used to redisplay or modify a rate quote.

21. A display of the lowest available rates offered by all participating vendors in a specific market.

22. The entry code that is used to display the lowest available rates.

23. The entry code that is used to sell a car segment.

24. The entry code that is used to modify an existing car segment.

25. The entry code that is used to display vendor policies.

Answers:

21. rate shopper display; 22. CF; 23. OC; 24. CM; 25. CP*.

tional rates; 14. corporate rates; 15. package rates; 16. C; 17. N; 18. off-airport location; 19. CQI; 20. CQ*;

ity; 6. CAR; 7. SS; 8. pickup date; 9. pickup point; 10. CQ; 11. rate plans; 12. standard rates; 13. promo-

1. vendor code; 2. Y/CAR; 3. Standard Interline Passenger Procedures (SIPP); 4. car type; 5. car availabil-

REVIEW QUESTIONS

Write the correct code for each of the following:

1. economy car with two or four doors, manual shift, and no air conditioning

2. intermediate-sized car with automatic shift and air conditioning

3. standard-sized wagon with automatic shift and air conditioning

4. compact car with two or four doors, manual shift, and no air conditioning

5. standard-sized car with two or four doors, automatic shift, and air conditioning

6. premium sports car with two or four doors, manual shift, and air conditioning

7. weekend rates

8. weekly rates

9. promotional rates

10. travel industry rates

11. Write the entry to display car availability after segment 4 of an itinerary.

12. Write the entry to display car availability without rates in GVA on 8 April.

13. A client will arrive in Denver on 22 June. Write the entry to display car availability without rates.

14. Write the entry to display rates offered by Hertz in Madrid (MAD) for pickup on 22 July at 10 A.M. and return on 25 July at 9 A.M.

15. Write the entry to display rates for economy cars offered by Avis after segment 2, obtaining the drop-off date and time from segment 3.

16. Write the entry to display weekend rates for Avis in New Orleans for pickup on 19 July at 8 A.M. and return on 22 July at 8 A.M.

17. Write the entry to display rates for compact cars offered by Budget in Seattle for pickup on 15 April at 2 P.M. and drop-off on 18 April at 9 A.M.

18. Write the entry to display rates for a standard-sized car from National for pickup after segment 1, obtaining the drop-off date and time from segment 2.

19. Write the entry to display the lowest weekly rates for an intermediate-sized car from all vendors in Miami, for pickup on 26 March at 4 P.M. and return 31 March at 8 A.M.

20. Write the entry to display rates for economy cars for pickup in Seattle on 6 August at 11 A.M. and return 8 August at 9 A.M.

21. Write the entry to display the lowest weekend rates for a standard-sized car from all vendors after segment 4, obtaining the drop-off date and time from segment 5.

22. Write the entry to display Budget's rental policies in Honolulu.

23. Write the entry to sell a car from line 3 of a rate display.

24. Write the entry to sell three cars from line 2 of a rate display.

25. Write the entry to sell one car from line 5 of a rate display with a car company I.D. code of 724335.

26. Write the entry to display only policies pertaining to insurance and collision damage waivers from Hertz in St. Louis.

27. Write the entry to modify a car reservation in segment 2 to change the pickup date to 24 March.

28. Write the entry to sell two cars from line 4.

29. Write the entry to modify a car reservation in segment 3 to change the drop-off date to 12 May.

30. Write the entry to modify a car reservation in segment 5 to change the car type to ECAR.

31. Write the entry to display car rules from line 3 of a rate shopper display.

APPLICATIONS

Read the following scenario, and decide what actions should be performed to satisfy the client's preferences and needs. Briefly describe how you would handle the situation, and then write the required entries.

Your agency previously made travel arrangements for Ms. Page. In her PNR, the name field and itinerary appear as follows:

```
1.1PAGE/H MS
1  CO   591Y  21MAR   S   DTWABQ   HK1    540P   852P
2  CO   550Y  22MAR   M   ABQDEN   HK1    845A   956A
3  HHL  HY  SS1  DEN  IN22MAR-OUT27MAR  5NT  3012  HYATT  DENVER
     1B1Q-1/85.00USD/AGT08920391/SI-CF/33421567
4  CO   524Y  27MAR   J   DENDTW   HK1   1035A   317P
```

Your client requests a car rental in Denver. She will pick the car up at the airport on arrival and will return it on 27 March at 9:30 A.M. She prefers a compact car with automatic shift and air conditioning, and she wants the lowest rate offered by any car company. When you display the rates, your client selects the vendor, car type, and rate in line 3.

Chapter 16

Reference
Information

Chapter Objectives

After you complete this chapter, you should be able to:

1. Use the direct reference system to display information by category and subject.

2. Obtain format help from the FOX system.

3. Verify flight information.

4. Use the calculator and calendar functions.

5. Display weather reports and forecasts.

6. Display currency exchange data and convert currencies.

PROBLEM

A client in Atlanta has booked flight arrangements for a trip to Seattle. She would like to know the weather conditions so she can plan her wardrobe. She would also like to know the total flight time and whether a movie will be shown on the flight.

SABRE SOLUTION

Display a weather forecast for the Seattle area. Then use the flifo function to verify the total elapsed flight time. To determine if a movie will be shown on the flight, access the direct reference system, and display the category for in-flight movies.

In this chapter, you will learn how to access the Direct RS, operate the calculator and calendar functions, and retrieve currency exchange data.

The **direct reference system (DRS)** stores information about travel industry vendors, entertainment events, immigration requirements, and numerous other topics.

DRS subjects are indexed by category. Each category is identified by a three-letter abbreviation, called a **keyword**. Airline reference information is stored in four primary categories, as follows:

AAL	American Airlines
SYS	System cohosts
SY1	More system cohosts
OTH	Other airline information

American Airlines has its own reference category, identified by the keyword *AAL*. **System cohosts** are any participating airlines other than American Airlines. Participating airlines are those that permit reservations to be booked through SABRE. The categories *SYS* and *SY1* both refer to system cohosts. Information for other travel vendors is stored in the category *OTH*.

Displaying a Subject

The entry code **Y/** is used to display a subject index for a primary category. The category is identified by the three-letter keyword, as follows:

FORMAT   Y/<Category>

EXAMPLE   Y/AAL

This example requests the subject index for American Airlines reference information. SABRE responds as follows:

```
SUBJECT FOR CATEGORY -AAL- AA INFORMATION
01 AAA-*                        02 ACC-ACCEPTANCE
02 ADS-INTERFACE                04 ADV-AADVANTAGE
05 AD2-AADVANTAGE DATA          06 AEC-AMERICAN EAGLE
07 ARP-AAIRPASS                 08 BAG-BAGGAGE INFO
09 BBB-*                        10 BDA-BERMUDA FARES
11 BPS-BOARDING PASS            12 BUL-BULLETINS
13 CAN-CANADA                   14 CAT-CATEGORIES AVAIL
```

The complete subject index consists of several screens. For illustration, only the first eight lines are shown in this example. Each subject has an item number, a three-letter keyword, and a title. Either the item number or the keyword may be used to display a subject. Both the category and the subject must be input. For example, using the keyword, the following entry would be used to display American Airlines baggage information:

Y/AAL/BAG

Using the item number, the following entry would be used:

Y/AAL/8

If the keywords for the category and the subject are already known, the subject can be displayed without displaying an index. For example, changes in airline policies, procedures, or fares are called *weekly implementations* and are referenced by the keyword *IMP*. The following entry will display a list of American Airlines' weekly implementations for the current week:

Y/AAL/IMP

Any week from 1 to 5 may be specified. For example, to display policy or fare changes implemented in the third week of the current month, the following entry can be used:

Y/AAL/IMP/WEEK3

AAL Hot News

The keyword *HOT* is used to display a daily update, as follows:

Y/AAL/HOT

This entry requests the most recent policy or fare changes for the current date. An update can be requested for a different date of the current month, as follows:

Y/AAL/HOT/15

This entry will display the daily update that was released on the fifteenth day of the current month. HOT information cannot be displayed for a different month.

Cohost Reference Information

The categories *SYS* and *SY1* refer to system cohosts. In some cases, both categories must be displayed to locate information for a desired airline.

For example, assume an agent wants to obtain display information for Bolivian Airlines. The agent displays the first cohost index as follows:

Y/SYS

The index is displayed as follows:

```
SUBJECTS FOR CATEGORY - SYS - COHOST PROGRAMS
  01 CKL-KLM              02 GFA-GULF AIR
  03 HOT-DAILY UPDATE     04 IMM-IMMIGRATION GUIDE
  05 KEY-KEYWORDS         06 NDX-INDEX
  07 QAC-AIR CANADA       08 QAF-AIR FRANCE
  09 QAL-USAIR            10 QAM-AERO MEXICO
```

Assume that after scrolling the display, the agent fails to locate Bolivian Airlines. To display the second cohost index, the agent inputs the following entry:

Y/SY1

The second cohost index is displayed as follows:

```
SUBJECTS FOR CATEGORY - SY1 - HOSTED CARRIERS
01 NDX-INDEX               02 QAN-ANSETT AIRLINES
03 QGF-GULF AIR            04 QKE-KOREAN AIRLINES
05 QKU-KUWAIT AIRLINES     06 QLB-BOLIVIAN AIRLINES
```

Bolivian Airlines (QLB) is the subject in line 6. The direct reference information may now be obtained by means of the following entry:

Y/SY1/6

The information can also be displayed by keyword, as follows:

Y/SY1/QLB

If the keywords for the desired category and subject are already known, the category index does not have to be displayed.

A keyword for cohost information consists of the letter *Q* followed by the carrier code, as illustrated by the following examples:

QAF   Air France

QBA   British Airways

QKL   KLM Royal Dutch Airlines

QNW   Northwest

QTW   TWA

QUA   United

QUS   USAir

Besides airline information, other reference information is also stored in the direct reference system. The following are examples of various DRS categories:

SHO   Theatrical shows

MOV   In-flight movies

IMM   Immigration information

REF   General reference information

Information about SABRE entry formats is stored in a data base called the **FOX system**. The information in this system can be displayed to obtain assistance with any SABRE format. FOX information is organized on three levels, as follows:

1. primary functions
2. entry formats
3. detailed format information

Primary SABRE functions are listed in an index called the *function list*. The entry **F*FOX** is used to display the function list, as follows:

    F*FOX

When this entry is made, SABRE responds as follows:

```
 1.  *** FOX INFORMATION ***      2.  *** FOX PRINT ***
 3.  AA TRAVEL ACADEMY            4.  AADVANTAGE PROGRAM
 5.  AAQUARIUS-QUEUE ANALYSIS     6.  AAQUARIUS-QUEUE BOUNCE
 7.  AAQUARIUS-QUEUE COUNT        8.  AAQUARIUS-QUEUE HISTORY
 9.  AAQUARIUS-QUEUE PLACE-QP    10.  AAQUARIUS-QUEUE TRANSFER
11.  AAQUARIUS-QUEUES           12.  AAQUARIUS-QUEUES 1-29
13.  AAQUARIUS-SELECT DISPLAY   14.  AAQUARIUS-SELECTION KEYS
15.  AAQUARIUS-SPECTRA          16.  AAQUARIUS-SPECTRA FILLIN
```

For illustration, only the first eight lines are shown here.

SABRE functions can also be listed by initial, as follows:

    F*FOX-C

When this entry is made, the function list will include only those functions that have the initial *C*. SABRE responds as follows:

```
 1.  CALCULATOR FUNCTIONS        2.  CANADIAN TELEX
 3.  CAREY LIMOUSINE             4.  CARIBBEAN TKTNG - PEAK
 5.  CARS                        6.  CITY PAIR AVAILABILITY
 7.  COMMERCIAL SABRE            8.  CORP TRAVEL POLICY
 9.  CORP TRAVEL POLICY-CONT    10.  CORP TRAVEL POLICY-MASKS
11.  CREDIT AUTHORIZATION       12.  CRT OPERATION
13.  CRUISE AMERICA RV          14.  CURRENCY CONVERSION
```

The entry code *F** is used to display information from the function list, as follows:

FORMAT   F*<Function>

EXAMPLE   F*5

This entry requests the information stored in item 5 of the function list. SABRE responds as follows:

```
------------------------------------CARS------------------------------------
1. 3 EASY STEPS/SELL  A  CAR FROM A SHOPPERS QUOTE
        1.  CF ITIN SEG NBR/CAR TYPE          CF2/IC
        2.  CF * LINE NBR OF VENDOR           CF*3
        3.  O  C  LINE  NBR
OTHER INFORMATION -
        1.  A PNR MUST BE IN YOUR WORKING AREA
        2.  STEP 1 DISPLAYS A SHOPPERS CAR QUOTE FOR
            INTERMEDIATE CARS  -IC- USING THE ARRIVAL
            CITY IN SEGMENT  2.
```

For illustration, only the first ten lines are displayed here. Each topic is identified by an item number on the left. The indented lines indicate subtopics within each topic. In the example above, the topic is item 1, and the indented lines are subtopics.

A typical FOX display is several screens long. To display more information, the following entry may be used:

MD

A specified topic within the function display can also be displayed by item number, as follows:

F**1

This example would redisplay item 1 after more information has been displayed.

Retrieving FOX Information by Keyword

The entry code *FOX* can be used to obtain format assistance by keyword, as follows:

FORMAT   FOX/<Keyword>/<Keyword>/<Keyword>

EXAMPLE   FOX/QUEUE/COUNT

In this example, the keywords *QUEUE* and *COUNT* are input to request format information for queue counts. To display format information by keyword, a slash must be typed before each keyword. A maximum of three keywords may be included in one entry. Note that, unlike DRS keywords, FOX keywords are not limited to three characters.

The following example will display information about how to retrieve a STAR:

FOX/STARS/RETRIEVE

Fox*/ stArs/Retrieve

An entry code may be used as a keyword to identify a function, as follows:

FOX/WP/SEGMENT/SELECT

In this example, the entry code *WP* is used to identify the itinerary pricing function. This entry requests format information for selecting segments when an itinerary is priced.

The entry code FOX may be abbreviated *FO*, as follows:

FO/FARE/QUOTE

This example may also be entered as follows:

FOX/FARE/QUOTE

Keywords used to obtain format information from the FOX system are referred to as *qualifiers*. If an invalid keyword is input in a FOX entry, SABRE will display a list of similar keywords or will display the message *NOT FOUND*.

Revision Tables

Recent changes and additions to the FOX system are stored in special records called *revision tables*. The following entry is used to display the revision table for the current date:

F*FOX*RT

The revision table for a previous date can also be displayed, as follows:

F*FOX*RT/24APR

A slash is typed before the desired date. A date range may be specified, as follows:

F*FOX*RT/24APR-28APR

A hyphen is typed to separate the first and last dates in the range.
The following are examples of valid FOX entries:

F*FOX	Displays the full function list
F*FOX-Q	Lists functions with the initial *Q*
F*8	Displays item 8 from a displayed function list
F*FOX/TICKET/REFUND	Displays format information by keyword
F*FOX*RT	Displays the revision table for today
F*FOX*RT/12JUN	Displays the revision table for a specified date
F*FOX*RT/12JUN-16JUN	Displays the revision table for a specified date range

Besides reference information and format assistance, other types of informational displays can also be obtained. The following entry codes are used for miscellaneous information displays:

V*	Flight verification
DU*	Participating vendors
T*	Time checks
¤WEA	Weather information
T¤	Calculator and calendar functions
W/	Quick fare calculation
DC*CUR	Currency conversion
CK*	Credit card approval

Flight Verification

The **flight information** function, called **flifo**, is used to verify the routing, departure and arrival times, meal service, equipment, and total flight time of a specified flight. The entry code **V*** is used for flight verification, as follows:

FORMAT   V*<Carrier><Flight>/<Date>

EXAMPLE   V*TW904/12MAR

This example will display flight information for TW 904 operating on 12 March. The entry code *2* may also be used for flight verification, as in the following example:

    2AA712/24JUN

If an air itinerary is present, flight information can be verified by segment reference, as follows:

    VI*2

This example will display flight information for segment 2. Multiple segments can be specified, as follows:

    VI*2/4/6

Flight information can also be obtained from an availability display, as follows:

    VA*1

This example will display flight information for line 1 of an availability display.

Flight Verification

Assume a client is booked on UA 418 departing on 21 October. The passenger inquires about the total travel time and the type of meal service on the flight. You use the following entry to verify the flight information:

V*UA418/21OCT

SABRE responds as follows:

21OCT		DPTR	ARVL	MEALS S	EQP	ELPD	ACCUM	MILES
SEA	SFO	805A	955A	B	DC8	1.50	1.50	872
SFO	MIA	1100A	847P	L		8.37	9.42	3024

The flight in this example originates in SEA, flies two segments, and terminates in MIA. The headings in the flifo display indicate the following information:

Heading	Information
DPTR	Departure time
ARVL	Arrival time
MEALS S	Meals served
EQP	Aircraft equipment
ELPD	Elapsed flight time
ACCUM	Accumulated travel time
MILES	Total miles flown

The elapsed flight time shows the total time that the aircraft is in flight. The accumulated travel time shows the total time from the originating point to the terminating point, including time spent on the ground. In this example, a passenger who boards the flight in SEA and disembarks in MIA will spend a total of 8 hours, 37 minutes in flight, but the accumulated travel time, including time spent on the ground, will be 9 hours, 42 minutes.

Assume your client will board the flight in SEA and disembark in SFO. The accumulated travel time is 1 hour, 50 minutes, and breakfast is served on the flight.

Participating Vendors

A **participating vendor** is any travel company, such as an airline, hotel, car rental company, or ship line, that permits bookings to be made through SABRE. The entry code *DU*/* is used to display a list of participating vendors by category, as follows:

FORMAT   DU*/<Category>

EXAMPLE   DU*/HTL

A three-letter keyword is used to specify the category. In the example above, the keyword *HTL* indicates hotel vendors. The following are examples of commonly used keywords for participating vendors:

CAR Car rental companies

HTL Hotels

BUS Bus lines

RAL Railways

SEA Ship lines

A list of participating vendors is called a **vendor table.**

Connecting Times

When a passenger must change aircraft in a connecting city, the minimum connecting time depends on the airport. The minimum connecting time must be sufficient to allow the passenger to disembark, proceed to the boarding gate, and board the connecting flight.

The entry code **T*CT-** is used to display the minimum connecting times at a specified airport, as follows:

FORMAT T*CT-<Airport>

EXAMPLE T*CT-GEG

This example will display minimum connecting times at the Spokane, Washington, airport (GEG).

The following is an example of a connecting time display:

```
STANDARD      D/D....D/I....I/D....I/I
ONLINE        .30   1.00  1.00  1.00
OFFLINE       .40   1.00  1.00  1.00
CO-CZ    DD   .40
UA-UA    DD   .20
DL-DL    DD   .20
NW-NW    DD   .25
CO-CO    DD   .15
```

The minimum connecting times are displayed in a table. The first line of the display, the header, indicates the type of connection. The following codes are used in the header:

D/D Domestic-to-domestic

D/I Domestic-to-international

I/D International-to-domestic

I/I International-to-international

The two lines below the header give the minimum connecting times for on-line and off-line connections. An **on-line connection** is a change of flights operated by the same airline. An **off-line connection** requires the passenger to change to a different airline. If the flight gates in an off-line connection are located in different airport terminals, the minimum connecting time is usually greater.

The time is given in hours and minutes. In the example, the minimum connecting time is 30 minutes for on-line domestic-to-domestic connections and 1 hour for on-line domestic-to-international connections.

Connecting times may also be displayed for specific carriers, as illustrated in the sample display. For on-line connections operated by Delta, the minimum connecting time is 20 minutes.

The connecting time for specific carriers may be requested as follows:

T*CT-GEG/COCZ

This example will display the minimum connecting time at GEG for connections from CO to CZ.

Weather information

Weather information can be obtained by means of the entry code ¤WEA. To obtain National Weather Service information for a particular city, the secondary code WX* is added to make the entry code ¤WEA/WX*, as follows:

FORMAT   ¤WEA/WX*<City>

EXAMPLE   ¤WEA/WX*PHX

Either a city code or an airport code may be used in this entry. The following is an example of a weather information display:

```
NATIONAL WEATHER SERVICE - APR 21
CURRENT                 FORECAST              FORECAST
  2:20  P  MT            TUE .......APR 22      WED....APR 23
WEA    TEMP   WIND   WEA   HI/LO          WEA      HI/LO
CLEAR   89    W  8   SUNNY 92/74          SUNNY  95/76
```

The weather display is based on the latest reported temperature and weather conditions and covers a two-day period. For most U.S. and Canadian cities, the display is updated twice daily seven days a week. For international cities, the display is updated once daily and only Monday through Friday.

To obtain a descriptive city forecast, the secondary code *CF** is input, as in the following example:

    ¤WEA/CF*PHX

The following is an example of a descriptive city forecast display:

```
NATIONAL WEATHER SERVICE PHOENIX AZ
222 PM  MST  MON  APR  21
.TONIGHT ....CLEAR AND WARM. LOW IN THE MID 70S. WEST WIND 8 TO 10 MPH.
.TUESDAY...SUNNY AND WARM.  HIGH IN THE LOW 90S.
```

Each city forecast covers a three-day period. If the entire text cannot be displayed in one screen, a selected page can be displayed as follows:

    ¤WEA/CF*PHX/2

This example will display the second page of the display. A page consists of the information in one screen.

The secondary code *EF** may be used to obtain an extended regional forecast, as follows:

¤WEA/EF*NYC

SABRE responds as follows:

```
EXTENDED FORECAST FOR EXTREME SOUTHEASTERN N.Y.
NORTHERN NEW JERSEY...AND LONG ISLAND NATIONAL WEATHER SERVICE
NEW YORK  NY  800A  EST  MON  SEP 18
THURSDAY THROUGH SATURDAY
MOSTLY SUNNY THURSDAY BECOMING PARTLY CLOUDY
FRI. MORNING WITH CHANCE OF RAIN SHOWERS SAT.
DAILY HIGHS 60 - 65 WITH OVERNIGHT LOWS IN THE
MID 40S INLAND TO THE HIGH 30S ON THE COAST.
```

The extended forecast covers a five-day period. If the display is longer than one screen, a selected page can be displayed as follows:

¤WEA/EF*NYC/2

If a forecast is requested for an international city, weather information will be displayed for the entire geographic area. For example, if a forecast is requested for Paris, weather information will be displayed for all of France. Either the city code or the airport code may be used to obtain a forecast.

Calculator Functions

The **calculator function** is used to perform an arithmetic operation, such as adding, subtracting, multiplying, or dividing. The entry code **T¤** is used for the calculator function. The symbol or sign that is used to perform an arithmetic operation is called the *operator*. The following arithmetic operators are used with the calculator function:

‡   Add
-   Subtract
*   Multiply
/   Divide

Calendar Functions

Besides arithmetic, the calculator function can also be used to add or subtract days from a calendar date. To illustrate, assume a fare has a 21-day advance-purchase requirement. The client plans to travel on 12 November. To determine the date by which the ticket must be purchased, the following entry can be used:

T¤12NOV-21

Calculator Functions

Assume an agent desires to add 225 and 18. The following entry can be used to calculate the sum:

   T¤225‡18

SABRE responds as follows:

   243.00

Note that decimals are included in the response, though they were not included in the calculator entry.
   Now assume the agent desires to multiply 300 by .11. The following entry may be used to perform the calculation:

   T¤300*.11

SABRE responds as follows:

   33.00

This entry will subtract 21 days from November 12. SABRE responds as follows:

   *22OCT THU

The entry code **T¤** can also be used to display a calendar for a specified month. For instance, to display a calendar for June 1999, the following entry would be used:

   T¤JUN/99

The calendar is displayed as follows:

```
              JUN   1999
    S     M     T     W     Q     F     J
    -     -     -     -     -     -     -
                1     2     3     4     5
    6     7     8     9    10    11    12
   13    14    15    16    17    18    19
   20    21    22    23    24    25    26
   27    28    29    30
```

In the calendar display, the days of the week are indicated by the same one-letter codes that are used in flight segments.

Dates can be displayed for a specified day of the week, as well. As an example, the following entry can be used to determine the date of each Friday in December 1999:

T¤FR/DEC99

In this entry, the day of the week must be indicated by the first two letters. In this example, *FR* is input to indicate Friday. SABRE displays the dates as follows:

03 DEC   10DEC   17DEC   24DEC   31DEC   1999

The secondary code *ET* may be used to calculate elapsed time. The arrival point and the departure point must be specified for each time, as follows:

T¤ET845PSFO-610AANC

This entry requests the elapsed time from 8:45 P.M. San Francisco time to 6:10 A.M. Anchorage time.

To calculate elapsed time between international points, the city codes must be input, as follows:

T¤ET1200NHKG/22MAY-400PTYO/25MAY

Quick Fare Calculation

You will recall from Chapter 1 that the entry code **W/** is used to encode and decode terms. This code can also be used to calculate the base fare and tax from a total fare. To illustrate, assume the total fare for a flight segment is $359. The following entry can be used to determine the base fare and tax:

W/359

Note that the dollar sign or currency code must not be typed in this entry. SABRE responds as follows:

326.36/32.64

In this example, the base fare is $326.36, and the 10 percent U.S. transportation tax is $32.64. Cents will be included in the response, even if they are omitted in the fare calculation entry.

The secondary code *B* can be used to calculate the tax and total fare from a base fare, as follows:

W/B298.18

The code *B* is typed before the amount to indicate that the amount is a base fare. When this entry is input, SABRE will respond as follows:

29.82/328.00

In this example, the tax is $29.82, and the total fare is $328.00

Time Checks

The entry code **T*** can be used to determine the local time in a specified city, as follows:

FORMAT   T*<City or airport code>

EXAMPLE   T*LHR

This example requests the local time in London. Note in this example that the airport code *LHR* is input for the London-Heathrow airport. When this entry is input, SABRE will respond as follows:

    * 1422 18JUL

The time is displayed in 24-hour format. In this example, the local time at London-Heathrow was 2:22 P.M. at the time the entry was input.

Currency Rates

The entry code **DC*** is used to display currency exchange rates based on the bank buying rate. The data is updated weekly to reflect changes in the international exchange rate. The following entry is used to display currency conversion rates:

FORMAT   DC*<Currency>

EXAMPLE   DC*ATS

In this example, the three-letter currency code *ATS* specifies Austrian schillings. Exchange rates can also be displayed by country name, as follows:

    DC*AUSTRIA

When either entry is input, SABRE will respond as follows:

COUNTRY	CURRENCY	CODE	DEC.	RATE	EFF DATE	NEW RATE
AUSTRIA	SCHILLING	ATS	0	.08569	10AUG	.08571

The response gives the country, currency name, and ISO currency code. The "Dec." column indicates the number of decimals that are used in the currency. A number from 1 to 3 may appear in this column. In this example, decimals are not used in Austrian currency.

The current currency exchange rate is given in the "Rate" column. In this example, the exchange rate for Austrian schillings (ATS) is .08569. Thus, one schilling is equal to 8.569 cents in U.S. currency. If a rate change is anticipated, the effective date and the future rate are also shown. In this example, on 10 August, the exchange rate will change to .08571.

To display the exchange rates for all international currencies, the code *CUR* is input instead of a currency code, as follows:

DC*CUR

The entry code *DC** displays the current bank buying rate. To display the current market rate, the entry code **DZ*** can be used, as follows:

DZ*FRANCE

Currency Conversion

To convert an amount from one currency to another, the following format can be used:

FORMAT   DC‡<Currency><Amount>/<Currency>

EXAMPLE   DC‡GBP245.50/CAD

This example will convert 245.50 British pounds to Canadian dollars. When an amount is input with a specified currency, the currency code is typed before the amount. For example, 2340 Austrian schillings is input as ATS2340. If decimals are used with the currency, they must be included. For example, 752 Australian dollars would be input as AUD752.00.

If the currency code of the amount to be converted is omitted, SABRE will use the currency of the country where the terminal is located. For example, assume an agent in New York desires to convert USD389.00 to Japanese yen. The following entry can be used to perform the conversion:

DC‡389.00/JPY

In this example, *JPY* is the currency code for Japanese yen. Because the agent set is located in a U.S. city, the currency code USD may be omitted.

Summary

The direct reference system (DRS) stores information about travel industry vendors, entertainment events, immigration requirements, and numerous other topics. DRS subjects are indexed by category. Each category is identified by a three-letter keyword. Information about SABRE entry formats is stored in the FOX system. Recent changes and additions to the FOX system are stored in revision tables.

Besides reference information and format assistance, informational displays can also be obtained for flight verification, connecting times, participating vendors, time checks, weather information, calculator and calendar functions, quick fare calculation, and currency conversion.

New commands included in this chapter:

Y/AAL	Displays the DRS index by category
Y/AAL/BAG	Displays the DRS index by category and keyword
Y/AAL/8	Displays the DRS index by category and item number
Y/AAL/HOT	Displays the daily AA information update
Y/SYS	Displays the first cohost index
Y/SY1	Displays the second cohost index
F*FOX	Displays the FOX function list
F*FOX-C	Displays the FOX function list by initial
F**1	Displays a specified paragraph
FOX/QUEUE/COUNT	Displays FOX information by keyword
F*FOX*RT	Displays the FOX revision table
F*FOX*RT/24APR	Displays the FOX revision table by date
V*TW904/12MAR	Displays flight verification data (flifo)
VI*2	Displays flifo from an itinerary
VA*3	Displays flifo from an availability display
DU*/HTL	Displays a vendor table
T*CT-GEG	Displays minimum connecting times
T*CT-GEG/COCZ	Displays connecting times by carrier
¤WEA/WX*PHX	Displays weather information
¤WEA/CF*PHX	Displays a descriptive city weather forecast
¤WEA/EF*NYC	Displays an extended weather forecast
T¤225‡18	Performs an arithmetic calculation
T¤12NOV-21	Subtracts days from a calendar date
T¤JUN/99	Displays a calendar
T¤ET845PSFO-610AANC	Determines elapsed time
W/359	Calculates base fare and tax from total fare
W/B298.18	Calculates total fare and tax from base fare
T*LHR	Displays local time
DC*SWEDEN	Displays currency bank buying rate
DZ*AUSTRIA	Displays currency market rate
DC‡GBP245.50/CAD	Converts from one currency to another

STUDENT REVIEW

KEY CONCEPTS AND TERMS

Identify the word, phrase, or symbol for each of the following concepts:

1. A SABRE program for retrieving such travel industry information as vendor news, entertainment event schedules, and immigration requirements.

2. Three-letter abbreviations that can be used to display topics from a menu.

3. Any participating airline other than American Airlines.

4. The entry code that is used to display a subject index for a primary category.
5. A SABRE program for retrieving information about CRS functions and entry formats.
6. The entry used to display the SABRE function list.
7. The function that is used to verify the routing, departure and arrival times, meal service, equipment, and total flight time of a specified flight.
8. The entry code that is used to verify flight information.
9. A travel company, such as an airline, hotel, car rental company, or ship line, that permits bookings to be made through SABRE.
10. A list of travel companies that permit bookings to be made through SABRE.
11. The entry code that is used to display the minimum connecting times at a specific airport.
12. A connection requiring a change of flights operated by the same airline.
13. A connection requiring the passenger to change to a flight operated by a different airline.
14. The entry code that is used to obtain National Weather Service information for a specific city.
15. The function that is used to perform arithmetic operations.
16. The entry code that is used to perform arithmetic or display a calendar.
17. The entry code that is used for quick fare calculations.
18. The entry code that is used to determine the local time in a specified city.
19. The entry code that is used to display currency exchange rates based on the bank buying rate.
20. The entry code that is used to display currency exchange rates based on the current market rate.

Answers:

1. direct reference system (DRS); 2. keywords; 3. system cohost; 4. Y/; 5. FOX system; 6. F*FOX; 7. flight information (flifo); 8. V*; 9. participating vendor; 10. vendor table; 11. T*CT-; 12. on-line connection; 13. off-line connection; 14. ¤WEA/WX*; 15. calculator function; 16. T¤; 17. W/; 18. T*; 19. DC*; 20. DZ.

REVIEW QUESTIONS

1. Write the entry to display an index of subjects for American Airlines information.
2. Boarding pass information is item 16 in the American Airlines category index. Write the entry to display the subject by item number.
3. A DRS subject keyword has how many letters?
4. What entry would be used to display baggage information for American Airlines?
5. American Eagle is a commuter airline that has a code-sharing agreement with American Airlines. The keyword for American Eagle in the American Airlines category index is *AEC*. Write the entry to display the subject by keyword.
6. Write the entry to display the first index for co-host information.
7. Air France is a subject in the first co-host index. Write the entry to display the subject by keyword.
8. Write the entry to display the second index for co-host information.
9. Write the entry to display late-breaking news from American Airlines.
10. Write the entry to display the list of FOX functions beginning with the letter *S*.

11. When a DRS index is displayed, what entry will display item 4?

12. What entry will display the complete FOX function list?

13. When the FOX function list is displayed, what entry will display item 12?

14. Write two different entries that can be used to display FOX information about the fare quote format.

15. When FOX information is already displayed, what entry can be used to display additional information?

16. Write the entry to display recent format changes for the current date.

17. Write the entry to display format changes that were implemented on 14 January.

18. When FOX information is already displayed, what entry can be used to display paragraph 24?

19. Write the FOX entry to display format information about city pair availability, using the keyword *CPA*.

20. What entry would be used to display recent format changes implemented between 24 August and 29 August?

21. Write the entry to display participating hotel vendors.

22. What entry would be used to display minimum connecting times in Honolulu?

23. What entry would be used to display connecting times at LHR for connections from UA to SR?

24. Write the entry to display current weather information for Honolulu.

25. Write the entry to display a descriptive city weather forecast for Denver.

26. Write the entry to display an extended weather forecast for Seattle.

27. Write the entry to multiply 189 by 13.

28. Write the entry to display a table of all international currencies.

29. Write the entry to convert AUD2307.24 to JPY.

30. Write the entry to display a calendar for April 1995.

31. Write the entry to add 1456 and 299.

32. Write the entry to convert GBP439.00 to CAD.

33. What entry would be used to determine the date 21 days before 13 June?

34. Write the entry to divide 7823 by 9.

35. Write the entry to calculate the base fare and the tax from a total fare of 688.

36. Write the entry to calculate the total fare and the tax from a base fare of 320.

37. What entry will display the local time in BKK?

38. Assume a flight departs from HNL at 8:30 A.M. and arrives in Denver at 8:35 P.M. What entry can be used to calculate the elapsed time?

39. Write the entry to verify flight information for US 599 on 17 March.

40. Write the entry to verify the flight information for segment 3 of a displayed itinerary.

APPLICATIONS

Read the following scenario, and decide what actions should be performed to satisfy the client's preferences and needs. Briefly describe how you would handle the situation, and then write the required entries.

Your client would like to transport a trunk containing photographic equipment. He inquires about the excess baggage charge for an American Eagle commuter flight. However, you are uncertain of the correct SABRE format to use to obtain the information. When you access the baggage information, you find that the maximum dimensions are 62 inches. Your client's trunk is 48 inches long, 30 inches wide, and 18 inches deep.

The passenger's itinerary involves stopovers in Tegucigalpa, Honduras; Belize City, Belize; and Mexico City. He inquires about the currency exchange rate in each country.

Chapter 17

Tours

Outline

The Tourfinder Plus System

Tour Index

Tour Descriptions

Tour Availability

Hotel Descriptions

Selling Tour Segments

Chapter Objectives

After you complete this chapter, you should be able to:

1. Display tour availability.

2. Display a property description for a tour.

3. Sell a tour segment.

4. Modify a tour segment.

PROBLEM

A client would like to purchase a package vacation that includes airfare, hotel accommodations, airport transfers, and golf fees at one price.

SABRE SOLUTION

Use the Tourfinder Plus system to display tour availability, specifying airfare, transfers, and golf as inclusives. Then sell a tour segment based on the client's budget, needs, and preferences.

In this chapter, you will learn how to obtain tour availability, display a property description, and sell, modify, or cancel a tour segment.

The word **tour** may refer to either a package vacation or a trip escorted by a guide. When a tour is a package vacation, it may be any type of prearranged, prepaid trip that combines two or more travel components. A typical tour includes airfare, airport transfers, accommodations, and selected activities. An **airport transfer** is prearranged transportation between the airport and a hotel. The components that are included in the price of a package tour are called **inclusives**.

The SABRE tour system is named *Tourfinder Plus*. It consists of five basic functions, shown in Table 17-1.

A vendor that sells package tours through retail travel agencies is referred to as a **wholesaler**. Each participating wholesaler is identified by a two-letter code. The following are examples of major wholesalers that permit tours to be sold through SABRE:

AD	Adventure Tours USA
AF	Adventure Tours Canada
AX	American Express Travel-Related Services
CF	Cosmos Tourama
GO	Go Go Tours
GL	Globus Gateway
JS	Jet Set Tours
MF	Mayflower Tours
NT	Nippon Travel
SQ	Sunquest Vacations
WD	Walt Disney Travel

Tour Index

The entry code **TOP** is used to obtain an index of tours available in a particular city, as follows:

FORMAT   TOP<City>

EXAMPLE   TOPOGG

Table 17-1 SABRE's Five Basic Functions for Tourfinder Plus.

1. Tour index
2. Tour descriptions
3. Tour hotel availability
4. Hotel descriptions
5. Tour segment

This example requests tour packages in Kahului, Hawaii. SABRE responds as follows:

```
ALL TOURS IN OGG
1*SP   ITAAJJA2              5NTS MAUI INDEPENDENT    TT
       MAUI INDEPENDENT VACATIONS
2*ZV   ITAAKJH1              3NTS MAUI A LA CARTE     TT
       3NT PKG INCLUDES HOTEL AND CAR
3*JT   ITCUST-IHTFC02        1NT CUSTOM VACATIONS     TT
       PRE-PLAN A CUSTOM VACATION
```

Each tour is identified by a line number. An asterisk after the line number indicates that the tour has multiple inclusives. Each listing shows the vendor, the tour code, the number of nights, and the tour name. The code on the right indicates the tour type. The tour type codes may be found in Table 17-2. In this example, **TT** indicates a basic independent tour. The second line of each listing includes a brief description of the tour.

Obtaining a Tour Index From an Air Segment

If an air itinerary is present, a tour index can be obtained as follows:

FORMAT   TOP<Segment to follow>

EXAMPLE   TOP2

In this example, tours will be displayed for the date and arrival point of segment 2. If the tour destination is different from the arrival point, the city should be specified as follows:

TOP2/MKK

Specifying a Tour Type

When a tour index is requested, a tour type can be specified as follows:

TOPOGGCT

Table 17-2 Tour Type Codes.	
Code	**Tour Type**
TT	Basic independent tour
CT	Condominium package
HT	Honeymoon package
ET	Escorted tour
XT	Extended/multistop tour
PT	Promotional package
ST	Sports package

This example will display only condominium tours. If a segment reference is included, a cross (‡) must be typed to separate the segment number and tour type, as follows:

TOP2‡CT

Specifying Inclusives

The secondary code **I** is used to request an inclusive, as follows:

TOPOGG/I-RC

This example requests an index of tour packages that include rental cars. The following codes are used to specify inclusives in a tour index entry:

SK	Ski tour
TN	Tennis tour
GF	Golf tour
SS	Sightseeing
TR	Transfers
AF	Airfare
RC	Rental car
CR	Cruise

Multiple inclusives may be specified as follows:

TOPPHX/I-AF,RC,GF

A comma is typed to separate the inclusive codes. This example will display only tours that include airfare, a rental car, and golf.

Date Qualifiers

The date qualifiers that are used to display a hotel index may also be used to display a tour index. For instance, assume a client inquires about package tours in Denver, with arrival on 10 May for a five-night stay. The accommodations will be occupied by two adults. The following entry can be used to display tours:

TOPDEN/10MAY-5NT2

If an air itinerary is present, the number of nights can be indicated as follows:

TOP2/5NT2

This example requests tours for the date and arrival city of segment 2, for a five-night stay. The accommodations will be occupied by two adults.

When a tour index is displayed, the entry code **TOD*** can be used to display a description, as follows:

FORMAT   TOD*<Line number>

EXAMPLE   TOD*3

This example will display a description of the tour in line 3 of the tour index.

— C L I E N T   F O C U S —

Tour Description

Assume an agent has obtained the following tour index:

```
ALL TOURS IN OGG
1*SP    ITAAJJA2              5NTS MAUI INDEPENDENT    TT
        MAUI INDEPENDENT VACATIONS
2*ZV    ITAAKJH1             3NTS MAUI A LA CARTE     TT
        3NT PKG INCLUDES HOTEL AND CAR
3*JT    ITCUST-IHTFC02       1NT CUSTOM VACATIONS     TT
        PRE-PLAN A CUSTOM VACATION
```

The client inquires about the Maui à la Carte tour in line 2. The following entry can be used to display a description:

```
TOD*2
```

SABRE responds as follows:

```
ZV       ITAAKJH1      3NT      AIRPORT-OGGTT
EFF    10APR - 30JUN
*** 14 DAYS ADVANCE RESERVATION REQUIRED ***
TOUR NAME - MAUI A LA CARTE
DESC - 3NT PKG INCLUDES HOTEL AND CAR
MEAL PLAN - EP
CHILDRENS RATES - ON REQUEST
PACKAGE INCLUDES - 3 NIGHTS HOTEL, HOTEL TAX
                   3 DAYS CAR RENTAL
                   INFORMATION KIT
OPTIONS OFFERED - NONE
OTHERS - EXTRA NIGHTS AVAILABLE
INDEXES -                        OGGTT
```

(continued)

The tour description includes the following sections:

1. **Header notes** The wholesaler, tour code, number of nights, airport, and tour type are shown in the first line.

2. **Effective dates** In this example, the tour price is valid from 10 April until 30 June.

3. **Booking requirements** The tour in the example must be booked a minimum of 14 days prior to departure.

4. **Tour name** The tour in the example is named Maui à la Carte.

5. **Description** The tour in the example is a three-night package and includes hotel accommodations as well as a rental car.

6. **Meal plan** In the example, the European plan (EP) is the only meal plan offered.

7. **Children's rates** In the example, rates for children must be requested.

8. **Tour inclusives** The tour in the example includes hotel accommodations for three nights and a car rental for three days. An information kit is also provided.

9. **Options offered** In the example, no optional inclusives are available.

10. **Other information** In the example, additional nights may be added to the tour package to extend the stay.

11. **Indexes** The tour in the example is listed in the index for OGG.

Tour Availability

The tour index indicates the tours that are offered in a particular destination, but it does not show hotel availability. The entry code **TOA** is used to display tour hotel availability. When a description is displayed, a hotel availability display can be obtained by means of the following format.

FORMAT   TOA<Qualifiers>

EXAMPLE   TOA

If a tour index is displayed, the following format may be used to obtain availability:

FORMAT   TOA*<Line number>

EXAMPLE   TOA*2

This example requests hotel availability for the tour in line 2 of the tour index. SABRE will respond by displaying hotel availability for the property or properties in the tour package.

Secondary codes can be used in the tour availability entry to request a maximum price or a particular room location, as follows:

TOA/R-1000   Requests availability with maximum price
TOA/L-OV   Requests availability with specified room location

A hotel name can be specified by means of the secondary code *HN*, as follows:

TOA/HN-MARR

Only the first three or four characters in the hotel name are entered. This example requests availability at a Marriott hotel, as indicated by the abbreviation *MARR*. Similarly, Sheraton may be entered as *SHE* or *SHER*, and Hilton as *HIL* or *HILT*.

Hotel Descriptions

When a tour index is displayed, the entry code **HOD*** can be used to obtain a hotel description. For instance, to display a hotel description for the tour in line 3 of a tour index, the following entry can be used:

HOD*3

The hotel description for a tour includes the following sections:

1. Hotel name, address, and phone number
2. Tour effective dates
3. Room rates
4. Booking requirements
5. Tour package rate periods
6. Tour location
7. Tour name
8. Hotel facilities
9. Hotel services
10. Other information

Selling Tour Segments

When tour availability has been requested, the following format is used to sell a tour segment:

FORMAT   0<Rooms><Room type><Line>/P<Total price>

EXAMPLE   01DLX2/P120000

This example will book one room of type DLX from line 2 of a tour availability display, at a total price of $1,200. The secondary code */P* is typed before the total price. The number of rooms and the room type are mandatory.

The total price is the price for all travelers in the party. Note that the cents are included but the decimal point is omitted. Thus, $898.00 would be entered as 89800, and $2,400.00 would be entered as 240000.

If, for some reason, the total price cannot be calculated at the time of booking, *NN* should be entered in place of an amount. For example, assume that children's rates have been requested, but a response has not yet been received from the vendor. The following entry indicates that the price cannot be calculated:

01DLX2/PNN

Tour Accommodations

A wide range of room type codes is used to indicate tour accommodations. For example, the following codes may be used to indicate the room category:

DLX	Deluxe room
SUP	Superior room
STD	Standard room
EC1	Economy room

The room type code may also indicate the rate range, as follows:

MAX	Maximum rate
MOD	Moderate rate
MIN	Minimum rate

At all-suite properties, the following room types are often used:

AJS	Deluxe junior suite
APT	Apartment
AST	Deluxe studio
A1T	Single accommodations
A2T	Double accommodations
BST	Superior studio

The following room types are commonly used by condominium properties:

CA1	Deluxe one-bedroom condominium
CA2	Deluxe two-bedroom condominium
CB1	Superior one-bedroom condominium
CC1	Standard one-bedroom condominium
CD1	Moderate one-bedroom condominium

At some properties, the room type is based on the number of adults per room, as follows:

DBLB	Double accommodations
SGLB	Single accommodations

Japanese-style hotels may have the following room types:

JA0   Japanese deluxe room without bath

JA1   Japanese deluxe room with bath

At tropical resorts, the following room types are often used:

BUG   Bungalow

GDV   Gardenview

OCF   Oceanfront

OVW   Oceanview

The code **ROH** may also be displayed, indicating "the run of the house." This type of accommodation is the best room that is available at check-in.

Selling a Tour From a Hotel Description

When a hotel description is displayed, the following entry can be used to sell a tour segment:

FORMAT   0<Rooms><Room type>/P<Total price>

EXAMPLE   01DLX/P120000

Booking Extra Nights

The secondary code *N* is used to book extra nights, as follows:

FORMAT   <Basic entry>/N<Extra nights>-<Rate per night>/N<Total nights>

EXAMPLE   01DLX/P73000/N1-7500/N5

The total number of nights must be included in the entry. The example above would book one extra night at a rate of $75, for a total of five nights.

When selling tours, observe the following guidelines:

1. Include the total package price for all members of the party.

2. If the total price cannot be calculated, enter *NN* instead of the total price.

3. When booking extra nights, indicate the charge per night per person, and indicate the total number of nights.

Booking Extra Nights

Assume an agent has obtained a tour description. The client requests a standard room at the package price of $899 per person. The party will consist of two travelers; thus, the total price is $1,798. Let us say that extra nights are offered at $49 per night per person, and the clients desire to stay two extra nights. Based on this information, the agent uses the following entry to book the tour:

01STD/P179800/N2-4900/N7

Guarantee Information

Most tours must be guaranteed or prepaid by credit card, tour order, or miscellaneous charges order (MCO). A tour order or MCO may be issued if the client makes a cash deposit or pays in full. Guarantee information should be included when the tour segment is sold.

The secondary code *G* is used to enter guarantee information, as follows:

01DLX/P120000/GAX6550587610029EXP 12 99-GULLIVER

In this example, a credit card number is used to guarantee a tour reservation. If an MCO will be issued, the document number and value should be included as follows:

01DLX/P120000/G65176543298-1200.00

Note that a decimal is included in the amount paid by the client.

Modifying Tour Segments

The entry code **TOM** is used to modify an existing tour segment, as follows:

FORMAT   TOM<Segment><Qualifier>/<New data>

EXAMPLE   TOM2R/1DLX-2

The example will modify a reservation in segment 2, changing the room information to one DLX room for two travelers. The following qualifiers are commonly used to modify a tour segment:

R/   Room information
D/   Dates
O/   Optional information

For example, to change the dates in a tour in segment 3, the following entry can be used:

TOM3D/4JAN-10NT

The SABRE tour system is named *Tourfinder Plus*. It consists of five basic functions. Each participating tour wholesaler is identified by a two-letter code. A tour index can be obtained to display tours available in a particular city. A tour type and one or more inclusives may be specified when the index is displayed.

A tour description can be obtained from a tour index display. The entry code *TOA* is used to display tour availability. When a tour index or availability display has been obtained, the entry code *HOD* can be used to display a hotel description. When a tour segment is sold, the number of rooms, the room type, and the total package price must be specified. Extra nights and guarantee information may also be included in the entry. The entry code *TOM* is used to modify the room information, the dates, or optional information in an existing tour segment.

New commands included in this chapter:

TOPOGG	Displays a tour index by city
TOP2	Displays a tour index from an air segment
TOPOGGCT	Displays a tour index by city and tour type
TOP2‡CT	Displays a tour index by segment and tour type
TOPOGG/I-RC	Displays a tour index with a specified inclusive
TOPPHX/I-AF,RC,GF	Displays a tour index with multiple specified inclusives
TOPDEN/10MAY-5NT2	Displays a tour index by date range and number of adults per room
TOD*3	Displays a tour description from a tour index
TOA	Displays availability from a tour description
TOA/R-1000	Displays tour availability with maximum price
TOA/L-OV	Displays tour availability with specified room location
TOA/HN-MARR	Displays tour availability with specified hotel name
HOD*3	Displays a hotel description from a tour availability display
01DLX/P120000	Sells a tour segment from a displayed tour description
01DLX2/P120000	Sells a tour segment from a tour availability display
01DLX/P73000/N1-7500/N5	Sells a tour segment with extra nights

01DLX/P120000/
  GAX 6550587610029
  EXP 12 99-GULLIVER
	Sells a tour segment with guarantee information

TOM2R/1DLX-2	Modifies an existing tour segment

KEY CONCEPTS AND TERMS

Identify the word, phrase, or symbol for each of the following concepts:

1. Any package vacation or a trip escorted by a guide.
2. Prearranged transportation between the airport and a hotel.
3. A component that is included in the price of a package tour.
4. A vendor that sells package tours through retail travel agencies.
5. The entry code that is used to obtain an index of tours available in a particular city.
6. The tour type code for a basic independent tour.
7. In a tour index entry, the secondary code that is used to request an inclusive.
8. The entry code that is used to display a tour description.
9. The entry code that is used to display tour hotel availability.
10. The entry code that is used to sell a tour segment.
11. When a tour segment is sold, the secondary code that is typed before the total price.
12. The accommodations code that refers to the best room type that is available at check-in.
13. The entry code that is used to modify an existing tour segment.

Answers:

1. tour; 2. airport transfer; 3. inclusive; 4. wholesaler; 5. TOP; 6. TI; 7. I; 8. TOD*; 9. TOA; 10. 0; 11. /P; 12. ROH; 13. TOM.

REVIEW QUESTIONS

1. Write the entry to display the tour index for ACA.
2. Write the entry to display the tour index for the destination city in segment 3, specifying honeymoon packages.
3. What entry would be used to request the tour index for cruise packages in ATH?
4. Write the entry to request the tour index for golf packages in CHC.
5. When a tour index is displayed, what entry will display a tour description for line 2?
6. Write the entry to display the tour index for the arrival city in segment 4 of an itinerary.
7. Write the entry to display the tour index for the arrival city in segment 2, specifying packages that include airfare.
8. What entry would display the tour index for FLL, including only those packages that include airfare, transfers, and golf?
9. Write the entry to display the tour index for STT, including only those packages that include a rental car and skiing.
10. Write the entry to display the tour index for HNL, including only those packages that include a rental car.

11. When a tour index is displayed, what entry will display a hotel description for the tour in line 2?

12. Write the entry to display hotel availability from a tour index.

13. Write the entry to display tour availability with a maximum package price of $900.

14. When a tour index is displayed, what entry will display availability for the tour in line 3?

15. Write the entry to display the tour index for MOW, specifying extended multistop tours that include airfare and transfers.

Refer to the following tour index to answer questions 16–20:

```
ALL TOURS IN MOW
1*AX    ITAX9987            9NTS THE MOTHERLAND    XT
        10 DAYS INCLUDING AIRFARE
2*GO    ITGOKJ3W            14NTS RUSSIA BY RAIL    XT
        MOSCOW - TRANS-SIBERIAN RAIL
3*JS    ITJSB230            12NTS WHITE NIGHTS      XT
        MOSCOW AND ST PETERSBURG
```

16. What is the tour code for White Nights?

17. What entry would display tour availability for Russia by Rail?

18. What wholesaler offers The Motherland?

19. What entry would display a description for Russia by Rail?

20. What entry would display availability for White Nights?

21. When tour availability is displayed, what entry will book one room at the STD rate for the tour in line 1, at a total price of $840?

22. When tour availability is displayed, what entry will book one room at the MOD rate for the tour in line 3, at a total price of $758?

23. Write the entry to book two rooms at the DLX rate for the tour in line 3 of a tour availability display. Assume the price cannot be calculated at this time.

24. When a tour description is displayed, what entry will book one room at the CA2 rate at a total price of $526?

25. When a tour description is displayed, what entry will book one room at the OVW rate at a total price of $1240?

26. Write the entry to book two rooms at the DBL rate from a displayed tour description. Assume the price cannot be calculated at this time.

27. Write the entry to book one room at the DLX rate for two adults for the tour in line 2 of a tour availability display. The price for each adult is $650. Include two extra nights, at a charge of $112 per person for a total of seven nights.

28. Assume a tour description is displayed. The package price is $1250 per person, and the charge for extra nights is $80 per person. Write the entry to book one room at the STD rate for two adults and include three extra nights for a total of nine nights.

29. Write the entry to modify a tour booking in segment 4 to change the travel dates to 18 July through 21 July.

30. Write the entry to modify a tour booking in segment 3 to book two rooms at the MAX rate with two adults per room.

APPLICATIONS

Read the following scenario, and decide what actions should be performed to satisfy the client's preferences and needs. Briefly describe how you would handle the situation, and then write the required entries.

Mr. and Mrs. Santiago are planning a vacation. Your clients would like to depart on 12 October from Boston to London. When availability is displayed, a nonstop NW flight in line 2 has seats available in B class. The passengers will return on 20 October. When availability is displayed for the return trip, the same carrier operates a flight in line 1 and has seats available in B class. Mrs. Santiago is diabetic. Meal service is provided on both flights. Tickets should be issued on 22 September.

The travelers would like to purchase a package vacation in London and prefer a basic independent tour that includes airfare, transfers, and sightseeing. When the tour index is displayed, your clients inquire about the hotels in the London Highlights tour in line 2.

The package for a DLX room includes five nights at a total price of $634 per person. Extra nights are available at a rate of $104 per night, per person. Your clients would like to stay eight nights. The reservation will be guaranteed by credit card. The account number is VI4343002172830012. The account expires September 1998.

The passenger names are Mr. Carl Santiago and Mrs. Martha Santiago. Your agency phone is 617-555-2039. Mrs. Santiago's business phone is 617-555-4345, and the clients' home phone is 617-555-1430. The reservation was received from Mrs. Santiago. Your clients will need a passport to travel to London, but a visa is not required.

Access Function

Assume you wish to access United's reservation system to display flight availability from Seattle to Honolulu on 10 May, departing around 8 A.M. The following direct-access entry may be used to display availability:

¤QUA/110MAYSEAHNL8A

SABRE responds as follows:

```
   UA  RESPONSE
7  UA   181   F9   Y9   B9   M9   SEAHNL   845A    435P   747   B   0
8  UA   276   F9   Y9   B9   M9   SEASFO   915A   1205P   D9S   B   0
9  UA   192   F9   Y9   B9   M9          HNL   220P   1010P   747   D   0
```

The availability display appears in the standard SABRE format. The header "UA Response" indicates that the availability display was obtained from United's reservation system. Observe that the first line in the display is numbered line 7. Line numbers in a direct-access availability display will always start with line 7 and may go as high as line 16. The direct-access data will remain in the agent's work area for two minutes.

When availability has been requested from a participating reservation system, seats can be sold with the normal entry. For example, to sell one seat in Y class on UA 181 in the display above, you use the following entry:

01Y7

SABRE books the segment as follows:

```
1  UA  181Y  10MAY   SEAHNL      SS2   845A   435P/TA UA
```

A tag is added to the end of the segment, indicating the computer system on which the segment was sold. The sell entry must be made within 2 minutes of displaying availability. After that, availability must be redisplayed before a segment can be booked.

Redisplaying Availability

The following entries may be used to modify a direct-access availability display:

1¤R	Displays return flights
1¤*	Displays additional availability
1¤*5P	Changes the departure time
1¤*OA	Redisplays original availability
1¤DL	Changes the host carrier
1¤DL*5P	Changes the host carrier and departure time
1¤AA	Redisplays availability through SABRE

Fare quotes can also be obtained through the direct-access system, as follows:

¤QDL/FQMIACHI23MAY-DL

This example will obtain a fare quote from the Delta reservation system. Many fare type codes used by other systems differ from those used in SABRE entries. For instance, to request adult excursion fares, **AX** must be input with the Delta system, but **EXA** must be used with the United system. When fare quotes are requested from these systems, the correct fare type code must be input.

To illustrate, the following example will display only adult excursion fares from the Delta reservation system:

¤QDL/FQMIACHI23MAYAX-DL

The following is an example of a fare quote obtained from the Delta system:

MIACHI-DL	23MAY	AA CO	NW TW UA US			
AX	FARE	TAX	OW	RT	RTG	BOOK
MLHAP21	307.27	20.73		338.00	1	M
MLEX7	331.82	33.18		359.00	1	M
QLHAP7	343.64	34.36		376.00	1	Q
QLE2	356.36	35.64		392.00	1	Q
BAP30	372.73	37.27		410.00	1	B

Note that the Delta fare display is different from a standard SABRE fare quote. Fare quotes obtained through direct access are always displayed in the format of the host system.

The following entry will obtain a fare quote from the United system for the same travel date, city pair, and fare type:

¤QUA/FQMIACHI23MAYEXA-UA

The following is an example of a fare quote obtained from the United system:

MIA	ORD	NORMAL	VALID	12APR	THRU	19OCT
FARE BASIS		OW FARE	RT FARE		AIRLINES	
1 VAP21		189.00	378.00	R	UA	
2 HAP14		204.00	408.00	R	UA	
1 QAP14		189.00	378.00	R	UA	
2 MAP14		204.00	408.00	R	UA	
3 B7PE25		239.00	478.00	R	UA	

Whereas direct-access availability displays are shown in the normal SABRE format, fare displays appear in the format of the host system.

Verifying Flight Information

The direct-access function can also be used to obtain flifo, or verified flight information, from the system of a participating carrier. For example, the following entry will obtain flight information from the Continental system:

¤QCO/4130/19JUN

The flight information is displayed as follows:

```
4130/19JUN
FLIGHT  ROUTINE
SKED    JAX    ORIG    855A
        EWR    1100A   1130A
        BTV    1230P   TERM
```

In this example, CO 4130 originates in Jacksonville and stops in Newark before terminating in Burlington, Vermont. A flifo display always remains in the format of the host system.

Displaying Seat Maps

The direct-access function can also be used to display seat maps on flights operated by participating carriers. To illustrate, assume an agent desires to display the seat map for Y class on UA 220 on 18 January from Denver to Los Angeles. The agent uses the following entry to obtain the seat map from the United reservation system:

¤QUA/4G*220Y18JANDENLAX

In this example, *QUA* is the host key for the United reservation system. The seat map request is in the standard SABRE format. The UA seat map is displayed as follows:

```
UA 220        18JAN DEN SEAT MAP *DC10*
        A     B     C     D     E     F     G     H     J
11      N     NA    NA    N     N     N     NA    NA    N
12      S     S     NA    N     N     S     S     S     S
13      R     R     R     S     S     S     S     S     S
14W     N     NA    NA    N     N     N     S     S     S
15W     S     NA    NA    N     N     N     NA    S     S
16W     S     NA    NA    N     N     N     NA    S     S
17W     S     NA    NA    N     N     N     NA    S     S
```

The seat map is displayed in the host carrier's format. In this example, the code *N* indicates an available no smoking seat, *S* indicates a seat that has already been assigned, and *R* indicates a reserved seat. An available aisle seat is indicated by the secondary code *A*.

As mentioned previously, the exact functions that can be used with a host system vary, depending on the carrier.

Multi-Access

The **multi-access** function can be used to build, retrieve, and modify PNRs on a host system. Multi-access can also be used to (a) access cruise ship information, (b) book Amtrak tickets, and (c) obtain Club Med information. The exact multi-access functions that can be used with a host system vary, depending on the carrier.

A host system can be accessed under multi-access, as follows:

FORMAT   ¤¤<Host key>

EXAMPLE   ¤¤QAF

This example will establish a multi-access link with the Air France reservation system. When the link has been established, standard SABRE formats can be used to build a reservation. To exit from the host system, the following entry is used:

QUIT

Multi-access displays appear in the host carrier's format. As an example of multi-access capabilities, the following functions can be used with the Air France reservation system:

¤¤QAF	Access Air France host system
FQNYCCDG10MAY	Fare quotation
110MAYJFKCDG8A	City pair availability
1*	More availability
1*OA	Original availability
1R17MAY5P	Return availability
9212-555-2222-A	Phone field
7T-A	Ticketing field
6P	Received from
5CAR/HTL TBA	Remarks (one line maximum)
V*2/10MAY	Verify flight information
01Y1	Sell air space
X4	Cancel segment
*4/10MAYJFKCDG-JONES	Retrieve PNR
4G*2Y10MAYJFKCDG	Display seat map

Summary

The total-access function is used to obtain flight availability, fare quotations, direct reference material, flight information, seat maps, and other information directly from the reservation system of a participating airline. Each total-access host is identified by a three-letter host key. Availability displays appear in the standard SABRE format, but most other displays remain in the host carrier's format. The multi-access function can be used to book a reservation directly on a host carrier's system.

New commands included in this chapter:

¤QUA/110MAYSEAHNL9A	Displays direct-access availability
1¤R	Displays direct-access return flights
1¤*	Displays additional direct-access availability
1¤*5P	Changes the direct-access departure time
1¤*OA	Redisplays original direct-access availability
1¤DL	Changes the host carrier
1¤DL*5P	Changes the host carrier and departure time
1¤AA	Redisplays availability through SABRE
¤QDL/FQMIACHI23MAY	Displays a direct-access fare quote
¤QCO/4130/19JUN	Displays direct-access flight verification
¤QUA/4G*189Y10MAYSEAHNL	Displays a direct-access seat map
¤¤QAF	Establishes a multi-access link
QUIT	Exits from the host system to SABRE

STUDENT REVIEW

KEY CONCEPTS AND TERMS

Identify the word, phrase, or symbol for each of the following concepts:

1. A three-letter code identifying an airline that participates in the total access program.
2. The entry code that is used to input direct-access entries.
3. The entry to display return flights after a direct-access availability display has been obtained.
4. The fare type code that is used to request adult excursion fares from the Delta Air Lines reservation system.
5. The fare type code that is used to request adult excursion fares from the United Airlines reservation system.
6. The function that is used to build, retrieve, and modify PNRs on a host system.
7. The entry code that is used to establish a link to build a PNR on a host system.
8. The entry to exit from a host system after building a PNR through the link.

Answers:

1. host key; 2. ¤ followed by the host key; 3. 1¤R; 4. AX; 5. EXA; 6. multi-access; 7. ¤¤; 8. QUIT.

REVIEW QUESTIONS

1. What host key is used to access the United reservation system?
2. What host key is used to access the TWA reservation system?
3. What host key is used to access the Delta reservation system?
4. What entry code would be used to perform direct-access functions with the British Airways reservation system?

5. Indicate whether the following statement is true or false: Fare quotes cannot be obtained with a direct-access entry.

6. Indicate whether the following statement is true or false: When a direct-access availability display has been obtained, an air segment can be sold with the normal SABRE entry.

7. Indicate whether the following statement is true or false: Direct-access seat maps are displayed in the normal SABRE format.

8. What entry code would be used to establish a multi-access link with the Continental reservation system?

9. Indicate whether the following statement is true or false: When a multi-access link has been established, standard SABRE entries can be used to make a reservation on the host system.

10. Assume you want to link with the QF reservation system to display availability from SYD to AKL on 12 March, with departure around 10 A.M. Write the direct-access and multi-access entries for this situation.

11. Assume a client will travel from DTW to IND on 27 June, departing around 9 A.M. Write the entry to display direct-access availability from the Delta reservation system.

12. Write the entry to display direct-access availability from the Continental reservation system, from DEN to LHR on 16 May departing around 12 noon.

13. What entry would be used to display direct-access return flights for question 12?

14. What entry would be used to display additional direct-access availability for question 12?

15. Assume a client will travel from ANC to TUS on 18 October and would like to depart around 10 P.M. What entry would be used to obtain a direct-access display from the Alaska Airlines reservation system?

16. What entry would be used to change the direct-access departure time to 6 A.M. in question 15?

17. What entry would be used to display direct-access return flights for question 15?

18. What entry would be used to redisplay the original direct-access availability display in question 15?

19. What entry would be used to change the host carrier to United?

20. What entry would change the host carrier to Northwest and also change the departure time to 6 P.M.?

21. Write the entry to redisplay availability through SABRE after direct-access availability has been obtained.

22. Assume you would like to obtain a fare display from the United reservation system for travel from Boston to Seattle on 22 April. What direct-access entry would be used to display only adult excursion fares?

23. Assume you would like to obtain a fare display from the Northwest reservation system for travel from Detroit-Wayne County Metro Airport to Ft. Lauderdale on 8 December. Write the access entry to display adult excursion fares.

24. Assume you would like to verify flight information for US 497 on 16 June. What direct-access entry would be used to obtain the flight verification from the USAir reservation system?

25. Assume you would like to verify flight information for CO 144 on 23 March. What direct-access entry would be used to obtain the flight verification from the Continental reservation system?

26. Write the entry to establish a multi-access link with the Delta reservation system.

27. What entry would be used to establish a multi-access link with the Continental reservation system?

28. After establishing the link in question 27, what entry would you use to display availability from Greensboro to Newark airport on 18 July, with departure around 11 A.M.?

29. After obtaining the availability display in question 28, what entry would you use to sell two seats in Y class from line 2?

30. After a multi-access link has been established, what entry will exit the host system and return to SABRE?

APPLICATIONS

Read the following scenario, and decide what actions should be performed to satisfy the client's preferences and needs. Briefly describe how you would handle the situation, and then write the required entries.

A client who plans to travel from St. Louis to Papua New Guinea inquires about flight schedules and fares for the trip. The passenger would like to travel from St. Louis to Los Angeles in V class, at a discount fare advertised by TWA. She will depart on 12 March at around 6 A.M. The SABRE availability display does not show any seats in this class on any early morning flight. However, on the TWA system the availability display shows one seat available in V class on a flight in line 2.

Flight information for the international portion of the journey can be obtained from the Qantas reservation system. The passenger will travel from Los Angeles to Sydney on 12 March, departing around 2 P.M. On 17 March the passenger will travel from Sydney to Port Moresby, and on 27 March she will travel from Port Moresby to Los Angeles via Cairns and Honolulu. She will return to St. Louis on 30 March. Book two seats in Y class on the first flight in each availability display.

Besides the flight times and fares, your client would also like to know the elapsed time of each international flight. The passenger is booked on QF 12 from LAX to SYD, QF 44 from SYD to POM, QF 90 from POM to CNS, QF 25 from CNS to HNL, and QF 17 from HNL to LAX.

The host key for TWA is TWA, and the host key for Quantas is QQF.

Chapter 19

Phase IV Pricing and Ticketing

Outline

Phase IV Pricing

Creating a Ticket Record

Inserting Data in the Ticket Record

Phase IV Ticketing

Chapter Objectives

After you complete this chapter, you should be able to:

1. Create a manual ticket record.

2. Enter price and ticketing information in a ticket record.

3. Store a ticket record.

4. Issue tickets from a manual ticket record.

PROBLEM

A client previously booked a reservation to travel from Pittsburgh to Paris. Now the passenger would like to book a side trip from Paris to Athens, returning to Paris in time for the return flight to Pittsburgh. After booking the side trip, you discover that SABRE cannot autoprice the itinerary.

SABRE SOLUTION

Use the Phase IV Pricing function to input the price information manually, enabling SABRE to ticket the PNR. In this chapter, you will learn to use Phase IV to create a ticket record, store a ticket, and issue tickets.

Phase IV Pricing

Although SABRE can correctly autoprice most domestic and many international itineraries, occasionally the fare information must be entered by the agent. This situation may occur if a carrier's fares or routes are not stored in the SABRE data base, or if the routing is too complex to autoprice. In such cases, the agent must manually enter all the information required to price the itinerary. This procedure is referred to as *Phase IV pricing and ticketing*. PNRs with itineraries priced by the Phase IV method must be ticketed by a special format.

The **Phase IV** function is used to create a ticket record for PNRs with itineraries that SABRE cannot price. The fare information can then be inserted into the ticket record manually. In general, the following information can be inserted:

1. Line entitlement (fare basis)
2. Fare calculation
3. Agency commission
4. Base fare and tax

Depending on the itinerary, other fare information may also be inserted, such as a tour code, validity dates, endorsement/restrictions information, and international fare information.

Creating a Ticket Record

The entry **W‡C** is used to create a ticket record, as follows:

W‡C

To illustrate, assume SABRE cannot price the following itinerary:

```
1  DL1236Y  12JUN   M   ATLMCI   HK1   927A    1030A
2  UA 247Q  19JUN   M   MCIDEN   HK1   725A     809A
3  UA 234Q  19JUN   M   DENPHX   HK1  1245P     152P
```

The following entry can be used to create a ticket record:

W‡C

SABRE responds with the following display:

```
FAIL CODE - 02
TA-ADT
1    0    ATL     DL1236Y      12JUN   927A   OK
2    0    MCI     UA 247Q      19JUN   725A   OK
3    0    DEN     UA 234Q      19JUN  1245P   OK
          PHX
```

Pricing qualifiers can be added to the entry to specify passenger type or segment selection. For example, to create separate ticket records for adult and child passengers, the passenger types would be included, as in the following example:

W‡C‡PADT/CHD

To ticket only a portion of the itinerary, segment selection would be included, as in the following entry:

W‡C‡S1/3/4

Name selection may also be included, as follows:

W‡C‡N1.2

Pricing qualifiers may be combined in one entry as follows:

W‡C‡N2.1‡S1/3

Inserting Data in the Ticket Record

When a ticket record has been created, the next step is to insert the required fare information. At a minimum, the record must include the fare basis, the base fare and tax, the agency commission, and the fare calculation.

The following secondary action codes identify the fare information inserted in a ticket record:

L	Line entitlement
C	Fare calculation
K	Commission
Y	Base fare/tax
U	Tour code
*	Validity dates
RF	Routing, foreign
RD	Routing, domestic
RT	Routing, transborder

The entry code **W‡I** is used to insert information in the ticket record. A secondary action code is input to designate the type of information that is to be inserted.

Inserting the Fare Basis

The secondary action code **L** is used to insert the fare basis for each segment as follows:

FORMAT W‡I‡L<Line>-<Fare basis>

EXAMPLE W‡I‡L1-Y

This example inserts the fare basis Y for segment 1.

Multiple segments with the same fare basis can be indicated as follows:

W‡I‡L2/3-Q

This entry inserts the fare basis Q for segments 2 and 3.

To insert different fare bases for multiple segment lines, separate the fare bases with a cross (‡) as follows:

W‡I‡L1-Y‡L2/3-Q

The fare basis codes will be printed on the ticket in the fare basis box on each line of the itinerary. These codes are referred to as the **line entitlement**.

Inserting Validity Dates

Validity dates are printed in the NOT VALID BEFORE/AFTER box on the passenger ticket. The dates are inserted in the ticket record along with the line entitlement, as follows:

FORMAT   W‡I‡L<Line entitlement>*<Validity dates>

EXAMPLE   W‡I‡L1-YXIT21*10MAY01JUN

In this example, the fare basis YXIT21 in segment 1 is valid from 10 May through 1 June. The code * is typed before the validity dates when fare basis codes are input in a ticket record.

Inserting the Commission

The agency commission must also be inserted in the ticket record. The secondary action code **KP** is used to insert the commission as a percentage, as follows:

FORMAT   W‡I‡KP<Pct>

EXAMPLE   W‡I‡KP10

If the commission is entered as a dollar amount, *K* should be used instead, as in the following example:

W‡I‡K24.00

The percentage or amount will be printed in the commission box on the ticket. If a commission is not entered in the ticket record, it will not be printed on the ticket.

Inserting the Fare Calculation

The fare calculation breaks down the base fare by segment and carrier. As an example, assume a PNR has the following itinerary:

```
1  DL  683Y  12JUN  M  GSODAB  HK1  450P  815P
2  US  802Y  19JUN  M  DABGSO  HK1  115P  412P
```

The fare calculation for the itinerary appears as follows:

```
GSO DL DAB150.00Y US GSO130.00Y 280.00 END
```

In this example, Delta is the carrier from Greensboro to Daytona Beach, and the base fare is 150.00. USAir is the carrier from Daytona Beach to Greensboro, and the base fare is 130.00. The total base fare for the itinerary is 280.00. In a fare calculation, the city code (not the airport code) is used to indicate each point in the itinerary. The fare basis code appears after each base fare. In this example, the fare basis is Y for both segments.

The fare calculation is inserted with the secondary code **C**, as follows:

FORMAT   W‡I‡C<Fare calculation>

EXAMPLE   W‡I‡CGSO DL DAB150.00Y US GSO130.00Y 280.00 END

Special symbols are used in the fare calculation to indicate a connecting point, a stopover charge, a local surcharge, a fare differential, or a surface segment.

-X	Connecting city
S	Stopover charge
Q	Surcharge
D	Differential
/-	Surface segment

As an example, consider the following fare calculation:

```
ATL DL SFO230.00Q7 /-SJC AA DFW260.00Q2 490.00 END
```

In this example, a surface segment exists between SFO and SJC.

Inserting the Base Fare and Tax

The secondary action code **Y** is used to insert the base fare and tax for each line, as follows:

FORMAT   W‡I‡Y<Base fare>/<Tax>

EXAMPLE   W‡I‡Y420.38/33.62

The code *Y* is always input, regardless of the booking class or fare basis. The amounts must be entered with decimals and cents but without a dollar sign. The base fare and tax will be printed in the base fare and tax boxes on the ticket.

Fare Calculation

Assume you want to insert the fare calculation in the following ticket record:

```
1  O  PDX  AS   85Y   22SEP   705A  OK
2  O  ANC  YC  143Y   26SEP   500P  OK
      ENA
```

Assume the base fare from PDX to ANC on AS is 210.00, and the base fare from ANC to ENA on YC is 90.00. Thus, the total base fare is 300.00. The fare basis is Y for both segments. Using this information, you input the following entry to insert the fare calculation:

W‡I‡CPDX AS ANC210.00Y YC ENA90.00Y 300.00 END

On the ticket, this information will be printed on the fare calculation line.

Displaying the Ticket Record

The entry **W can be used to display the fare information in a ticket record, as follows:

**W

When this entry is input, SABRE will respond as follows:

```
T-ADT O CNT
1      O   PDX        AS      85Y   22SEP  705A   OK
2      O   ANC        YC     143Y   26SEP  500P   OK
           ENA
PDX    AS  ANC210.00Y         YC          ENA90.00Y      300.00  END
```

Inserting Tour Codes

A tour itinerary requires additional information in the ticket record: the tour number and the routing code. The qualifier **RF** is used to indicate that the routing is foreign. A tour number is entered with the secondary action code **U**.

FORMAT   W‡I‡U<Tour number>‡R<Routing>

EXAMPLE   W‡I‡UAMF3131‡RF

If a routing code is not inserted in the ticket record, SABRE will assume the routing is domestic.

Using Phase IV Pricing

Let us follow an example from the creation of a ticket record to the insertion of fare information. Assume that SABRE cannot autoprice the following itinerary:

1	HP	598Y	12JUL	M	PHXMCI	HK1	1021A	152P
2	TW	620M	14JUL	W	MCISTL	HK1	142P	221P
3	TW	247M	14JUL	W	STLCVG	HK1	355P	702P
4	DL	319Y	17JUL	J	CVGPHX	HK1	852A	1045A

The first step is to create a ticket record, as follows:

W‡C

SABRE responds as follows:

```
FAIL CODE - 02
TA-ADT
1 O PHX HP  598Y 12JUL 1021A OK
2 O MCI TW  620M 14JUL 142P  OK
3 X STL TW  247M 14JUL 355P  OK
4 O CVG DL  319Y 17JUL 852A  OK
    PHX
```

Let us say the fare basis is Y3 in segments 1 and 4, and MA3 in segments 2 and 3. The following entry is used to insert the fare bases for all segments:

W‡I‡L1/4-Y3‡L2/3-MA3

The commission is inserted as follows:

W‡I‡KP10

(continued)

Several types of information may be inserted in a ticket record with one entry, as follows:

W‡I‡L1-YXIT21‡L2-YWIT21*10MAY01JUNE‡Y637.00/3.00‡KP8‡UA3113‡RF

This example will insert the line entitlement, validity dates, the base fare and tax, the commission percentage, the tour code, and the routing indicator.

Now assume the base fare from Phoenix to Kansas City on America West is 150.00, the throughfare from Kansas City to Cincinnati on TWA is 180.00, and the base fare from Cincinnati to Phoenix is 160.00. The fare calculation is inserted as follows:

W‡I‡CPHX HP MKC150.00Y3 TW-XSTL TW CVG180.00MA3
DL PHX160.00Y3 490.00 END

The total base fare is 490.00, and the 10 percent transportation tax is 49.00. The following entry is used to insert the base fare and tax:

W‡I‡Y490.00/49.00

The ticket record may now be displayed, as follows:

**W

SABRE responds as follows:

```
TA-ADT 0      CNT
1  O  PHX  HP   598Y   12JUL  1021A  OK  Y3
2  O  MCI  TW   620M   14JUL   142P  OK  MA3
3  X  STL  TW   247M   14JUL   355P  OK  MA3
4  O  CVG  DL   319Y   17JUL   852A  OK  Y3
      PHX
PHX HP MKC150.00Y3 TW-XSTL TW CVG180.00MA3
DL PHX160.00Y3 490.00 END
```

Other Phase IV Pricing Entries

The secondary code **ED** is used to input information in the ticket record to print in the endorsements/restrictions box on the ticket, as follows:

W‡EDSUBJ GVT APVL

This example would be used to indicate that the ticket is subject to government approval.

Multiple tax amounts may be input if more than one tax applies. Each tax should be identified by the two-letter country code, as follows:

W‡I‡Y290.00/29.00US/4.75CA

In this example, the U.S. tax is 29.00, and the Canadian tax is 4.75.

If a fare is tax-exempt, the secondary code *TE* is inserted in place of the tax, as follows:

W‡I‡Y250.00/TE

In this example, the base fare is 250.00, but the fare is tax-exempt. This entry might be used for special government travel for which U.S. transportation tax does not apply.

Multiple Ticket Records

When passengers are to be ticketed using different passenger types, SABRE creates a separate ticket record for each passenger type (one for ADT, one for CHD). The following entries may be used with multiple ticket records:

**W1	Display first ticket record
**W2	Display second ticket record
W‡CR1	Recreate first ticket record
W‡CR2	Recreate second ticket record

Phase IV Ticketing

The entry code **W‡T** is used to issue tickets from a Phase IV ticket record as follows:

FORMAT   W‡T<Option>

The PNR must be ended and retrieved before tickets can be issued. To end the transaction and print tickets with one entry, the following entry may be used:

EW‡T

An option, such as the form of payment or issuing carrier, may be included in the ticketing entry, as in the following example:

W‡T‡FCK‡ADL

This entry will print *CK* in the form-of-payment box on the ticket and will print *Delta Airlines* in the issuing-airline box. If a carrier is not specified, the first carrier in the itinerary is used as the issuing airline.

The same form-of-payment formats that are used with demand ticketing can be used with Phase IV entries.

Summary

If SABRE cannot autoprice an itinerary, the agent must enter the fare information manually, using the Phase IV pricing function. The fare information is inserted in a ticket record. To enable tickets to be issued, the fare basis, fare calculation, agency commission, base fare, and tax must be input. In a tour itinerary, the tour number and the routing code are also required. The entry code *W‡T* is used to issue tickets from a Phase IV ticket record. The entry code *EW‡T* is used to end the transaction and print tickets.

New commands included in this chapter:

W‡C	Creates a ticket record
W‡C‡PADT/CHD	Creates ticket records for specified passenger types
W‡C‡S1/3/4	Creates a ticket record for specified segments
W‡I‡L1/2-Y	Inserts the fare basis code
W‡I‡L1-Y‡L2/3-Q	Inserts multiple fare basis codes
W‡I‡KP10	Inserts the commission
W‡I‡CATL AA MIA49.07Y DL ATL46.28Y 95.35 END	Inserts the fare calculation
W‡I‡Y420.38/33.62	Inserts the base fare and tax
**W	Displays the ticket record
W‡I‡UAMF3131‡RF	Inserts tour code and routing code
W‡I‡L1-YXIT21*10MAY01JUN	Inserts validity dates
W‡EDSUBJ GVT APVL	Inserts endorsements/restrictions
W‡I‡Y296.15/14.58US/4.75CA	Inserts multiple tax amounts
W‡I‡Y250.00/TE	Inserts a tax-exempt fare amount
W‡CR	Recreates a ticket record

STUDENT REVIEW

KEY CONCEPTS AND TERMS

Identify the word, phrase, or symbol for each of the following concepts:

1. The function that is used to create a ticket record for PNRs with itineraries that SABRE cannot price.
2. The entry that is used to create a Phase IV ticket record.
3. The entry code that is used to insert information in a ticket record.
4. The secondary code that is used to insert the fare basis for each segment.
5. The fare basis codes that will be printed on the ticket in the fare basis box on each line of the itinerary.
6. The code that is typed before the validity dates when fare basis codes are input in a ticket record.
7. The secondary code that is used to insert the commission as a percentage.
8. The secondary code that is used to insert the fare calculation.
9. The secondary code that is used to insert the base fare and tax for each line of the ticket record.
10. The entry used to display the fare information in a ticket record.
11. The qualifier that is used to indicate a foreign routing.
12. The secondary code that is used to input a tour number in a ticket record.

13. The secondary code that is used to input information in the ticket record to print in the endorsements/restrictions box.

14. The entry code that is used to issue tickets from a Phase IV ticket record.

15. The entry to end the transaction and print tickets from a Phase IV ticket record.

Answers:

14. W‡T. 15. EW‡T.

1. Phase IV. 2. W‡C. 3. W‡L. 4. L. 5. line entitlement. 6. *. 7. KP. 8. C. 9. Y. 10. *W**. 11. RF. 12. U. 13. ED.

REVIEW QUESTIONS

1. Write the entry to create a ticket record.

2. Write the entry to create a ticket record for segments 1 and 5 only.

3. Write the entry to create a ticket record to use both adult and child fares to price the itinerary separately for adults and children.

4. Write the entry to create a ticket record to price the itinerary with only senior fares.

5. What entry will insert the fare basis YLE3 for segments 1 and 5?

6. Write the entry to insert the fare basis QA7P50 for segments 2 and 4.

7. What entry will insert the fare basis QA3 for segment 1 and the fare basis ME3N for segment 2?

8. Write the entry to insert a commission rate of 10 percent.

9. Write the entry to insert a flat commission of 23.80.

10. Write the entry to insert the fare calculation for the following itinerary:

```
1  BA   24Y  T  12MAR  SFOLHR  HK1  145P  ‡610A
2  BD  100Y  W  13MAR  LHRAMS  HK1  900A  1000A
```

The fare from San Francisco to London is 942.00, and the fare from London to Amsterdam is 180.00. The fare basis is Y in both segments.

11. Assume a PNR has the following itinerary:

```
1  WN 803Q  W  11JAN  SANABQ  HK2  805A  1135A
2  WN 669Q  S  15JAN  ABQSAN  HK2  310P   400P
```

What entry would be used to create a ticket record for the San Diego-Albuquerque segment only?

12. Assume that in question 11 the fare basis is QA21. Write the entry to insert the fare basis in the ticket record.

13. Assume that in question 11 the base fare is 132.00. Write the entry to insert the fare calculation.

14. Write the entry to insert a base fare of 340.00 and a tax of 34.00.

15. What entry will insert a base fare of 413.64 and a tax of 41.36?

16. Write the entry to redisplay the ticket record.

17. What entry would be used to insert the tour code AWA1924 and indicate that the routing is foreign?

18. Write the entry to issue a ticket from a Phase IV ticket record.

19. Assume the client will pay by check, and the issuing airline is AA. Write the entry to issue the ticket from a Phase IV ticket record and enter a 10 percent commission.

20. Assume the client will pay by cash, and the issuing airline is BA. Write the entry to issue the ticket from a Phase IV ticket record and enter an 8 percent commission.

APPLICATIONS

Read the following scenario, and decide what actions should be performed to satisfy the client's preferences and needs. Briefly describe how you would handle the situation, and then write the required entries.

A client will travel from Albuquerque to Akutan, Alaska. His PNR has the following itinerary:

1	WN	963K	12JUN	ABQSFO	HK1	330P	520P
2	AS	93Y	14JUN	SFOANC	HK1	855A	150P
3	RV	23Y	14JUN	ANCDUT	HK1	305P	330P
4	RV	12Y	14JUN	DUTKQA	HK1	430P	835P

SABRE cannot autoprice the itinerary. The passenger is booked at the KA3 fare basis on segment 1 and at the Y fare basis in all other segments. The base fare from Albuquerque to San Francisco is 200.00, and the base fare from San Francisco to Anchorage is 240.00. The base throughfare from Anchorage to Akutan is 112.73. The total tax for the itinerary is 53.82.

Study Guide

To the Student

This Study Guide is designed to assist you in learning the important concepts presented in each chapter of the text. Each section corresponds to one chapter and consists of a series of paragraphs with one or more blank lines. The missing word or phrase that belongs in each blank may be found by reading the chapter.

Chapter 1

1. Until the 1950s, flight reservations were made either by _____ or at _____.

2. SABRE was developed in 1976 by the parent company of _____.

3. Relations between CRS vendors and subscribers are regulated by _____.

4. Information that consists only of numbers is referred to as _____. Information that consists only of letters is referred to as _____. Information that consists of both numbers and letters is called _____.

5. The _____ of a data processing system performs arithmetic and logic operations and coordinates the communication, storage, and retrieval of information.

6. The part of a data processing system that keeps data for future retrieval is referred to as _____.

7. Together, the central processor and permanent storage area constitute a _____.

8. A _____ is located at each site to link the agent sets to the central processor.

9. A _Modem_ converts computer data into signals that can be transmitted over a telephone line.

10. _ARINC_ maintains a data communications network linking SABRE with the airlines and other travel-related vendors.

11. _____ is a display of regularly scheduled flights between a specified origin and destination.

12. On each flight, the display shows the number of seats that can be sold in each _____.

13. Booking an airline reservation is called _Selling_.

14. A waitlisted reservation may eventually be confirmed, if other passengers with confirmed reservations later _Hanzel_.

15. Pertinent information about each reservation is stored in a _PNR_.

16. The passenger data items are entered by the agent in an electronic holding area called the _Queue_.

17. SABRE can autoprice most air itineraries, by automatically calculating _Total_, _Base fare_, and _Tax_.

18. On many flights, SABRE can reserve seats automatically, based on the client's preference for _Any Airline_

19. Cigarette smoking is not permitted on any domestic flight of _Any Airline_.

20. Each line of a _Item. Invoice_ contains a SABRE entry to input passenger data, such as the name, home telephone number, and form of payment.

21. An _____ is a document that provides detailed flight information for each segment and a summary of all the charges.

22. Bookings such as hotel reservations, car rentals, cruises, and tours are referred to as _____.

23. When a PC is used to communicate with SABRE, the _____ is displayed when the backwards slash key is typed.

24. When the _____ is typed, a solid box is displayed.

25. When the _____ is typed, a symbol called a cross is displayed.

26. When all the data relating to a reservation has been assembled, the agent inputs the command to _____.

27. Each work area is identified by _____.

28. The _Agent SI_ procedure identifies the agent who will be using the computer and the work area in which he or she will be working.

29. Before leaving the agent's set for an extended period of time, or at the end of the work day, the agent must _SO_.

30. A _____ at the bottom of the screen indicates that additional data exists.

31. The entry code _W/_ is used to encode and decode.

Chapter 2

1. Each portion of an _Segment_ is referred to as a segment.

2. If a trip involves a connection, _Seperate Segments_ included in the itinerary for each connecting flight.

3. Together, the departure point and arrival point make up a _____.

4. If a departure date is not specified in an availability entry, SABRE will display _Only that day_

5. The date 4 August may be input as either _04 Aug_ or _4Aug_.

6. The time 12:00 noon may be input as either _12N_ or _12P_.

7. In an availability display, the header indicates the _departure time_ and day of the week, and the _city pair, timezone_

8. SABRE will display a maximum of _~~4~~ 6_ flights at one time.

9. The maximum number of seats that can be sold in each class of service is referred to as the _Seat quota_.

10. Except on American Airlines flights, if fewer than 4 seats are available in a class of service, SABRE will display _4_.

11. In an availability display, the departure and arrival points are indicated by the appropriate _on time preformance_

12. In the SABRE availability display, _____ is indicated by a digit, called the dependability factor.

13. When a departure time is specified in an availability entry, SABRE searches for the first flight departing within _1 hour_.

14. In an availability display, the departure and arrival times are given in _Am/Pm_.

15. The _free_ refers to the days of the week on which a flight operates.

16. _exception_ are days on which the flight does not operate.

17. The one-letter code for Thursday is _Q_.

18. The code _X6_ in an availability display indicates that a flight does not operate on Saturday.

19. In an availability display, the _dep. Point_ of an onward connecting flight is omitted.

20. When an availability display has been obtained, the entry code ___1R___ may be used to display flights for the return trip.

21. After an availability display has been obtained, the entry ___1≠2___ would redisplay the same city pair two days later.

22. The entry ___1¥E___ would be used to change the departure point of an availability display to EWR.

23. When the entry 1*OA is input, SABRE will display _____.

24. A connecting point can be specified by typing the city or airport code at the _____ of the availability entry.

25. To specify a carrier in an availability entry, ___+___ is typed before the carrier code.

26. The option _____ may be included in an availability entry to display only direct flights.

27. The _total Access_ function is used to obtain data directly from an airline's own computer system.

28. To change an availability display to a total access display, _1 change_ is typed before the carrier code.

29. Availability may be checked on a specific flight, if the _carrier_ and _flight #_ are known.

30. When availability is requested on a specific flight, the response ___0A CL___ indicates that the flight is closed, but seats may be waitlisted.

Chapter 3

1. The act of booking an airline reservation is called _Selling_.

2. If the requested seats are not available, the reservations may be placed on a _Wait list_.

3. The entry code ___0___ is used to sell an air segment.

4. If an agent attempts to sell more seats than the maximum number displayed, the reservation will _PN_.

5. Each segment line is numbered based on the order in which _____.

6. In an air segment, the code ___SS___ indicates that the seats will be confirmed immediately when the transaction is ended.

7. When a transaction is ended, a confirmed segment has the status ___HK___.

8. If the number of seats requested exceeds the maximum number shown in the availability display, the segment status will be _____.

9. On most domestic connections, the class of service must be the same on all legs in order to obtain _____.

10. The secondary code _LL_ is used to waitlist seats.

11. When a transaction is ended, a waitlisted segment has the status _____.

12. The _____ key is labeled DSPL on some SABRE keyboards, as a reminder that this key is used to display information.

13. The entry code _0 D5_ is used to direct-sell a flight.

14. An _Open Segment_ is a reservation to travel on an unspecified flight operated by a specified carrier.

15. The action code _Cake Sewken - open_ is used to book open segments.

16. A passive segment may be input using the action code _GK_ or _BK_.

17. If a reply to a requested (NN) segment is not received within 24 hours, the seats may be re-requested with the action code _IN_.

18. An _ARUNK_ segment is input to indicate surface travel in an air itinerary.

19. The best possible guarantee can be obtained by selling an air segment from a _Total Access Display_.

Chapter 4

1. The _____ field stores the names of all the passengers traveling together in the same reservation.

2. Names are grouped together by _____.

3. A PNR may have several passengers, but only one _____.

4. A maximum of _____ passengers can be stored in the name field.

5. The _____ field is used to store the passenger's business and home phones.

6. Each telephone number stored in a phone field is referred to as a _____.

7. The location code _____ indicates the agency phone, B indicates the _____, and _____ indicates the passenger's home phone.

8. The _____ is the date on which tickets will be issued.

9. When an agent _____, the PNR is removed from the work area, but is not transmitted to the processor for storage.

10. The _____ field may be used to store any free-form text.

11. Two fields, _____ and _____, are used for service information.

12. Most airlines prefer _____ to be used in name entries to clarify the sex, age group, and marital or professional status of each traveler.

13. The field identifier _____ is used to input name items.

14. If a ticket will be prepaid for pickup at a different location, the _____ should be input in the name field.

15. In name entries, _____ is typed before optional reference information, such as an employee identification number.

16. When an AAdvantage account number is input in the name field, _____ is typed before the account number.

17. The _____ must be included as the first phone item in every PNR created by a travel agency.

18. The field identifier _____ is used to input phone items.

19. If the name field has more than one passenger, the business and home phone of each passenger should be identified by _____.

20. The field identifier _____ is used to input ticketing items.

21. The code _____ is input to arrange ticketing for a specified date.

22. The entry code _____ is used to enter a time limit.

23. The field identifier _____ is used to input received-from items.

24. The entry _____ will display all the data items in the current work area.

25. The entry _____ will display just the itinerary.

26. When the transaction is ended, a 6-character code called a _____ is displayed.

27. The _____ key can be used to input multiple items with one entry.

Chapter 5

1. The _____ field is used to store the agency name and address.

2. The _____ field may be used to store any general information about the reservation.

3. The general facts and AA facts fields are used to communicate _____ to the airlines.

4. The field identifier _____ is used to input free-form notes and reminders in a PNR.

5. A(n) _____ may be used to input two or more text lines simultaneously.

6. The entry code 5- causes the inputted text to be printed on the ticket in the _____.

7. In a form-of-payment entry, if _____ is typed before a credit card code, automatic credit approval will be requested.

8. When a credit card is entered as the form of payment, _____ is typed before the expiration date.

9. A _____ is a document issued by a government agency authorizing a travel agency or airline to issue a ticket.

10. The entry code _____ is used to store an address to print on an invoice.

11. A(n) _____ is a message stored in the remarks field to print on an invoice.

12. The secondary code _____ may be used to enter free-form text in the PNR history.

13. The entry code _____ is used to input the travel agency's address in a PNR.

14. A minimum of _____ lines and a maximum of _____ lines may be entered in the address field.

15. The field identifier _____ is used to enter service information for carriers other than AA.

16. To include name reference in an SSR entry, the _____ must be stored in the PNR.

17. If an SSR request applies to all passengers in the PNR, name reference may be _____.

18. When descriptive text is included in an SSR entry, _____ is typed before the text.

19. The entry code _____ is used to enter service information for an AA flight.

20. An unaccompanied minor is a child _____ years or younger traveling without an adult.

21. The SSR code _____ is used to request assistance for an unaccompanied minor.

22. The SSR code _____ is used to input frequent traveler account numbers for carriers other than AA.

23. The entry code _____ is used to input an OSI item for carriers other than AA.

24. If an OSI message applies to all the carriers in the itinerary, the code _____ is typed in place of the carrier code.

25. When the entry code 4OSI is used to input an OSI message, the _____ is omitted.

Chapter 6

1. When a PNR is created and _____, the record is transmitted to the central processor for storage.

2. The _____ key is used to retrieve and display PNRs.

3. When a PNR is stored, a _____-digit code, the record locator, is displayed.

4. When a PNR is stored, SABRE changes the status of a waitlisted segment from _____ to _____.

5. The _____ identifies the travel agency, and the _____ identifies the agent who created the PNR.

6. Retrieving a PNR created by another booking source is called _____.

7. If PNRs are stored for more than one passenger with the same surname, a _____ is displayed if an agent attempts to retrieve one of the PNRs by surname.

8. To retrieve a reservation by flight number, the carrier code, flight number, _____, _____, and _____ must be input.

9. The entry _____ is used to display only the passenger data fields.

10. The entry code _____ is used to cancel segments.

11. After cancelling a segment, if a new segment is not booked, the itinerary must be _____ to reset the order.

12. Whenever a PNR is created or changed, a _____ must be input.

13. The _____ key can be used to cancel and rebook with one entry.

14. When multiple segments are canceled with one entry, _____ is typed to separate the segment numbers.

15. When multiple segments are canceled, the next segment that is sold will replace _____.

16. The entry _____ will cancel only the air segments in an itinerary.

17. The entry code _____ is used to insert a new segment in an existing itinerary.

18. The _____ key may be used to insert and sell with one entry.

19. When a waitlisted segment is confirmed, the segment status is changed from _____ to _____.

20. The entry code _____ is used to change segment status.

21. If an agent sells more than 4 seats on a flight that shows a maximum of 4 seats in the availability display, the segment will have the status _____.

22. When a segment has the status KK, the status must be changed to _____ before a ticket can be issued.

23. If a segment has the status PN after 24 hours, the status code _____ will cause another seat request to be transmitted to the carrier.

24. If a segment has the status UC, the agent must _____.

25. When an American Airlines flight is affected by a schedule change, the original segment will have the status _____, and the alternative segment will have the status _____.

Chapter 7

1. The _____ key is used to delete or change information in a passenger data field.

2. The entry _____ will delete the third item in the phone field.

3. The entry _____ will delete only the second passenger in name item 2, without deleting any other names.

4. When an entry is input to change a data item, the new data is typed after _____.

5. When a name item is changed, the item number may be omitted if _____.

6. The entry code _____ is used to reduce the number of seats.

7. When a party is reduced, no action is taken on _____.

8. To increase the number of seats, an agent must _____.

9. When a PNR is divided, a separate record is created for _____.

10. The entry code _____ is used to divide a PNR.

11. The entry code _____ is used to file a new PNR created as a result of dividing a party.

12. After a party has been divided, an OSI item should be input in each record to _____.

13. The entry _____ will divide only the third passenger in name item 2.

14. The entry _____ will divide the passengers in name items 1 and 3.

15. The entry _____ will divide the passenger range from 1.3 through 1.5.

Chapter 8

1. _____ fares apply to travel outside the United States, Canada, Mexico, the Caribbean, and Bermuda.

2. Each fare basis has a primary code and one or more _____.

3. The valid dates for travel or ticketing, and any restrictions that apply to a particular fare basis are set forth in _____.

4. If a _____ applies, the ticket must be purchased within a predefined period of time after the reservation is made, or by a specified date.

5. A _____ determines whether a particular booking code or fare basis can be combined with other booking codes or fare bases.

6. A fare quote is a display of fares for a specified carrier, listed from _____ to _____.

7. The entry code _____ is used to obtain a fare quote.

8. The fare type _____ refers to normal and excursion fares.

9. In a fare quote display, the currency on which the fares are based is shown in _____.

10. The _____ is shown in the F/B column.

11. The fare application _____ indicates that a fare is valid only for round-trip travel.

12. If a fare has an advance purchase requirement, the number of days is given in the _____ column.

13. The _____ for each fare appears at the bottom of the fare quote display.

14. The secondary code _____ is used to specify a fare basis.

15. The secondary code ‡B is used to specify _____.

16. The secondary code _____ is used to request joint fares.

17. The entry _____ will redisplay a fare quote for departure on 12 March.

18. The entry _____ will redisplay an existing fare quote and change the fare type to normal and excursion fares.

19. The entry code _____ is used to obtain a fare shopper display.

20. If a fare type is not specified when a fare shopper display is requested, _____ fares will be displayed.

21. The entry code _____ is used to obtain a fare quote from a city pair availability display.

22. If an international fare is based on _____, only the specified intermediate points may be used.

23. The entry code _____ is used to display fare rules from a fare quote display.

24. The secondary code _____ can be used to display a menu of rule categories.

25. The entry code _____ is used to display a specific category from the fare rules menu.

Chapter 9

1. When an itinerary is priced, any _____ or fare applications are applied.

2. The entry code _____ is used to price a displayed itinerary.

3. In the first line of a price display, SABRE indicates the last date on which _____.

4. In a price display, the _____ is shown to the right of the total fare for each passenger.

5. The _____ line itemizes the base fare by segment and carrier.

6. A _____ may be input in a pricing entry to specify an alternative fare type.

7. The secondary code _____ is used to specify a passenger type in a pricing entry.

8. If a passenger type is not specified, SABRE will price the itinerary at _____ fares.

9. The secondary code _____ is used to price only selected itinerary segments.

10. The secondary code _____ is used to price only selected passengers.

11. When an itinerary includes a valid connection with a connecting time of four hours or less, the itinerary is priced based on _____.

12. The secondary code B is used to indicate a _____.

13. The secondary code _____ is used to price an itinerary using a specified fare basis.

14. The entry _____ is used to price an itinerary at the lowest available fare without rebooking.

15. The entry code _____ may be used to change the class of service after a WPNC entry has been input.

16. The entry _____ will price an itinerary at the lowest available fare and automatically rebook any applicable segments.

17. The entry code _____ is used to store price instructions for ticketing on a future date.

18. In a future pricing entry, the secondary code A is used to specify the _____.

19. The secondary code _____ is used in a future pricing entry to specify the commission percentage.

20. The secondary code U may be input in a future pricing entry to print _____ on the ticket.

Chapter 10

1. Each ticket printer has a unique six-digit code that identifies the _____ and printer.

2. The entry code _____ is used to issue tickets from a retrieved PNR.

3. After tickets have been issued, SABRE changes the ticketing field to indicate the _____, duty code, agent sine, and _____.

4. When tickets are issued, the secondary code _____ is used to specify the issuing airline.

5. The secondary code KP is used to specify the _____.

6. The secondary code _____ is used to ticket selected passengers.

7. The secondary code S is used to ticket selected _____.

8. To specify a passenger type for pricing, the secondary code _____ is input.

9. If all passengers are to be priced at _____, a passenger type code is not required.

10. The secondary code _____ is used to specify the form of payment.

11. When a credit card number is input, a ticket entry _____ is typed between the month and day of the expiration date.

12. The secondary code ED is used to input information to print in the _____ box on the ticket.

13. The secondary code Q may be used to specify a _____.

14. The secondary code _____ is used for exchange tickets.

15. Before tickets can be issued, the PNR must be _____ and then retrieved from storage.

16. If the issuing airline is not specified, SABRE will use _____ as the issuing airline.

17. The entry code _____ is used to input data on an accounting line.

18. The entry code DIN is used to print _____.

19. Special ticket stock, called _____ stock, is used to print a ticket and boarding pass.

20. The entry _____ will request 200 consecutive ticket numbers for issuing tickets and boarding passes.

21. The entry _____ will issue a boarding pass only.

22. The entry _____ will issue a ticket with a boarding pass, specifying a 10-percent commission.

Chapter 11

1. On American Airlines flights, seats can be reserved up to _____ before departure.

2. Passenger seating is referred to by _____.

3. If cigarette smoking is permitted on a flight, the code _____ refers to the no-smoking section, and _____ refers to the smoking section.

4. The entry code _____ is used to request automatic seat assignment on a confirmed flight segment.

5. When prereserved seats are requested, _____ is added to the flight segment.

6. When seats are assigned on selected multiple segments, _____ is typed between the segment numbers.

7. If an itinerary has _____ segments, the secondary code A may be used to request prereserved seats on all segments.

8. If the requested location or zone is not available, _____ will be displayed.

9. A _____ shows the status of all the seats on a particular flight.

10. The entry _____ will request a seat availability map for segment 3.

11. If a seat is available for advance seat assignment, _____ is displayed.

12. The locations of the wings are indicated by the code _____.

13. The code X indicates a(n) _____.

14. A seat that does not recline, or that has an obstructed view of the movie screen, is indicated by the code _____.

15. The entry _____ is used to display prereserved seat data.

16. The entry _____ will cancel previously assigned seat 14F on segment 2.

17. If an airline does offer advance seat assignment through SABRE, _____ may be input to request a seat reservation.

Chapter 12

1. The term *queue* is derived from the French word meaning _____.

2. Each queue has a unique number that identifies _____.

3. A PNR that awaits attention or action in a queue is said to be _____

4. A _____ is a summary of the messages or records currently on queue.

5. The entry _____ will display the number of messages or PNRs in all queues.

6. The entry _____ will display the number of PNRs in queues 2 and 11.

7. To obtain a queue count from the branch office of a multi-office agency, the _____ must be included.

8. The entry code _____ is used to access the records in a queue.

9. The entry _____ will access the records in queue 23 at branch office C9D0.

10. When an agent signs into a record queue, _____ is displayed automatically.

11. If a transaction is ignored while working a queue, the PNR is moved to _____.

12. The entry _____ is used to display the current queue number.

13. The entry QR is used to _____.

14. The entry _____ is used to exit from the queue and end the transaction.

15. If a client cannot be contacted to confirm a reservation, the record may be placed on the _____ queue to suspend the record for a set interval, usually 15 minutes.

16. If a message is left for the client to call back, the PNR may be placed on the LMC queue to suspend the record for an extended interval, usually _____.

17. When a PNR is placed on queue, a _____ should be included to advise the agent who works the queue.

18. The entry _____ will place a PNR on queue 38 with the text SEE REMARKS.

19. The entry code _____ is used to initiate continuous queue ticketing.

20. SABRE can print a maximum of _____ tickets at one time.

21. A _____ is a summary of PNRs processed by SABRE during continuous queue ticketing.

22. The entry _____ will halt queue ticketing from queue 9 at branch office C9T0.

23. The entry code _____ is used to remove all the records from a specified queue.

Chapter 13

1. A client profile contains _____.

2. A _____ contains data for a primary client, such as a company, government agency, or school district.

3. An employee would have a _____ STAR.

4. A STAR ID code may consist of up to _____ alphanumeric characters.

5. The entry code _____ is used to display a STAR.

6. The subject line contains the _____.

7. A line coded P is called a _____ and contains important information.

8. If a line is coded _____, the item is a mandatory item that should always be transferred to the PNR.

9. If a line is coded O, the item is _____.

10. The entry code _____ is used to list STAR ID codes.

11. When an ID list is displayed, the entry _____ will display item 3.

12. The entry _____ will move all the data lines coded A from a displayed STAR to a PNR.

13. If an optional line is not specified, only _____ will be transferred to the PNR.

14. The entry _____ will move all mandatory data items along with optional line 5.

15. The _____ key may be used to transfer multiple optional lines from a displayed STAR.

16. The secondary code _____ can be used to prevent a line that is coded A from transferring to the PNR.

17. A STAR that is used to communicate information to SABRE subscribers is called a _____.

18. When the Universal STAR index is displayed, the entry _____ will display item 2.

Chapter 14

1. Each hotel vendor is identified by a two-letter _____ code.

2. The code _____ indicates a standard room.

3. The code _____ refers to a room with one king bed, and 2Q refers to a room with _____.

4. The room type A1K refers to a _____ room with _____.

5. The code _____ refers to rack rates, whereas COR refers to _____ rates.

6. The code _____ indicates that a hotel booking must be guaranteed.

7. The code 6 indicates that a reservation may be held until _____ without a deposit or guarantee.

8. The entry code _____ is used to display a hotel index.

9. In a hotel index, the location code _____ indicates the city center.

10. The location R indicates the _____ area.

11. The alphanumeric code following the address shows _____.

12. The one-letter code at the end of the first line of each listing indicates _____.

13. The qualifier R is used to specify a _____ in a hotel index entry.

14. The qualifier _____ is used to specify properties with a particular room location.

15. The qualifier _____ may be used to specify the maximum distance from the airport.

16. To display availability, if the stay will exceed one night, the number of _____ and _____ must be specified.

17. The _____ may be input in lieu of the number of nights.

18. The entry code HOD is used to display a _____.

19. A _____ displayed in the first screen of each hotel description lists the available room types, rate categories, and rates.

20. A _____ permits one to three children to stay in the same room as a parent at no charge.

21. The _____ plan includes three daily meals in the room rate.

22. The entry _____ will display policy information for the Marriott chain.

23. When a hotel description is displayed, the entry _____ will book one room of type B2Q at the rack rate.

24. The label _____ identifies a hotel segment.

25. The booking source is indicated by _____.

26. The secondary code _____ is used to indicate deposit or guarantee information.

27. The option code _____ is used to indicate an extra guest.

28. The option code RC is used to indicate _____.

29. The entry _____ will display only the hotel segments in an itinerary.

30. The entry code _____ is used to display hotel reference points.

31. When reference points are displayed, the entry _____ will display availability for properties near item 5.

32. To display reference points in foreign countries, the entry code _____ is used with the country code.

33. The entry code _____ is used to modify an existing hotel reservation.

34. The secondary code _____ is used to modify room information.

35. The secondary code D is used to modify _____.

36. The status/action code _____ is used to remove a direct hotel booking from the itinerary.

37. The entry _____ will display hotel chain codes.

Chapter 15

1. The entry _____ will display the car vendor table.

2. _____ provide a standard coding system for the CRS industry, enabling reservation systems to exchange data.

3. The code _____ indicates a standard size car, and T indicates a _____.

4. The code _____ indicates an automatic shift, and R indicates _____.

5. The code _____ indicates an intermediate car with automatic shift and air conditioning.

6. The entry _____ will display car availability in the arrival point of segment 3.

7. The entry code _____ is used to request the rates offered by a specified vendor.

8. The rate code E is used to specify _____.

9. If a rate plan is not specified, _____ will be displayed.

10. The category code A or ASC refers to _____ rates.

11. _____ rates are a vendor's normal unrestricted rates.

12. _____ rates are offered in conjunction with other travel products, such as hotel accommodations or a cruise.

13. In a rate quote, the code G after the line number indicates that the rate is _____.

14. The status _____ indicates that the car type is available on a request basis only, and _____ indicates that the car type is not available.

15. The entry code _____ is used to list off-airport offices.

16. The entry code _____ is used to redisplay or modify a rate quote.

17. In a rate shopper display, rates are listed from _____ to _____.

18. The entry code _____ is used to obtain a rate shopper display.

19. The secondary code _____ is used to request only rates that include unlimited mileage.

20. When a rate shopper display has been obtained, the entry code _____ is used to display the rules for a specified line.

21. When car rental rates are displayed, the entry _____ will sell a car segment from line 3.

22. The secondary code _____ is used to input optional service information.

23. The entry code _____ is used to modify an existing car segment.

24. The secondary code _____ is used to modify the pickup date, and the secondary code CT is used to modify the _____.

25. The entry code _____ is used to display policies for a specified vendor and city.

26. When a specified category is displayed, the entry CP* will display _____.

Chapter 16

1. Each DRS category is identified by a three-letter abbreviation called a _____.

2. Participating airlines other than American Airlines are referred to as _____.

3. The entry code _____ is used to display a subject index for a primary category.

4. When the DRS index is displayed, either the _____ or the _____ may be used to display a subject.

5. The category _____ specifies American Airlines reference information.

6. The categories SYS and SY1 refer to _____.

7. A keyword for co-host information consists of the letter _____ followed by the _____.

8. The entry _____ is used to display the main function FOX list.

9. The entry code _____ is used to display information from the function list.

10. When FOX information is displayed by keyword, the entry code FOX may be abbreviated as _____.

11. Recent changes and additions to the FOX system are stored in special records, called _____.

12. The entry code _____ is used for flight verification, or flifo.

13. In a flifo display, the _____ shows the total time that the aircraft is in flight, whereas the _____ shows the total time from the originating point to the terminating point, including time spent on the ground.

14. The entry _____ will display flight information for line 3 of an availability display.

15. The entry code DU*/ is used to display a list of _____ by category.

16. The entry code _____ is used to display the minimum connecting times at a specified airport.

17. The head I/D indicates _____ connecting times.

18. The entry code _____ may be used to obtain National Weather Service information for a specific city.

19. The secondary code _____ is used to obtain a descriptive city forecast.

20. The secondary code _____ may be used to obtain an extended regional forecast.

21. The entry code _____ is used for calculator and calendar functions.

22. The entry code _____ may be used to separate the base fare and tax from a total fare.

23. The entry code _____ can be used to determine the local time in a specified city.

24. The entry code _____ is used to display currency exchange rates based on the bank buying rate.

25. The entry code _____ is used to convert an amount from one currency to another.

Chapter 17

1. The entry code _____ is used to display an index of tours available in a specific city.

2. A vendor that sells package tours through retail travel agencies is referred to as a _____.

3. The entry code _____ is used to display a tour index for a specific city.

4. In a tour index, an asterisk after the line number indicates that the tour has _____.

5. The tour type _____ indicates basic independent tours, whereas ET indicates _____ tours.

6. If both segment reference and a tour type are used to display a tour index, _____ must be typed to separate the segment number and tour type.

7. The secondary code _____ is used to request an inclusive.

8. When multiple inclusives are requested, _____ is typed to separate the inclusive codes.

9. The date qualifiers that are used to display _____ may also be used to display a tour index.

10. The entry code _____ is used to display a tour description.

11. The entry code _____ is used to display tour availability.

12. When tour availability is requested, the secondary code HN may be used to specify the _____.

13. When a tour index is displayed, the entry code _____ may be used to obtain a hotel description.

14. When tour availability is displayed, the entry _____ will sell 1 room of type OCF from line 2, at a total price of $2400.00.

15. When selling a tour segment, the secondary code N may be used to _____.

16. If the total price cannot be calculated, _____ must be typed instead of the total price.

17. The secondary code G is used to enter _____.

18. If an MCO will be issued, the _____ should be included.

19. The entry code _____ is used to modify an existing tour segment.

20. The secondary code O/ is used to modify _____.

Chapter 18

1. Airlines that participate in the Total-Access system are referred to as _____.

2. The host key for British Airways is _____, whereas the host key for Northwest is _____.

3. The entry code for direct-access is _____ followed by _____.

4. The entry _____ will display total-access availability from Miami to Denver on 12 March, departing around 10 A.M.

5. When total-access availability is requested from the Continental reservation system, the header _____ will appear above the display.

6. Line numbers in a direct-access availability display will always start with _____.

7. When an air segment is sold from a total-access availability display, a tag is added indicating _____.

8. When a total-access availability display has been obtained, the entry _____ will change the host carrier to United.

9. Fare quotes obtained through direct-access are displayed in the format of _____.

10. The entry _____ will display direct-access flight information for TW 330 on 17 May.

11. The entry _____ will display the seat map for CO 510 in C class on 20 July from Seattle to Los Angeles.

12. The exact total-access functions that can be used with a host system vary depending on the _____.

13. The entry code for multi-access functions is _____ followed by _____.

14. The entry _____ is used to exit from a host system.

Chapter 19

1. The Phase IV function is used to create a ticket record for PNRs with itineraries that _____.

2. The entry _____ is used to create a ticket record.

3. At a minimum, a manual ticket record must include _____, _____, _____, and _____.

4. The entry code _____ is used to insert information in a manual ticket record.

5. The secondary action code _____ is used to insert the fare basis for each segment.

6. When different fare bases are inserted for multiple segment lines, _____ is typed between each pair of segments and fare bases.

7. When validity dates are inserted with a line entitlement, _____ is typed before the dates.

8. If the commission is inserted as an amount instead of a percentage, the secondary code _____ is used to insert the data.

9. The secondary code C is used to insert the _____.

10. The secondary code _____ is used to insert the base fare and tax for each line.

11. The entry _____ will display the fare information in a ticket record.

12. The secondary code U is used to insert _____.

13. If a fare is _____, the secondary code TE is inserted with the base fare.

14. The entry _____ is used to issue tickets from a Phase IV ticket record.

15. The same form-of-payment formats that are used with _____ may be used with Phase IV entries.

Glossary

A1SO Called *full pension*.

AA facts field The PNR field in which service information is stored for transmittal to American Airlines.

address field A PNR field that is used to store address information. In SABRE, the travel agency address is stored in the address field.

advance purchase A fare rule requiring the ticket to be purchased a set number of days prior to departure.

AFAX AA facts field.

air itinerary An itinerary containing only flight segments; the flight segments of an itinerary that also contain auxiliary segments.

air segment The representation of an airline flight in an itinerary. Also called a flight segment.

airline code An alpha or numeric code assigned to each airline by ARC and IATA. The alpha airline code, also called the carrier code, consists of two letters. The numeric airline code consists of three digits.

Airlines Reporting Corporation (ARC) A corporation jointly owned by major U.S. airlines to account for ticket sales by travel agencies.

airport code A three-letter code assigned to each airport by the Department of Transportation and IATA.

airport transfer Prearranged transportation between the airport and a hotel.

alpha Consisting only of letters of the alphabet.

alphanumerical Consisting of a combination of numbers, letters, or punctuation.

American plan (AP) A hotel rate that includes lodging and two or three daily meals.

Amtrak The trade name of the National Railroad Passenger Corporation, the unified American railway system created by the Rail Passenger Service Act of 1970.

AP American plan.

ARC Airlines Reporting Corporation.

ARINC An independent data communications network that links computer reservation systems with airlines.

ARNK Arrival unknown. The representation of a surface segment in an air itinerary to maintain continuity between flight segments.

arrival point   The second city or airport code in a city pair. Also called the destination point.

ATB stock   (ATB) Ticket forms for issuing an automated ticket and boarding pass.

autoprice   To use a CRS to price an itinerary automatically.

auxiliary segment   Any segment of an itinerary other than an air segment.

availability   A display of regularly scheduled flights between a specified origin and destination. Also, a display of room types or car types available during a specified period.

bargain finder   The SABRE entry to price an itinerary at the lowest available fare regardless of the classes in which the segments are booked.

bedding code   A code that indicates the number and size of beds provided at a specific room rate.

board point   Any point where a passenger boards an aircraft; the first point in a city pair or air segment. Also called a *departure point*.

book   To arrange a reservation for transportation or accommodations; to sell a travel product or service.

booking agent   A person or business that books reservations on behalf of a travel vendor; the travel agent responsible for a specific reservation.

booking class   Booking code.

booking code   The code for the class of service, used to obtain a selected fare basis when an air segment is sold.

booking source   The travel agency or other seller that is responsible for a reservation.

business class   A class of service on an airline flight, priced higher than standard coach class but lower than first class.

cabin   A passenger compartment on an airline flight. The standard cabins are first class, business class, and coach (also called *economy class*).

cancel   To remove a segment from an itinerary and return the space to the vendor's inventory.

car   Any type of rental vehicle offered by an automobile and truck rental firm.

car availability   A display of vendors and car types for a specified city and date.

car company   Any vendor that rents automobiles on a daily basis.

car type   A code identifying the vehicle class, body type, type of shift, and air conditioning.

carrier   A company that provides transportation service.

central processor   In a data processing system, the component that performs arithmetic and logic operations, and coordinates the communication, storage, and retrieval of data.

chain code   A two-letter code identifying a participating hotel vendor.

chain description   A summary of policies regarding deposits, refunds, extra guests, family plans, credit card acceptance, and other information about a hotel chain.

child fare   A discount fare for children of a designated age.

circle trip   An itinerary in which the passenger returns to the origin point.

city code   A three-letter code designated by the International Standards Organization for a city served by passenger air carriers.

city pair   A six-letter code consisting of city or airport codes for a departure point and an arrival point.

claim a reservation   To retrieve a PNR created by another booking source for ticketing.

class   A designation of the level of service and price on an airline flight.

client profile   A computer record that contains passenger data items for a frequent traveler.

coach   The standard class of service offered by an airline; any large passenger vehicle operated for intra-city bus service or sightseeing excursions.

cohost   Airlines, other than American Airlines, that permit reservations to be booked through SABRE.

combinability   A fare rule that states whether a specific booking code or fare basis can be combined with other booking codes or fare bases. Also called a *combination rule*.

commission   A percentage of the sale price of a product, paid by a vendor to a third-party seller.

commission box   The part of an airline ticket where the travel agency's commission is printed. The commission is usually stated as a percentage of the base fare.

commuter carrier   An airline that operates small aircraft and provides service within a limited geographic area.

computer reservation system   (CRS) A computer system designed for use by booking agents to facilitate the sale of travel products and services of participating vendors.

configuration   The interior arrangement of an aircraft or other transportation vehicle.

connecting point   A city or airport where a passenger must change from one flight to another.

connection   Air transportation requiring a transfer from one flight to another.

continental United States   The 48 contiguous U.S. states (i.e., excluding Alaska and Hawaii).

continuous queue ticketing   The function used to issue tickets for all PNRs with ticketing arrangements for the current date.

corporate rate   A discounted hotel rate offered to business travelers. A discounted car rental rate that has been negotiated with a corporation.

cross-reference   To input an OSI message in PNRs for passengers who will travel together on a portion of their itineraries.

CRS   Computer reservation system.

CRS vendor   A company that operates a CRS for use by subscribers.

cruise   A pleasure trip by boat or ship; a business or ship that is used for a cruise.

cruise line   A transportation carrier that operates cruise ships.

cruise ship   A ship, especially a large ocean liner, used for cruises.

data   Information that can be processed by a computer.

data communications   The process of transmitting and receiving computer data.

data field   The part of a record in which a data item is stored.

data item   An item of information, such as a name, telephone number, or remark, stored in a PNR data field.

days of operation   Days of the week on which a flight operates; also called *frequency of operation*.

decode   To determine the name or word represented by a code such as a city, carrier, equipment, or vendor code.

Department of Transportation   (DOT) U.S. Department of Transportation.

departure point   The first point in a city pair; any point from which a traveler departs.

dependability factor   The percentage of flights that have the same flight number and that depart and arrive within 15 minutes of the scheduled times; also called *on-time performance*.

deplane   To disembark from an airplane.

destination   A traveler's intended arrival point; the last stopping point of an itinerary; the point of an itinerary to which the highest one-way full coach fare applies.

destination point   The second city or airport code in a city pair or air segment. Also called the *arrival point*.

diabetic meal   A meal that is fit to be eaten by a person who has diabetes, in conformance with medical instructions or guidelines.

direct flight   A flight that does not involve a change of flight number.

Direct Reference System   (DRS) A SABRE program by which information can be retrieved about travel industry vendors, entertainment events, immigration requirements, and other topics.

direct-sell   To book an airline reservation by inputting the carrier, flight number, class, date, city pair, action code, and number of seats.

disembark   To leave an aircraft or ship.

domestic   Within or belonging to a particular country.

domestic fare   A fare that applies to travel between points in the United States, Canada, Mexico, the Caribbean, and Bermuda; a fare stored in the North American Fare Data Base (NAFDB). Also, any fare for a domestic flight.

domestic flight   A flight that both departs and arrives within the United States and the Canadian buffer zone.

DOT   Department of Transportation.

double bed   A bed with a mattress size of 54 inches by 75 inches, designed to accommodate two people. Also called a *French bed*.

double occupancy   A hotel room that is occupied by two adults.

double rate   A hotel rate for a room that will be occupied by two adults.

downline space   Any segment of an itinerary after the originating flight.

DRS   Direct Reference System.

economy class   Coach class on an international flight.

elapsed flight time   The total elapsed time of an airline flight from departure to arrival.

encode   To determine the code for a name or word such as a city, airline, aircraft equipment, or hotel chain.

end transact   End the transaction.

end the transaction   To transmit an assembled PNR to the central processor for permanent storage.

endorsement   On an airline ticket, written authorization from an airline permitting the passenger to travel on a different carrier.

endorsement/restrictions box   The part of an airline ticket where endorsements or restrictions are printed.

equipment   In aviation, the type of aircraft used for transport.

equipment code   A three-letter code designating the type of aircraft used for a passenger flight or cargo transport.

EP   European plan.

escorted tour   A package tour that includes the services of an escort.

ETA   Estimated time of arrival.

ETD   Estimated time of departure.

European plan   A hotel rate that includes accommodations only, without meals.

exception   Days of the week on which a flight does not operate; also called *frequency exception*.

exchange   In ticketing, the issuance of a new ticket to replace a ticket that was issued previously, as a result of an itinerary change.

excursion   A short journey that returns to its starting point.

excursion fare   A round-trip fare that is less expensive than the combined cost of the component one-way fares.

family plan   In the lodging industry, a policy permitting children of a specified age to stay free in the same room as their parents; in the transportation industry, a discount plan offered to members of a family traveling together.

fare   The fee paid by a traveler for transportation on an airline, bus, or train.

fare basis   A preset price level for air travel, designated by a code and defined by a combination of travel restrictions.

fare calculation   The itemization of the total fare for an itinerary by departure point, carrier, and arrival point, based on the fare basis and base fare for each segment.

fare construction   The calculation of international fares based on IATA guidelines and Neutral Units of Construction (NUC).

fare quote   A display of fares between a specified origin and destination. Also called a *fare* or *tariff display*.

fare rule   A description of the booking code, validity or ticketing dates, and any restrictions that apply to a particular fare basis.

fare shopper display   A display of competitive fares for all carriers, listed from least expensive to most expensive.

field   A part of a PNR in which a passenger data item is stored.

field identifier   A code that indicates the PNR field where information is to be stored.

first class   The premium class of service and highest fare offered by an airline; also called *premium class*.

flight   A regularly scheduled air service.

flight information   (Flifo) The function that is used to verify the routing, departure and arrival times, meal service, equipment, and total flight time of a specified flight.

flight number   A number consisting of one to four digits assigned to each flight.

flight segment   The portion of an itinerary representing a reservation to travel on an airline flight.

form of payment   An abbreviation or other text indicating the method by which airline tickets will be purchased—usually check, cash, or a credit card account number.

form-of-payment box   The part of an airline ticket where the form of payment is printed.

frequency   Days of the week on which a flight operates.

frequency exception   Days of the week on which a flight does not operate.

general facts field   The PNR field in which service information is stored for transmittal to airlines other than American Airlines.

GFAX   General facts field.

government travel request   (GTR) A document issued by a government agency authorizing a travel agency or airline to issue a ticket.

group rate   A hotel rate offered to members of a group such as a trade association, corporation, or fraternal organization, based on a guarantee to occupy a set minimum number of rooms.

GTR   Government travel request.

guarantee   A promise to pay for a hotel reservation whether or not it is fulfilled. Common guarantee instruments include a cash deposit, credit card number, or corporate address.

guaranteed flight segment   A flight segment that was booked by linking with the carrier's reservation system.

header   In a city pair availability display, the line that indicates the departure date, day of the week, and the time zone of each point.

high season   A period of high demand; also called a *peak period*.

host key   A three-letter code identifying an airline that participates in the total access program.

hotel availability   A display listing hotels and rate categories that are available during a specified date range.

hotel description   A detailed record containing data about facilities, credit card policies, family plan, and other information about a specific property.

hotel index   A list of hotels that are located in a specified city and permit reservations to be booked through SABRE.

IATA   International Air Transport Association.

ignore   To remove a PNR from the work area without transmitting the record to the central processor for permanent storage.

inclusive   A product or service included in a package tour.

inclusive tour   A tour that is offered at a set price and includes such components as transportation, accommodations, and transfers.

in-flight service   Entertainment, meals, beverages, or miscellaneous items provided during a flight.

in-plant   A department or division of a company set up to handle the travel requirements of the company or its employees.

input   To enter data to a computer for processing.

inter-line   Between different carriers. An inter-line connection utilizes flights operated by different carriers, and an inter-line agreement is a contract between two airlines.

in-terminal   Located in an airport terminal.

international airline   Any airline that provides service to or from a foreign point; an airline that is based in a country other than the one where the travel agency is located.

International Air Transport Association   (IATA) A voluntary organization of international airlines established to coordinate airfares, establish service standards, and provide a unified system of worldwide air transportation.

international fare   A fare that applies to travel between points outside the United States, Canada, Mexico, the Caribbean, and Bermuda.

international transportation tax   A tax imposed on passengers who depart from the United States to a foreign point.

issuing carrier   The airline that authorizes a ticket to be issued by a retail travel agency and certifies that the ticket is valid for carriage over the designated routing.

item number   The information that is typed before the change code when one data item of a multiple-item field is deleted or changed.

itinerary   A list of points, routes, and transportation carriers for a trip.

itinerary/invoice   A document that provides detailed flight information for each segment and a summary of all the charges.

itinerary pricing   A CRS function that is used to determine the total fare for an itinerary, including tax.

joint fare   A fare using two or more carriers via a specified routing.

journey time   Total trip time, including transportation time and layovers.

keyword A code consisting of three or more alpha characters that can be used to retrieve information from storage or select an item from a menu.

king bed A bed with the largest mattress size, 76 inches by 80 inches.

kosher meal A meal that meets Jewish dietetic and/or ceremonial laws.

lacto-ovo vegetarian meal A meal that is prepared only from vegetables, milk, and eggs.

last-seat availability A city pair availability display obtained by linking with an airline's reservation system.

layover A time interval between points in an itinerary; actual connecting time.

leg A segment of a connection or, if a direct flight involves a change of aircraft, any portion between a departure point and an arrival point.

level-1 STAR A STAR that contains data for a primary client, such as a company, government agency, or school district.

level-2 STAR A STAR that contains data for a passenger associated with a level-1 STAR.

local fare A fare published in the currency of a specified country for air travel originating in that country or utilizing a carrier based in that country.

local time The time in a specified location.

location indicator A code in a phone entry designating whether the telephone number is for a travel agency, client business, client home, or hotel. A code in a hotel index or availability display indicating the geographical area in which the property is located.

low season A period of low demand; also called an *off-peak period*.

MAP Modified American plan.

mainframe Computer hardware consisting of a powerful central processor and a large storage area.

market The geographical area served by a specific flight, hotel, or car rental outlet.

maximum permitted mileage In international fare construction, the maximum number of miles permitted between two points to obtain a designated point-to-point fare.

MCO Miscellaneous Charges Order.

meal plan A hotel rate that includes one or more daily meals.

menu A list of options that can be selected by an item number or keyword.

message queue   A queue in which agents can leave text messages for other agents in the office.

mileage system   A method of calculating international fares based on the maximum permitted mileage between two points.

military passenger   A traveler who is a full-time active member serving in the U.S. Army, Navy, Air Force, Marines, or Coast Guard.

minimum connecting time   The minimum time permitted between connecting flights.

Miscellaneous Charges Order   (MCO) A document issued by a travel agency or vendor authorizing a travel service for a specified individual.

modem   (modulator/demodulator) A device that converts computer data into signals that can be transmitted over a telephone line.

modified American plan   (MAP) A hotel rate that includes accommodations and two meals, usually breakfast and dinner.

mpm   Maximum permitted mileage.

NAFDB   (North American Fare Data Base) Fares that apply to travel between points in the United States, Canada, Mexico, the Caribbean, and Bermuda.

name field   The PNR field in which the names of all the passengers traveling together in the same reservation are stored.

Neutral Unit of Construction   (NUC) A standard monetary unit used to calculate international fares, adjusted to international currency rates.

nonstop   Without any stops.

NUC   Neutral Unit of Construction.

numerical   Consisting only of numbers.

off-line   Services provided by a carrier other than the ticketing airline. An airline other than the host carrier.

off point   The second point in a city pair; any point at which an airline passenger disembarks.

off-premises   Not located on the premises of an airport.

on-line connection   A connection requiring a change of flights operated by the same airline.

one-way   An itinerary in which the traveler will not return to the originating point.

on-premises   Located on the premises of an airport.

on-time performance   The percentage of flights that depart within 15 minutes of the scheduled departure time and arrive within 15 minutes of the scheduled arrival time. Also called *dependability factor*.

onward segment   The next flight segment after a specific segment.

open jaw   A circle trip with a surface portion at the outward destination or just before the return segment to the originating point.

open segment   A reservation to travel on a specific carrier without a specified flight number.

operator   In mathematics, a symbol used to designate an arithmetic operation such as multiplication or division.

origin   Any point from which a traveler departs; the first departure point in an itinerary.

originating carrier   The first carrier in an air itinerary.

originating point   The first point of departure in an itinerary.

OSI   (other service information or optional service information) A message that is input to a CRS to advise an airline about some aspect of a reservation, such as a child's age, an elderly passenger, or a VIP.

outbound segment   The first segment in an air itinerary; the segment that departs from the originating point.

output   To generate data from a computer for display, printout, or storage.

overbook   To intentionally book more reservations than the capacity of the flight or hotel, to compensate for no-shows and cancellations.

package rates   Rates that are offered in conjunction with other travel products, such as hotel accommodations or a cruise.

package tour   A prearranged trip that includes a combination of components such as transportation, accommodations, and activities.

passenger   A person who travels on a transportation carrier.

passenger facility charge   (PFC) A surcharge imposed by an airport for construction or improvements.

passenger name record   (PNR) A computer record containing the itinerary, passenger names, contact telephone numbers, ticketing arrangement, and other data relating to a reservation.

passenger type code   (PTC) A code used, for pricing purposes, to indicate whether a passenger is an adult, child, military passenger, senior citizen, stand-by passenger, etc.

passive segment   A segment representing air space that was booked directly with a carrier rather than through the CRS. Passive segments are input in SABRE using the action code GK or BK.

peak period   A period of high demand; also called a *high season*.

permanent storage   The type of storage that is used to maintain reservations, fares, and flight schedules.

PFC   Passenger facility charge.

Phase IV   A SABRE function that is used to create a ticket record for PNRs with itineraries that cannot be autopriced.

phone field   The PNR field in which contact telephone numbers are stored.

PNR   Passenger name record.

prefatory instruction code   (PIC) A code input when a PNR is placed on queue, specifying a message to be displayed when the queue is accessed and the record is displayed.

Prepaid Ticket Advice   (PTA) An authorization to issue a ticket at a location other than the point of purchase.

prereserved seat   A seat assignment that is made prior to check-in.

priority line   A line that is coded P and contains important information but is not used in a PNR.

promotional fare   A reduced fare offered by a carrier during a special promotion or to encourage sales during a period of low demand.

promotional rate   A special room rate offered by a hotel in conjunction with an advertising campaign. A car rental rate that has specific restrictions, such as an advance reservation requirement or a minimum rental period.

pseudo city   A code that identifies each site where CRS terminals are installed.

PTC   Passenger type code.

queen bed   A bed with a mattress size of 60 inches by 80 inches, larger than a double bed but smaller than a king bed.

queue   An electronic holding area for messages or passenger records awaiting special attention by an agent.

queue count   A summary of the messages or records currently on queue.

quota   A preset quantity of a product or service; in computer reservations, the maximum number of airline seats that may be sold in one transaction with immediate confirmation.

quote   To communicate a fare or rate to a prospective client; a price quotation.

rack rates   The normal room rates that are offered by a hotel to the general public.

rate category   Special car rental rates, such as association, corporate, promotional, and convention rates.

rate plan   The basis for a car rental rate, such as daily, weekly, monthly, and weekend rates.

rate quote   A display of available car types and rates in a specific market.

rate shopper display   A display of the lowest available rates offered by all participating car rental vendors in a specific market.

rate type   The price level for a room rate, such as rack, corporate, promotional, and group rates.

reconfirm   To state an intention to fulfill a reservation.

received-from field   The field in which text is stored to indicate the source of the reservation.

record   A collection of related data, such as a passenger reservation.

record locator   A six-digit code that is displayed when a transaction is ended, and by which the PNR can be retrieved from storage.

reference-sell   To sell a segment by line number from an availability display.

remarks field   The PNR field in which free-form text is stored to communicate information to other agents in the office, or to remind the agent to take some future action.

reservation   An arrangement to occupy an accommodation on a transportation carrier or in a lodging establishment.

restricted fare   A discounted coach fare subject to restrictions.

restriction   A condition, such as advance purchase or a minimum stay, for travel at a specific fare basis.

retail   The sale of products or services directly to the public.

return availability   A display of flights for the opposite city pair of the previous availability display. For example, if flights are displayed from ORD to SFO, return availability will display flights from SFO to ORD.

return segment   In a circle trip, the segment that arrives at the originating point.

room option   An optional request input with a hotel reservation, such as a charge for an extra guest, an adult or child rollaway, or a crib.

room rate   The charge for a specific room type based on the rate type and category.

room type   A code consisting of the room category and bedding offered for a specific room rate.

round trip   A circle trip with one stopover.

round-trip fare   A fare that requires round-trip travel on the same carrier in an equivalent class of service on all segments.

round-trip indicator   A code in an air tariff or fare display designating a round-trip fare.

route   To arrange or specify connecting points.

route system   The network of cities and airports at which an airline has regularly scheduled departures and arrivals.

routing   The permitted connecting and stopping points for a particular fare.

rule   Fare rule.

SABRE   A computer reservation system operated by AMR, Inc., the parent company of American Airlines. (Acronym for Semi-Automated Business Research Environment)

screen   Video display terminal; an information display.

scroll   To move text vertically on the screen to search for specific information.

seat assignment   A record of the row and seat to be occupied by a passenger on a specific flight segment.

seat availability map   A display showing the status of all the seats on a specific flight. Also called a *seat map*.

seat configuration   The seating arrangement on a passenger aircraft.

seat quota   On a specific airline flight, the number of seats that can be sold in each class of service in one transaction, based on the carrier's agreement with SABRE.

segment   A specific portion of an itinerary, such as an airline flight or hotel reservation; in an air itinerary, any point-to-point flight reservation.

segment line   A line of an air itinerary that shows the carrier, flight number, class, departure date, day of the week, and departure and arrival airports of a specific flight.

segment status   A two-letter code indicating the status of a reservation. For example, HK indicates a confirmed reservation, and HL indicates a waitlisted reservation that has not yet been confirmed.

senior citizen   A passenger 65 years of age or older.

sign on   To input an entry to identify the agent and gain access to the CRS.

sign off   To input an entry to exit the CRS.

similar name list   A display of the names and departure dates of PNRs that have the same or similar surnames.

sine   Sign-on code.

single occupancy   A hotel room that is occupied by one adult.

single rate   A hotel rate based on single occupancy.

single supplement   A surcharge assessed to a client who will travel unaccompanied but purchases a product that is priced on the basis of double occupancy.

Standard Interline Passenger Procedures   (SIPP) A standard coding system for the CRS industry, enabling airline reservation systems to exchange data with airlines, hotel chains, and car rental chains.

space   A reservation to travel on a transportation carrier.

special meal   A meal ordered on an airline flight, other than that normally served to passengers.

SSR (special service requirement or request) Special service or assistance not normally provided to passengers, such as a wheelchair or special meal. Also called a *special service request*.

stand-by Travel offered or arranged without a confirmed reservation, based on available space at the time of departure.

stand-by fare A reduced fare for stand-by travel.

STAR (Special Traveler's Account Record) A SABRE client file containing passenger data items for a frequent traveler.

stopover Any point in an itinerary that is not a connecting point; a point where the interval exceeds *4* hours between domestic flights or *12* hours between international flights.

subject line The line in a STAR that is coded S and contains the account name.

supplemental data Information stored in the address, remarks, general facts, or AA facts field.

surcharge A charge added to a basic fare for airport improvements or security, travel during a peak period, or other reasons.

surface segment A segment in which the passenger will travel by a means other than air transportation. Surface segments are represented in an air itinerary as ARNK (arrival unknown).

system cohost Any participating airline other than American Airlines.

tariff A printed reference book containing price information for transportation carriers; any schedule of airfares.

terminal Airport facilities used by an airline. Also, a computer workstation consisting of a keyboard and a video display screen.

throughfare A fare covering all legs of a connection and less than the combined fares of each leg if priced separately.

ticket A document that entitles the bearer to passage on a transportation carrier.

ticket exchange See exchange.

ticket stock Ticket forms issued to travel agencies by Airlines Reporting Corporation.

ticketing field The PNR field in which ticketing details are stored.

time limit An arrangement by which tickets must be purchased by a pre-set date and time to prevent automatic cancellation of the itinerary.

title An abbreviation such as MR, MRS, MISS, MSTR, DR, or REV, used in a name entry to clarify the sex, age group, and marital or occupational status of each traveler.

total access A SABRE function that can be used to obtain data directly from the reservation system of a participating airline.

tour   A package trip consisting of two or more components such as airfare, accommodations, a car rental, or other services; any travel product offered for resale by a tour wholesaler.

tour basis   A reduced fare for a passenger who purchases a prepaid tour.

tour number   A code identifying a specific travel product offered for resale by a tour wholesaler.

tour wholesaler   A travel vendor that assembles package vacations for resale to the public by retail travel agencies.

travel agency   A retail business authorized to sell travel products on behalf of vendors such as airlines, ships, rail companies, and lodging establishments.

travel agent   An owner, employee, or sales representative of a retail travel agency.

travel consultant   An employee of a retail travel agency responsible for providing information to travelers and arranging transportation and accommodations; also, *travel counselor*.

turn-around point   In an itinerary, the destination point used to determine the round-trip fare or maximum permitted mileage.

twin bed   A bed with a mattress size of 39 inches by 75 inches, designed for one person.

unaccompanied minor   A child *11* years or younger traveling without an adult.

Universal STAR   A STAR created by the SABRE customer service department to communicate information to subscribers.

U.S. Department of Transportation   (DOT) A branch of the federal government responsible for certifying and regulating transportation carriers. (When the Civil Aeronautics Board was dismantled after the airline industry was deregulated, its remaining regulatory powers were transferred to the DOT.)

validate   To imprint an airline or rail ticket with the trademark and airline code of the issuing carrier and the name, address, and ARC/IATA number of the issuing agency.

validating carrier   The airline that issued the validation plates that are used to validate a ticket; also called the issuing carrier.

validation   Authorization by an airline that a ticket is valid for carriage on the designated airline(s) and routing.

validity dates   The dates between which a special fare or hotel rate is valid.

vegetarian meal   A meal that does not contain any meat or dairy proucts.

vendor   A person or business who offers a product or service for sale.

vendor table A list of hotel, car, tour, or ship vendors that permit bookings to be made through SABRE.

video display terminal (VDT) A component of a data processing system, consisting of a keyboard used to enter data and a video screen used to display data.

VIP A very important passenger such as a high-ranking airline executive, diplomat, or government representative.

waitlist A list of passengers who desire a confirmed reservation for accommodations that were sold out at the time the reservation was requested; to place a reservation on such a list.

wholesale The sale of products or services to retail businesses for resale to the public.

wholesaler A vendor that sells products or services at wholesale; a tour operator.

work area An electronic holding area in which passenger data items are assembled before they are transmitted to the central processor.

Index

Photo Credits

Cover, KS Studios; 1, Life Images; 21, Pete Saloutos/TSW; 43, 59, 79, 99, Doug Martin; 123, Life Images; 139, Doug Martin; 161, 177, Life Images; 193, Jon Feingersh/The Stock Market; 205, Life Images; 219, Jon Gray/TSW; 235, John F. Mason/The Stock Market; 259, 279, Life Images; 301, Walter Hodges/Westlight; 315, 325, Life Images.